Handbook of Learning Disabilities

Volume II: Methods and Interventions

Handbook of Learning Disabilities

Volume II: Methods and Interventions

Kenneth A. Kavale, Ph.D.

Professor and Chair
Division of Special Education
The University of Iowa
Iowa City, Iowa

Steven R. Forness, Ed.D.

Director of Mental Retardation and
Developmental Disabilities Program
Principal, Neuropsychiatric Hospital School
Professor of Psychiatry and Biobehavioral Sciences
UCLA School of Medicine
Los Angeles, California

Michael Bender, Ed.D.

Vice President of Educational Programs
The Kennedy Institute
Professor of Education
The Johns Hopkins University
Joint Appointment, Department of Pediatrics
The Johns Hopkins School of Medicine
Baltimore, Maryland

A College-Hill Publication

Little, Brown and Company
Boston / Toronto / San Diego

College-Hill Press
A Division of
Little, Brown and Company (Inc.)
34 Beacon Street
Boston, Massachusetts 02108

Library of Congress Cataloging in Publication Data
Main entry under title:

Handbook of learning disabilities.

    Includes bibliographies and index.
    Contents: v. 1. Dimensions and diagnosis — v. 2.
Methods and interventions.
    1. Learning disabilities — Handbooks, manuals, etc.
2. Learning disabilities — Treatment — Handbooks, manuals,
etc. I. Kavale, Kenneth A., 1946-   . II. Forness,
Steven R. III, 1939-   . Bender, Michael, 1943-   . [DNLM:
1. Learning Disorders — handbooks. WS 39 H236]
LC4704.H365 1987   86-26396
ISBN 0-316-48368-0 (pbk. : v. 1)

ISBN 0-316-48370-2

Printed in the United States of America

Contents

Preface

Over the past twenty five years, the field of learning disabilities (LD) has witnessed amazing growth. From modest beginnings, it has become the special education category serving by far the most individuals. Accompanying this unprecedented growth has been a significant increase in the literature available about all aspects of LD. Consequently, it has become a challenge for even the most dedicated professional to keep abreast of the latest information. The many books now available tend to be either texts, providing basic information but little critical evaluation, or highly technical publications focusing on specific topics.

The *Handbook of Learning Disabilities* volumes are intended to occupy a place between these two extremes. The comprehensive coverage of these two books will provide the basic information, as well as a more in-depth critical evaluation. Our main goal is to provide students and practitioners with ready access to the essentials for understanding and treating LD.

Our thesis is that, although an individual with learning disabilities may have an underlying neurologic processing difficulty that may indeed have had something to do with the development of the learning disability, the documentation of such problems is only necessary to the extent that federally or locally mandated procedures now call for such evidence in determination of eligibility for services. Such information has not proven critical in determining which approaches need to be used or in planning remedial programs. Therefore, there are no chapters on visual processing or sensory–motor integration, since these areas have not been shown to be areas of prime importance to remediation; nor are there separate chapters on attention and memory or on information processing, since these areas are still inchoate and have not yet led to specific remedial strategies. Each of these areas is discussed, however, and possible principles or guidelines that can be gleaned from existing evidence are suggested. There is a focus on direct instruction of academic skills, on language strategies to the extent that these are integrated into the reading lesson or taught as skills valuable unto themselves, on increasing the time the child actually spends in reading instruction or in the experience of reading, and on related matters such as social functioning, family issues, and maturational outcomes.

It is clear that learning disabilities is a field fraught with controversy, even in terms of its most basic diagnostic criteria and remedial methods. The focus of these *Handbooks* is on a balanced evaluation of these issues and on what can reasonably be deduced, from existing knowledge, about the nature of LD, the diagnostic process, and the basic strategies of remediation. Our purpose is not an extensive review of controversial ideas, although these will be presented periodically throughout as preambles to specific procedures or approaches.

These volumes stand somewhere between "edited" and "authored" texts; most contributed chapters were first published as papers in *Learning Disabilities: An Interdisciplinary Journal,* but they have been substantially updated and adapted in collaboration with the original authors. In these chapters, we have credited the original author(s) on the first page of the chapter. However, it should be understood that we made editorial changes and additions to the original material in every case. Other chapters were written by us expressly for these volumes. Our primary goal throughout has been to provide the best and most recent information possible for understanding, assessing, and treating individuals with learning disabilities.

Introduction

Regardless of what you believe a learning disability (LD) is or how you believe it should be identified, students will still be classified LD and some form of remediation will be necessary. The methods and interventions used for remedial purposes form the basis of this volume of the *Handbook of Learning Disabilities*. Once classified, an LD student is provided with an educational plan, but the components of that plan can be as variable as the concept of LD itself. It is, therefore, the purpose of this volume to explore the methods and interventions that are commonly associated with LD.

How should an LD student be treated? The wide variety of options available make this a difficult question. Beyond a general statement that treatment should be tailored to meet the student's needs, no single answer is either correct or appropriate. Therefore, the LD professional must be aware of the possibilities and possess an assortment of methods and techniques in order to design an optimal program. The practitioner armed with rational choices is in the best position to make sound decisions about the most effective program. This volume is designed to provide a basis for those rational choices by offering an overview of the multitude of treatment possibilities for the LD student.

The volume is divided into three parts. The first part provides an overview of major intervention methods. Specifically, behavioral and cognitive methods are analyzed critically in the first two chapters. Efforts at empirically identifying subtypes of LD are reviewed in the third chapter along with their implications for remediation. The second part focuses on "basic skill" interventions in the areas of reading, written expression, arithmetic, and social skills. Basic approaches in these areas are described and analyzed with respect to how they may be included in a total intervention package. The third part deals with adjunct and alternative interventions. A variety of practices are described that may be included for an LD student.

The second volume in the *Handbook of Learning Disabilities* focuses on methods and interventions. The many choices available to the LD professional make it difficult to choose among methods and interventions. This volume is designed to assist that process by providing fundamental information about LD methods and interventions on which the LD professional can begin to design an optimal program for an LD student.

Contributors

Ann M. Bain, Ed.D.
Educational Specialist
Comprehensive Evaluation Unit
University of Maryland School of
  Medicine
Department of Behavioral Pediatrics
Baltimore, Maryland

Jeannette E. Fleischner, Ed.D.
Associate Professor
Department of Special Education
Teachers College, Columbia
  University
New York, New York

Kenneth D. Gadow, Ph.D.
Professor
Department of Psychiatry
SUNY at Stony Brook
Stony Brook, New York

J. Stephen Hazel, Ph.D.
Research Associate
Kansas Institute for Research in
  Learning Disabilities
Department of Human Development
University of Kansas
Lawrence, Kansas

Benjamin B. Lahey, Ph.D.
Professor of Psychology
Department of Psychology
University of Georgia
Athens, Georgia

**Judith M. Levy, M.S.W.,
A.C.S.W.**
Director of Social Work
The Kennedy Institute
Baltimore, Maryland

G. Reid Lyon, Ph.D.
Clinical Associate Professor of
  Neurology
University of Vermont
Faculty of Special Education
St. Michaels College
Winooski, Vermont

Eileen S. Marzola, Ed.D.
Adjunct Associate Professor
Department of Special Education
Teachers College, Columbia
  University
New York, New York

Ronald Neeper, Ph.D.
Mayo Medical School
Rochester, Minnesota

David M. O'Hara, Ph.D.
Associate Director and Associate
  Professor of Preventative Medicine
  and Psychiatry
Mental Retardation Institute
New York Medical College
Valhalla, New York

Jean B. Schumaker, Ph.D.
Associate Professor
Kansas Institute for Research in
  Learning Disabilities
Department of Human Development
University of Kansas
Lawrence, Kansas

Bernice Y. L. Wong, Ph.D.
Professor of Special Education
Faculty of Education
Simon Fraser University
Burnaby, British Columbia, Canada

Major Methods and Approaches

T he chapters in Part I provide an overview of major methods used with LD students. Chapter 1 focuses on the role of behavioral methods for the remediation of academic and social deficits. The behavioral approach is compared and contrasted with the medical model, and inappropriate and appropriate targets for behavioral remediation are discussed. A model of behavioral intervention is presented, based on the premise that the focus should be on direct modification of academic behavior. The chapter closes with a discussion of what we know and do not know about behavior therapy with LD students.

Chapter 2 deals with cognitive methods that emphasize the individual as an active information processor who participates in learning and who learns to monitor and evaluate their own behavior. The role of metacognition in the remediation of reading difficulties and social deficits is discussed. The advantages of metacognitive theory for LD remediation are noted, and the constraints in application are discussed regarding the proper evaluation of metacognitive interventions and the role of metacognitive variables in explaining an LD student's task failure.

The third chapter demonstrates how a theoretical research activity can be applied to LD instructional practices. There has been considerable interest in the empirical identification of homogeneous subtypes of LD as a means of reducing heterogeneity. Are there practical implications from the research in LD subtypes? An affirmative answer is given in this chapter, which demonstrates how instructional practices can be matched to subtypes to provide a subtype-by-treatment interaction.

CHAPTER 1

Behavioral Approaches

Ronald Neeper
Benjamin B. Lahey

A n impressive body of research suggests that the methods of behavior
therapy can be applied to the remediation of academic and behavioral deficits in LD children (Lahey, 1976, 1979). Behavioral conceptualizations treat learning disabilities as forms of maladaptive behavior. Viewed in this way, the same techniques used to modify other types of maladaptive behavior may be applied to learning disabilities. The focus of treatment is on the dysfunctional behavior itself rather than on deficits in attentional, neurological, perceptual-motor, psycholinguistic, or other processes believed to be responsible (Lahey, Delameter, Kupfer, & Hobbs, 1978). Second only to this emphasis on direct modification is behavior therapy's emphasis on measurement. A thorough behavioral assessment is the first and last step in the behavioral remediation of any problem. The behaviors that are to be the focus of change must be clearly identified and measured prior to, during, and following treatment.

MEDICAL MODEL THEORIES

Theories of the etiology and treatment of learning disabilities fall within one of two broad theoretical approaches: medical and behavioral

---

This chapter originally appeared as an article by **Ronald Neeper** and **Benjamin B. Lahey** in *Learning Disabilities: An Interdisciplinary Journal* (Vol. III (5), 51–61, 1984) and was adapted by permission of Grune & Stratton for inclusion in this *Handbook*.

models. Medical model theories view learning problems as overt manifestations or symptoms of an underlying pathology. The inferred pathology has been conceptualized by different theorists as lying in perceptual (Fernald, 1943; Frostig & Horn, 1964), perceptual-motor (Barch, 1967; Cratty, 1969; Kephart, 1971), neurological (Cruickshank, 1967; Delacatto, 1959; Orton, 1937), or psycholinguistic (Bush & Giles, 1969; Kirk, McCarthy, & Kirk, 1968) systems. In spite of their differences, however, these theories endorse remedial procedures aimed at remediating the underlying process deficits (the pathology) as a prerequisite to enhancing academic performance (the symptom) (Lahey, 1979; Vellutino, Steger, Moyer, Harding, & Niles, 1977; Wong, 1979). There has been a proliferation of commercially marketed training kits based on various medical model theories that have been used extensively in educational settings and have been subjected to frequent empirical scrutiny.

For example, perceptual and perceptual-motor programs (e.g., Frostig, Getman, Kephart, Barsh) have been the focus of many research investigations. Numerous reviews of this research (Glass & Robbins, 1967; Goodman & Hammill, 1973; Lahey, 1976; Ross, 1976; Spache, 1976; Stone, 1972) point to two major conclusions. First, most of the experiments are characterized by methodological flaws that make interpretation impossible. Second, the studies that meet minimal criteria for experimental design show that no improvement in academic performance is obtained when groups given perceptual and/or perceptual-motor training are compared to untreated control groups.

Remedial programs developed from psycholinguistic theories (e.g., Kirk & Kirk, 1971) do not fare any better when empirically scrutinized. Hammill and Larsen (1974) surveyed the available literature and concluded that psycholinguistic training methods were not effective in changing academic performance. The sensory deprivation approaches (Strauss & Lehtinen, 1974) based on minimal brain damage theories have not been researched as extensively as other programs. Hallahan and Kauffman (1976) reviewed this literature, however, and concluded that little benefit is derived from this restrictive approach. In perhaps the most comprehensive and convincing review to date, Arter and Jenkins (1979) similarly argued that the medical model approach to assessment and remediation does not lead to effective remediation of academic deficits.

The consistent lack of support for medical model-based remedial programs is not unexpected when these programs are examined in terms of basic learning principles. That is, children are trained in behaviors (e.g., crawling, balance-beam walking, copying abstract geometric forms) without consistent feedback or reinforcement. They are subsequently expected to show transfer to educational tasks that are only remotely related to the training (i.e., reading, mathematics, writing). There are three plausible reasons for the continuation of these approaches in spite of the lack of sound empirical support for their efficacy: (1) some methodologically flawed experiments provide apparent evidence of the beneficial results of these approaches, (2) the selection of treatment regimens is often not based on empirical evidence in the applied sciences, and (3) educators and other professionals have not been provided with viable alternatives.

BEHAVIORAL APPROACHES

The behavioral approach differs markedly from the traditional medical model conceptualizations of learning disabilities in that it does not focus on inferred etiological factors. Rather, the LD child is viewed simply as exhibiting *deficient academic behaviors* that can be altered through techniques commonly used with other behavior disorders. On a short-term basis, the behavioral approach has been successful in alleviating academic deficits in a variety of populations, including mentally retarded (e.g., Bijou, Birnbrauer, Kidder, & Tague, 1966; Brown & Perlmutter, 1971; Clark & Walberg, 1979), emotionally disturbed (e.g., Drabman, Spitalnik, & O'Leary, 1973; Hewett, Taylor, & Artuso, 1968; O'Leary & Becker, 1967), disadvantaged and underachieving (e.g., Chadwick & Day, 1971; Evans & Oswalt, 1968; Hart & Risley, 1968; Miller & Schneider, 1970; Wolf, Giles, & Hall, 1968), and normal (e.g., Harris & Sherman, 1972; Harris, Sherman, Henderson, & Harris, 1973). The lack of experimental evidence on the long-term effectiveness of the behavioral approach, however, severely limits any conclusions that can be drawn. Still, the demonstrated ineffectiveness of medical model approaches certainly suggests that alternative treatments be tried.

The behavioral approach to the remediation of academic-related behaviors is defined by three characteristics: (1) individualization and mastery learning, (2) direct teaching, and (3) emphasis on measurement. The child's strengths and weaknesses are assessed and progress is made at the child's own rate after the successful mastery of each task. Basic principles of learning are used in directly modifying the behaviors that need to be altered (e.g., remediating reading itself rather than trying to remediate an unseen processing deficit). Continuous measurement of the behavior that is being treated results in immediate feedback about the effectiveness of the treatment program and permits changes when appropriate.

Two major strategies have been used in the behavioral approach to the treatment of learning disabilities. Initial studies attempted to modify behaviors that were believed to be incompatible with learning (e.g., distractibility, impulsivity, hyperactivity) in hopes that once these incompatible behaviors were eliminated, improvements in academic performances would follow (Madsen, Becker, & Thomas, 1968; O'Leary & Becker, 1967; Wolf et al., 1968). Later studies attempted to modify specific academic deficits (Lahey, 1976, 1979).

Inappropriate Targets for Remediation

A number of false starts were made in the early search for the best targets for academic behavior modification. Much can be learned from these mistakes, however. Each of these approaches was based on the assumption that it was both necessary and sufficient to modify behaviors that were believed to be *incompatible* with effective learning to produce improvements in academic performance. In other words, it was believed that if the behavioral barriers to effective learning were removed, improved learning would be the automatic result.

Impulsivity

Research has shown that children experiencing academic difficulties often respond to academic questions faster than do normal children (Hemry, 1973; Massari & Schack, 1972). Kagan (1966) suggested that such children have an impulsive cognitive style. They do not take the time to consider all the alternatives and consequences of their actions. Thus, it was reasoned that to enhance academic performance it was necessary for LD students to delay their responses. Williams and Lahey (1977) tested this hypothesis on a group of impulsive preschool children. Their results indicated that reinforcement of correct responding produced increases in accuracy, but not in latency. Similarly, reinforcement for increased latency in responding did not produce accompanying improvements in accuracy. Furthermore, reinforcement of both latency and correct responding was no more effective than reinforcement for accurate responding alone. Apparently, it is not necessary to modify latency to produce improvements in accuracy; it is sufficient to directly target correct responding.

Attention Deficits

It has been suggested that attention deficits play a significant role in the underachievement of LD children (Barkley, 1981a; Douglas, 1972; Ross, 1976). Two meanings of the term *attention* are confused in these theories and need to be distinguished. First, reference is often made to overt attending behaviors, such as "being on-task," grossly looking at academic work, and directing eye movements toward reading stimuli. In this sense, LD children are said to be "inattentive" and "distractible," meaning that they frequently fail to direct peripheral attending behaviors to academic tasks. Second, it is often suggested that LD children have central deficits in attention. They are described as having difficulties in selecting relevant stimuli, filtering out irrelevant stimuli, and maintaining concentration.

Behavioral interventions cannot be directly focused on central attention deficits, but a number of studies have attempted to modify peripheral attending behaviors in an attempt to improve academic performance (e.g., Novy, Burnett, Powers, & Sulzer–Azaroff, 1973). Although positive reinforcement for attending does produce increases in this class of behavior, it does not result in academic gains (Marholin & Steinman, 1977). Like the proverbial horse that was led to water but would not drink, reinforcing children for peripheral attending behaviors leads them to look at their schoolwork but not to learn from it.

The appropriateness of peripheral attention deficits as targets for behavioral intervention is further questioned by the results of two studies that found that LD children do not show the erratic patterns of eye movements during reading that suggest peripheral attention deficits (Lahey, Kupfer, Beggs, & Landon, 1982; Lefton, Nagle, Johnson, & Fisher, 1979).

Excessive Motor Activity

A large percentage of LD children are also classified as hyperactive, with the overlap estimated as ranging from 50% (Lambert & Sandoval, 1980) to as high as 80% (Safer & Allen, 1976). Factor analytic studies usually identify a cluster of behaviors indicating hyperactivity (i.e., short attention span, distractibility, and impulsivity) that is frequently associated with LD children. Behavior modification programs have been successful in decreasing hyperactive behaviors (Kent & O'Leary, 1976; O'Leary & Becker, 1967). However, no investigation has shown that reducing hyperactivity produces corollary improvements in academic performance.

The clearest demonstration that it is not necessary to reduce hyperactivity before remediating academic deficits comes from a study by Ayllon, Layman, and Kandel (1975). The subjects were three children who had been classified as both learning disabled and hyperactive and whose activity levels had been successfully controlled by methylphenidate (Ritalin). When medication was discontinued, all subjects evidenced marked increases in hyperactive behavior. A token reinforcement system was incorporated for correct responses in a math workbook, in which the teacher made a checkmark on a record card for each correct response. At the end of the day, checkmarks were exchanged for various prizes or periods of free time. This program resulted in immediate improvement in the percentage of correct responses in math while performance in reading remained at low baseline levels. The children's hyperactivity in the math class dropped to baseline medication levels, while in the reading class the level of hyperactivity remained unchanged. In the last treatment phase, the token reinforcement system was implemented during the reading period as well. Similar results were obtained with significant improvements in academic performance being noted while hyperactivity levels dropped to baseline medication levels. These results have been confirmed in a number of similar studies (Ayllon & Roberts, 1974; Broughton & Lahey, 1978; Marholin & Steinman, 1977).

In these studies, direct reinforcement of academic behaviors (e.g., correct academic responses) resulted in improved academic performance while significant declines were seen in behaviors incompatible with learning, such as inattentiveness, disruptiveness, and motor activity. This latter finding is extremely important since earlier studies that focused on the elimination of disruptive behaviors through behavior modification (Ferritor, Buckholdt, Hamblin, & Smith, 1972) or medication (Rie, Rie, Stewart, & Ambuel, 1976) were unsuccessful in improving academic performance.

Appropriate Targets for Remediation

Since, by definition LD children show deficits in academic performance (Hallahan & Kauffman, 1976; Ross, 1976), academic performance should be a primary target for remediation (Lahey, Vosk, & Habif, 1981). To reiterate, the traditional approach has involved remediation of unseen process deficits that are believed to cause academic problems. The behavioral approach has shown that significant improvements in academic performance can be obtained without dealing with inferred process deficits (Lahey, 1976, 1979). This is not to say that LD children do not have process deficits; rather that direct treatment of these inferred deficits is neither possible nor necessary for academic improvements to occur. This assertion is not a statement of faith, but a conclusion based on empirical evidence. Two studies provide examples of the kind of data that support such a position. Lahey, Busemeyer, O'Hara, and Beggs (1977) worked with four LD children with severe deficits in handwriting. The children wrote in mirror image or could not write at all in spite of normal intelligence and several years of education. When reinforcement was made contingent upon correctly written words, dramatic changes occurred in handwriting. If it is reasonable to assume that these children had severe deficits in the underlying process of perceptual-motor integration, then we must also assume that reinforced practice remediated both the academic behavior and the underlying perceptual-motor deficit. However, it is not necessary to add inferred process variables to a conceptualization of learning disabilities, but simply to focus on overt academic deficits.

A study of reading comprehension by Lahey, McNees, and Brown (1973) illustrated that it is not necessary to remediate process deficits to modify academic behavior. The subjects were two sixth-grade children who showed major discrepancies between their oral reading (both at a 6.5 grade level) and reading for comprehension (both at a 4.5 grade level). During the first baseline phase the subjects answered 65% to 85% of the questions correctly. When reinforcement (social praise and money) was provided, correct responses rose immediately to 80% to 100%. The percentage of correct answers dropped during the second baseline, but increased to at or above 90% correct when the treatment phase was reinstated. In fact, the subjects' accuracy rose to grade level as soon as the treatment periods began. These findings illustrate the significant short-term effects that appropriate reinforcement procedures can have on a complex cognitive/academic skill without treating underlying process deficits (e.g., poor sequencing skills, inadequate memory).

In addition to handwriting and reading comprehension, direct behavioral intervention has been successful with a variety of academic targets, including letter identification (Stromer, 1975, 1977), sight-word vocabulary (Lahey & Drabman, 1974), arithmetic (Broughton & Lahey, 1978; Kirby & Shields, 1972; Lovitt & Smith, 1974; Smith, Lovitt, & Kidder, 1972), and oral reading (Ryback & Staats, 1970; Staats & Butterfield, 1965).

Educational assessments and interventions that are aimed directly at academic performance deficits rather than underlying process deficits are typically *molecular* in nature. That is, they focus on highly specific problems such as phonics skill, visual letter discrimination, and multiplication skills. The educational programs based on molecular assessments are generally individually tailored to the specific deficits identified in the LD child and are often implemented in a tutoring format. Some behavioral studies indicated, however, that it may be possible to modify more global or *molar* units of academic behavior without specifically modifying the molecular deficits associated with these molar units (Lahey, 1979). For example, a number of studies (reviewed by Lahey, 1977) demonstrated that reinforcing disabled readers for correctly reading aloud entire sentences (a molar unit of reading behavior) led to increases in oral reading accuracy, regardless of what molecular deficits led to poor oral reading.

TOWARD A MODEL FOR BEHAVIORAL INTERVENTION

Research in behavioral interventions with academic deficits leads to the following conclusions. First, intervention should focus on direct modification of academic behavior, not on behavior believed to be incompatible with effective learning. Second, remedial programs should focus directly on the deficient academic behavior rather than on inferred process deficits.

Research to date has focused primarily on two issues: (1) can specific academic deficits be modified and (2) are specific academic behaviors independent (in the sense that modifying one does not lead to changes in other academic areas)? For example, reading can be thought of as consisting of a number of separate behaviors that are functionally independent. Lahey, McNees, and Schnelle (1977) tested this hypothesis by giving token reinforcement contingent upon correct responses in one of three different reading subject areas: comprehension, oral speed, and oral accuracy. Reinforcement resulted in significant improvements in each behavior, but no interdependence among the three reading behaviors was observed. That is, improvements in one area of reading did not have any effect on the other two reading behaviors.

SPECIFYING TARGET BEHAVIORS

Since research has confirmed that all significant aspects of academic performance can be modified and that they are generally independent of one another, the next step is to develop and test a model that specifies target behaviors. Such a model must be judged by four criteria: (1) feasibility, (2) adequate assessment, (3) identification of functional units of academic behavior, and (4) efficient use of learning principles.

Feasibility

Teachers usually adopt intervention strategies that are convenient and feasible within the restrictive demands of the classroom. Intervention methods that require one-to-one instruction, excessive preparation time, or that detract from other instructional programs are less likely to be used.

Adequate Assessment

Lahey and colleagues (Lahey et al., 1981) recommended a protocol for the behavioral assessment of LD students. Assessment included the use of standardized tests, a review of written work, and direct observation. A summary of Lahey's protocol follows.

Standardized achievement tests provide useful global estimates of academic performance. Tests should assess a wide variety of skills and should employ test items that closely *resemble the academic tasks performed in the classroom.* Only by measuring what is being taught can standardized tests provide useful quantification of classroom progress. At a minimum, the test battery should include: (a) a spelling test in which the child is required to actually write the words to be spelled, (b) a math test in which the child writes the calculations to be performed, and (c) a reading test in which the child reads orally or silently and is required to answer comprehension questions like those required in the classroom.

Standardized tests of language functioning may be useful in screening for problems in this area. An emphasis should be placed on selecting a test that yields objective (targetable) results.

Repeated assessment in an essential part of a behavioral approach (Ross, 1981). Daily samples of written academic work provide an unobtrusive means of continuously collecting assessment data. In addition to providing information about basic achievement skills, written samples can provide data on perceptual and fine-motor performance directly related to actual classroom performance.

If feasible, *all* written work (not just potentially biased samples) should be collected to provide an assessment of typical performance. Several days of written work (5 to 10) should be collected prior to any intervention to provide a stable baseline against which to assess any improvements produced by the intervention.

Direct observation of behavior can be a useful adjunct to standardized tests and written work samples. In addition to providing information on such academic skills as oral reading, direct observation provides data on environmental factors that may be contributing to academic performance deficits (e.g., inadvertent reinforcement from the teacher for not attending or disruptive peers). Based on these observations, a functional analysis of environmental factors is possible. Often direct observation is not feasible, however, due to time and staffing constraints. Teacher ratings of behavior (using standardized rating scales) may provide a summary statement of a child's typical behavior in the classroom (Barkley, 1981a). These ratings may also provide data regarding psychiatric classification.

Identification of Functional Units of Academic Behavior

The goal of remedial educational programs is to allow a child to perform the daily academic tasks that occur in a classroom. An intervention will only be judged to be successful if it eliminates deficiencies in functional units of academic behavior. Remedial methods may focus on other aspects of academic behavior, but benefit must be seen in the classroom if intervention is to be considered a success. For example, this suggests that the target of reading intervention should, at least initially, be the functional, or molar, unit of reading in a child's classroom. If the teacher wants the child to answer more questions in the reading workbook, reinforcement should be made contingent upon each correct answer.

Research indicates that significant improvements in molar units of academic behavior can be obtained without focusing on finer deficiencies in behavior (Ayllon, Layman, & Kandel, 1975; Lahey, 1979). Ayllon et al. (1975) used a highly molar strategy to improve the academic performance of three children who were diagnosed as both learning disabled and hyperactive. The study, conducted using a replicated multiple baseline design across reading and math classes, evaluated the use of a token reinforcement system targeting correct academic responding in workbooks. All three children were taking medication (Ritalin) at the start of the study. Baseline observations indicated that the medication controlled their motor activity, but their academic performance was consistently low. After a drug wash-out period, baseline observations of behavior and workbook performance were repeated. No changes in academic performance were found during this phase, but dramatic increases in motor activity and disruptive behavior were observed.

Treatment began in the third phase of the design. The teacher administered token reinforcement (checkmarks on a daily report card) contingent on correct performance in the math workbook. Checkmarks were later exchanged for prizes of differing value. The results of this contingency were both immediate and clinically dramatic. Hyperactive behavior decreased to levels equivalent to those while the children were medicated, and concurrent increases in correct responding to math problems were observed. The final phase of treatment included both the math and reading workbooks in the reinforcement program. Low levels of hyperactive behavior in both settings resulted along with concurrent increases in reading and math performance.

Lahey, McNees, and Brown (1973) used a tutoring method to modify reading comprehension. In this study, children read short passages aloud and answered questions based on the passages. Treatment consisted of contingent feedback regarding accuracy and reinforcement for correct answers. Reinforcement consisted of praise and money (pennies). Accurate responses to comprehension questions increased upon initiation of treatment. While the children were being reinforced, their comprehension levels rose two grade levels.

Researchers have found that major improvements in oral reading can be achieved solely by reinforcing correct oral reading, rather than by setting reinforcement contingencies for elimination of specific molecular reading problems (Haring & Hauck, 1969; Ryback & Staats, 1970; Wadsworth, 1971). This approach has been successful with other academic behaviors, including reading comprehension (Lahey, McNees, & Brown, 1973), handwriting (Lahey et al., 1977), and arithmetic (Cullinan, Lloyd, & Epstein, 1981; Kirby & Shields, 1972; Lloyd, Saltzman, & Kauffman, 1981).

In some cases, it may be necessary to also take a more molecular approach to remediation. Molecular interventions teach skills that are not the goal of education per se, but are components of the desired educational skills. For example, reading sentences is a goal of education, whereas visually discriminating letter shapes is considered a subsidiary skill; in this sense, visual discrimination is a molecular reading behavior. Molecular interventions not only focus on "smaller" units of academic behavior, but use a more complex treatment strategy that can often best be implemented in a tutoring format tailored to the needs of the individual child.

Hallahan et al. (1983) noted that molecularly focused programs may be conceptualized as having three main treatment components: modeling, practice, and reinforcement. Initially, the desired academic behavior (such as writing specific letters) is modeled by the teacher or tutor. Students practice the modeled skill, receiving feedback regarding accuracy as they practice. The final component of the procedure is reinforcement, which ranges from simple praise to tokens that may be exchanged for desired objects or activities.

Lahey and Drabman (1974) used modeling and reinforced practice to enhance oral reading of sight words. They compared simple performance feedback, which is analogous to traditional modes of classroom instruction, to performance feedback in combination with tangible reinforcement (pennies). The children who received feedback plus reinforcement outperformed the children who received feedback alone by a large margin. The children who received the combination treatment not only required half the number of learning trials, but retained their newly acquired vocabulary words longer.

Lahey, Weller, and Brown (1973) used a molecular strategy to train adults with extensive histories of underachievement in a basic phonics discrimination task. Treatment included providing contingent feedback and reinforcement for correct responding. Training appeared to generalize. Verbally presenting the subjects with rules of phonics (as is the traditional mode of education) did not increase their abilities to phonetically decode words. In this study the authors generated six lists of 15 words, each containing the five primary vowels in both long and short sound forms. All of the words were of the format consonant-vowel-consonant, with the letter "e" at the end of half of the words. All of the words with an "e" at the end were pronounced with a long medial vowel (e.g., rate, bite), and all of the words without a final "e" were pronounced with a short medial vowel (e.g., rat, bit). The words were presented one at a time on 3×5 cards. Four adults were trained in this general rule for decoding vowel sounds with these lists of words.

Initially, the subjects were asked to read the first set of words, without feedback or instruction, as a baseline assessment. Following this phase, the general phonics rule was verbally presented by the experimenter and the students were again required to read the word list. Little improvement was noted even after the instructional component of the treatment was introduced. The third phase of the treatment protocol consisted of the experimenter providing contingent feedback and reinforcement for correct responding while the subjects read the initial word list repeatedly until a criterion of two consecutive trials without error was met. Following this phase, a baseline condition was reinstituted where the subjects read the original word list without feedback. Little or no decrement in performance was observed. The five additional sets of words served as generalization probes. The subjects were trained on each of these sets following the procedure outlined above. It was noted that fewer training trials were required for each successive set of words introduced, hence the training appeared to generalize.

Lahey et al. (1977) demonstrated the effectiveness of a simple behavioral intervention conducted in a tutoring format for the treatment of severe graphomotor (handwriting) disturbance. These investigators treated four children in two different protocols. Two children were recruited from an LD classroom where they were placed due to their high frequency of reversing letters and letter sequences ("mirror writing"). Treatment for these two children consisted of contingent feedback and monetary reward (pennies) for appropriate handwriting. Rather than focusing on molecular skills of forming letter strokes or individual letters, the children were asked to copy complete words one at a time before feedback was given. The criteria for appropriate handwriting were that productions needed to be legible, with the letters in proper sequence, and in the correct spatial orientation. To assess the generalization of treatment, the children also copied unpracticed words. The treatment produced dramatic and generalized improvement in the number of reversals, sequencing errors, and general legibility of the children's handwriting.

The second group of students demonstrated more severe graphomotor problems than did the first two students; they could not produce legible letters or words at all. As in the previous treatment program, reinforcement given contingent upon correctly writing each word resulted in dramatic improvement in the legibility of the children's handwriting. Generalization to the actual classroom did not occur for one of these students, emphasizing the need to extend the contingencies to the classroom environment.

Several authors have attempted to correct visual letter reversals and substitutions using stimulus-fading techniques (Gibson & Levin, 1975; Ross, 1976, 1981). Generally these techniques are based on the assumption that children who reverse or substitute letters that are similar in appearance, are "overattending" to the common characteristics between the letters and ignoring the distinguishing characteristics. For example, it is proposed that a child who is confusing P with R, may be ignoring the distinguishing stem of the R and focusing attention only on the features in common with P. To remediate this using a stimulus fading technique, the two letters would be presented simulataneously. However, the stem of the R would be highlighted in some manner to draw attention to it as a distinguishing characteristic. Several discrimination trials would be conducted in which the child would be asked to correctly name and write the two letters. Over a series of discrimination learning trials, the amount (area) of highlight on the stem of the R would be decreased until it faded out completely, with the result that the child would be able to distinguish the letters correctly without highlight. In his review of these studies, Ross (1981) provided a generally favorable evaluation of their effectiveness. It must be pointed out however, that stimulus-fading techniques have not been used beyond the laboratory and their effects on actual classroom performance are not known.

Remediation of molecular deficits does not focus on the molar goal of a remedial program and often involves additional preparation and one-to-one instruction. Thus, molecular instruction should only be provided when direct remediation with the functional classroom units of academic behavior is not successful, or when particular deficits are so obvious that it is clear that molecular instruction will be needed. This necessity may be less common than first anticipated until experience is gained with the molar approach of reinforcing classroom academic performance.

Efficient Use of Learning Principles

Because LD children are, by definition, less able than most children to benefit from classroom instruction, it is necessary to maximize their learning conditions. This means that teaching methods must be based on the principles of learning. Specifically, it is essential to reduce the size of the response unit to create a high probability of success, and to provide consistent positive reinforcement for correct performance.

BEHAVIOR THERAPY AND LEARNING DISABILITIES: CONSTRAINTS

There is still much to learn about the remediation of academic deficits. Research has provided some effective ways to modify targeted academic behaviors (primarily by operant reinforcement) and has shown that it is generally more effective to directly modify academic behavior than to eliminate behavior patterns that are believed to be incompatible with learning. However, we do not know if the population of LD children consists of dissimilar subtypes that would benefit from different treatment strategies. We do not know whether it is better to target molar units of academic behavior or to target more molecular units. Treiber and Lahey (1983) recommended a strategy of targeting molecular aspects of academic performance only when molar strategies prove ineffective, but this is a pragmatic strategy based on lack of data rather than an empirical resolution of the problem. We do not know which molar or molecular units of academic behavior should be targeted for remediation in which order.

In short, we know a considerable amount about how to use the principles of learning and cognition to improve the learning of LD children, but we do not know how to best use this knowledge to teach them.

As noted, earlier, the behavioral approach to remediating learning disabilities is neither completely developed nor without problems. Still, given what we now know, behavior therapy is the treatment of choice, if only because other methods appear to be less effective and are more problematic. The following protocol is offered, therefore, with the understanding that the reader has been made aware of the current limitations of a behavioral approach to learning disabilities.

Operant techniques are generally effective in remediating academic deficits (Lahey, 1977). This is true with regard to both molar academic behavior and molecular academic behavior. Operant procedures targeting molar behaviors appear to be cost efficient means of modifying academic problems. For reasons of cost-effectiveness and demonstrated remedial efficacy, initial interventions should consist of operant treatment with a molar focus (Treiber & Lahey, 1983).

Several precautions should be taken when initiating an operant program for learning problems. Teachers and parents are often placed in the position of carrying out treatment. For both practical and ethical reasons, their input in selecting goals and designing the treatment procedures is essential (Lahey et al., 1981). Selecting reasonable, achievable goals along with a flexible schedule for reaching them, is the first step in treatment. Problems in reaching goals indicate a need to reassess factors that may be interfering with the progress of treatment. Variable academic performance during treatment often indicate the operation of environmental factors external to treatment (e.g., disruptive peers). Setting unrealistic goals or using weak reinforcement will, in contrast, tend to produce consistently low performance.

Molar operant procedures will not be effective with all children. Children who do not respond to such procedures are probably experiencing difficulties of a more severe degree. For these children, a molecular operant focus may be in order (Treiber & Lahey, 1983). In some severe cases, the remedial educator may need to resort to very basic and time-consuming techniques, such as stimulus fading and behavioral language training. Ross (1981) provided a comprehensive review of these techniques, which may be considered, because of difficulty of implementation, the treatment of last resort.

SUMMARY

Years of research attempting to identify specific cognitive processing deficits in LD children that may be targeted for remediation have yielded few conclusive results. It seems that for each study that indicates LD children possess a specific cognitive processing deficit, there is another study that indicates they do not. These muddled results may be due to the fact that research populations have included heterogeneous types of learning disabilities (Torgesen, 1981). Additionally, many studies have suffered from inadequate methodology and control.

A similar dilemma exists regarding the development of effective treatments. If we cannot define subtypes of LD children and, therefore, cannot delineate the behavioral and cognitive processing deficits shown by the various subtypes, we are limited in our ability to develop specific remedial techniques and evaluate their effectiveness. It seems then, that the logical first step to further understanding and treatment of learning disabilities is to empirically derive objective and operationally definable subtypes of learning disabilities. Following this step, we can systematically determine which remedial technique is most effective with each subtype.

A final note addressed specifically to the development of remedial techniques is in order. To date, no behavior therapy study of learning disabilities has included a long-term follow-up. Additionally, behavioral techniques have rarely been directly compared with more traditional methods of treatment, and specific behavioral techniques (e.g., stimulus fading, operant reinforcement) have not been compared with one another. Future research with behavioral techniques must address these issues.

CHAPTER 2

Cognitive Methods

Bernice Y. L. Wong

Cognitive intervention research with LD students represents several independent efforts. Many within the LD field have adopted the models and experimental paradigms of psychology, particularly Skinner's behaviorism. Skinner's notions of stimulus control, shaping, and reinforcement radically changed the approach to learning disabilities. LD practitioners began to examine variables in the environment that affect learning disabilities instead of blaming them for all the adverse consequences of a handicap (Bryan & Bryan, 1977).

Techniques derived from behavior modification have been used with LD students. One such technique is direct instruction, which emphasizes active effort by the teacher to elicit as many responses from students as possible within a certain time. Direct instruction focuses attention on the amount and type of environmental structuring necessary to assure controlled and consistent student achievement. Environmental structuring includes grouping by immediate instructional needs, careful sequencing of academic skills, modeling, rapid pacing to provide many response opportunities, using response signals to control attention and pace, choral and independent responding, immediate corrective feedback, including adequate, contingent reinforcement, and frequent, teacher-monitored practice. These techniques can be used in all

Portions of this chapter originally appeared in an article by **Bernice Y. L. Wong** which appeared in the *Journal of Special Education* (Vol. 20 (1), 9–29, 1986) and was adapted by permission of Grune & Stratton for inclusion in this *Handbook*.

aspects of curriculum and across a range of learner characteristics (e.g., Becker, 1977; Becker & Carnine, 1981; Carnine, 1983; Englemann, 1969; Lloyd, 1975; Lloyd, Cullinan, Heins, & Epstein, 1980).

The LD field has also profited from measurement techniques developed in educational psychology. Evaluative research has provided methodologies for special educators to measure the effectiveness of educational programs and to evaluate the impact of specific government and nongovernment policies on disabled individuals (Bryan & Bryan, 1977). Wang and Birch's (1984) evaluative study of the implementation and impact of a full-time mainstreaming program in an urban school system represents the application of sophisticated evaluation methodologies to special education.

Descriptive and explanatory models of learning failure borrowed from cognitive psychology could be used to differentiate student needs and to design instructional interventions (Farnham-Diggory & Nelson, 1984). Cognitive psychologists emphasize the individual as an active information-processor (Anderson, 1975; Mandler, 1981; Reeves & Brown, 1985) who actively interacts with the environment and does not passively react to impinging stimuli. Cognitive psychologists conceptualize two systems of internal organization: the representational system and the executive system (Anderson, 1975). The *representational system* deals with how information input is selectively organized, attended to, and meaningfully interpreted. The *executive system* is posited to explain control processes manifested in the planning, monitoring, checking, and evaluating of our actions. These control processes direct and edit our behavior (Miller, Galanter, & Pribram, 1960).

A cognitive approach to educating LD students advocates the following. First, LD students must actively participate in their learning and must assume control of the learning situation (Brown, 1980; Reid & Hresko, 1981a). Second, it is important for teachers to inculcate in LD students self-monitoring, planning, and self-evaluation skills (Wong, 1985a). Reid and Hresko (1981a) provided many illustrations of how the preceding two points can be translated into teaching practices.

The relevance of a cognitive approach to educating LD students can be seen by examining learning style and attributional patterns, two factors that critically affect learning outcomes. Children who think they are in control of their environment and are oriented to mastery learning appear to be the most successful learners. However, as the result of persistent academic failure, LD students often develop a passive, maladaptive learning style (McKinney, McClure, & Feagans, 1982; Torgesen, 1977) and acquire maladaptive traits typical of learned helpless children. When they succeed, LD children attribute it to luck; when they fail, they attribute it to lack of ability (Pearl, 1985; Pearl, Bryan, & Herzog, 1983). Teaching LD students to become active learners and, through reattribution training, to acquire adaptive reactions to failure appears to be a logical remedy for their maladaptive learning mode and attributions.

COGNITIVE PSYCHOLOGY AND LEARNING DISABILITIES

The influence of cognitive psychology on learning disabilities can be seen in the burgeoning studies of various forms of metacognitive strategy interventions, including the application of cognitive behavior modification (Hallahan, 1980; Harris, 1985; Wong, 1985a), training packages involving cognitive and/or metacognitive components (Alley & Deshler, 1979; Palincsar, 1982; Wong & Jones, 1982), and strategy generalization (Brown Campione, & Barclay, 1979; Kendall, Borkowski, & Cavanaugh, 1980).

Metacognition is the introspective awareness of one's own cognitive processes and one's self-regulation. Flavell (1976) originated the theoretical concept of metacognition to explain young children's failure to generalize trained mnemonic strategies in his research on memory processes. He proposed that children failed to generalize learned strategies because they were not aware of the parameters governing the outcome of their recall performance. In contrast, Flavell illustrated that adults realize the need to spend more time studying items that are harder to remember and thereby demonstrate *metamemory*, i.e., metacognition concerning memory processes. Metacognition enables us to use suitable strategies to deal effectively with task demands. Thus, the failure of younger children to generalize learned mnemonic strategies is seen as their lack of metamemorial knowledge.

Brown (1980) underscored the crucial role of metacognition in effective reading. However, it should be pointed out that notions akin to metacognition have long been held in reading. For example, Huey (1968) defined reading as "thought-getting and thought manipulating," Thorndike (1917) contended that "reading is reasoning," and Gray (1952) said "reading is a form of clear and vigorous thinking."

Researchers in cognitive developmental psychology and instructional psychology have obtained valuable insights into metacognitive processes and discovered the complex relationship between metacognition and strategy use (Borkowski, Johnston, & Reid, in press). Equally important, they have outlined specific steps in teaching metacognitive strategies that have been empirically validated and could easily be adapted by teachers (André & Anderson, 1978-79; Collins & Smith, 1980; Garner & Kraus, 1982; Palincsar, 1982; Taylor 1982; Taylor & Beach, 1984; Wong & Jones, 1982).

Metacognition has made important contributions to the LD field. By highlighting the critical role of phonemic awareness in the process of learning to read, metacognition provides an understanding of why certain children do not learn to read. Metacognitive skills underlie efficient reading and effective studying. LD students lack these skills, and their poor scholastic achievement reflects not only deficient basic skills, but also deficient metacognitive skills. Metacognition also contributes to understanding the failure of LD students to maintain and generalize learned skills/strategies.

METACOGNITION AND READING

Phonemic awareness is knowledge of the abstract nature of language. Children must learn that a word is made up of a string of separable sounds, that a word can be segmented into its constituent components (phonemes), and that constituent sounds can be blended into a word. Unless children acquire this phonemic awareness, they will experience difficulties in learning to read (Libermann, 1973, 1982; Seymour, 1970). Williams (1986) summarized the data on the important role of phonemic awareness in learning to read. However, an alternative view is that reading instruction can promote the phonemic skills of analysis and blending and phonemic awareness. Ehri (1979) maintained that when children learn to read and spell, they acquire "print" (written language), and this knowledge of print affects the way they perceive language. For example, when children use their knowledge of spelling to help them in a phonemic segmentation task, they end up with incorrect answers. They would claim that "boat" has four phonemes since they count the silent *a*. (Space does not permit an elaborate discussion on these opposing views except to note that they have been reconciled.)

At present, the consensus among researchers is that there is a reciprocal relationship between phonemic ability and reading instruction (Williams, 1986). However, a child's lack of phonemic awareness can result in the subsequent development of reading disabilities (Fox & Routh, 1975; Snowling, 1980). Baker and Brown (1984a, 1984b) provides excellent summaries of further metacognitive research in reading.

Metacognitive skills "involve predicting, checking/self-monitoring, reality-testing, coordinating and control of deliberate attempts to solve problems or to study and learn" (Brown, 1980, p. 454). A good reader possesses metacognitive skills in reading, is aware of the purpose of reading, and differentiates between task demands by seeking to clarify the purpose of reading a given material (Anderson, 1980). This awareness leads to use of suitable reading strategies. For example, a good reader varies reading rate and concentration level as a function of the material being read — text or magazine. Such awareness leads to self-monitoring of reading comprehension. For example, good readers who encounter comprehension difficulties use debugging strategies, which indicate self-regulation (Anderson, 1980; Brown, 1980). Fluent readers are rarely conscious of their own comprehension monitoring. When a comprehension failure arises, the fluent reader immediately slows reading rate and reviews the difficult section or reads on seeking enlightenment in subsequent text (Anderson, 1980). In contrast, learning-disabled readers show little indication of coordination between demands and suitable reading strategies. They lack the requisite metacognitive skills in reading (Wong, 1985a).

Awareness of the Purpose of Reading

Younger, poorer readers perceive the purpose of reading to be decoding rather than reading for meaning (Canney & Winograd, 1979; Garner & Kraus, 1982). This is an understandable result of the emphasis in the early grades on decoding, auditory and visual discrimination (Seymour, 1970), and remedial phonics drills. But for older, poor readers who have learned to decode sufficiently, the perception of reading as decoding reflects deficient awareness of the purpose of reading, that is, a failure to develop the appropriate metacognition about the reading task.

Canney and Winograd's (1979) study illustrated the developmental shift in children's metacognition about the purpose of reading. They found that by grade 6, good readers showed a shift in their perception of what reading entails. They attended more to the comprehension aspects of reading, whereas poor readers still appeared to retain a decoding focus in reading. Garner and Kraus (1982) reported similar findings. Lack of awareness of the proper purpose of reading impairs reading efficiency.

Knowledge of Reading Strategies

Using 144 children from grades 3 and 6, and 24 children at three reading levels (good, average, poor) per grade, Forrest and Waller (1980) investigated children's knowledge about decoding, comprehension, and strategies of reading for a purpose, such as skimming or studying. In individual interviews, each child was asked standardized questions about the reading skills of decoding, comprehension, and advanced strategies. They found that younger and poorer readers possessed fewer strategies, knew less about decoding, comprehension, and reading proficiency, and were less sensitive to problems, such as recognition of a comprehension problem, and less able to solve problems. Reading skills increased with grade level and reading proficiency.

A reader's sensitivity to important parts of a text enables efficient allocation of attention and efforts in focused study of relevant information. Poor readers may lack such sensitivity and awareness.

Winograd (1984) investigated summarization difficulties in eighth graders. He found that good and poor comprehenders had strikingly different notions of important sentences in given passages. Poor comprehenders selected sentences that contained details, especially details of a highly visual nature. Good comprehenders, in contrast, selected main idea or topic sentences. Their choice of important sentences parallelled that of adult readers. When poor comprehenders summarized given passages, there was a low correlation between their summary contents and the rated importance of the sentences in the summaries. That is, poor comprehenders included information in their summaries that was less important based on their own rating. In contrast, good comprehenders were consistent; they included information that they rated as important in their summaries and deleted information that they rated as less important. Winograd's findings indicated that the eighth-grade poor comprehenders lacked sensitivity to important parts of the text. This deficiency affected adversely the adequacy of their summaries of given passages.

Comprehension Monitoring

Many investigators have reported that students with poor reading comprehension and LD adolescents do not monitor reading comprehension (Garner, 1980, 1981; Garner & Kraus, 1982; Garner & Taylor, 1982; Wong & Jones, 1982). Garner and Kraus (1982) investigated seventh-grade good and poor comprehenders' conceptions of reading and their detection of intersentence and intrasentence inconsistencies. Narrative passages were designed to include conflicting information in the first and last sentences (intersentence inconsistency) or only within the last sentence (intrasentence inconsistency). The subjects were asked to determine whether any of the passages needed revision by the writer. Garner and Kraus found that of 15 good comprehenders, 4 detected intersentence inconsistency and 12 detected intrasentence inconsistency. None of the 15 poor comprehenders detected either type of information inconsistency. Clearly, poor comprehenders had not engaged in comprehension-monitoring.

Debugging Strategies

Debugging refers to strategies that a person employs to resolve a comprehension difficulty. Although good comprehenders are reported to monitor their listening and reading comprehension (Garner, 1981; Garner & Kraus, 1982; Markman, 1977), data on whether they also spontaneously employ debugging strategies and on the nature of these strategies were not obtained until a study by Garner and Reis (1981). Nineteen poor comprehenders in grades 4 through 10, with a median of grade 7, and an equal number of good comprehenders participated in the study. For the purposes of their study, Garner and Reis devised a passage and comprehension test questions that would require the subject to review the passage. The passage was broken into three segments, each on a separate sheet, to facilitate the experimenter's recording of subjects' review behaviors. On each page, the text of the passage apppeared on the top half, and the questions appeared on the bottom half of the page. The subjects were seen individually and told to read the first segment silently, and then answer questions. After completing the first segment and the attached questions, students were told to continue with the second segment. The page containing the first segment of the passage was left at a 90-degree angle to facilitate the experimenter's observation and recording of the subject's review behaviors. (Some of the questions on the second segment of the passage entailed referring to the first segment for accurate answers.)

Garner and Reis (1981) found that good comprehenders had a higher frequency of correct responses in instances of recorded review behavior. However, further examination of the data indicated that there was an unexpected age-experience factor at work among the good comprehenders. The six oldest poor comprehenders showed no differential performance from the group of poor comprehenders in successfully answering question's on which they reviewed the text; however, the six oldest good comprehenders were substantially more successful than their entire group. Based on frequency of reviewing and percentage of accuracy in comprehension test questions, poor comprehenders and younger good comprehenders differed from the six oldest good comprehenders in using review as a debugging strategy. More important, only the oldest good comprehenders showed spontaneous use of review with high frequency.

One important finding was that comprehension monitoring is not necessarily followed by a debugging strategy when a comprehension problem is met. Garner and Reis found that sixth- and seventh-grade good comprehenders did show comprehension monitoring, but monitoring was not followed by review. Only the oldest eighth-grade good comprehenders showed *both* comprehension monitoring and spontaneous lookbacks. The investigators concluded that in the developmental sequence of detecting and resolving comprehension breakdowns, monitoring precedes deployment of debugging strategies.

Garner and Reis's study is important not only because of their purpose of inquiry and the data obtained, but also because of the use of quantitative *and* qualitative data. They recorded observations of nonverbal and verbal indices of noncomprehension in the subjects, such as shrugging shoulders, making faces, and verbalizations such as, "That's a hard one; can we skip it?" Using both quantitative and qualitative information enables a more comprehensive picture of the subjects' cognitive and metacognitive behaviors.

METACOGNITION AND REMEDIATION

The impact of metacognitive theory and research on the LD field is evident in the development of specific prescriptive approaches in remediation. Alley and Deshler (1979) designed specific remedial procedures and curricula. A prototypical example of their work is the COPS error monitoring strategy used in teaching LD adolescents to monitor errors in their written assignment. COPS stands for capitalization, overall appearance, punctuation, and spelling. Similarly, the 5-step self-questioning procedure used in Wong and Jones' (1982) study induced systematic self-monitoring in LD adolescents and consequently enhanced their reading comprehension. The self-questions in Wong and Jones' study were: (1) Why read this passage? (To answer questions later.) (2) Find the main idea(s) in a paragraph, and underline it (them). (3) Think of a question about the main idea you have underlined (a *good* question targets the main idea and paraphrases it). (4) Learn the answer to the question. (5) Always look back at the questions and answers to see how each successive question and answer add more information.

Metacognition has generated a new orientation in remedial instruction of LD students in which self-monitoring procedures and basic skills building now receive equal emphasis. Implicit in this remedial orientation is the adoption of the basic tenet in cognitive psychology, namely, the centrality of the students' active participation in and responsibility for their learning (Brown, 1980; Wittrock, 1978). We not only need to improve LD students' academic skills, we need to improve them to the extent that they can function *autonomously* like their non-LD peers. To attain such a remedial criterion for LD students typically lacking in autonomy, a self-monitoring component must be included within any remedial program. In designing self-monitoring training, reseachers and practitioners can draw on the theory and research in cognitive behavior modification (Meichenbaum, 1977; Meichenbaum & Asarnow, 1978).

Metacognitive Intervention

If LD students can be characterized by the fact that they learn at a slower rate than their non-LD peers, can metacognitive methods be used to address specific obstacles encountered during acquisition of basic academic skills and produce accelerated learning? Metacognition might be applied whenever acquisition roadblocks are confronted or might be a formal part of the everyday curriculum (Borkowski & Cavanaugh, 1979; Borkowski & Konarski, 1981).

Corno and Mandinach (1983) sugested that metacognitive research has underscored the need to develop better conceptualizations of "self-regulated" learning in classroom settings and not only in laboratories. It is in actual day-to-day teaching of LD learners that the need for guidelines to modify metacognitive methods becomes apparent. Self-regulated learning implies that students have the ability to be efficient and effective on specific learning tasks and the competence to learn cumulatively, independent of task content. The problem, from both a theoretical and applied point of view, is whether there exists a unified metacognitive approach that can be applied simultaneously to specific and general learner competence and that can also be implemented, with reasonable economy of time and effort, in real classrooms.

Self-Monitoring

Some of the theoretical and practical problems are illustrated in research investigating the effectiveness of metacognitive techniques for training LD students to monitor and to record their attention to task. Training students to pay attention to task, where "attention" means cognitive engagement with task content as well as resistance to distraction, should result in generalized improvement in learning, independent of task.

Systematically developed studies (Hallahan, Lloyd, Kauffman, & Loper, 1983), have shown that that training similar to that used by Meichenbaum and Goodman (1971) resulted in LD students learning how to regulate their task orientation behavior to match a behavioral model of appropriate attention to task. These studies found that students trained to self-monitor and record attention showed marked improvements in academic productivity. However, this improvement was observed almost entirely during drill activities, which led to the conclusion that self-monitoring may work best with LD students who have attention problems, not skill deficiencies. How, then, can metacognitive methods be used to improve skill learning?

In a review of 27 studies of the effects of training self-questioning on the processing of prose, Wong (1985) differentiated three approaches to intervention that were generally based on three different conceptual frameworks. These are loosely classified as active processing and metacognitive and schema theories. She noted that active processing theories result in interventions that use "higher order" self-questions to induce a more thorough processing of material. Self-questioning routines based on metacognitive theories tend to emphasize self-monitoring of discriminable aspects of prose material or responses that can be compared to a set of guidelines. Schema theory emphasizes self-statements designed to help students access prior knowledge that might be relevant for completing their present task.

Cognitive Strategies

A primary concept in metacognition is "strategy," which suggests a means of inferring links between covert and overt actions. Although useful conceptually as a bridging device between cognitive phenomena, it has been argued that the concept strategy is often invoked uncritically to explain experimental results related to a variety of different theoretical positions and applied purposes. Gerber (1983) warned that the concept would become obscured and lose its explanatory power unless its meaning was clarified. Lloyd (1980), for example, described strategies as "a series of steps ... through which students proceed in order to solve a problem" (p. 53). According to Lloyd, these steps can be abstracted as general plans for any task, or they can be very task-specific. Related discussion in the literature concerning differentiation of cognitive and metacognitive activity does little to clarify the central notion of a strategy. Rather, the concept appears to drift in response to particular purposes, sometimes describing an overt behavior, sometimes a presumptive self-verbalization, and sometimes mental activity. Are strategies collections of rote memorized rules or abstract algorithms? Are strategies organized problem-related thoughts or thoughts about organizing problem-related thoughts? Are they plans to control thinking or are they the controls themselves? The answers are unclear and often contradictory, but are nontheless critical to how cognitive-behavioral training methods are designed and implemented.

Hall (1980) suggested that concern for organization and reduction of information load is common to all metacognitive interventions. The primary goal is to discover ways in which LD students can be taught to approach learning tasks in a more structured and more efficient manner. Structure, in Hall's argument, implies organization. It would also seem to imply a transactional relationship between operations devoted to searching a knowledge base for relevant information and the structure of that knowledge base. For example, how quickly and efficiently one can reduce uncertainty by using what is known may determine to some degree both the reliability and future accessibility of newly appended knowledge. Conversely, the degree of organization with which knowledge has accumulated in the past may severely constrain the possible speed and efficency of search procedures selected in response to learning problems in the present.

Strategies impose structure by controlling the organization and sequencing of information and the timing and rate of response demand. It is a matter of pedagogical indifference whether they are defined as overt behaviors or as internalized, cognitive habits. It becomes clear how teaching can affect different learners. For mildly handicapped students particularly, effective teaching, as in direct instruction, provides highly constraining structure that serve as an environmental proxy for absent or ineffective strategies (e.g., see Corno & Mandinach, 1983).

METACOGNITIVE THEORY AND
LEARNING DISABILITIES: CONSTRAINTS

Despite the strength of the rationale for metacognitive skills and strategy training for LD students, certain constraints warrant consideration. The issue of constraints in applying the theory and research of metacognition to LD resides in the broader context of advantages and disadvantages in one discipline adopting theoretical constructs or paradigms from another (see Holyoak & Gordon, 1984). Because LD lacks the rich tradition of research and the empirical base that other scientific disciplines possess, intellectual exchanges between LD and these disciplines tend to have an asymmetrical relationship, with LD increasingly adopting the customs of other disciplines. One inadvertent consequence is that LD practitioners may forget important aspects of their own heritage in special education, such as an insight into cognitive and noncognitive problems of the LD student. The purpose in considering constraints in applying metacognitive theory to learning disabilities is to counter the possibility of a faddish impact on the field. Fads within a field occur as a result of the adopting discipline's failure to tie adopted constructs and paradigms to central issues and problems. A case in point is the frequency with which studies reported in the *Journal of Learning Disabilities* employ paradigms from experimental psychology with LD samples, producing atheoretical and fragmented data. A consideration of certain constraints on the application of metacognitive theory to special education would ensure a proper relationship between this adopted construct and the field. Essentially, these constraints point out the limitations in the application of metacognitive theory to learning disabilities, thus setting the boundaries of its usefulness.

The first constraint concerns the interpretation of the successful outcome of metacognitive strategy training. It would be wrong to imply that the sole cause of poor performance at any given task is the lack of an appropriate metacognitive strategy. Failures at any given task — academic or experimental — have many causes, one of which may be strategic deficiency or inappropriateness. More important, in some situations, strategy may be relatively unimportant and other factors, such as effort and ability, may assume more prominence (Anderson & Jennings, 1980; Jennings, 1981). Thus, a proper perspective on strategic intervention with LD persons is necessary. Occasionally, the best response to a task failure consists of *more* than a strategy, such as improved knowledge base, and it would be harmful and erroneous to presume that only strategic variables are of concern. Special educators must refrain from inadvertently promoting this erroneous idea.

A second constraint concerns a proper perspective on the contributions of metacognition to LD students. It is pertinent to note that metacognitive problems do not explain the entirety of LD students' poor learning and achievement in school. Other equally important aspects in their academic problems cannot be explained by the metacognitive construct: For example, metacognition cannot explain the cognitive deficiencies such as decoding problems in LD students (Stanovich, 1982a; Torgesen, 1982). Basic decoding problems affect LD students' reading comprehension because their slow and laborious decoding exhausts their information-processing capacities, leaving little cognitive resources for understanding what is read (Perfetti & Lesgold, 1977).

An exclusive focus on metacognitive training may neglect the need for an adequate knowledge base. Because of the interdependence between knowledge and strategy, we cannot afford to overlook increasing content knowledge in the domain upon which metacognitive strategy is to be applied (Wong, 1985b).

The interdependence of knowledge (in a particular area) and strategy has been clearly shown by Chi (1981) and emphasized by Voss (1982). Chi showed that 7-year-old children with expert knowledge of dinosaurs categorized them more according to abstract than perceptual (physical) features. For example, the expert children categorized the dinosaurs into meat eaters and plant eaters. The novice children categorized the dinosaurs according to visual resemblance and similarities. The categorizing behaviors of the expert children resembled those of adults. Chi's findings suggested that the development of classification strategies interacts strongly with knowledge about the stimulus domain.

Studies by Chi (1981) and by Miyake and Norman (1979) confirmed the interdependence of knowledge and strategy use. They indicate that a metacognitive perspective does not suffice in academic interventions with LD and EMR students.

A metacognitive perspective does not cover noncognitive variables that affect LD students' academic learning and performance. Emotions, self-perceptions, belief systems, self-esteem, and attributions of success and failure greatly affect motivation to learn and achievements. For example, LD children and adolescents tend to have low self-concepts and perceptions of their own abilities (Battle, 1979; Boersma & Chapman, 1981; Hiebert, Wong, & Hunter, 1982). When encountering difficulty, LD children are more likely than non-LD peers to attribute it to insufficient ability (Butkowsky & Willows, 1980) than to inadequate effort (Butkowsky & Willows, 1980; Pearl, 1982; Pearl, Bryan, & Donahue, 1980). LD students have low expectations for future success and show a greater decrement in success expectations following failure than their non-LD peers (Boersma & Chapman, 1981; Pearl, Bryan, & Herzog, 1983).

SUMMARY

Clearly, noncognitive variables exert as much influence as metacognitive variables on the learning and achievements of LD students. To view their academic problems through a metacognitive angle alone distorts the picture, and leads to treatments that focus exclusively on "cold" cognition (Zajonc, 1980). Such treatments are incomplete (Borkowski, Johnston, & Reid, in press). Indeed, the future direction in strategic interventions for LD students emphasizes investigations of the best means of combining strategy training with affective training for LD (Licht, 1983). Including affective variables recognizes that metacognition and motivation appear to be equal partners in strategic maintenance and in generalization. Already, conceptual models of intervention accord equal weight to metacognition and affective variables (Borkowski, Johnston, & Reid, in press; Palmer & Goetz, 1985). Future research stemming from conceptual models that incorporate metacognitive and affective variables appears promising in enabling clearer understanding of the complex phenomenon of LD.

CHAPTER 3

Subtype Remediation

G. Reid Lyon

A lthough considerable progress has been made as the result of research in learning disabilities, the field still lacks an empirically sound theoretical focus to guide educational practice and policy. A major factor that continues to inhibit progress is the great diversity among students who are eligible for special education according to the present definiton of LD. The problem of heterogeneity among LD students has not only frustrated efforts to build a generalizable body of knowledge, but also has contributed greatly to the present controversy over misclassification and what constitutes appropriate special education for LD students.

The term *learning disability* was first used in the 1960s to describe a broad collection of disorders related to school failure that could not be attributed to other known forms of exceptionality or to environmental disadvantage. The advent of this category of exceptionality reflected the belief by scientists, educators, and parents that some children had learning handicaps that did not fit existing categories. It also reflected a general lack of consensus about the principal manifestations of LD, and its prevalence, etiology, and appropriate treatment. Subsequently, the federal definition of LD that was incorporated into PL 94-142 included children

Portions of this chapter originally appeared in an article by **G. Reid Lyon** which appeared in *Learning Disabilities Focus* (Vol. I (1), 21–35, 1985) and was adapted by permission of the Division for Learning Disabilities for inclusion in this *Handbook*.

who did not achieve at a level commensurate with their age and ability. Eligibility for special education services was established when other categorical forms of exceptionality and environmental disadvantage could be excluded.

Over the past decade, the field of LD has grown to represent over one third of the students receiving special education nationally. At the same time, it is one of the least understood of the various disabling conditions that affect school-age children. Although much of the confusion in the field could be attributed to its newness, existing practice has often been based on fragmentary evidence and largely speculative theories that provide little understanding about what processes might be involved in the development of learning disabilities.

RATIONALE FOR SUBTYPE RESEARCH WITH LEARNING-DISABLED STUDENTS

Prevalence studies indicate that children with difficulties in developing basic reading skills who have average or above-average intelligence and adequate opportunity to learn comprise 3.5% to 6% of the school-age population (Rutter, 1978). Further, clinically based studies such as those carried out by Duffy and his associates at Harvard (Duffy, Denckla, Bartels, & Sandini, 1980) and by Lyon at the University of Vermont (Lyon, 1985b) show that 60% to 80% of the LD children seen for diagnosis or remediation manifest primary deficits in basic reading skills or reading comprehension. However, despite this high frequency of occurrence and long-standing history of research interest in the psychological and educational correlates of specific learning disabilities in reading, we still have neither (1) a consensual description of the reasons for the manifestation LD nor (2) an identification of teaching tactics and materials that can be selected and implemented systematically on the basis of learner characteristics.

This persistent difficulty in understanding, describing, and remediating LD can be attributed to at least two major factors. First, traditional research with LD children has typically involved grouping subjects into heterogeneous samples and comparing the reading behavior of children in those samples to the reading behavior of normal controls. In general, the LD children are selected for study on the basis of exclusionary definitions. That is, children whose reading deficits might be attributed to below-average intelligence, low socioeconomic status, or emotional or physical factors are parsed from the sample, leaving youngsters who are apparently average in intelligence and who ostensibly have had an adequate opportunity to learn. Such sampling procedures produce enormous interpretation problems, primarily because exclusionary definitions of LD vary from state to state and even within states. For example, in some states the psychometric definition of "average" intelligence is one standard deviation above and below the mean (85 to 115), whereas in others, two standard deviations above and below the mean (70 to 130) denote the range of "average" intellectual functioning. Given the significant relationships between general IQ and reading development (Chalfant & Scheffelin, 1969), it is not surprising that there are significant differences between studies in terms of the characteristics of LD children and their ability to respond to instruction. In short, this heterogeneity has produced confusion in the measurement and interpretation of learning disabilities such that consistent findings regarding the correlates of reading failure, the prediction of response to instruction, and the discovery of etiological factors are virtually nonexistent.

Second, several recent studies have indicated consistently and clearly that even when samples of LD children are grouped according to attribute variables such as IQ (e.g., 90–110), socioeconomic status (e.g., middle to upper-middle class), and adequate opportunity to learn (e.g., not educationally disadvantaged), the youngsters within a given sample still differ significantly in their development of skills that are correlated with basic reading development (Lyon, 1985a). Thus, even within well defined samples of LD children, there is a large within-sample variance. This indicates that not all children read poorly for the same reasons and, as such, might not respond equally well to the same teaching tactics. This explains to some degree why LD children have been reported to differ, but not always, from controls on so many variables related to reading (Rourke, 1978).

Given the practical issues of teacher effectiveness and cost efficiency and the persistent finding that LD children form a group that, in itself, is significantly diversified in terms of learning characteristics, it is clear that attempts should be made to reclassify this heterogeneous group of children objectively into smaller homogeneous subtypes to promote more precise study of learner reading behavior and the effects of different forms of instruction on improving such behavior. The virtue of a reliable classification of learning disabilities is that for each subtype identified, differential intervention, prognosis, and specific correlation with educational, behavioral, physiological, and neuropsychological functions are far more reliable than what has been accomplished so far. Thus, detailed studies of LD subtypes and their responses to different types of educational interventions can help to identify and describe relations among cognitive skills, information-processing characteristics, linguistic and perceptual capabilities, and reading skill development far more precisely than if the LD population was investigated as a heterogeneous whole. Furthermore, studies designed to identify and describe subtype cognitive, linguistic, and perceptual characteristics related to reading skills and to behavior changes in reading shown by LD students during remediation should aid future development of practical guidelines for teachers selecting particular methods and materials for LD students.

SUBTYPE IDENTIFICATION

Recent research conducted with LD readers suggests that a number of subtypes in the LD population can be identified on the basis of how their members perform on measures of cognitive–linguistic, perceptual, and achievement skills (Doehring & Hoshko, 1977; Lyon, 1983, 1985a, 1985b; Lyon & Watson, 1981; Lyon, Rietta, Watson, Porch, & Rhodes, 1981; Lyon, Stewart, & Freedman, 1982; Mattis, French, & Rapin, 1975; Petrauskas & Rourke, 1979; Satz & Morris, 1981). The data from these studies support a model that assumes that learning disabilities can result from several independent deficiences in information-processing skills rather than from a single unitary deficit. This model is more convincing than a traditional unitary deficit perspective, because it helps explain the significant heterogeneity observed in the LD population and provides a heuristic base for the systematic study of learner characteristics and the efficacy of teaching interventions.

Empirical support for subtype structure in the LD population has been provided by a number of studies. In general, these investigations have been conducted according to one of two methodological approaches and can be grouped accordingly. The first subtype identification studies to appear in the literature were carried out using a clinical-inferential approach (see Lyon, 1983, and Lyon and Risucci, in press, for a comprehensive review of these studies). The subtypes were delineated on the basis of visual inspection of interrelated achievement or neuropsychological test scores (e.g., Boder, 1971; Mattis et al., 1975). More recently, subtypes have been identified by applying multivariate statistical classification approaches (e.g., Q-factor analysis or hierarchical cluster analysis) to neuropsychological, psychoeducational, or information-processing scores obtained by LD and low-achieving youngsters (e.g., Doehring & Hoshko, 1977; Fisk & Rourke, 1979; Lyon et al., 1981, 1982; Lyon & Watson, 1981; Petrauskas & Rourke, 1979; Satz & Morris, 1981; Speece, McKinney, & Applebaum, 1984). In the main, the results of the multivariate studies have indicated that the LD population, traditionally described as heterogeneous, can be conceptualized more adequately as composed of a number of independent homogeneous subtypes, each manifesting different strengths and weaknesses in skills and abilities related to the developmental reading process.

Doehring and Hoshko (1977) published one of the first reports in which statistical classification methods were successfully applied to the analysis of reading problems. This work was later validated by Doehring, Hoshko, and Bryans (1979). In these two studies, measures closely related to the reading process were used. In the most recent work, Doehring, Trites, Patel, and Fiedorowicz (1981) included measures of language and neuro-psychological functions in addition to the reading measures. Within this series of investigations, Doehring and his colleagues identified three reliable subtypes of retarded readers through the application of Q-factor analysis. These include (1) Type O (oral reading disability); (2) Type A (associative reading disability), in which the deficit is in the association of spoken and written words, letters, and syllables; and (3) Type S (sequential reading disability), in which the deficit is in reading sequences of letters with adequate auditory-visual matching of letters and numbers.

As a result of Doehring's work with Q-factor analysis, Petrauskas and Rourke (1979) and Fisk and Rourke (1979) also analyzed the performance of reading disabled and normal subjects on a broad array of neuropsychological variables. In the first investigation, Petrauskas and Rourke (1979) identified three subtypes of reading disabled children. One subtype appeared to be a language-disordered group, with the largest Verbal IQ-Performance IQ split on the *Wechsler Intelligence Scale for Children-Revised* (Wechsler, 1974), and with associated significant deficits in verbal fluency and auditory memory. Another subtype appeared to exhibit a sequencing disorder, with poor performance on Wechsler Sequencing tasks and poor finger localization. A third subtype had impaired concept formation, involving verbal coding and poor hand-eye coordination. A second investigation by Fisk and Rourke (1979) was carried out to determine whether the same subtypes would be obtained at different age levels. Subjects who were significantly underachieving in spelling, arithmetic, and reading were identified by objective criteria. Two of the subtypes were found across the three age levels (9–10, 11–12, and 13–14 years). These included the language disability group and a group with poor sequencing and finger localization.

In a study by Satz and Morris (1981), achievement and neuropsychological test data of LD and normal children were cluster analyzed in two separate phases. In the first phase, WRAT (Jastak & Jastak, 1978) reading, spelling, and arithmetic achievement scores obtained by 236 boys (mean age = 11) were submitted to a hierarchical cluster analysis to identify a target group of LD children and a contrast group containing normal readers. Nine subtypes emerged from the analysis. Subgroups 1 through 7 had low-average to superior scores on all three WRAT subtests, whereas subtypes 8 and 9 contained members who had significantly low scores on the reading and spelling subtests in the presence of average or above-average intelligence.

In the second phase, neuropsychological test data obtained from the 89 LD subjects (subtypes 8 and 9) were submitted to a series of additional

cluster analyses. Five LD distinct subtypes were identified. Subjects in subtype 1 (30%), labeled a global language impairment group, were characterized by deficiencies in verbal fluency and receptive language comprehension and strengths in visual-motor integration. Members of subtype
2 (16%) were selectively impaired on a measure of verbal fluency and thus
were diagnosed as manifesting a naming disorder. Subtype 3 (11%) showed
deficits on all language and visual-perceptual-motor measures. Satz and
Morris classified this subgroup as a mixed-deficit type. Subtype 4 (26%)
was labeled a visual-perceptual-motor type because all of its members were
selectively impaired on only the nonlanguage perceptual tests. Finally, in
contrast to Satz and Morris' expectations, children in subtype 5 (13%) were
found to perform normally on all measures within the neuropsychological
battery. Thus, this subgroup was defined as an unexpected LD subtype.
This particular study represents a unique application of cluster analysis in
that this empirical method was employed to distinguish normal from LD
subjects before identifying subtypes within the LD sample.

Recently, McKinney and his associates extended the application of
empirical multivariate classification procedures to three major domains
identifying LD subtypes. Their first study (Speece, McKinney, & Applebaum, 1985) involved the classification and validation of behavioral subtypes based on classroom teacher ratings of independence/dependence,
task-orientation/distractibility, extroversion/introversion, and considerate-
ness/hostility. The resulting subtypes were interpreted as follows:

Cluster 1. Attention deficit (28.6%) — This subtype was characterized by
deficiences in task-oriented behavior and independence but displayed normal personal/social behavior.
Cluster 2. Normal behavior (25.4%) — Although this subtype showed
slightly elevated ratings on considerateness and introversion, all
profile points were within ± one standard deviation of the normal sample means.
Cluster 3. Conduct problems (14.3%) — These children displayed mild
attention deficits combined with elevated hostility and distractibility.
Cluster 4. Withdrawn behavior (11%) — This cluster was composed primarily of LD girls and was rated as overly dependent and
introverted.
Cluster 5. Normal behavior (9.5%) — Like cluster 2 all of the profile
points for this subtype were in the normal range, but with
slightly elevated ratings on hostility.
Cluster 6. Low positive behavior (6.3%) — Children in this small subgroup
showed uniformly low ratings on all positive behaviors but no
corresponding elevation on negative behaviors.

Cluster 7. Global behavior problems (4.8%) — This very small subgroup of 3 boys was rated as significantly impaired on all classroom behaviors.

The interpretation of subtypes 2 and 5 as normal patterns of behavior was supported by the fact that 85% of the non-LD children were classified into these two subtypes. Subtypes 3, 7, and 6 (problem behavior types) differed from all others with respect to gross motor inappropriate behavior and aggression. Similarly, the frequency of observed off-task behavior differentiated the normal clusters from the other five as well as subtypes 4, 6, and 7 from the others. Generally, the seven subtypes conformed to expectation based on contemporary theories of adaptive classroom behavior (McKinney & Feagans, 1984; Schaefer, 1981).

Feagans and Applebaum (1986) used six measures of syntax, semantics, and discourse skills to identify the following six language subtypes:

Cluster 1. Narrative deficit (n = 9, 16%) — This subtype showed poor comprehension and accuracy of communication relative to adequate syntax and semantics with marginal verbal output.

Cluster 2. Production deficit (n = 9, 16%) — Although these children displayed superior vocabulary, they showed subaverage verbal output and language complexity with marginal narrative performance.

Cluster 3. Hyperverbal (n = 8, 14%) — This subtype displayed great output (words) and high complexity in relation to much lower (but average) comprehension, vocabulary, and syntax.

Cluster 4. Structural deficit (n = 15, 27%) — These children displayed lower semantics and syntax scores compared to better-than-average narrative scores.

Cluster 5. Normal-structural (n = 9, 16%) — Normal profile with better narrative and production scores than vocabulary and syntax scores.

Cluster 6. Normal-narrative (n = 5, 9%) — Normal-appearing profile but with low narrative and production scores relative to semantics and syntax scores.

As in the Speece et al. (1985) study, the interpretation of normal subtypes in this study was supported by forecasting procedures that classified 71% of the non-LD sample into normal appearing LD clusters. The six clusters did not differ in nonverbal IQ. Based on previous studies (Feagans, 1983), Feagans and Applebaum (1986) hypothesized that children with narrative language deficits would score lower on reading tests initially and make less progress longitudinally compared to children with better narrative skills relative to poorer structural skills and/or to those without language deficits. Clusters 1, 2, and 6 had lower achievement scores than clusters 4 and 5 when the children were classified in the first and second grades. Similarily, longitudinal analyses showed that LD children with narrative language deficits progressed at a slower rate over the 3 years of the study compared to those with structural language deficits, hyperverbal children, and those without apparent language deficits.

McKinney, Short, and Feagans (1985) used six measures to index perceptual cognitive subtypes: visual recognition (match-to-sample), sequential problem-solving (information units), perceptual-motor skills (WISC-R coding), linguistic comprehension (trials to criterion in an instructional problem), liniguistic production (information communicated), and semantics (WISC-R vocabulary). The following subtypes were identified:

Cluster 1. Normal (n = 6, 11%) — This subgroup of LD children had profile points within $\pm$ 1 SD of the means of the average achieving comparison sample with one exception; their performance in sequential problem solving (pattern including bits) was above average.

Cluster 2. Severe perceptual deficit (n = 4, 7%) — All of the LD children in this subgroup showed deviations of –3 SD or greater on the match-to-sample task as well as slightly subaverage linguistic comprehension and production. Sequential, perceptual-motor, and semantic skills were within the normal range.

Cluster 3. Severe comprehension deficit (n = 15, 27%) — This subgroup showed a marked deficiency in language comprehension as assessed by the instructional task, as well as subaverage language production. Semantic and perceptual-motor skills were marginal relative to adequate visual recognition and sequential skills.

Cluster 4. Normal (n = 12, 22%) — Although three children in this cluster showed significant deviations on the match-to-sample task, the general pattern of profile points for the group as a whole was within the average range, with a tendency toward marginal performance on WISC-R coding.

Cluster 5. Mixed perceptual-linguistic deficits (n = 8, 14%) — This subgroup showed a mixed pattern of deficits and was the least homogeneous of the six subtypes. Generally, these children showed a combination of mild deficits in visual matching, language comprehension, and language production compared to relatively good semantic and perceptual-motor skills. However, three children showed severe perceptual deficits combined with either severe comprehension or production deficits.

Cluster 6. Marginal perceptual semantic problems (n = 10, 18%) — Unlike clusters 1 and 4, all children in this subgroup showed strengths in perceptual-motor skills with generally adequate sequential and language comprehension skills. Six out of ten of these children showed mild deficits in visual matching and four out of ten showed marginal vocabulary and communication skills.

The results of this study were similar to others in this section, which reported distinct perceptual, linguistic, and mixed perceptual-linguistic subtypes (e.g., Lyon & Watson, 1981; Satz and Morris, 1981).

In the second study in the cognitive domain, Speece (1985) sought to identify theoretically based subtypes by using experimental measures of information processing that were related to various single deficit hypotheses of reading disability. Seven measures were selected to index sustained attention, phonetic and semantic encoding, speed or recoding, short term memory capacity, and strategic organization in memory.

Six clusters were identifed:

Cluster 1. Short-term memory deficit (n = 9, 15%) — Children in this subtype showed subaverage performance on memory for digits and speed of recoding (naming) compared to average encoding and memory skills.

Cluster 2. Speed of recoding deficit (n = 12, 20%) — These children had severe deficits in their ability to recode (name) both digits and words. They were weak in short-term memory, but displayed good memory organization and adequate encoding.

Cluster 3. Mild recoding/attention deficit (n = 10, 17%) — Although this subtype showed strengths in phonetic encoding, performance was subaverage for both recoding tasks and marginal for sustained attention.

Cluster 4. Mild encoding/severe recoding deficit (n = 10, 17%) — The most salient feature of this subtype was strength in sustained attention relative to weakness in both phoenetic and semantic encoding and recoding of words.

Cluster 5. Marginal performance (n = 9, 15%) — The profile for this subtype was the "flattest" of the six. Although these children showed adequate memory, the general impression was one of borderline performance.

Cluster 6. Mild memory/recoding deficit (n = 9, 15%) — This subtype showed strength in semantic encoding with marginal performance on both short-term memory and memory organization with deficits on both recoding tasks.

With respect to external validation, Speece (1985) found no differences among the information-processing subtypes on the WISC-R or reading subtests of the Woodcock-Johnson Achievement Battery. Nevertheless, Speece's study does provide important information on the relative frequency of various information-processing deficits that have been reported in the experimental literature, but studied from a univariate as opposed to a multivariate perspective. Her categorization of the sample as a whole indicated that most LD readers exhibited a speed deficit (76%), which supports previous research in this area (Denckla & Rudel, 1976). Short-term memory capacity was the next most frequent problem (51%), followed by semantic encoding (29%), and sustained attention (24%) (Hallahan & Reeve, 1980; Swanson, 1984a; Torgesen & Licht, 1983). Memory organization and phonetic encoding were the most frequent deficits (15% and 9%, respectively).

SUBTYPE REMEDIATION AND VALIDITY

The subtyping studies carried out by Doehring, Rourke, Satz, and McKinney cited previously are similar in the sense that they all have identified LD subtypes by empirical statistical classication procedures and then validated the identified subtypes by demonstrating that they differed significantly from one another on diagnostic or observational measures not included in the initial cluster or factor analysis. Thus, the obtained subtypes have psychometric and educational relevance. (See Rourke, 1985, and Lyon, 1985a, for a thorough discussion of subtype validation procedures).

In contrast to this form of subtype identification and validation process are studies that first empirically identify subgroups and then validate them, in part, by determining how the subtypes respond to a teaching procedure or procedures. Obviously, if subtypes respond differently to various forms of instruction and if these interactions are systematic and replicable, then the educational validity of the subtypes is well established. Unfortunately, the methodological demands inherent in subtype-educational intervention (aptitude-by-treatment) studies are extremely difficult to satisfy. For example, for the requirements of an A-T-I (aptitude-by-treatment interaction) design to be met, children from each subtype must be equated on preintervention academic variables (the dependent variables) or must be randomly assigned to a variety of different teaching conditions. Both of these methodological conditions require that sample sizes be large and teaching conditions be highly controlled (see Lyon, 1983, 1985a, for a discussion of these issues).

Unfortunately, large samples are difficult to obtain and the LD children's previous educational histories and teaching programs are difficult to control. As such, no intervention study carried out with LD subtypes to date can be considered methodologically sound. However, a series of subtype remediation pilot studies carried out by Lyon and associates have yielded some interesting findings that indicate that large-scale investigations of how LD subtypes respond to dissimilar types of teaching materials and methods might be very valuable indeed. These pilot studies, reviewed briefly below, are part of a larger subtype research program initiated in 1975. Readers are referred to earlier studies (Lyon, 1983; Lyon et al., 1981, 1982; Lyon & Watson, 1981) as well as recent comprehensive reviews (Lyon & Risucci, in press) for more complete background information.

EDUCATIONAL STUDIES:
SIX SUBTYPES — ONE TEACHING METHOD

The Subtype Identification Phase

In one of the first investigations in our series of subtype identification studies (Lyon & Watson, 1981), a battery of auditory receptive language, auditory expressive language, and visual perceptual, memory, and integration tasks chosen because of their use in previous research and in the public schools was administered to 100 LD children and 50 normal readers (NR) matched for age (M = 12.4 years) and full-scale IQ (M = 105.7). Standard Z-scores, derived from a comparison of each LD child's score with the NR group's performance on each diagnostic task, were cluster analyzed (using hierarchical cluster analysis) to identify subtypes within the LD sample. The results of the cluster analysis yielded six homogeneous LD subtypes. Table 3-1 shows how each of the six subtypes performed across the battery of language and perceptual measures. Specific subtype diagnostic profiles are presented in Lyon and Watson (1981).

Subtype reading, decoding, and spelling characteristics were also assessed and analyzed in the Lyon et al. (1981) study. These characteristics, along with subtype diagnostic characteristics, are described briefly below.

Inspection of Table 3-1 indicates that subtype 1 (n = 10) exhibited significant deficits in receptive language comprehension (Token; Disimoni, 1978), auditory memory (Detroit; Baker & Leland, 1967), the ability to blend phonemes (ITPA; Kirk, McCarthy, & Kirk, 1968), visual-motor integration (VMI; Beery & Buktenica, 1967), visual-spatial skills (Raven, 1956), and visual memory skills (MFD; Graham & Kendall, 1960), with some strengths in naming (Naming), and auditory discrimination (Wepman, 1975) skills. Analysis of the reading and spelling errors made by members of subtype 1 indicated significant deficits in the development of both a sight word vocabulary and word attack skills. For example, when reading single words orally, many subtype 1 youngsters confused visually similar letters and words (*d/b, n/m, play/bay, jump/pond*), inverted letters (*m/w*), and committed reading errors involving internal details (*lodge/ledge, rain/run*). These oral reading problems could be related to deficiencies in orthographic coding, visual-spatial and visual memory skills. However, the majority of children in subtype 1 also manifested oral reading deficits that seemed to be

TABLE 3-1
Auditory Receptive Language, Auditory Expressive Language, and Visual Perceptual Characteristics of Subtypes Identified by Lyon and Watson (1981)

Task Domains and Instruments	Auditory Receptive Language			Auditory Expressive Language		Visual Perception, Memory, and Integration		
Subtypes	Auditory Discrimination (Wepman, 1975)	Language Comprehension (Token Test; Disimoni, 1978)	Auditory Memory (Detroit; Baker & Leland, 1967)	Retrieval (Naming) (Naming Test; Mattis et al., 1975)	Sound Blending (ITPA; Kirk, McCarthy, & Kirk, 1968)	Visual-Spatial Reasoning (Raven, 1956)	Visual Memory (Memory for Designs; Graham & Kendall, 1960)	Visual-Motor Integration (VMI; Beery & Buktenica, 1967)
1 (n = 10)	+*	-(1.0)**	-(1.5)	+	-(2.0)	-(1.3)	-(2.0)	-(2.8)
2 (n = 12)	+	-(2.0)	-(1.9)	+	+	+	+	-(2.2)
3 (n = 12)	+	-(1.5)	+	+	-(1.2)	+	+	+
4 (n = 32)	+	+	+	+	+	+	+	-(1.5)
5 (n = 12)	+	+	-(2.4)	+	(1.9)	+	+	+
6 (n = 16)	+		+	+	+	+	+	+

*+ = Not significantly different from normal readers.

** ( ) = Number of standard deviations below normal readers (signficant difference) associated with their significant deficits in retaining and recalling phonological information and sound blending. For example, frequent vowels errors were noted (*wagon/wiglin, colt/callip*), as were problems in reading words with consonant blends (*smile/silo*) and in pronouncing all syllables in words (*elegant/elgan*).

Subtype 1 children's spelling behavior also reflected the significant linguistic and orthographic problems observed in diagnostic testing (Table 3–1). Similar to their oral reading errors, many of the children confused visually similar words when spelling (*brush/dush*), inverted letters (*comb/cowp*), made frequent vowel errors (*key/kal, ring/tamy*), and at times produced bizarre nonphonetic spellings (*pencil/erwich, spoon/pone, toothbrush/thothurwlhy*). Subtype 1 members were the most deficient oral readers and spellers in this sample and also produced the lowest scores on a reading comprehension measure.

Children in subtype 2 (*n* = 12) also exhibited a pattern of mixed deficits but in a milder form than observed in subtype 1. Specifically, significant problems in receptive language comprehension (Token; Disimoni, 1978), auditory memory (Detroit; Baker & Leland, 1967), and visual-motor integration (VMI; Beery & Buktenica, 1967) were observed and may have accounted for the reading problems of these subjects. No deficits were seen in these youngsters' performance on naming, auditory discrimination, sound blending, visual-spatial, and visual memory tasks.

Subtype 2 members produced mixed visual and phonetic errors when reading but to a much milder degree than did subtype 1 children. It appeared that their auditory comprehension and auditory memory problems impeded a strong phonic attack, as many of the oral reading errors reflected labored auditory analysis and blending (*run/r-a-l, fishing/figet*). Surprisingly, many of the children could read phonetically irregular words adequately (*ruin, yacht*). The spelling errors produced by subtype 2 children also appeared more closely related to their auditory receptive and expressive deficits than to their problems in visual-motor integration. Again, many children could approximate the length of the target word dictated to them, but the letters included in the words often bore no relationship to the sound of the word (*pencil/pillup, ring/ralg, spoon/sasen*). Frequent vowel errors were noted (*toothbrush/tethbras, crayon/kenon*), as were omissions of final sounds (*toothbrush/totbu, crayon/cao*).

Members of subtype 3 (*n* = 12) manifested selective deficits in receptive language comprehension (Token; Disimoni, 1978) and sound blending (ITPA; Kirk et al., 1968) with corresponding strengths in all other linguistic and visual perceptual skills measured. The oral reading errors made by subtype 3 youngsters were primarily auditory in nature, as would be expected from their diagnostic profile (Table 3–1). Specifically, their significant deficiencies in receptive language comprehension and sound blending appeared to be related to an inability to read words with consonant combinations (*smile/soll, blaze/bus, flour/fir, stylish/sold*) and multisyllables (*dangerous/ding, exercise/exen*). The errors cited here also indicate frequent vowel errors. The spelling errors produced by the majority of subtype 3 members were also nonphonetic in nature, ranging from misspellings of simple words (*run/dab, play/bek*) to misspellings of more complex targets (*fishing/falup, igloo/ilit*).

Children in subtype 4 (*n* = 32) displayed significant deficiencies on the visual-motor integration task (VMI; Beery & Buktenica, 1967) and average performance on all other measures. These youngsters displayed an assorted sample of oral reading errors, though most errors were made when attempting to read phonetically irregular words. For example, in the majority of cases, the words, *run, jump, wagon,* and *fishing* were read correctly, though laboriously. Conversely, words such as *brook, gloves, ruin, anchor,* and *gaudy* were often mispronounced.

Similar error patterns were also observed in subtype 4 members' spelling behavior. In general, the misspellings were phonetic in nature, especially when the target words were dictated by the examiner (*pencil/pensl, ring/rin, spoon/spune, crayon/craon*). Some spelling pattern differences were observed, however, when these youngsters spelled the same words spontaneously in sentences (*pencil/people, ring/rige, spoon/spon*). This difference in spelling error topography could be due to the removal of auditory cues that are provided by the examiner in dictating spelling.

Subtype 5 (*n* = 12) members displayed significant deficits in receptive language comprehension (Token; Disimoni, 1978), auditory memory (Detroit; Baker & Leland, 1967), and sound blending (ITPA; Kirk et al., 1968), with corresponding strengths in all measured visual-perceptual and visual-motor skills. These characteristics appeared related to the severity of their oral reading and written spelling errors. The major academic characteristic that distinguished subtype 5 youngsters from the other children was their consistently poor application of word attack (phonetic) skills to the reading and spelling process. Quite frequently, even when reading high frequency one-syllable words, subtype 5 children could not approximate the correct pronunciation of the word (*run/wag, play/ban*). As would be expected, frequent mispronunciations also occurred when the children attempted to read more complex words (*wagon/winter, brook/ball, smile/silno*).

Analysis of subtype 5 members' spelling performance revealed similar error patterns. However, in addition to frequent vowel errors (*brush/blen, comb/kim*), omission of final sounds (*pencil/pen, crayon/caly*), and omission of syllables (*toothbrush/toth, penny/pol*), these children also produced poor spacing of letters and words and frequently confused letters (*brush/dus, pencil/danit, spoon/stom*).

The pattern of scores obtained by members of subtype 6 (*n* = 16) indicated a normal diagnostic profile. These results were unexpected, but not inconsistent with present-day notions concerning LD readers. It is possible, as Larsen and Hammill (1976) and others (Cohen, 1969; Kirk & Elkins, 1975) have pointed out, that many LD children read or spell poorly because of social, motivational, or educational factors rather than because of some neurobehavioral deficit. As might be expected from their diagnostic test data (Table 3-1), children in subtype 6 were the best decoders and spellers in the sample. Both reading and spelling errors were mixed in terms of topography, and no specific error patterns could be discerned. Oral reading errors involved faulty pronunciation of multisyllabic phonetically irregular words. Although spelling was below age and grade expectation, written formulation and syntax were generally intact with these youngsters.

The Subtype Remediation Phase

Following the Lyon and Watson (1981) subtype identification study, a pilot investigation (Lyon, 1983) was initiated to determine whether subtypes would respond differently to reading instruction. However, because of the relatively small sample size, a standard aptitude-by-treatment study could not be designed appropriately. Therefore, it was decided to explore the possibility that the six subtypes identified by Lyon and Watson might respond in significantly different ways to one teaching condition. Since the children for this exploratory study had to be matched for preintervention achievement levels and other relevant variables (age, IQ, sex, socioeconomic status), the initial subject pool available from the subtype identification study (Lyon & Watson, 1981) was reduced to 30. Thus, random assignment of children from each of the six subtypes to several teaching conditions was not feasible.

In light of these logistical difficulties, five subjects were selected from each of the six subtypes. They were matched on their ability to read single words, age, IQ, race, and sex. All 30 subjects were white males ranging in age from 12.3 years to 12.7 years and in full-scale IQ from 103.5 to 105. Peabody Individual Achievement Test (Dunn & Markwardt, 1970) Reading Recognition preintervention grade equivalents ranged from 3.0 to 3.3, with percentile ranks ranging from 4 to 8. Unfortunately, it was not possible to control for the amount and type of previous reading instruction experienced by the children, their present curriculum, and the amount of time spent in LD classrooms. Thus, the results obtained from this study must be evaluated in light of these confounding features.

The teaching method selected for the study was a synthetic phonics program (Traub & Bloom, 1975). This program was chosen because of its well-sequenced format, its coverage of major phonics concepts, and its familiarity to the teachers in training who were providing the instruction. All subjects were provided 1 hour of reading instruction per week (in addition to their special and regular classroom instruction) for 26 weeks.

In the Traub and Bloòm (1975) program, children are first required to supply the appropriate sounds for all single letters and letter combinations learned. This is followed in the instructional sequence by naming and writing the letters that correspond to letter sounds given by the teacher. Children are then introduced to consonant-vowel-consonant (CVC) words made up of letters learned to date. All children are then taught to write the CVC words from dictation prior to reading them. The instructional sequence progresses through writing and reading words with different consonant and vowel combinations (CCVC, CCVCC, CVVC) and writing and reading sentences constructed from known, phonetically regular words and "sight" words. Systematic movement from one level of the reading program was made possible in the present study by requiring that all children meet an accuracy criterion of 85% on all lesson components before moving to an instructional objective at a higher level.

Following 26 hours of phonics instruction, the 30 children were posttested with the PIAT Reading Recognition subtest (Dunn & Markwardt, 1970), and gain scores employing percentile ranks and grade equivalents were computed. A one-way analysis of variance indicated significant differences among the six subtypes for both types of gain scores achieved from preintervention to posttesting. An analysis of subtype gain scores and subsequent pair comparisons indicated that members of subtype 6 made the most progress (mean percentile rank gain = 18.0), followed by members of subtype 4 (mean percentile rank gain = 8.2). On the other hand, subtypes 1, 2, 3, and 5 made minimal gains in percentile ranks and were not significantly different from one another in terms of gain achieved. Subtypes 4 and 6 were both significantly different from one another and from all other subtypes with respect to their improvement in the oral reading of single words. Figure 3-1 displays the mean percentile rank gains made by each of the six subtypes. The number in paretheses to the right of each of the subtype identification numbers reflects the amount of gain rounded to the nearest percentile point.

The data obtained in this subtype remediation study indicate that, for some subtypes, a synthetic phonics teaching intervention appeared to enhance significantly the ability to read single words accurately. Clearly, members of subtypes 4 and 6 demonstrated robust improvements in their decoding capabilities. Whether or not the absence of auditory-verbal and specific phonological deficits in these two subtypes was associated with their good response to instruction cannot be clearly answered at this time, but one could hypothesize that this may be the case. This hypothesis is made more tenable by the observation that those subtypes with the most severe auditory receptive and auditory expressive language deficits made either minimal gains (subtypes 2 and 3) or no gains (subtypes 1 and 5) in the ability to pronounce single words accurately and efficiently.

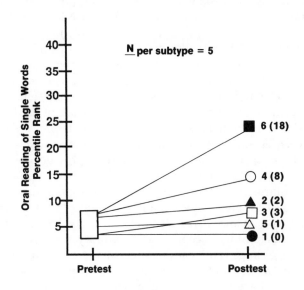

Figure 3–1.
Mean gains in the oral reading of single words made by six
subtypes in response to one teaching method.

Identifying specific relationships between student response to the type of reading intervention employed and the particular patterns of strengths and impairments displayed by each of the subtypes is very difficult in this study because of the methodological weaknesses inherent in its design. Clearly, the effect of previous and additional on-going remediation could have had an effect on student gains. Further, the dependent variable chosen for measurement (oral reading of single words) was limited in its ability to indicate the full effects of synthetic phonics instruction. Moreover, the number of hours of intensive remediation with the synthetic phonics program may not have been great enough to develop decoding capabilities in children with moderate to severe oral language deficits.

EDUCATIONAL STUDIES:
ONE SUBTYPE — TWO TEACHING METHODS

The Subtype Identification Phase

In 1980, a second subtype identification study was initiated (Lyon et al., 1982) with younger LD children (6.5 to 9.0 years of age) to control, as best as possible, for lengthy previous exposures to reading instruction. As in the Lyon and Watson (1981) study, a battery of linguistic and perceptual tasks assumed to assess subskills related to the developmental reading process was administered to both LD (N = 75) and NR (N = 42) children matched for age (8 to 9 years) and full-scale IQ (102 to 105). Standard (Z-scores were then derived and submitted to a series of hierarchical cluster analyses to identify empirically independent and homogeneous LD subtypes. The results of these analyses revealed the presence of five LD subtypes. Eleven LD children could not be located consistently and were excluded from the study. Table 3–2 indicates how each of the five subtypes performed, relative to their normal reading classmates, across each of the diagnostic tasks. A summary of the language, perceptual, and reading characteristics for each of the five subtypes is provided below.

Subtype 1 (n = 18) manifested significant deficits in visual perception (Motor Free; Colarusso & Hammill, 1972), visual-spatial analysis and reasoning (Raven, 1956), and visual-motor integration (VMI; Beery & Buktenica, 1967). Visual memory was also below average but not significantly so. All measured auditory receptive and auditory expressive skills were within the average range. The reading errors made by members of subtype 1 appeared to be related to their diagnostic deficit profile (see Table 3–2). Specifically, their lowest scores were generally obtained when reading phonetically irregular single words aloud. Frequent mispronunciations due to confusion of visually similar words were noted (*work/word, what/where, duck/back*), as were reading errors involving medial vowels and vowel combinations (*love/live, watch/witch, bear/bore*). Several children also made errors when attempting to decode phonetically regular nonsense words (*bim/dim, bed/ded, tob/tobe, laip/lap, wips/wids*).

Children in subtype 2 (n = 10) displayed selective deficits in morpho-syntactic skills (ITPA; Kirk, McCarthy, & Kirk, 1968), sound blending (ITPA), receptive language comprehension (Token; Disimoni, 1978), auditory memory (Detroit; Baker & Leland, 1967), auditory discrimination (Wepman, 1975), and naming ability (Naming; Mattis et al., 1975), with corresponding strengths in all measured visual-perceptual skills. These deficits across auditory receptive and auditory espressive language domains appeared to seriously impede their ability to decode single words and to apply decoding principles to the pronunciation of nonsense words. Frequent mispronunciations of vowels in the medial position hampered oral reading (*big/bog, sit/sat, ship/shot, most/men*), and a lack of automaticity in blending sounds together was noted in almost all subtype 2 members. Analysis of these children's errors on a word attack measure indicated that auditory discrimination, sound blending, and morphological deficits hampered the ability to decode unknown nonsense words. For example, frequent substitutions of initial and final consonants were noted (*maft/naft,*

TABLE 3-2
Auditory Receptive Language, Auditory Expressive Language, and Visual Perceptive Characteristics of Subtypes Identified by Lyon, Stewart, and Freedman (1982)

Task Domains and Instruments	Auditory Receptive Language			Auditory Expressive Language			Visual Perception, Memory, and Integration			
Subtypes	Auditory Discrimination (Wepman, 1975)	Language Comprehension (Token Test; Disimoni, 1978)	Auditory Memory (Detroit; Baker & Leland, 1967)	Retrieval (Naming) (Naming Test; Mattis et al., 1975)	Grammar & Syntax (ITPA Gram. Clos.; Kirk, McCarthy, & Kirk, 1968)	Sound Blending (ITPA; Kirk, McCarthy, & Kirk, 1968)	Visual Perception (Motor Free; Colarusso & Hammill, 1972)	Visual-Spatial Reasoning (Raven, 1956)	Visual Memory (Benton, 1974)	Visual-Motor Integration (VMI; Beery & Buktenica, 1967)
1 (n = 18)	+*	+	+	+	+	+	-(1.6)**	-(1.0)	+	-(1.1)
2 (n = 10)	-(1.8)	-(1.6)	-(2.0)	+	-(2.4)	-(2.1)	+	+	+	+
3 (n = 13)	+	+	+	+	+	+	+	+	+	+
4 (n = 15)	+	-(4.9)	-(1.0)	-(1.4)	+	-(1.8)	-(1.4)	+	+	+
5 (n = 9)	+	+	+	+	-(1.7)	-(1.5)	-(2.0)	-(1.6)	-(1.2)	-(1.2)

*+ = Not significantly different from normal readers.
** ( ) = Number of standard deviations below normal readers (significant difference)

bim/bin, weet/weed), as were omissions of word endings indicating tense (*rayed/nay*) and possession (*wip's/wap*).

Members of subtype 3 (*n* = 12) scored in the normal range on all diagnostic measures (Table 3-2) and thus can be compared to youngsters in the subtypes identified by Lyon and Watson (1981) and Satz and Morris (1981) who scored significantly below normal on reading tasks without concomitant low performance on diagnostic test batteries. As suggested earlier in the review of Lyon and Watson's (1981) subtype 6, it is possible that many children identified as learning disabled in public school settings may read inefficiently for social or affective reasons rather than because of inherent oral language or perceptual deficiencies. It is also quite possible that the diagnostic batteries employed did not effectively assess all relevant skills related to the developmental reading process. As was the case with Lyon and Watson's (1981) subtype 6 (normal diagnostic profile), members of subtype 3 scored higher than all other subgroups on the reading measures. These youngsters did have relatively more difficulties in comprehending reading passages than in the other measured reading skills. No systematic patterns of errors could be identified from analysis of their performance on word recognition and word attack measures.

Children in subtype 4 (*n* = 15) displayed significant deficiencies in sound blending (ITPA; Kirk et al., 1968) receptive language comprehension (Token; Disimoni, 1978), auditory memory (Detroit; Baker & Leland, 1967), naming ability (Naming; Mattis et al., 1975), and some aspects of visual perception (Motor Free; Colarusso & Hammill, 1972). The difficulties manifested by subtype 4 members in remembering, analyzing, synthesizing, and correctly sequencing verbal and visual information appeared to have a significant effect on their ability to decode phonetically regular real and nonsense words. For example, on measures of oral reading and word attack skills, a large proportion of subtype 4 youngsters could not approximate the correct pronunciation of many words (*my/yip, water/walk*). Further, most of the children laboriously attempted to "sound out" the individual letters of nonsense words and then blend them together, making a number of vowel errors (*weet/wat, maft/miftl, laip/tobe*), sequencing errors (*plen/pelm, hets, hest*), and errors of omissions (*telequick/tolchip*) in the process.

Members of subtype 5 (*n* = 9) manifested significant mixed deficits in morphosyntactic skill (ITPA; Kirk et al., 1968), sound blending (ITPA), visual perception (Motor Free; Colarusso & Hammill, 1972), visual-motor integration (VMI; Beery & Buktenica, 1967), visual-spatial analysis (Raven, 1956), and visual memory (Benton, 1974) (see Table 3-2). These youngsters committed primarily visual errors when reading single words (both real and nonsense), apparently reflecting their deficiencies in visual analysis and memory. Specifically, a large number of these youngsters confused visually similar words (*of/on, work/word, bed/ded, nudd/nupp*), and some confused letters in the letter identification tasks (*m/n, U/W, J/L*).

The Subtype Remediation Phase

Similar to the Lyon (1983) subtype remediation study, a relatively low sample size and other logistical difficulties (funds, sample migration) prohibited any attempts to randomly assign members from each of the five identified subtypes to a variety of teaching approaches. However, rather than teaching all subtype members with the same general methods and materials as in the 1983 study, it was decided to split one subtype (subtype 2) and teach half the group using a synthetic phonics approach and the other half with a combined sight word-analytic phonics method. Although this approach represents a significant departure from the experimental design necessary for an aptitude (subtype)-by-treatment (teaching method) interaction study, we thought we could gain preliminary information about how children who are similar to one another diagnostically would respond to different teaching methods. Subtype 2 ($n = 10$) was chosen as the target subtype for this pilot study because all its members displayed both significant auditory receptive deficits (auditory discrimination, auditory comprehension, auditory memory) and auditory expressive deficits (retrieval, syntax, sequencing) within a context of robust visual-perceptual-motor-memory strengths (see Table 3–2). Since all of the subtype 2 members also manifested significant difficulties reading single words and connected language, we had the opportunity to determine how two different reading approaches affected these skills in the presence of a number of linguistic subskill impairments.

For this pilot study, five children were randomly assigned to a synthetic phonics approach (Traub & Bloom, 1975) and the remaining five were randomly placed in a combined sight word, contextual analysis, structural analysis, and analytic phonics group. Preintervention assessment using the Woodcock Reading Mastery Word Identification subtest (Woodcock, 1973) indicated that the five children in each remediation group were reading between the 8th and 10th percentile ranks for age. The mean percentile ranks for the two groups were not significantly different (Mann Whitney $Z > .05$) prior to the initiation of the remediation programs.

Both remediation groups received approximately 30 hours of individualized instruction (3 hours a week for 10 weeks). Unfortunately, it was not possible to control for the type of previous exposure to reading instruction or for the type of ongoing regular and special class instruction the children were receiving in their typical school day. Thus, any conclusions drawn from the results of this study must be interpreted in light of these confounding factors.

The synthetic phonics remediation group was taught via the scope and sequence presented in the Traub and Bloom (1975) reading program. A brief description of the instructional format for this approach was presented earlier.

The combined remediation group learned to label whole words (three nouns, three verbs) rapidly by first pairing the words with pictures, then recognizing the names of the words (by pointing), and finally reading the words in isolation. Following the development of rapid reading ability for these six words, function words (*the, is, was, are*) were introduced and taught. Following stable reading of these words, short sentences using combinations of the sight and function words were constructed and read to introduce the concept of contextual analysis and to develop metalinguistic awareness of reading as a meaningful language skill. Following contextual reading drills, the combined group received instruction in structural analysis and the reading and comprehension of the morphosyntactical markers *-ed, -s,* and *-ing.* These morphemes were written on anagrams and introduced into context so that the children could readily grasp their effect on syntax and meaning. Finally, analytic phonics drills were initiated to develop letter-sound correspondences within the context of whole words. Specifically, phonetically regular words that could be read rapidly by sight were presented, and children were first asked to recognize a particular letter-sound correspondence ("Point to the letter that mades the /a/sound") and then to give a recall response ("What sound(s) does this letter(s) make?") As children become more adept at recalling grapheme-phoneme relations, drills in auditory analysis and blending were initiated.

Following the 30 hours of remediation, children in both groups were posttested with an alternate form of the Woodcock Reading Mastery Word Identification subtest (Woodcock, 1973). Significant differences were found between the two remediation groups with respect to postintervention reading percentile rank scores (Mann-Whitney $Z < .0003$). Children within the combined remediation group gained, on the average, 11 percentile rank points, whereas members of the synthetic phonics group gained approximately 1 percentile rank point. These differences are clearly illuminated in Figure 3-2.

There is little doubt that subtype 2 members responded signficantly differently to two forms of reading instruction. Clearly, the auditory receptive and auditory expressive language deficits that characterized each member of subtype 2 (see Table 3-2) impeded their response to a reading instructional method that required learning letter-sound correspondences in isolation followed by blending and contextual reading components. A tentative hypothesis might be that subtype 2 children did not have the auditory language subskills necessary for success with this approach but could deploy their relatively robust visual-perceptual and memory skills

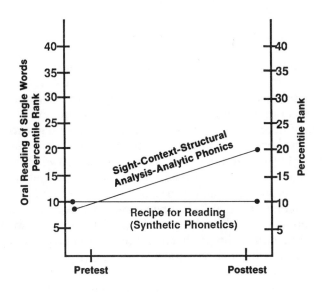

Figure 3–2.
Mean gains in the oral reading of single words made by children
in one subtype taught by two different teaching methods.

more effectively with whole words, as seen within the combined remediation group.

However, with the six-subtype remediation study (Lyon, 1983), the specific nature of the relationships between subtype 2 learner characteristics and response to two particular forms of reading instruction is virtually impossible to determine with the experimental design employed in this particular study. Very simply, conclusions and generalizations cannot be offered because we do not know how the additional instruction being received in special and regular classrooms affected subtype 2 members' responses to the two teaching methods. Moreover, the data collected in this pilot investigation only indicate that the oral reading of single words may have been influenced by the remediation methods. Clearly, in future studies, measures that specifically assess word attack skills, the ability to read connected language, and the ability to comprehend what is read must be used to establish a clearer understanding of the relationships between subtype characteristics, type of reading method, and the magnitude of response to teaching. Finally, the relatively limited time (30 hours) spent in the remediation programs with instruction being presented by teachers in training are factors that could negatively influence student response.

CAUTIONS

If the studies reviewed and the data presented in this chapter can be considered a fair representation of some of the recent research conducted in the area of learning disabilities, we can conclude future research should include more precise differentiation among, and description of, subtypes of LD children. Without precision in identification and diagnosis, many research findings — whether educational, psychological, or neurological — will be obscured by the contaminating factors associated with heterogeneity.

At present, however, the information presented here has limited clinical and practical utility, primarily because the studies reviewed represent exploratory attempts to identify subtypes and to determine how they respond to different forms of teaching. A significant amount of work must be accomplished in both subtype identification and subtype remediation if the findings derived from such studies are to contribute to our knowledge base. It must be remembered that the ability of empirical classification procedures (e.g., cluster analysis) to identify meaningful subtypes within large groups depends on the researcher's ability to (1) select and implement valid and reliable tasks; (2) ensure that the tasks are theoretically, conceptually, and pragmatically related to the area being studied for subtyping (e.g., reading); (3) choose and apply the appropriate data analysis procedure and the most appropriate statistical algorithm; and (4) validate, internally and externally, any subtypes identified to ensure that they are in fact reliable in their occurrence and meaningfully different from one another. All of these procedures must be carried out in detail because the statistical procedures employed in the majority of studies cited in this chapter can literally identify clusters or subtypes in any data and on the basis of performance on any tasks or measures.

This particular phenomenon can be clearly seen in the subtype identification studies published during the last 10 years. Although there is some degree of subtype similarity and pattern concordance across the independent studies (e.g., Lyon et al., 1982; Satz & Morris, 1981), the majority of investigations have not been replicated because researchers come to the subtyping task with a wide variety of theoretical assumptions and measurement batteries. In reviewing the literature, one can find "linguistic" subtypes, "perceptual" subtypes, "achievement" subtypes, and "neuropsychological" subtypes. Which of these subtype "frames of reference," if any, characterize the LD population in the most valid and efficient way is not known. What is known is that such diversity in theoretical backgrounds, assessment task batteries, and statistical methodologies does not bode favorably for the development of a concise and coherent framework for learning disabilities. Unless we begin to combine our talents and resources in a search for a common conceptual and measurement base, subtyping is prone to failure even as a heuristic.

As mentioned earlier, the data derived from the exploratory subtype remediation studies are tenuous at best. In effect, these investigations have taught us more about what to do and what not to do in future studies than about the relationships between subtype learning characteristics and magnitude of response to different teaching methods. This is primarily because we have been unable, with our present funding resources, to study LD cohorts for several years while controlling the vast number of influences that affect academic learning. Thus, if a particular teaching method appears to have a demonstrable effect on some subtype but not on others, we do not know if the gain should be attributed to the subtypes' characteristics, the instructional format, the interaction between the two, the teacher, the time spent in remediation, or previous or concomitant experience. Because the children we study are located not only in different schools, but in different states, we cannot assume that the error variance introduced by each of the confounding factors cited here is randomly distributed throughout our research samples. Thus, if we expect major contributions to emerge from our collective subtype research efforts, we must solve the extensive problems that are associated with our difficulties in identifying and maintaining samples of appropriate size, controlling for educational experiences and teaching variables that possibly contaminate response to instruction, using appropriate experimental designs in our investigative efforts, and, importantly, arriving at a theoretical and conceptual consensus about how best to describe and measure the attributes of children we assign to subtypes. As Kavale and Forness (1987) pointed out, "the present classification efforts in LD may be somewhat ahead of their time . . . we must retreat . . . . and devote greater attention to description. This description can then be the grist for subtyping efforts which can take both conceptual and empirical forms . . . It would behoove the field to strive for more communality and consensus in measurement and methodology." (p. 381)

Although some progress has been made through our subtyping efforts, the problems and pitfalls are many. Bringing more order out of our continued state of chaos relies on our collective ideas, skills, ingenuity, and the ability to design and carry out the many investigations needed to replicate and extend this exploratory line of research.

SUMMARY

With the preceding cautions in mind, the data obtained from the subtype identification and remediation studies do support many teachers' clinical hunches that difficulties in reading decoding and spelling are related to deficits in the ability to distinguish sounds from one another, comprehend words and connected language, retain and recall auditory information (sounds, words), retrieve words to label objects, retrieve sounds to label letters, and distinguish among and remember visual stimuli (e.g., shapes, letters, and letter sequences). Clearly, not all LD readers manifest all of these deficits. Moreover, many LD children differ significantly from one another in the pattern of difficulties they do present.

On the practical side, the data suggest that it may be useful for teachers to consider the information-processing demands that readers are faced with and to creatively circumvent particular demands for individual readers by controlling variables within the teaching task. In the second subtype teaching study (Lyon et al., 1982), it was clear that youngsters who had difficulty distinguishing sounds from one another, blending sounds, and labeling letter graphemes with their phonemic counterparts had significant problems learning to decode words using a highly structured synthetic phonetics approach. Thus, the demands placed on subtype 2 readers by the snythetic phonics methodology created a significant mismatch between learner and task expectations that had to be corrected by teaching letter sounds within the context of whole words.

As mentioned previously, the data presented here are not "strong" enough to provide practitioners with "cookbook" procedures for applying various instructional tactics with various LD subtypes. What is indicated from these studies is that reading is an exceedingly complex and difficult task for those who are not inherently able to efficiently and automatically decipher its code. For these children, even the most well thought out sequence on instruction and the most powerful application of reinforcement principles will not reduce the complexity and difficultly unless a systematic analysis of the interface between learner characteristics and task demands is carried out.

PART II

Academic and Social Interventions

P art II is the heart of this volume. Since deficits in academic and social functioning are always associated with learning disabilities, the primary focus of intervention activities is in academic and social areas. The chapters in this section provide a comprehensive overview of intervention techniques for reading, arithmetic, written expression, and social skills.

The first three chapters deal with basic academic areas. Chapter 4 focuses on the remediation of reading difficulties and describes teaching techniques emphasizing language, attention, memory, and other cognitive processes. Although many remedial reading techniques are based on particular models, most evaluations stress the necessity for highly individualized instruction that focuses on direct teaching of reading skills. Chapter 5 discusses the remediation of written language problems, an increasingly important area for LD intervention. It begins with a discussion of assessment for written language difficulties and reviews specific assessment and remediation techniques for handwriting, spelling, and written expression. Chapter 6 provides an overview of the remediation of arithmetic difficulties. It includes discussions of assessment issues, the establishment of a conceptual base for arithmetic, and possible instructional techniques. Chapter 6 also describes instructional possibilities for topics such as precomputational skills, the four basic operations, fractions and decimals, problem solving, and money and time concepts.

The final chapter in Part II deals with the remediation of social skills deficits. Although LD students manifest primarily academic deficits, the social and emotional difficulties experienced by LD students compound academic problems. Consequently, social skills training has become an integral part of most LD intervention packages. Chapter 7 discusses the theoretical foundation for social skills training, the content of social skills training programs, assessment of social skills, and specific intervention approaches. The chapter concludes with a summary of research methodology and a discussion of ethical concerns about social skills training.

CHAPTER 4

Reading

A n acceptable definition of reading disability is critical to the development of effective remedial approaches (Rutter, 1978). Applebee (1971) suggested that specific reading disability is a residual disorder; it is the part of reading retardation that has not been explained and that possibly represents the lower end of a continuous distribution of varying reading ability (Rutter & Yule, 1975). Consequently, identification and diagnosis inevitably become processes of exclusion — extraneous factors that might account for a reading deficit must first be ruled out. Establishing the existence of one or more underlying process disorders that account for a reading disability is, then, the next critical step toward developing an effective remedial approach (Stanovitch, 1985). Torgesen (1977), however, noted that it is often difficult to determine whether a poor reader is simply deficient in the underlying ability, or whether the ability is present but the task situation does not elicit it. A lack of consensus is revealed by the low reliability of diagnostic judgments about reading disability (Visonhaler, Weinshank, Wagner, & Polin, 1982; Ysseldyke, 1983) and the differential weighting of information by different professionals based on their own theoretical biases (Kavale & Andreassen, 1984; Weisberg, 1984).

The definition of Public Law 94-142, however, stresses that a learning disability is a disorder in one or more of the basic psychological processes involved in understanding or in using language, spoken or written, that may manifest itself in an imperfect ability to listen, think, speak, read, write, spell, or to do mathematical calculations (*Federal Register*, Dec. 29, 1977). The emphasis in this definition is on the disability as a disorder in some underlying process, which, perhaps unfortunately, tends to underscore the need for remediation of the deficient process (Senf, 1978).

The syndrome of specific reading disability may include children with many different types of disorders, each of which may call for specific remedial approaches. The failure of previous research to demonstrate the effectiveness of a particular approach may have been due to the diversity of the population studied. There continues to be a need for acceptable criteria for a reading-disability diagnosis and some means of identifying meaningful subgroups of poor readers. Early attempts at classification include grouping poor readers by auditory or visual deficits (Myklebust & Johnson, 1962), visuospatial problems correlating (symbol-sound) difficulties, or speech difficulties (Ingram, 1969), or by primary reading disability or disability secondary to neurological deficits or emotional and environmental influences (Rabinovitch, 1962). Such models, however, are valid only if poor readers represent a homogeneous population deficient in a single ability. Then good and poor readers would differ clearly on measures of this essential ability, and there would be no overlap between groups (Kerns & Decker, 1985).

Recently, there have been more sophisticated attempts to arrive at suitable subclassifications (Aaron, Baker, & Hickox, 1982; Dobbins, 1985; Doehring, Trites, Patel, & Fiedorowicz, 1981; Fisk & Rourke, 1979; Newcombe & Marshall, 1981; Petrauskas & Rourke, 1979; Pirozzolo, 1979; Satz & Morris 1981). Typically, there is an attempt to find a coherent structure that can be used to define the observed pattern of variation. The structure is considered taxonomic since it positions individuals at distinct clusters of points. For example, Boder's (1971) scheme has three categories: *dysphonetic* readers, who are poor in phonics, *diseidetic* readers, who are poor in remembering the appearance of letters or words, and a *mixed* group who are deficient in both phonetic and sight-vocabulary skills. Mattis (1978; Mattis, French, & Rapin, 1975) grouped reading-disabled people into those with language disabilities, articulatory and graphomotor difficulties and visual perceptual disorders. Denckla (1977) found the same three categories plus additional groups with verbal memory and sequencing problems. Lyon and Watson (1981) found similar clusters but also found a group with no "process" disorders whatsoever, a group they suggested might be children with motivational problems or poor previous instruction. Relatively little research has been done using such groupings to test the effectiveness of various remedial programs (Harris, 1982; Lyon, 1985a; Mattis 1981; Rourke & Finlayson, 1978). More on this issue is contained in Chapter 3.

The difficulties surrounding classification attempts are complicated by the finding that poor readers are not characterized by different sets of deficiencies (Reed, 1968). For example, Guthrie (1973) compared tests of grapheme-phoneme association skills and found that the strength of sub-skills in the poor reading group was virtually identical to the comparable subskills in a comparison group. Both groups were inferior to normal read-ers matched by age who had mastered the subskills. High positive intercor-relations among subskills were found for normal readers but were largely insignificant for the poor reading groups, suggesting the source of dis-ability was a lack of integration and interfacilitation among subskills.

Not only are there few empirically valid subclassifications of reading disability, but rarely is there strict adherence to an acceptable definition of the syndrome in general (Keogh, Major-Kingsley, Omori-Gordon, & Reid, 1982; Tucker, Stevens, & Ysseldyke, 1983; Ysseldyke, Algozzine, Richey, & Gardner, 1982). Most authors would agree that reading-disabled children chosen for study should meet the following diagnostic criteria: (a) a severe level of reading impairment, usually two or more years below grade level, preferably demonstrated on one or more individual standardized tests; (b) an intelligence quotient in at least the normal range, as measured by an individual test of intelligence; (c) an absence of uncorrected visual or audi-tory acuity problems, gross neurological or physical abnormalties, or pro-nounced emotional disorders or environmental disadvantage; and (d) a reasonable period of exposure to adequate instruction in the regular grades.

As Vellutino (1979) pointed out, the problems of meeting such criteria are formidable, but not insurmountable. Lack of adherence to a definition of reading disability has hampered the search for significant underlying deficits, usable subclassifications, and effective remedial programs. Forness (1982) suggested that relatively mild forms of remediation, i.e., those that can be incorporated into standard reading instruction, might ameliorate certain reading problems before more complex and specialized programs need to be used. Indeed, recent attempts to modify the Public Law 94-142 definition of learning disabilities as well as the definition of the National Joint Committee for Learning Disabilities (1981) stress that inappropriate pre-vious instruction first be ruled out before a diagnosis is made.

ISSUES IN READING REMEDIATION

A number of issues related to remediation were previously introduced, in Chapter 7 in Volume I and Chapter 3 in this volume, that need not be further reviewed here. Among the initial observations that need to be stressed is that early intervention seems essential. Keeney and Keeney (1968) have shown that when a child is identified as reading disabled in grades one or two, the prognosis for remediation is good in nearly four of every five cases, but the prognosis diminishes rapidly with later identification. More recent studies have confirmed this outcome, especially for the most severely disabled readers (Rourke & Orr, 1977; Satz, Taylor, Friel, & Fletcher, 1978). Educators are therefore understandably eager to initiate early intervention programs even in kindergarten, when possible.

The leap from identification to remedial approaches is hazardous, however, in light of suggestions by Koppell (1979), Torgesen (1977), Vellutino (1979), and others that a child's approach to tasks may result in performance that does not necessarily reflect actual deficits. 4oor performance on a visual-perceptual task, for example, might reflect intermittent attention, short-term memory problems, subtle linguistic disorder, or even poor self-concept. Furthermore, Senf (1972) suggested that deficits in certain skills may be more critical at different ages. Indeed, a recent study by Glazzard (1982) illustrated differences in the predictability of tests each year from grades one through six. Results of certain tests were effective predictors of reading outcome at some ages but not at others. Furthermore, when Jenkins and Pany (1978) compared content of five commonly used achievement tests with that of five popular reading programs, grade equivalent scores varied as much as two years at a single grade level, in the early grades, depending on which test was used to measure reading skills in a particular program. Similar variability has been found in other studies (Coleman & Harmer, 1982; Deno, Mirkin, & Chang, 1982).

It seems almost redundant to note that teachers need to be cautious of results and recommendations based on standard psychoeducational test batteries (Bateman, 1964). Coles (1978) reviewed 10 tests or procedures commonly used in evaluation and diagnosis of children with learning disabilities and concluded that their validity is suspect. Low performance on such tests may often be due to a variety of causes that may be unrelated to the test in question. Forness (1982) suggested that teachers should be especially critical of recommendations for diagnosis or remediation that are based on only one test of a particular function. Poor performance in copying designs on the Bender Gestalt test, for example, should not be accepted as evidence of poor, visual perceptual skills. If low performance is also evident on visual subtests of other tests of the WISC-R and on visual-perceptual functioning, such as the VMI, and if such functioning is significantly below a child's functioning in other processing areas, then a teacher can feel more confident in planning remediation.

A child's approach to test items should be observed carefully. The process of test taking often provides more important data than the test score does. A teacher may produce more effective data for remediation by observing a child's approaches to reading or asking the child to describe his or her own reading difficulties (Rhodes, 1985).

Forness (1981) described a model in which teachers might order a psychoeducational assessment only *after* a child has failed to respond to a well-balanced program of developmental and remedial instruction. Specialty testing would not include a complete diagnostic assessment but only an assessment of those specific functions a teacher suspects are impaired. Testing would occur only after careful observation and diagnostic teaching have taken place. Such approaches, of course, call for considerable modification of current special education identification and referral procedures (Bognar & Martin, 1982; Heron & Heward, 1982; Swanson, 1982).

The choice of the most effective remedial program for a child with a reading disability is complicated by problems in definition (Dinsmore & Isacson, 1986). Few valid subclassifications exist that enable teachers to group children for instructional purposes or to match a particular remedial program to an individual child (Zigmond, 1978). Specific training in perceptual skills as requisite to reading success is not emphasized. Conclusions from comprehensive reviews of remediation (Guthrie, 1978; Hall & Humphreys, 1982; Johnson, 1978; Myers & Hammill, 1982; Savage & Mooney, 1979; Stanovitch, 1982a, 1982b; Zigmond, 1978b) seem, instead, to stress intense individualized instruction that focuses on direct teaching of reading skills, with ongoing clinical observation as the criterion for selection of techniques and materials (Andrews & Shaw, 1986).

Difficulties in choosing remedial methods are compounded by disagreements over the nature of the reading process (Gough & Turner, 1986). Although there is general agreement that the purpose of reading is getting meaning from print, how that occurs is the subject of debate. One position postulates a "bottom-up" or "outside-in" theory emphasizing a sequential processing of information from print to meaning (Gough, 1972; La Berge & Samuels, 1974). An opposing theory offers a "top-down" or inside-out" conceptualization wherein letter and word perception are controlled by linguistic context to make reading analogous to hypothesis testing behavior (Goodman, 1967; Smith, 1971). Recently, synthesis of these views is emerging in the form of models emphasizing fully interactive parallel processing of "top-down" and "bottom-up" components (Lesgold & Perfetti, 1981; Levy, 1980; Rumelhart, 1977; Stanovitch, 1980).

However, levels of processing vary according to the beliefs of theorists. For example, conceptualizations concerned with higher levels of discourse processing (e.g., Frederickson, 1979) might include only a stage of feature detection prior to syntactic analysis, whereas those emphasizing the initial stages of processing (e.g., Mattingly, 1972) place little emphasis on levels beyond word recognition. Between these views are models attempting to explain how the reader deals with the lack of correspondence between speech and print by interposing a phonological (Liberman & Shankweiler, 1979), syllabic (Gleitman & Rozin, 1977), morphophonemic (Levy, 1978), orthographic (Venezky & Massaro, 1979), or lexical (Perfetti &

Lesgold, 1979) level of processing between feature extraction and semantic analysis.

Although reading involves a confusing conglomerate of activities and it seems difficult to formulate a single theory of reading (Gibson & Levin, 1975), assumptions about reading instruction and remediation are based on models about how reading is, or, at least, should be. Remedial procedures reflect theoretical differences between the view of reading as the translation from printed to spoken language (coding or phonic approaches) and the view of reading as an autonomous language processing activity (whole word or look-say approaches) (Carr, 1982; Resnick & Beck, 1976). "Bottom-up" theorists would favor a heavy phonics approach whereas "top-down" theorists would favor remedial efforts emphasizing language experience. The role of metacognition (i.e., awareness of one's own cognitive activity) (Baker & Brown, 1981; Brown, 1978) and the role of metalinguistic awareness (i.e., one's conception of language) (Hakes, Evans, & Tunmer, 1980; Sinclair, Jarvella, & Levelt, 1978) differ with respect to theoretical perspective. Those favoring top-down processing suggests that understanding the metalinguistic insights that reading is language and written language differs from spoken language are required for reading (Goodman & Goodman, 1979; Smith, 1977), whereas those favoring bottom-up processing argue that metalinguistic awareness of phonemic structure is essential for learning how letters correspond to speech sounds (Gough & Hillinger, 1980; Liberman, Shankweiler, Liberman, Fowler, & Fischer, 1977; Massaro, 1975). Comprehensive models attempt to incorporate both positions (Otto & Smith, 1983). For example, LaBerge and Samuels (1974) suggested a model in which lower-level processes such as letter recognition, phonological recoding, and whole-word recognition must be overlearned to facilitate higher-level processes. Other models suggest the necessity of lower-level coding skills for the acquisition of higher levels of reasoning and inference to gain meaning (Chall, 1979; Sticht, 1979). A primary feature of such comprehensive models is emphasis on teaching decoding and comprehension, not as subskills, but as conceptual systems related to each other (Gibson, 1972). Remediation must be based on knowledge of how different reading programs make use of various sources of information (graphophonemic, syntactic, and semantic) and how individual readers may benefit from specific aspects of particular programs (Calfee & Drum, 1978; Pearson, 1978).

Some reading theories suggest that children experiencing reading difficulty may have to progress through an entire sequence of lower level skills to achieve reading proficiency, whereas "normal" children may be able to gain meaning more directly without any particular emphasis on decoding skills. Although such generalizations may be valid, it is important to note that remedial activities often reveal ordinal interactions wherein good readers are likely to do well under all conditions and poor readers are likely to do poorly under all treatment conditions, at least within the range of available treatments (Bracht, 1970; Levin, 1973). This should not imply, however, that poor readers cannot be remediated but that little benefit accrues by shifts in remedial activities. The best strategy is probably found in the application of a single remedial program based on sound and complete diagnostic information. A sustained effort with only one form of intervention is likely to show improvement, albeit slow, when compared to a "shot-gun" approach marked by repeated changes in the form of remedial activities (Gittelman, 1985).

REMEDIAL GUIDELINES

Some general guidelines emerge from what has been discussed thus far concerning remediation. The finding that poor readers often lack a conceptual understanding of both language and reading (Downing, 1970, 1972, 1978; Downing & Oliver, 1974) might serve as the initial focus for remedial efforts. Downing (1979) outlined a "cognitive clarity" theory of reading in which instruction attempts to remove the cognitive confusion surrounding language and reading processes. The focus should be on decoding skills (Williams, 1979) that may emphasize individual elements (Gillingham & Stillman, 1960; Hegge, Kirk, & Kirk, 1936), letter clusters (Glass, 1973), whole words (Fernald, 1943), or psycholinguistic elements (Kavale & Schreiner, 1978). As reading skill develops, increasing emphasis should be placed on word meaning and on developing semantic and syntactic relationships among words through a taxonomy of reading tasks (Gregg & Farnham-Diggory, 1979) that combines "top-down" and "bottom-up" concepts (Anderson, 1977; Fleischer, Jenkins, & Pany, 1979; Pflaum & Pascarella, 1980; Posner, 1979). Comprehension skills may also be approached directly through the language experience approach (Allen & Allen, 1970), the Directed Reading Thinking Activities (DRTA) (Stauffer, 1975), the cloze procedure (Jongsma, 1971), questioning strategies (Wong, 1980), and psycholinguistic processes (Altwerger & Bird, 1982; Rhodes & Shannon 1982; Smith & Goodman, 1971).

An accepting emotional climate, opportunities to develop listening skills (e.g., being read to), and a child's expectation about success or failure in reading (Entwisle, 1976) affect learning to read. A unique study by Neeley and Lindsley (1978) seems to reiterate some of these principles. They studied 3 years of performance charting on individual pupils by "precision" teachers who used 17 commonly used reading curricula. Not only did different programs yield almost identical learning, but findings suggested that reading errors were important opportunities for new learning. It has also been shown that simply increasing time devoted to direct reading instruction by 5 or 10 minutes a day can markedly improve progress (Leinhardt, Zigmond, & Cooley, 1981).

Beyond these general principles, however, recent concepts suggest further possibilities. For example, attention and memory problems may necessitate special strategies for certain reading-disabled children (Trieber & Lahey, 1982). Techniques designed to teach impulsive children to monitor, evaluate, and reinforce their own behavior in problem-solving situations have been reviewed (Masson, 1982; Polsgrove, 1979). Such approaches involve having children pause before responding in order to select or rehearse appropriate strategies and then guide themselves through the task. Emphasis should be on moving away from external reinforcers and toward assisting children to develop their own internal monitoring and reinforcement systems (Blair, 1972; Brown, 1980; Forness, 1983; Palmer, Drummond, Tollison, & Zingraff, 1982). Parents and peers can also be influential in teaching or demonstrating these strategies (Glenwick & Barocas, 1979; Nagle & Thwaite, 1979). The more extreme attention problem of hyperactivity may require combining these approaches with other forms of treatment, such as medication that, contrary to earlier opinion, tends to both decrease hyperactivity and increase academic performance (Kavale, 1982a). Modifying a child's diet, on the other hand, does not seem to result in improved behavior, despite its popular appeal (Kavale & Forness, 1983).

More to the point, however, are techniques directing a child's attention to reading processes. For example, Schworm (1979) demonstrated how training poor readers to focus their attention selectively on the middle of words, along with pretraining on patterns of vowel sounds, significantly improved reading performance. Fayne and Bryant (1981) also found that directing a child's attention to specific sound patterns rather than letter by letter decoding was an efficient strategy. For memory problems, Torgesen's ideas (Torgesen, Murphy, & Ivey, 1979) suggest techniques similar to the self-monitoring approaches just described. Teaching different memory aids (e.g., orienting, rehearsal, mnenonics) and helping a child to be aware of when to use each strategy may be effective with some reading-disabled children (Wong, 1980). Torgesen's research (1979, 1980) showed, however, that it is often difficult to predict which children will show improvement with these techniques.

Linguistic approaches should receive renewed attention. Although training directed at specific linguistic deficits seems possible (Kavale, 1981a), there is no clear evidence that this results in improved reading performance, Vellutino (1979), an advocate in this area, suggests instead a somewhat broader approach, in which teachers emphasize language in the context of direct reading instruction. He suggested that a child's limitations might occur in any or all aspects of language, including pronunciation, word meaning, or grammar and syntax. Instruction should be well- balanced, with emphasis on both phonics and whole-word strategies and with training in dividing words phonetically and in discriminating between printed letters (as long as the latter does not take place out of context). Letter sounds should be taught according to syllables whenever possible. Words, on the other hand, should be presented both within sentences for meaning and in isolation for analysis of their structure (see Fleisher & Jenkins, 1983). Vellutino feels that general language enrichment may prove helpful and that teachers should encourage "cross referencing," in which the presentation of a word emphasizes its appearance, pronounciation, meaning, function, derivative forms, and use in various contexts. Language enrichment activities include having a child generate sentences, listen to stories, tell stories, and participate in any related activities "that facilitate elaborated use of new words ... (and) render the structure and unique characteristics of language itself the object of study" (Vellutino, 1979, p. 362).

Although research on such remedial approaches is sparse these techniques have the advantage, as mentioned earlier, of focusing on direct instruction of reading skills (Valtin, 1978-1979). Giordano (1978) reviewed research on language and reading and supported the notion of incorporating at least one other language modality into every reading exercise. Allington and Flemming (1978) suggested that poor readers profit from being able to use semantic and syntatic cues in word recognition, although developing vocabulary knowledge prior to reading may not necessarily prove effective and frequently depends on the type of reading materials used (McCormick & Moe, 1982; Pany, Jenkins, & Schreck, 1982) and how gradually new words are introduced (Hargis, 1982). Children in reading programs that stress phonetic decoding, however, have been shown to do significantly better than those in other types of curricula (Silberberg, Iverson, & Goins, 1973; Stanovich, 1982a; Wallach & Wallach, 1976). Given Satz's contentions (Satz, Taylor, Friel, & Fletcher, 1978) that visual skills lag more significantly in younger reading-disabled children, however, some caution might be warranted. Silver, Hagin, and Beecher (1978) have demonstrated success with more visually oriented programs for very young children. The nature of reading instruction needed for adolescents and adults with reading disorders may require a great deal of accompanying strategic training (Deshler, Schumaker, Alley, Warner, & Clark, 1982; Frauenheim, 1978; Lindsey & Kerlin, 1979).

The marked success of DISTAR programs (Becker & Engleman, 1977) argue convincingly for direct, language-based reading instruction. Renewed interest in both the Fernald method (Blau & Loveless, 1982; Miccinati, 1979) and color phonics techniques (Johnson, 1978) might occur because of their structure and emphasis on direct instruction in sound-symbol relationships. Such approaches seem to include components that could attenuate attention and memory deficits as well. The amount of instructionally engaged time also is an important variable (Rosenshine & Berliner, 1978). Since poor readers are inferior to normal readers in the rate of learning reading skills (Calfee, Venezky, & Chapman, 1969; Mackworth & Mackworth, 1974), it is necessary to commit a substantial amount of time to remedial activities to achieve gains (Guthrie, Martuza, & Seifert, 1979; Guthrie & Siefert, 1978; Harris & Sarver, 1966).

Special education for reading-disabled youngsters has largely taken place in special classes until fairly recently, when federal law began to encourage mainstreaming. Reanalysis of outcome studies (Carlberg & Kavale, 1980) has shown, however, that regular class placement has generally been less efficacious for LD children. It should be noted that this conclusion was based on analysis of studies grouped for both learning-disabled and behavior-disordered children. Definitive conclusions for reading-disabled children in particular could not be drawn from the data.

Review of long-term follow-up studies of outcome in reading-disabled youngsters (Watson, Watson, & Fredd, 1983) are generally inconclusive with respect to treatment or type of classroom placement. This may be related to the fact that, although remedial groups score higher immediately after intervention, the gains typically "wash out" in a relatively short period of time after remediation ends (Balow, 1965; Silberberg & Silberberg, 1969). As mentioned earlier, this frequently has to do with the general lack of discernible subgroups of reading-disabled children that would permit meaningful comparisons to be made among groups or treatment approaches. Algozzine and colleagues (Algozzine and Ysseldyke, 1981; Ysseldyke, Algozzine, & Richey, 1982; Ysseldyke, Algozzine, Richey, & Gardner 1982) have shown that considerable confusion exists as to who actually gets referred for LD placement. Potentially large numbers of non-LD children are mistakenly identified as learning-disabled and relatively little critical data in diagnosis is considered in placement decisions. The fact that social adjustment of reading disabled children is frequently impaired (Bryan, 1982; Osman, 1982) leads to possible confusion between effects of academic and social variables. Finally, it is clear that large numbers of children placed in LD classes fail to meet even the basic criteria for learning or reading disabilities, which is intelligence in the normal range (Smith, Coleman, Dokecki, & Davis, 1977). It is thus understandable that specific recommendations on even the *setting* of remediation, let alone techniques or approaches, are difficult to make.

A final caution seems in order at this point. Much of what has been concluded in this chapter, as well as in most research reviews, is based on results of traditional experimental research. These procedures have been critically analyzed (Singer, 1982), particularly in relation to the concept of dyslexia (Valtin, 1978/1979). The available research is faulted for two primary methodological difficulties that limit interpretation. The first is subject selection resulting in (a) variance due to the use of matched pairs in selecting comparison groups, (b) variance due to selection on the basis of total IQ, since subtest patterns may differ, or (c) variance due to the lack of standard identification criteria that alters the composition of the subject populations studied. The second methodological problem is the failure to provide an explicit theoretical model of the reading process, which has led to an emphasis on psychophysiological functioning with no demonstrable causal relationship to reading difficulties. That such research is normally conducted in relatively controlled situations on carefully isolated variables should serve as a caution to practitioners. Forness (1981) noted that research is conducted in situations far removed from actual classroom settings. Many researchers are psychologists who are not currently, or in many cases have never experienced, teaching reading disabled children in a classroom. Cohen (1976), Carver (1978), and Blatt (1980) criticized educational researchers for using research methodology that is ill-suited to drawing conclusions about real-world practices in school settings. Arter and Jenkins (1977) indeed wrote that teachers continued to use and believe in a techniques that empirical research had failed to validate. Theirs was not an isolated lament. The difficulty, however, lies not with the failure of teachers to heed researchers but with the translation of research findings into practice and a certain sense of perspective about research.

Even in a study that fails to demonstrate the efficacy of a particular approach, despite appropriate methodology and correct statistical inference, it is rare when *every* subject in an experimental group does less well than controls or performs worse in the nonexperimental condition. It is also uncommon to see *several* independent or dependent variables studied simultaneously in demonstrating the efficacy of a particular technique (Forness & Kavale, 1987). A particular child's cognitive, linguistic, perceptual motivational, or social functioning in the classroom may cancel out the effectiveness of an approach that research has supported or may enhance performance with a technique empirical study has concluded is invalid. The key for practitioners is to know as much as possible about remedial reading approaches and to be able to match the appropriate strategy to an individual reading-disabled child.

SUMMARY

A great deal of often conflicting evidence about the nature of reading disabilities and the process of remediation has been presented in this chapter. It should be stressed that considerable overlap exists among recent approaches to reading disability. Definitional problems and conflicting evidence make it difficult to give definitive recommendations to practitioners. Resurgence of conceptual linguistic theories and agreement on the efficacy of direct instructional approaches seem, nontheless, to characterize much of the thinking of the last decade. A reasonable conclusion is Benton's (1978) statement that effective clinical teaching continues to be a process of manipulating multiple instructional and related variables to discover the unique learning patterns of each disabled reader.

CHAPTER 5

Written Expression

Ann M. Bain

W ritten language disabilities is an amorphous area in need of experts. The sheer complexity of unraveling the psycholinguistic process involved in the act of writing calls for a joint effort from those helping LD students. English teachers, reading specialists, LD specialists, and speech-language pathologists working separately are analogous to blind men who describe an elephant in terms of their own experiences with isolated sections. An assessment may produce an incomplete mosaic and remediation may highlight isolated skills, forcing the LD student to attempt to integrate these new skills into the regular English curriculum without guidance. Not surprisingly, poorly integrated splinter skills with concomitant frustration and poor self-esteem may be the product.

The lack of solid development data and the uneven quality of assessment tools exacerbate both theoretical and practical assessment and remediation problems. Accruing more longitudinal information on the writing skills of non-LD and LD students would be of enoromous help in answering the following questions. To what extent are LD students' skills merely delayed? Are LD deficits unique and specific? Should assessment focus on documenting a *severe discrepancy* between ability and achievement or on

This chapter originally appeared as an article by **Ann M. Bain** in *Learning Disabilities: An Interdisciplinary Journal* (Vol. I (5), 49–61, 1982) and was adapted by permission of Grune & Stratton for inclusion in this *Handbook*.

delineating strengths and weaknesses? How does the LD student's connected writing correlate with performance on objective writing tests? To what extent can written discourse be objectively quantified? How can a subjective area such as handwriting be measured? And, most important, if written language can be quantified, what information is directly applicable to the development of remedial strategies for the LD student?

ASSESSMENT ISSUES

The assessment of written language disorders should be conducted within the framework of a psychoeducational evaluation. The student's age, cognitive abilities, and educational history are important. Present levels of academic functioning, particularly in reading, and receptive and expressive language skills should be evaluated. The assessment of written language is actually part of an extensive evaluation to determine current skill levels as the basis for the best overall remedial plan.

The case of FK illustrates why a comprehensive assessment is so important in understanding written language disorders. FK was a 37-year-old female who requested an evaluation of her academic skills because of difficulty at work. Her diagnostic profile and educational history presented a

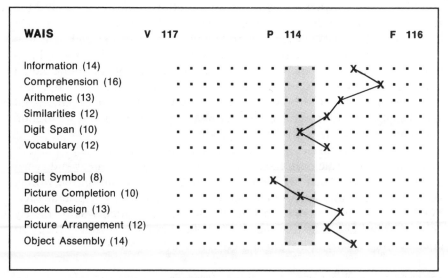

Figure 5–1
FK's WAIS profile.

picture of a bright woman with minimal schooling. Despite this, FK had managed to develop adequate reading and computational skills. Poor written expression skills were in sharp contrast to good oral language skills, cognitive ability, and academic skills. If only written expression had been evaluated, a completely different picture of FK would have emerged; expectation and prognosis would have been greatly diminished.

Ideally, written language skills are assessed within the context of a thorough educational history and a complete psychoeducational evaluation. The testing profile is viewed in terms of cognitive ability, educational skills, and the personal goals of the individual. The assessment of written language includes a number of different tasks that provide information about handwriting, spelling, punctuation, capitalization, syntax, written vocabulary, organization and structure, ideation, style, point of view, and audience awareness.

HANDWRITING

Although handwriting is a critical component of written expression, there are a few assessment instruments and little research to support remediation techniques.

Assessment

The few instruments desinged to evaluate handwriting are riddled with technical problems. The Ayres Handwriting Scale (1917) is still most widely used in clinical evaluations. First published in 1912 and later revised in 1917, it was designed to assess the quality and speed of handwriting. In this timed test, the student is instructed to copy the Gettysburg Address. The number of letters written correctly in one minute is determined and a raw score is obtained and converted into a grade level equivalent. The Ayres Handwriting Scale affords the clinician an opportunity to observe how a student writes the same sample over a period of time. There is, however, a great deal of subjectivity involved in determining what is a well-formed letter. Moreover, little information is available on the reliability and validity of the Ayres. Osburn (1953) noted that it is not designed to yield diagnostic information. Consequently, the assessment of handwriting disorders generally relies on careful observation of a student and the written production.

The Handwriting Survey (Bain, 1980) is an informal tool for recording and systematically describing various handwriting difficulties (Figure 8-2). A variety of handwriting activities, appropriate to the age of the student, are selected and observations of posture, grip, handedness, and paper posi-

Student: Observer:

Age: Date:

Grade:

Handwriting skills should be compared on the following activities to determine the type of problem and the extent of difficulty.

1. Write the lowercase alphabet
2. Write upper- and lowercase letters from dictation
3. Write single words from dictation
4. Near Point Copy
5. Far Point Copy
6. Creative Writing
7. Note Taking

Assessment of Component Skills:
Organization of Paper
Handedness
Pencil Grip
Pencil Pressure
Position of Paper
Anchor Hand Position

Letter Formation
Letter Size
Letter Slant
Letter Spacing
Letter Alignment

Word Spacing
Word Slant
Omissions
Substitutions
Additions
Reversals
Mixed (Cursive/Manuscript)
Mixed (Lower/Upper Case)
Erasing
Speed
Fluency

Additional Comments:
On Task?

Student's Attitude Towards Handwriting:

Figure 5–2
Handwriting Survey.

tion as well as the actual written production are recorded. Writing the alphabet and writing dictated letters focus on letter formation. A sample of the way a student writes dictated words can be taken from a spelling test. A student might exhibit handwriting deficits, inaccurate spelling, or a combined deficit. The observer should be alert to the possibility of a bright youngster masking spelling errors with equivocal letter formation. With a little imagination, most of the cursive, lowercase alphabet could be rendered by four or five loosely formed letters.

The difference in a student's performance on various writing activities can be instructive, particularly when observing the student's approach to a task. Slow rate, for instance, may be the result of inattentive behavior, laboriously copying one letter at a time, frequently losing one's place, or writing and then erasing and rewriting.

A pattern of strengths and weaknesses frequently emerges when comparing a child's handwriting of dictated words, near- and far-point copy, and compositions. Writing might break down at the level of the composition, indicating that the integration of spelling, punctuation, developing ideas, and generating sentences might be overwhelming. A skill breakdown at the copying level might indicate inefficient copying and monitoring strategies, or visual or kinesthetic memory deficits for letters and letter sequences. A skill breakdown on a spelling task might suggest a spelling deficit or inadequate auditory processing.

For older students, academic success in some classes is often dependent on efficient note-taking skills. Students evidencing a slow rate and inadequate letter formation will probably have difficulty. Inadequate organizational skills coupled with inefficient handwriting and slow auditory processing produce incomprehensible notes that are virtually useless in preparing for exams.

A series of transparent overlays (Helwig, 1976; Jones, Trap, & Cooper, 1977) has been used to provide a standard description of handwriting disorders. Transparencies may lead to the development of an efficient, valid, and reliable tool for assessing handwriting. Perhaps a series of sketches showing hands in various poses gripping writing utensils could be included. The SEARCH Test (Silver & Hagin, 1976) contains a partial set of sketches to describe pencil grips.

The Children's Handwriting Evaluation Scale (CHES) (Phelps, Stempel, & Speck, 1982) was developed at Scottish Rite Hospital and Crippled Children in Dallas, Texas and standardized on 1,372 Dallas County students in grades 3 through 8. Like the Ayres, it contains a near-point copy task that is scored by counting the numbers of letters written correctly within 2 minutes. The more subjective quality scale of the CHES addresses general appearance, slant, rhythm, letter formation, and spacing. A projective component is included, but technical information on the validity and reliability is minimal.

The development of a standardized instrument for assessing note-taking skills would be useful for the older student. A restandardization of the Ayres or a similar instrument would be helpful in measuring rate of handwriting. Another useful tool would include both near- and far-point copy tasks. Although unstandardized, the Slingerland Screening Tests for Identifying Children with Specific Language Disability (Slingerland, 1970) represent a positive step. An instrument including copying skills as well as spontaneous writing would be a welcome addition to the field.

Remediation

Handwriting materials and instructional procedures seem to be based on tradition rather than on research. Materials used in development programs, such as the type of writing instrument and its diameter or the exact amount of space between lines on a paper, are not well documented (Coles, & Goodman, 1980).

Remedial methods for handwriting disorders are based on clinical observation. Johnson and Myklebust (1967) presented a comprehensive, task-analysis model for the development of a treatment plan. The Johnson Handwriting Program, Level 3 and Ungraded (Johnson, 1977) focuses on a systematic analysis of cursive writing by dissecting and labeling various control strokes. Madison (1970) developed a kinesthetic technique, with initial writing activities done in fingerpaints. Kaliski and Iohga (1970) suggested that the rhythmic nature of handwriting be reinforced with music. Haworth (1971), however, concluded in a study of educable mentally retarded children that rhythmic motor skills were not useful in developing handwriting. Ramming (1970) and Helms (1970) stressed the use of chalkboards and Kimmel (1970) emphasized readiness activities. Verbal explanations of required handwriting motions were advocated by Sovik (1976) and Kirk (1978). An interesting trend involves the use of transparencies for helping students evaluate their own letter formation (Helwig, 1976; Jones, Trap, & Cooper, 1977). This idea may prove invaluable for developing remedial procedures. Other technological advances such as Parker's photoelectric pen (1975) may be applicable to remedial programs for LD students.

Although many specialists have advocated the use of cursive writing for LD students (Fernald, 1943; Gillingham & Stillman, 1960; Mullins et al., 1972), little data actually support this notion (Peck & Fairchild, 1980). In fact, manuscript writing appears to be easier and more legible for children with handwriting problems. The debate over cursive and manuscript will continue until an adequate research base is developed. Careful clinical studies should produce a profile of the child most likely to succeed with manuscript or cursive rather than attempt to generalize to all LD children.

For students with persistent handwriting difficulties, the development of compensatory strategies may be vital for academic success as well as a positive self-image. Oral testing can be substituted for written exams or objective tests can be substituted for ones containing written essays. Students can use tape recorders to prepare oral reports in lieu of written essays. The tape recorder can be an invaluable aid for the student who is an inefficient note-taker because of handwriting or auditory processing deficits. Another alternative is to teach the student typing skills (Duffy, 1974; King, 1985; Nash & Geyer, 1983) for a typewriter or word processor (Daiute, 1985).

The possibilities for compensatory devices seem almost limitless. Two points, however, should be kept in mind. First, whatever compensatory device is used, time and supervision will be needed for student mastery: typing, word processing, or efficient use of a tape recorder are not overnight projects. Second, compensatory devices are not a substitute for a carefully designed remedial program.

SPELLING

Traditionally, spelling has been measured by tasks involving dictated words written in isolation and misspelled words identified in a multiple-choice format. Although both tasks are labeled *spelling,* they are, of course, fundamentally different. Selecting an error is best classified as an editing skill whereas spelling a single word from memory actually includes skills needed for the real task — spelling words in connected language. It is uncertain, however, how well any of the typical spelling tests measure an LD student's ability to write words in spontaneous language.

Assessment

Most spelling instruments include a range of words culled from spelling programs at various grade levels. Word length and frequency of occurrence generally determine at which grade level a particular word is tested, though spelling lists differ greatly. The grade level or percentile is usually obtained from these norm-referenced tests. The dictation subtest of the Woodcock-Johnson Psycho-Educational Battery (1977) is a 40-item test including monosyllabic and multisyllabic words, punctuation marks, plural forms, and abbreviations. The dictated spelling subtests of the Wide Range Achievement Test-R (Jastak & Wilkinson, 1984) provide a larger and broader sample of words. Norm-referenced tests, allow comparison of students' achievement but contribute little diagnostic information. What, after all, is a fifth-grade spelling level? In an effort to make the best of norm-referenced instruments, Warwick (1968) offered a number of practical suggestions, including an analysis of individual errors and patterns of misspellings.

The development of criterion-referenced spelling tests represents a positive direction in the field of spelling; however, multiple problems still

exist. The Kottmeyer Diagnostic Spelling Tests (1959) do not provide sufficient samples of various sound/symbol relationships or generalizations
and many basic skills are not included. The Test of Written Spelling (Larsen & Hammill, 1976) and its shortened version, the spelling subtest on the
Test of Written Language (Hammill & Larsen, 1978), are disappointing
even though they are based on adequate research. These instruments include only a few skills in a relatively unsystematized fashion. The Lincoln
Diagnostic Spelling Tests (1949), although fraught with serious technical
problems, offer a more comprehensive format for evaluating spelling. On
these 100-word tests, every tenth word is designed to evaluate a specific
skill. A grid of all the numbered items provides a profile of a student's
strengths and weaknesses.

One important testing problem is designating errors that do not relate
to the skill being tested. Scribner (1953) noted, for example, that the word
awful on one of the forms of the Lincoln is supposed to evaluate student
knowledge of the suffix *-ful*. However, significantly more errors occurred in
spelling *aw*.

Although the most logical terminal goal for any spelling program
would be to increase a student's abilitiy to spell words correctly in written
discourse, spelling is not formally assessed in context. Experienced clini-
cians recognize that LD students might spell words correctly in isolation
but not in written compositions. LD students could limit their spelling
vocabulary to high frequency words that they could spell automatically.
However, students who attempted a more sophisticated vocabulary might
have a higher ratio of misspelled words. Perhaps a spelling instrument could
be constructed to include a scale for frequency as well as for misspellings.

Remediation

Spelling, reading, and phonics are treated as separate subjects in most
classrooms. The scope and sequence of spelling and reading programs differ markedly, as do the actual vocabulary words taught in each program.
Many spelling programs include arbitrary word lists, sometimes relating to
a theme, on the assumption that the English language is capricious. Spelling words are usually selected by frequency of occurrence and emphasis is
placed on visual and visual-motor memory. Systematic reviews are generally not provided although a cumulative review may be included. Students
who fail spelling tests are usually given new word lists so they can *keep up
with the rest of the class.* Poor spellers in such programs accumulate a long
list of spelling failures as the year progresses.

Some developmental programs emphasize linguistic patterns and others
claim to be "phonetic." Phonic programs usually stress sound/symbol
relationships while introducing irregular words at a slower rate. For all
practical purposes, the "phonic" series that simultaneously introduces

phoneme/grapheme correspondence and irregular "challenge" words, with only sporadic review, are indistinguishable from frequency-based programs. Highly structured phonic programs, such as KISP (Knight, 1975), present skills systematically and provide structured practice of sound/symbol relationships and spelling rules.

Surprisingly, few developmental or remedial programs has comprehensive research bases, such as those developed by Venezky (1970) or Hanna, Hodges, and Hanna (1971), who presented a skeleton outline of morphological and contextual clues and phonological principles in a systematic study of language — vocabulary as well as spelling. Based on a computerized study of words most frequently used by literate adults, Hanna et al. (1971) noted the importance of teaching useful spelling generalizations. A computer was *programmed* to spell 17,000 words using commom generalizations. The computer "spelled" 50% correctly and produced only one error on an additional 37%.

Many remedial spelling programs, such as those developed by Gillingham and Stillman (1960) and Slingerland (1981), organize words by common phonological elements and present them in a multisensory format for both reading and spelling. S.O.S., simultaneous oral spelling, is part of a multisensory strategy designed for spelling (Gillingham & Stillman, 1960). Students say the word, name each letter as they write it, and pronounce the word after it is written. Students are encouraged to trace, copy, write from memory, and check finished work for correctness. Generalizations are gradually introduced while irregular words are carefully controlled. Some generalizations emphasize phonological elements and other emphasize structural elements:

/l/, /f/, /s/, and /z/ tend to be spelled *-ll, -ff, -ss,* and *-zz* directly after a short vowel in words of one syllable.
hi*ll*, sta*ff*, gra*ss*, fu*zz*
some common exceptions: bus, gas, this, quiz
/k/ directly after a short vowel in a one syllable word is often spelled *-ck.*
pa*ck*, ro*ck*, lu*ck*, sti*ck*, de*ck*
/k/ is spelled *-k* after consonants, vowel combinations, and long vowels.
for*k*, as*k*, boo*k*, oa*k*, ca*k*e
/k/ in initial position is usually spelled with a *c* before *a, o, u,* and consonants.
*c*at, *c*ow, *c*ut, *c*lap
/k/ is often spelled with a *k* before *e* and *i.*
*k*ing, *k*ite, *k*ey
/k/ is usually spelled with *ch* in words of Greek derivation.
*ch*emistry, *ch*aos, psy*ch*ology
/k/ is generally spelled with *c* at the end of a multisyllabic word.
lila*c*, franti*c*, authenti*c*

Some remedial specialists advocate a "discovery" approach to learning generalizations whereas others treat spelling rules didactically. Few programs emphasize morphological markers. When a student spells *jumped/jumpt* or *yelled/yeld,* the problem is generally treated as a phonological error or irregular pattern. Since LD youngsters frequently evidence difficulty with inflected endings, this aspect of spelling is particularly important.

Another area of spelling difficulty is the schwa or obscure vowel in multisyllabic words. Most programs ask the student to memorize these difficult words. Chomsky (1970), however, noted that learning related words with different stress patterns can be quite helpful: aristocrat/aristocracy, emphatic/emphasize, historical/history, prepare/preparation. Chomsky suggested that teaching related words also helps students to develop a problem-solving strategy for silent letters and equivocal sounds: critic/criticize, quest/question, crumble/crumb, signature/sign. Hodges (1977) provided a detailed list of games and activities that help foster the development of spelling rules and generalizations.

Many remedial programs don't stress phoneme-grapheme correspondence or rules. Fernald (1943) developed a multisensory, remedial approach. Students say the whole word they are attempting to spell, then pronounce each syllable while tracing it. When the students think they can spell the word, they write it from memory while pronouncing each syllable. Students then compare the product with the original model. If correct, they write the word several times for reinforcement. If incorrect, they return to the tracing stage and repeat the procedure.

Another popular strategy for learning troublesome words is to develop appropriate mnemonics. For example, "there's *a rat* in sep*arat*e" or accounting for *ss* in de*ss*ert by remembering *s*trawberry *s*hortcake. Other techniques include color-coding (Kimmel, 1968; Madison, 1968) and writing words on the student's back (Glusker, 1968). Spelling activities in workbooks often include unscrambling words, rhyming, and completing sentences with words from the spelling list. A modified cloze procedure de-emphasizes the phonological component:

w e r e
w e r __
w __ r __
w __ __ __
__ __ __ __

_____

There is a surprising lack of research supporting spelling strategies. Procedures are poorly documented and little evidence links diganostic-testing profiles with the efficacy of any particular strategy. Studying a student's approach to learning words as well as studying normal and deviant spelling patterns should eventually lead to the development of a comprehensive language program — not just a spelling program.

Research Trends

A promising research trend has been the recognition of the strong parallel between normal language acquisition and normal spelling development. Most children progress through invariable stages of generating and modifying language rules (C. S. Beers, 1980; Reed, 1968). Zutell (1980) related children's spelling development to Piagetian stages: (1) letter–name–sound correspondence, (2) structural patterns, (3) inflectional patterns, and (4) derivational patterns.

Other researchers are beginning to note the error patterns of reading disabled and learning disabled children (Cromer, 1980; Nelson, 1980; Seymour & Porpodas, 1980). Henderson (1980) suggested the practical implications for an instructional program. Applying developmental research to the LD student should help focus attention on the psycholinguistic process as well as on the written product.

WRITTEN LANGUAGE

Although written language is valued by our society, few comprehensive assessment instruments are available. Lloyd–Jones (1977) classified writing tests into two broad categories: *atomistic* and *holistic.*

Atomistic Assessment

Atomistic tests are concerned with the visible features of written language, such as vocabulary level, spelling, usage, punctuation, and handwriting. They are prevalent because they are relatively easy to construct, score, and administer. Four atomistic tests are frequently used in assessing the written language of LD students: the Picture Story Language Test (Myklebust, 1965), the Test of Written Language (Hammill & Larsen, 1983), the Test of Adolescent Language (Hammill, Brown, Larsen, & Wiederholt, 1980), and the Written Language Cluster of the Woodcock–Johnson Psycho-Educational Battery (Woodcock & Johnson, 1977).

The Picture Story Language Test (PSLT) requires the student to write a story based on a picture. The test was designed to measure productivity, correctness, and meaning. The test directions are purposefully unstructured and the examiner may answer questions in such a way as to encourage the student but may not offer help or suggestions.

The PSLT can provide useful diagnostic information through each of its rating scales. The productivity scales give a rough estimate of the length and complexity of the writing sample. The syntax scale provides a weighted score based on errors. The abstract/concrete scale attempts to quantify the idea level expressed by the student. Numerous examples and specific criteria are provided.

The PSLT provides useful diagnostic information about a student's ability to integrate ideas, grammar, and punctuation in spontaneous writing. It includes samples written by hearing impaired, mentally retarded, emotionally disturbed, learning disabled, and culturally disadvantaged children and by children considered the products of poor teaching.

The PSLT presents problems in administration and scoring. Some children do not relate to the prompt: a black and white photograph of a small boy with a crew cut who is playing with dolls. Consequently, some students produce short, concrete compositions but, given a different picture, writing skills appear strikingly better. Although the test was norm-referenced to age 17, the text suggests that the PSLT may provide useful diagnostic information for adults. Some adult test-takers interpret the directions to mean a concrete description and not an imaginative story. The PSLT may not elicit a sample of the writing style most often used by adults. There is little evidence to suggest that the ability or inability to produce an imaginative story predicts an adult's ability to generate non-fiction. Scoring may present problems for some evaluators. Those who are not well versed in the conventional rules of American English may find the syntax scale difficult to use. For those who are not mathematically inclined, the formula for deriving the percentage of syntax errors may seem cumbersome.

The Test of Written Language, or TOWL, (Hammill & Larsen, 1983) can be administered to students through the age of 18 years and 11 months. Given three sequenced pictures relating to a spaceship theme, students are asked to write a story. The composition is scored for thematic maturity, vocabulary, and handwriting. The TOWL includes separate subtests for usage, spelling, and style, including capitalization and punctuation. The word usage subtest uses a cloze procedure to survey knowledge of grammar. The style subtest requires children to copy sentences and insert correct capitalization and punctuation. The spelling subtest is a shortened form of the Test of Written Spelling (Larsen & Hammill, 1976). All subtest scores are converted into scaled scores and a total score, a written language quotient, is derived.

The TOWL can be a useful diagnostic tool if caution is exercised when interpreting subtest results and comparing the writing sample to other work by a student. Characteristically, LD students present a wide range of uneven skills. Some LD students may spell words correctly in isolation and punctuate single sentences accurately but may not use these skills in compositions. Their inability to integrate multiple skills in writing a composition may, in fact, be an LD characteristic. The TOWL measures spelling, grammar, and punctuation on atomistic tests but not within the actual writing sample.

Students seem to enjoy the TOWL pictures and, with this kind of external support, many write clever, imaginative stories. However, the organizational skills needed for school writing assignments are not required for the TOWL. The appropriateness of the highly structured picture prompt is particularly questionable for the high school population.

The vocabulary subtest is based on the premise that longer words represent a higher level of vocabulary than shorter ones. Thus, "animals" and "planted" would be awarded more points than "crux" and "alien." A student's handwriting is compared to a 10-point scale, but there are no stated criteria for each of the 10 levels. On occasion, a student's writing is not comparable to any of the samples in the test manual. The style subtest yields information about a student's near-point copying, handwriting, and proofreading skills, but some items don't provide sufficient space for the student's response.

The Test of Adolescent Language (TOAL) (Hammill, Brown, Larsen, Wiederholt, 1980) contains some written language features for older students. The writing grammar subtest assesses a student's ability to combine simple sentences into more complex structures. The written vocabulary subtest measures a student's ability to appropriately use specified vocabulary words in sentences. The TOAL also includes listening and reading subtests. It does not, however, ask the student to write a composition.

The written language cluster of the Woodcock–Johnson Psycho-Educational Battery (Woodcock & Johnson, 1977) is composed of two subtests, dictation and proofing. The dictation test is primarily a dictated spelling task that includes abbreviations, punctuation, and plural markers. Proofing requires the student to identify spelling and grammatical errors presented on the test. Typical of atomistic tests, very specific skills are evaluated. The written language cluster does not require the student to write a composition.

Dozens of other atomistic tests and informal diagnostic procedures assess written vocabulary, sentence structure, and various mechanical skills. Written vocabulary, for instance, is sometimes assessed using readability formulas. Sentence structure can be measured by T-units (Hunt, 1977). Mechanical skills are assessed using instruments that require a student to insert or select correct capitalization and punctuation in a multiple choice format. Poteet (1980) offered a number of practical suggestions for informal diagnostic procedures that could enhance formal assessment.

However, the major question posed by atomistic tests is one of content validity. Does measuring the parts constitute measuring the whole? Can a test that measures selected, discrete skills, measure written language? If a student can select correct punctuation on a multiple-choice test, does that suggest that the student will produce correct punctuation in connected written language? These questions are particularly important for the LD student who is, by nature, a person with a range of skills that are vulnerable to the task.

Holistic Assessment

Holistic scoring procedures attempt to evaluate the overall effectiveness of a composition as a vehicle for communicating. According to Cooper (1977), a holistic procedure is, "Any procedure which stops short of enumerating linguistic, rhetorical, or informational features of a piece of writing" (p. 4). Holistic scales are divided into seven broad categories: general impression, essay, "center of gravity," dichotomous, analytic, feature analysis, and primary trait. Of these, primary trait is currently being adopted in many states for the evaluation of functional writing. It appears to be applicable to the written work of LD students.

Primary Trait Scoring (Mullis, 1980), developed for the National Assessment of Educational Progress (NAEP), is a highly structured holistic scoring system. The premis of the NAEP Primary Trait Scoring is that the ability to write effectively in one mode of discourse does not necessarily predict the ability to write in other modes. Therefore, the NAEP developed a comprehensive guide for each assessed writing style. The guide includes the student exercise, a clear definition of the type of discourse, a statement about the kind of, performance that is expected, the scoring procedures, examples of student responses for each scoring category, and an explanation of the scoring for each sample assignment.

Tasks are carefully defined for Primary Trait Scoring. The assessment includes, for example, a factual reporting task. Students are given a list of facts about the moon, told to write a report including them, and after writing the report, are directed to revise their work. This form of assessment seems particularly appropriate for LD children. The specificity of the directions assures the kind of writing that is expected, and the variety of writing tasks allows an examination of more than one style of written discourse. The "primary trait," the expression of the idea, and not mechanical skills, is the focus of attention. The inclusion of revision skills is particularly useful in assessing the work of LD students who frequently have difficulty evaluating their own written work.

A combination of Primary Trait Scoring and several atomistic procedures would be most useful in assessing the writing skills of LD students. A remedial plan could be developed around one of several types of written discourse, and punctuation and capitalization skills could be taught in a useful context.

Remediation

The remediation of writing deficits in LD students is a field of myriad ideas and materials. Although some programs are specifically geared to areas of exceptionality, others are an outgrowth of new trends in normal language development.

Some remedial programs are transplanted directly from other areas of exceptionality. The *Fitzgerald Key* (1966) and the Fokes Kit (1976) have been widely used in the education of the hearing impaired and include a strong language base for developing writing skills. The *Fitzgerald Key* is a highly structured text emphasizing word order as the most important feature in understanding and generating English sentences. Syntactical structures are taught through geometrically coded components of a sentence. Visual ordering of langauge is also stressed. Phelps–Gunn and Phelps–Teraski (1982) suggested that the *Fitzgerald Key* can be used with LD students if the geometric symbols and grammatical rules are minimized. The Fokes Kit includes colorful, highly structured materials for the development of oral and written sentence structure.

Framing Your Thoughts (Greene & Enfield, 1979) is a written language program developed primarily for LD students. It relies on geometric shapes to enhance a child's understanding of the function of each word in a sentence. The program develops the concept of a sentence, explains subject and predicates, and introduces paragraph development and basic punctuation.

Sentences and Other Systems (Blackwell, Engen, Fischgrund, & Zarcadoolas, 1978) is another comprehensive language program developed for hearing impaired students. Based on Chomsky's (1965) transformational grammar, the program emphasizes the intent of language through an analysis of deep and surface structures.

The Phelps' program (1980) is an adaptation of the *Fitzgerald Key* and a modification of Laura Lee's work (1974, 1975). The Phelps' program was designed to be used withg children in regular and special education. A unique feature of the program is its emphasis on editing skills.

Since the early 1970s, the focus of research has gradually changed from a study of the final product to a study of writing processes. Research now includes more dynamic models in an attempt to describe what the writer needs to consider in shaping text. Flower (1985), for example, presented a detailed analysis of the writing process through specific writing assignments. Writing Across the Curriculum (Yates, 1983) views writing as a tool for learning content — writing to learn. Process research is just beginning to affect the LD field (Graves, 1985; Moulton & Bader, 1985). In light of the research on metacognitive awareness in LD adolescents (Wong, 1985), the application of the writing process approach will be a welcome addition.

SUMMARY

Assessment and remediation of written language disorders is a field in its infancy. Carefully designed testing instruments in handwriting, spelling, and written expression are still needed. The feasibility of applying testing procedures not originally designed for LD students, such as Primary Trait Scoring, should be carefully considered. Comprehensive remedial programs and procedures for eliminating specific deficits need to be refined and systematically field-tested to assure quality.

Ideas, methods, and materials from research in normal language development and from other areas of exceptionality can be used with LD students. Tailoring many of these programs to the needs of LD students is a priority as well as a challenge.

CHAPTER 6

Arithmetic

Jeannette E. Fleischner
Eileen S. Marzola

B y current estimates, approximately 6% of school-age children have
serious arithmetic achievement deficits (Badian & Ghublikian, 1982;
Kosc, 1974; McKinney & Feagans, 1980; Weinstein, 1980). Although average
mathematics performance in students aged 9 to 17 years has shown some
improvement in recent years (Lindquist, Carpenter, Silver, & Matthews,
1983), that same trend has not been evident for the population of students
with learning disabilities.

Most referrals for special education services for potential LD students
are precipitated by delays in reading skill acquisition. A large percentage
of these children, however, also have substantial arithmetic achievement
deficits (Fleischner & Garnett, 1983; McKinney & Feagans, 1980). When
teachers of LD students were questioned about their students' need
for remediation in mathematics, they reported that two out of three of
their students had a "significant" deficit in this area (McLeod & Armstrong, 1982).

Despite the fact that the current federal definition of LD includes disorders of mathematical calculations (*Federal Register,* August 23, 1977)
relatively few children are referred for evaluation specifically because of
deficits in mathematics. Even when a child has been classified as LD, adequate assessment procedures and remediation of arithmetic deficits are
rarely evident (Goodstein & Kahn, 1974). As a result, a potentially sizable
number of students with arithmetic disabilities are excluded from the help
they need (Badian, 1983).

Although research has indicated that math disabilities are as prevalent as difficulties in other academic areas (Cohn, 1971; Kosc, 1974; McKinney & Feagans, 1980; Otto, McMenemy, & Smith, 1973), only recently has research in this area increased significantly. In the past, much of the research was narrow in scope and, consequently, only limited information was made available to practitioners about the nature of children's arithmetic learning disabilities, effective diagnostic procedures, and the effectiveness of various teaching approaches (Cawley, 1981; Reid & Hresko, 1981; Wallace & Larsen, 1978). In comparison to the extensive research in reading, for example, the investigation of math disabilities has really just begun. However, interpretation of existing data, coupled with clinical experience, lends support to basic principles of math instruction for LD students.

PRINCIPLES OF ARITHMETIC INSTRUCTION

Assessment Issues

Arithmetic assessment includes an understanding of the scope and sequence of the curriculum; assessment that is based on the curriculum, and an analysis of errors.

Scope and Sequence

Appropriate assessment is a critical prerequisite for effective mathematics instruction. Teachers need to know what skills students already possess before they can make decisions about instructional objectives. Before accurate assessment of arithmetic skills can begin, however, teachers must understand the scope and sequence of the mathematics curriculum.

Because there is no national mathematics curriculum, states or local school districts determine the curriculum (Begle, 1979). Typically, the arithmetic curriculum is characterized by the skills selected by authors of the basal arithmetic series designated for use in grades K–8. Textbook series in mathematics typically provide information indicating precisely when specific skills are taught in scope and sequence charts provided by the publisher.

The order in which computational operations are taught is generally standard across curricula. At the first grade level, most arithmetic curricula begin by introducing addition of single digits with sums less than 10. In some texts, subtraction may be taught separately or introduced as the reverse operation of addition. Generally, by the middle of second grade, the basic addition facts with combinations adding up to 18 are introduced. The concept of place value becomes important at this stage. Without understanding the exchange of ones for tens, tens for hundreds, hundreds for thousands, etc., children will be limited to rote functioning when working with complex computation.

Multiplication and division are introduced in some curricula by the end of the second grade, and in others by the beginning of third grade. In third or fourth grade, children are becoming familar with the concept of part-whole relationships and fractional notation. In fourth or fifth grade, decimal notation is frequently introduced.

At the same time new information is presented, children are still required to practice periodically addition and subtraction facts to facilitate automatism. Basic fact proficiency is expected in all four operations during the elementary years. As school years progress, texts and teachers put increasing emphasis on algorithms required for more complex operations, including addition with renaming, subtraction with regrouping, multidigit multiplication and division, and all operations with fractions and decimals.

Curriculum-based Assessment

It is essential that assessment be based on the classroom curriculum. The administration of achievement tests at the beginning and end of the school year provides little useful information for instructional planning or evaluation (Freeman, Kuhs, Knappen, & Porter, 1982; Goodstein, 1985). These tests are given too infrequently to be useful for instructional decision making. Because test items are not necessarily tied to any particular curriculum, teachers cannot use the results to evaluate students' skills as they relate to the textbook used in class (Blankenship, 1985; Salvia & Ysseldyke, 1985). Another criticism directed toward standardized achievement tests is that they contain only a scattered sample of facts and concepts. As a result, teachers have to generalize from student performance on test items to performance on items that have not been tested (Salvia & Ysseldyke, 1985).

Unlike standardized norm-referenced or commercial criterion-referenced tests, curriculum-based assessment allows teachers to assess student performance by drawing objectives directly from the text used in the classroom (Blankenship & Lilly, 1981). Assessment occurs throughout the year to monitor maintenance of skill attainment.

Teacher's manuals or scope and sequence charts can serve as references for specific objectives. Using these sources as a base, the teacher decides what skills need to be assessed and what methods will be used to evaluate performance. Direct and frequent (often daily) measurement is used to evaluate performance on specific objectives.

Error Analysis

Error analysis is another effective tool for assisting teachers in determining a precise plan for remediation of their students' arithmetic skills deficits. Teachers who merely record an answer as right or wrong are missing an opportunity to analyze at exactly what point an error occurred in a student's work. By further probing, the teacher can have a more precise idea of where the student's level of competence in a specific skill breaks down. Students may make computational errors, not because they lack competence of a skill, but because they have misunderstood or misapplied one small step of an algorithm. Error analysis can be an extremely efficient way of isolating a stumbling block to problem solutions. Through error analysis, a teacher is encouraged to refrain from assigning drill activities such as worksheets, which only serve to reinforce incorrect strategies (Asklock, 1986).

By definition, error analysis is the process of examining and analyzing a sample of a student's work in a particular operation (e.g., addition with regrouping or subtraction with renaming) to determine if a systematic pattern of incorrect procedures is present. Ashlock (1986) cautioned that errors in computation are not necessarily the sole result of carelessness or lack of procedural knowledge. Almost 60 years ago, Brueckner (1928) was concerned with identifying types of errors in computation. Roberts (1968) identified four error categories or "failure strategies" in the written computation of mixed ability in math: wrong operation, obvious computational error, defective algorithm, and random response. Roberts found that using the wrong operation and making random responses were particularly prevalent among low ability third grade students. The largest number of errors in almost all ability groups was due to faulty algorithm techniques. Other researchers have affirmed that many students at all grade and ability levels, make systematic procedural errors rather than mere careless mistakes or errors due to lack of knowledge of basic facts (Ashlock, 1986; Brown & Burton, 1978; Engelhardt, 1977; Cox, 1975; Schacht, 1967).

An error interview is the most effective means of determining how a child thinks when computing. For the teacher who does not want to take the time to interview each child, Ashlock (1986) suggested distractors drawn from error patterns to give the teacher clues to a child's thought process. A multiple-choice test can be administered that contains distractors matched to erroneous procedures that may be used by a child. Garnett and Fleischner (1986) suggested that timed exams requiring only written responses may represent a misleading picture of the capabilities of LD students. By merely circling incorrectly computed problems and permitting students to recalculate in an untimed format, teachers may get a truer picture of the LD student's understanding of computational procedures.

The goal of the error interview is to get a child to solve incorrect problems aloud so that the teacher can see exactly where the solution process breaks down. (Does the child supply the wrong fact, know how to use the required algorithm, make wild guesses, or lack a basic understanding of the concept involved?) Ashlock (1986) reminded us that the actual process of commenting aloud can influence a child's thinking. He suggested encouraging retrospection by asking a child to comment on the solution process *after* completing it. The danger of this procedure, of course, is that the child may forget where the difficulty began. Ashlock (1986) proposed, therefore, that the two strategies, introspection and retrospection, be alternated to get the most detailed picture of a child's solution processes.

Establishing a Conceptual Base

Operations in math are based on an understanding of computational operations. Addition and multiplication require combining; subtraction, division, and basic fraction concepts involve partitioning objects. The use of concrete representations helps students to comprehend the rationale underlying computational operations. Although many young children develop these understandings intuitively before they begin formal math instruction, LD students may need to have direct, guided experiences with concrete objects to establish a conceptual base (Garnett & Fleischner, 1986). Ashlock (1986) noted that many children develop rigid concepts because they have seen these concepts represented by only one kind of material or manipulative device. A variety of manipulative materials are available, such as blocks, abacuses, Unifix cubes, Stern, Traub, or Cuisenaire rods, sticks, and straws. Different materials should be used to illustrate concepts, and children should be encouraged to vary materials to support computation during early stages of learning.

Use of manipulatives alone, however, is probably not sufficient to help children establish mathematical concepts. This is in contrast to the "Discovery Approach" to mathematics, in which students are expected to intuit the relationships between principles and to develop concepts on their own through manipulation of concrete materials. *Guided* practice, including verbal descriptions either preceding or accompanying the manipulation of materials, may also be needed for LD students. In addition, Ashlock (1986) stressed recording the step-by-step process involved when manipulatives are used for computation. This helps children to understand the symbols they are working with on paper. Addition with renaming and subtraction with regrouping, for example, become more than mere rote exercises when children have worked with manipulatives such as place value materials (e.g., sticks or straws used singly and bound in groups of 10). When children order manipulatives to reflect a written problem, and then record the computation process on paper, they gain a much better understanding of the process involved.

Directive Instruction and Mastery Learning

It has been hypothesized that learning problems exhibited by LD children occur because these children have difficulty processing information (Connor, 1983; Farnham-Diggory, 1979). Fleischner and Garnett (1983) viewed the information-processing difficulties of LD students from two perspectives: as cognitive delays or differences within the students themselves and as information-processing demands of the subject matter. They proposed that achievement deficits of LD students result from an interaction between information-processing limitations and the complex, often confusing presentation of the subject matter. Insufficient practice with new material compounds the processing demands. Precise teaching objectives coupled with practice to mastery may help the LD student cope with the information-processing demands of an arithmetic curriculum.

Although there are many possible causes of poor performance in arithmetic, inadequate teaching has been cited as one of the most significant contributing factors (Russell & Ginsburg, 1982). Bloom (1976) asserted that under favorable learning conditions, students are similar in their learning abilities and rates of learning. Carnine, Silbert, and Stein, (1981) who described direct instruction techniques in math, and Bloom (1976), who outlined the principles of mastery learning, attempted to provide all students with maximum opportunities to learn.

Research has shown that instructional techniques can produce significant improvements in academic achievement among students (Brophy & Evertson, 1976; Clark, Gage, Marx, Peterson, Staybrook, & Winnie, 1976; Fleischner & Shepherd, 1980; Hunter, 1979; Rosenshine, 1976; Silbert, Carnine, & Stein, 1981; Stebbins, Proper, St. Pierre, & Cerva, 1977). Silbert, Carnine, and Stein (1981) noted that learning mathematics may be made easier by breaking down complex tasks into more manageable subskills, teaching these skills to mastery, and then showing students how the subskills can be combined. Pretesting to pinpoint specific objectives for each student is critical to the success of directive teaching. Manipulation of instructional variables for which teachers are responsible is a main component of direct instruction methodology. Although concrete materials may be used in direct instruction programs, the teacher states explicitly the concept presented rather than allowing students to formulate their own rules through observation. This is in direct contrast to the "discovery approach" to math instruction outlined earlier.

Bloom (1976) proposed four requirements for success in mastery learning: developing separate units of analysis within a curriculum; pinpointing the source of difficulty and attacking it when problems occur; allowing sufficient time to reach mastery; and establishing a clear criterion for mastery. The principles of direct instruction and mastery learning are clearly compatible. Recent studies have shown the effectiveness of math instructional plans that employed both direct instructional and mastery learning principles (see, for example, Fleischner, Garnett, & Preddy, 1982; Marzola, 1985; Nuzum, 1982).

TOPICS OF INSTRUCTION

Instructional topics in arithmetic include precomputational skills, basic operations, whole number computation, part-whole relationships, problem solving, and related topics such as money and telling time.

Precomputational Skills

Children who have not yet been exposed to formal arithmetic instruction still come to school exhibiting mathematical knowledge, skills, and solution strategies (Carpenter, Hiebert, & Moser, 1981; Gelman & Gallistel, 1978; Ginsburg, 1983). This early knowledge of numbers is a precursor of more advanced mathematical thinking (Resnick, 1981). Research has explored early mathematical abilities including counting, subitizing (the direct awareness of numerosity without counting), beginning addition and substraction strategies, understanding the concepts of more or less, cardinality, equality, and problem-solving strategies (Katz, 1986). Children use these skills to solve practical problems such as sharing treats and matching silverware to place settings at a table. As they learn new vocabulary and symbols for these concepts, children see relationships between what they already know and what they are taught in school.

Although many children begin school with a rich store of prior knowledge in mathematics, some children experience difficulty with arithmetic skills and understanding concepts very early in their schooling (Cawley, 1984). Because new math concepts are highly dependent on previously acquired knowledge and skills (Sharma, 1979), the child who does not have an early conceptual base in mathematics is at risk for later difficulties (Fleischner, 1983; Katz, 1986).

Bley and Thornton (1981) identified eight areas within the early number program that are often difficult for the LD child: recognizing sight groups, writing numerals 0 to 10, naming consecutive numbers, counting on, writing two-digit numbers, counting and skip counting two-digit numbers, reading and writing larger numbers, and comparing numbers.

Skill deficits involving counting, subitizing, sequencing, and comparing numbers can be addressed through the use of a variety of manipulative materials. Activities such as counting, recognizing, and comparing rods or groups of cubes, sticks, coins, or chips can help children form meaningful number concepts. Stern and Stern (1971) developed a rich store of activities to help young children establish arithmetic knowledge through the use of manipulatives, particularly the Stern blocks. Many of the games and activities they suggested, however, are easily adaptable to other manipulative materials including Unifix cubes, Traub blocks, and Cuisenaire rods. Activities that reinforce sequencing skills include the use of walk-on number lines, rulers or number tracks used as number lines, and large numeral cards.

Children should be encouraged to relate numerals to specific quantities in different ways (Ashlock, 1986; Traub, 1985). After they have manipulated concrete objects, children should record what they have seen with written notation. When they are presented with written notation or comparisons between two numbers, they should be encouraged to construct sets of materials that represent the numbers they have seen.

Numeral reversals may be addressed by providing color cues suggesting where a numeral should start (green dot) and end (red dot) on a page. Writing in 1-inch graph paper squares also helps children establish boundaries for their efforts at writing individual numerals. Children can be encouraged to "talk through" their writing movements to reinforce appropriate orientation in space.

Basic Operations

Place Value

To understand the numeration system and the algorithms of the four basic operations, students must master place value concepts (O'Neill & Jensen, 1981). Initial exposure to place value should be through the manipulation of concrete materials (Fitzmaurice-Hayes, 1984; O'Neill & Jensen, 1981; Stern & Stern, 1971). Many commercial materials are available to help students develop place value concepts. Stern Structural Arithmetic materials, Cuisenaire rods, Unifix cubes, Dienes Multibase Arithmetic Blocks, and the abacus are only a few of the materials currently in use. For many years, teachers have created their own place value materials with Popsicle sticks, coffee stirrers — anything that could be bundled into groups of 10.

Place value instruction, like the teaching of numeral/quantity relationships should relate the symbolic to the concrete and the concrete

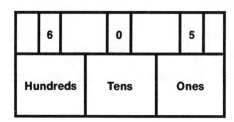

Figure 6–1
Pocket place value chart. As teacher dic-
tates a number, students may hold up
these miniature charts with number strips
in the appropriate pockets.

to the symbolic (Fitzmaurice-Hayes, 1984). When a numeral is written on the board, children should be required to represent the number using sticks and a variety of other manipulatives. They should also write the numeral after the bundled sticks have been presented. Older children who might rebel at the use of manipulatives but who still have a weak under-standing of place value can use a manual (nonelectric) hand calculator (Fitzmaurice-Hayes, 1985).

A personal pocket chart is a useful aid for students learning place value. It also permits the teacher to get immediate feedback about a student's grasp of the concepts being taught (O'Neill & Jensen, 1981). The pocket charts may be made by folding up the bottom third of a 5" × 8" file card and stapling the resulting pocket into divisions labeled thousands, hundreds, tens, and ones (see Figure 6–1). Students use strips of paper to represent numbers in each of the four columns. For the student who needs extra structure in this activity, specific colors can be assigned to each place. When the teacher reads a number or writes one on the board, students place the appropriate numerals in the proper column on their pocket charts. Overlapping place value cards suggested by O'Neill and Jen-sen (1981) can also help students to read longer numerals correctly (see Figure 6–2). They are also useful for illustrating the concept of an expanded notation. An accordion-folded index card can be used to show expanded notation (see Figure 6–3). Place value skills can be practiced by playing games like Concentration. Students match cards that have the same num-

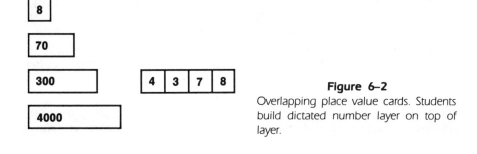

Figure 6–2
Overlapping place value cards. Students build dictated number layer on top of layer.

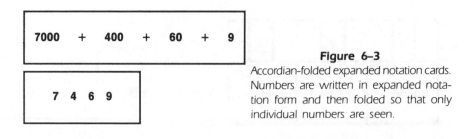

Figure 6–3
Accordian-folded expanded notation cards.
Numbers are written in expanded notation form and then folded so that only
individual numbers are seen.

ber written on them in different forms (e.g., 142 may also be written as 100
+ 40 + 2 or as 1 hundred + 4 tens + 2 ones). Place value stamps can also
be used to represent the picture form of manipulative materials on cards
(Beattie & Scheer, 1982). Distractor cards (e.g., 1,042) may be added to
encourage children to discriminate between similar numbers.

Basic Facts

Research during the last 10 years has revealed that LD students frequently have difficulty learning basic facts (Badian, 1983; Fleischner, Garnett, & Shepherd, 1982; Russell & Ginsburg, 1981) even when they have a
good understanding of math concepts (Russell & Ginsburg, 1981). There
are approximately 100 basic facts within each of the four whole-number
operations in arithmetic. They include all the number relations resulting in
sums and differences from 0 to 18, products from 0 to 81, and quotients
from 0 to 9. Mastery of addition and subtraction facts is stressed in grades
1 and 2. Efficient recall of multiplication and division facts is a fundamental goal for grades 3 through 5.

Fleischner, Garnett, and Shepherd (1982) showed that LD students
were able to compute basic facts in addition, subtraction, and multiplication as accurately as their non-LD peers in a timed-test format. However,
their speed of completion was greatly impaired. They attempted only about
half as many problems in the 3 minutes allotted for the completion of each
test of 98 problems. When the protocols of the LD students were examined,
it was discovered that they were covered with evidence of counting (e.g.,
number lines, hatch marks). Although these students obviously understood the process involved in the computation of basic facts, their failure
to commit the facts to memory slowed their performance considerably.
Groen and Parkman (1972) hypothesized that one of two methods, either
reproductive or reconstructive strategies, may result in successful computation of basic facts. Children who use a reproductive strategy are able to respond automatically as they retrieve their answers directly from memory.
They do not report any intervening cognitive manipulation of information.

Reconstructive strategies include counting and using better-known combinations as bridges to unknown facts.

Fleischner (1983) reported that LD students relied much more heavily on reconstructive strategies than did non-LD students. Furthermore, the reconstructive strategies used by the LD students were primitive (counting one number at a time, using fingers, marks, or number lines).

Mastery of basic facts is stressed in elementary school because proficiency at this level is seen as fundamental to more complex computation skills and problem solving (Fleischner & Garnett, 1983). Case (1982) discussed the problem of inadequately automatized operations at the basic fact level taking up more processing capacity than necessary. As a result, students find that the mastery of higher level concepts or algorithms is impaired.

In an attempt to analyze the effect of order of presentation on mastery and retention of basic facts, Fleischner, Garnett, & Preddy (1982) and Lieby (1981) compared a traditional fixed order of presentation of basic facts (referred to as a "Mastery/Motivation" approach) to instruction based on the relationships among facts (referred to as a "Strategies Generalization" approach). The principles of direct instruction and mastery learning were used to guide the construction of the lessons, which were modeled on suggestions made by Myers and Thornton (1977). Students practiced facts using a variety of motivational games and activities and charted their own progress. The students showed marked improvement in the number of basic facts they computed accurately in 3 minutes. Students did equally well in both modes of presentation. It was concluded that if direct instructional techniques were used, basic fact proficiency was improved no matter what sequence of facts was presented. Frequent systematic practice of learned facts was found to be important for retention.

Recently, a number of games and activity books have appeared that focus on the systematic teaching and practicing of basic facts. In addition to the teaching manuals compiled by the Research Institute for the Study of Learning Disabilities (Garnett, Frank, & Fleischner, 1983a, 1983b, 1983c, 1983d), publishers such as Creative Publications (Oaklawn, Illinois) have published workbooks (e.g., *Look Into the Facts* and *A Matter of Facts*) that systematically present and review math facts. Game boards such as *Faxactly Games* (also from Creative Publications) review single facts in a highly motivational format. Golick's book, *Deal Me In!* (1973), provides many card games that can reinforce learning. Traub's (1985) *Recipe for Math* gives teachers a dozen games, including those that use blank or regular playing cards and chips, to review math facts.

Traditional paper and pencil drills may have negative associations for a child who has failed repeatedly. As Biggs (1963) noted, "In arithmetic and mathematics, the inhibition produced by anxiety appears to swamp any motivating effect, particularly where the children concerned are already anxious. . . . Anxiety appears to be more easily aroused in learning mathematics than it is in other subjects" (quoted in Ashlock, 1986). Games are excellent devices for motivating practice under "safe" conditions, as in computer-based drill and practice. As Ashlock (1986) warned, however, these games should be used for reinforcement and practice, which must follow developmental instruction.

It is important to use manipulatives to teach a concept before assigning practice activities (Ashlock, 1986). For example, when teaching the concept of multiplication, a teacher should demonstrate that multiplication deals with equal-sized groups. The display of sets of rods or cubes on a number track or against a number line can demonstrate vividly the concept of multiplication as repeated addition. Division as the inverse of multiplication, and subtraction as the opposite of addition, can be seen easily when concrete materials are used. Children should be encouraged to use aids only as long as they are needed to make a concept clear. They should become familiar with a wide variety of representational materials and activities so that they do not limit their application of concepts to one set of conditions.

Children should be encouraged to record what they see. Traub (1985) advised teachers to have children record basic facts (e.g., addition combinations to 10) on 1/2" graph paper after they have formed these combinations with rods. In addition to the traditional flash cards with problems on one side and answers on the reverse, triangle flash cards can be made to emphasize the commutative properties of multiplication and addition as well as the organization of facts into "families" representing the relationships between addition and subtraction and multiplication and division (Figure 6-4).

Children learn to memorize facts in many different ways. Rathmell (1978) provided strategies that can be used to learn facts at different levels

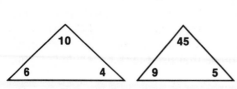

Figure 6-4
Triangle flash cards. Students use these cards for both addition/subtraction facts and multiplication/division facts. In the addition card on the left, the student covers up the number at the top (10) and adds 6 + 4. After verifying that 10 is the correct answer, the student then asks the related subtraction problem and covers up the 6: 10 − 4 = ? The same procedure is used to reinforce the understanding of the relationship between multiplication and division.

of skill development and maturity. These strategies include counting on, linking unknown facts to known facts, skip counting, doubling strategies, and seeing patterns. Traub (1985) suggested mnemonics to help children remember specific facts (e.g., 7 × 8 = ?). What two numbers come before 7 and 8? 5 and 6 come before 7 and 8. 7 × 8 = 56). Self-recording of progress is also a good motivational tool for basic fact acquisition. A grid can be drawn with room for all the facts to be recorded as they are learned. As an alternative procedure, the facts can be prerecorded on the grid and children can color in the boxes as they master the facts. Children soon begin to focus on how many facts they have mastered rather than how many they still have to learn. Children can also chart their speed in basic fact recall. Rather than competing against each other, children in a class can be encouraged to compete against themselves. Facts should not be considered "mastered" until children are able to recall them accurately on several different occasions.

Whole Number Computation

Competent performance in arithmetic does not stop with mastery of basic facts. As soon as problems with more than one digit are introduced, many LD children exhibit difficulty performing computations in the appropriate right/left order. The performance of LD students is frequently marked by impaired ability to grasp a concept and use the proper procedures for regrouping and renaming. These problems are magnified by poorly constructed textbook pages with too many examples crowded onto one page or too few opportunities to practice newly learned skills.

Multiplication instruction generally follows this order after basic facts are mastered:

- Single digits times 10, 100
- Single digits times other 10s (e.g., 20, 30) and by other 100s
- One digit times two digits without regrouping
- One digit times two digits with regrouping
- Multidigit multiplication (two digits times two digits; two digits times three digits, three digits times three digits)

Division follows a similar order after basic fact acquisition:

- Single digits into 10s, 100s (without remainders)
- Single digits into any two digits evenly
- Single digits into two digits with remainders
- 10s into two and three digits
- Two digits into two, three, or four digits evenly
- Multidigit division with remainders

Garnett and Fleischner (1987) outlined three principles for developing remedial plans for LD children with math deficits: clarifying underlying concepts by providing a variety of illustrations; ensuring reliable application of algorithms; and teaching the appropriate use of instructional aids, including number lines, calculators, and computers. Packets of manipulative and practice materials can be made available for students to use in remedial, special education, or regular classrooms. Packets may contain any or all of the following materials:

- Squared materials (1s, 10s, 100s)
- Number lines
- Fraction pieces
- Decimal squares
- Prompt cards for word problem solving strategies
- Color-cued prompt cards for complex computational processes (e.g., long division, multidigit multiplication)
- Flash cards containing facts (including both new and review facts) to practice alone or with a partner whenever possible

The difficulty LD children have in applying algorithms may be ameliorated in a number of ways. Bley and Thornton (1981) and Traub (1985) suggested color-cuing problems to reinforce right to left progression. Computation begins with green-coded numbers and ends with red-coded numbers. Some LD children may need to use a highlighter on multidigit examples to guide them in recording different steps (Garnett & Fleischner, 1987). These color cues are gradually deleted as children become more competent in their performance.

Workbook pages and worksheets can be structured to improve LD children's performance (Bley & Thornton, 1981). Examples in workbooks can be boxed off or students can use index cards with windows cut out of them to help focus on only one set of problems at a time. Worksheet pages can be accordion-folded or folded into fourths or halves to reduce frustration and to avoid "overloading." Examples may be written on graph paper to reinforce page organization and proper alignment of numerals.

Verbal mediation is another effective tool to master more complex computation. This strategy may help LD children monitor their performance on multistep problems. The use of mnemonics helps LD children to remember computation steps (e.g., Does My Spaghetti Cheese Bounce? for Divide, Multiply, Subtract, Check, Bring Down). Teacher modeling of proper algorithms helps LD students clarify strategies for their own use. Written examples may be used for reference. Encourage children to review the models before they begin a set of problems. Gradually delete cues as students achieve mastery, but have models available for review. Bley and Thornton (1981), Silbert, Carnine, and Stein (1981), and Traub (1985) suggested a variety of other teaching ideas to facilitate whole number computation.

Students need adequate practice time for each new skills. Teachers should provide short practice periods rather than long, concentrated periods of work. A skill learned one day is not necessarily mastered forever. Intermittent review is critical.

Part-Whole Representation

Part-whole relationships are often hard for LD students to understand. Fractions may seem more confusing than decimals.

Fractions

Both the understanding of fractional concepts and computing with fractions are often extremely critical for the LD child. Even the act of writing a fraction can be perceptually confusing (e.g., 2⅓ may be read as $\frac{1}{23}$ or $\frac{23}{3}$). It is essential to use manipulative aids to facilitate concept development of fractions (Bley and Thornton, 1981). Without the use of a variety of concrete examples, it may be confusing to the child to be told that ⅓ is greater than ¼. Unless children are shown otherwise, they tend to have misperceptions about fractions. In a series of interviews conducted with sixth graders, Peck and Jencks (1981) found that non-LD sixth graders did not fully understand fractions. Sketches that they made of fractions were only vaguely related to the correct meaning of the symbol represented (e.g., pictures of ⅕) had grossly misproportioned segments detailed in the circle). Although many children were able to recall examples of specific fractions (e.g. ½, ¼) they did not have a generalized concept of fractions.

Peck and Jencks (1981) also found that even those students who did understand fractions could not extend their ideas to operations on fractions. Less than 10% of the students interviewed were able to compare fractions. Because they had no conceptual base, they were not able to determine if the results of their attempts made any sense. Students frequently misapplied rules, and even those who applied them correctly were not sure of what they were doing. The only positive observation in Peck and Jencks' study was that when the students were provided with concrete materials, they were able to conceptualize fractions and make logical predictions. Once again, the need for helping students to develop concepts through the use of a variety of manipulative materials becomes apparent.

Children frequently have only circles as their models for fractions. Some workbooks (e.g., Rasmussen's *Key to fractions,* 1980) provide students with examples of fractions not only as circles, but also as squares, triangles, rectangles, hexagons, and other polygons. Colored-acetate fraction strips (either alone or in conjunction with a number line) can be used as an aid to compare fractions and to demonstrate their equivalency. Fractions may be seen as parts of geometric regions, but they may also be interpreted as parts of groups of objects (e.g., ⅗ of 15) or as points on a number line.

Fraction skills begin with concept development, particularly the identification of the function of the denominator and the numerator. Skill acquisition progresses through addition and subtraction of fractions with the same denominator, improper fractions, and mixed numbers. Computation of fractions continues with problems with different denominators, reducing answers to the lowest common denominator, and regrouping and renaming in addition and subtraction of fractions. Multiplication and division of fractions, including mixed numbers, are mastered last.

Traub (1985) emphasized the function of the denominator as the "down number that divides." It represents the total number of parts the whole thing was divided into. The concept of the numerator is taught by explaining that this top number indicates how many pieces a person "got" of the thing that was divided. Traub stressed that students should always write down what they have seen after they have worked with concrete objects.

Even after students appear to have acquired the conceptual base for understanding fractions, they may have difficulty. One of the first stumbling blocks is adding or subtracting fractions. Students frequently have problems finding the lowest common denominator. Bley and Thornton (1981) suggested preformatting worksheets and workbooks to encourage children to focus on denominators. By putting a box around each denominator and another box in the answer area, children are reminded to ask themselves whether the denominators are the same or different.

Many children merely multiply the denominators together to find the common denominator. After students understand the concept of the common denominator, they can be given a prompt card reminding them to try doubling or even tripling the largest denominator before resorting to multiplying the denominators by each other. Prompt cards or examples are also useful for helping students to remember the steps in multiplying and dividing fractions. More teaching suggestions for computing fractions and developing more advanced fraction concepts can be found in Bley and Thornton (1981), Carnine, Silbert, and Stein (1981), and Traub (1985).

Decimals

Computation with decimals is often easier for students than computation of fractions. This may be because they are already familiar with whole number comptutation, which is similar (Bley & Thornton, 1981). The results of the National Assessment of Educational Progress in 1981, however, indicated that students lack a firm understanding of the place value interpretation of decimals. As a result, more students can compute decimals than can interpret their meaning (Carpenter, Corbitt, Kepner, Lindquist, & Reys, 1981).

Decimals can be viewed as a special group of fractions with denominators in multiples of 10. Decimal instruction begins at about the fourth grade level with reading and writing decimals, comparing them, and being aware of column alignment in order to add and subtract tenths, hundredths, and whole numbers. During fifth grade, children are usually required to read and write decimals to the thousandths place, multiply and divide decimals, and round them off. The conversion of fractions (including mixed numbers) to decimals and decimals to fractions is also introduced in the fifth grade.

Decimal concepts are usually represented with manipulative aids. Base ten blocks can be used to illustrate units, tenths, and hundredths. Place value charts are indispensable aids for remembering the relative value of decimals. Numerals to the right of the decimal can be highlighted in a different color. Drawing attention to the difference between hun*dreds* and hun*dredths* through color cuing may also be useful (Bley & Thornton, 1981). Money can illustrate decimal concepts, with the dollar as the unit and dimes and pennies as tenths and hundredths.

To facilitate comparing decimals, Bley and Thornton (1981) suggested shading in hundreds squares to see which is greater. Another technique they sugested is aligning decimal points in numbers to help students compare decimal values. As soon as students see a difference in a column, the number with the greater digit has the greater value:

.8<u>4</u>2

.8<u>3</u>6

When the number of decimal places is different in two numbers, students may compare them more easily if zeroes are added to even out the number of decimal points:

.069 can be changed to .069
.66   .660

Traub (1985) suggested converting decimals to common fractions to facilitate reading them. When students want to change decimals to fractions, they underline them and stretch the decimal point down to make a one out of it. Finally, a zero is written under every number (Figure 6-5). To read a mixed decimal number, students read the digit before the decimal just as they would any whole number, then follow the same procedure (illustrated in

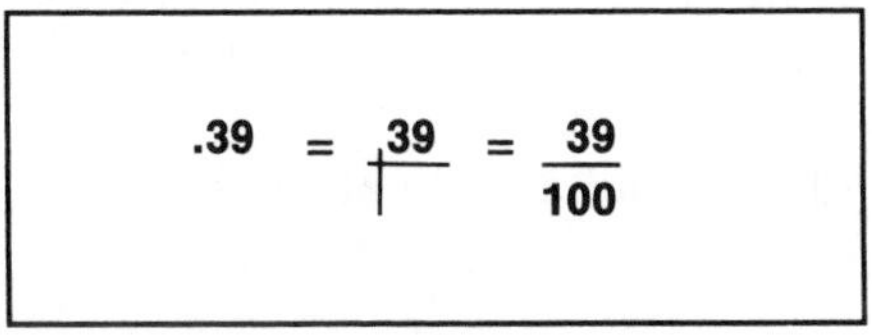

$$.39 = \frac{39}{1} = \frac{39}{100}$$

Figure 6-5

Reading decimals as fractions. Students draw a line under the decimal, extend the decimal point to make a 1, and then draw as many zeroes as there are numbers in the decimal.

Figure 6-6

Reading whole numbers and decimals. Repeat same procedure as for simple decimals. Draw a line under the decimal, extend the decimal to make a 1, and draw as many zeroes as there are numbers. Students learn to read decimals as fractions.

$$3.789 \;=\; \frac{3\ 789}{1000} \;=\; 3\ \frac{789}{1000}$$

Figure 6-5) for reading the numbers after the decimal point (Figure 6-6). Card games like Concentration, with decimal and fractional forms of numbers written on blank playing cards, can be used to practice reading and comparing fractions.

Typically, students experience difficulty in rounding decimals (Bley & Thornton, 1981). To structure the process, students can begin by drawing a line under the appropriate digit. For example, to round the number 3.981 to the nearest hundredth, draw a line under the 8 (3.981). Students look at the following digit. If it is a 5 or more, the underlined digit is increased by one. If it is less than 5, it remains the same.

Students who have demonstrated an understanding of place value and who have mastered addition and subtraction algorithms will probably have little trouble with addition and subtraction of decimals (Fitzmaurice-Hayes, 1985). The only difficulty they may have is remembering to line up decimal points before they begin to compute.

Bennett (1982) and Bley and Thornton (1981) presented many ideas for teaching concepts and computation of decimals using pictorial representations of decimal squares. Traub (1985) advised students to talk themselves through multiplication and division of decimals, referring to a model as needed. In multiplication, students are told to forget that there are decimals until after they finish the multiplication process. Then, students use a rubberband on their right hands to remind them to count the number of digits in both rows of the multiplication problem to the *right* of the decimal. Finally, they place the decimal in the answer the same number of places *from the right* as the total number of decimals in the problem. In division of fractions, students are told that they are not allowed to work with a decimal in the divisor. They must "chase" the decimal point to the end of the divisor so that it becomes a period at the end of the whole number. Students must remember how many places they moved the decimal point to the right. Whatever they do to the divisor, they must do to the dividend. Therefore, they move the decimal point in the dividend the same number of spaces to the right. Students remember this process by recalling the directions, "What we do outside, we do inside." In the final step, students place a decimal *directly* above the one in the dividend.

Problem Solving

Mastery of skills necessary for solving everyday problems has long been recognized as an important goal of the mathematics curriculum. To reach this end, teachers frequently design brief "story problems" as devices for applying computational skills to practical settings. Although it is expected that most students will be successful in making this transition to problem solving, LD students, even when they are proficient in computation, appear to have particular difficulty solving any but the simplest story problems (Bennett, 1981; Fleischner & Garnett, 1983; Marzola, 1985; Russell & Ginsburg, 1981)

Reisman and Kauffman (1980) described effective problem solving as having four necessary components: recognizing the salient aspects of a situation, appreciating the important information supplied, determining what information is missing, and abstracting essential from nonessential details. Information-processing disturbances evident in many LD children may make these problem-solving tasks inherently difficult (Farnham-Diggory, 1972).

Recent studies have identified prompts as powerful tools for improving problem-solving performance among LD students (Marzola, 1985; Nuzum, 1982; Quandt, 1986). Zweng, Garaghty, and Turner (1979) identified four prompts as being particularly effective with a group of low ability students: using small numbers, focusing on the action implied in the problem (e.g., objects put together, removed, or separated), focusing on the part-whole relationship of the quantities within the problem, and focusing on the size of the answer.

Some of the difficulty LD students have with solving word problems may not be the result of an intrinsic deficit but the result of poor instruction and teaching materials. Brannan and Schaaf (1983) found that problem solving was rarely a major part of instruction in either elementary or secondary schools. Zweng, Garaghty, and Turner (1979) reported that textbooks seldom employed *any* of the strategies their research found to be most effective in helping students to select the correct process for problem solving. On the contrary, they found that textbooks contained methods that have negative or negligible effects on problem solving. Explicit instruction in problem solving is rare. Instead of encouraging students to analyze problems, educators frequently use strategies that have the opposite effect. For example, some teachers might attempt to de-emphasize problem analysis by using problem sets in which the same operation is used throughout; or they might encourage students to look for key words or phrases to give clues to the correct operation. The first approach uses word problems only after a particular computation skill has been introduced and thus provides no selection process or any incentive to think. Studies have demonstrated that LD students spontaneously leap to calculation, seizing any numbers in a problem without regard to the problem's requirements (Fleischner, Nuzum, & Marzola, 1987).

The two instructional techniques that have been consistently effective in teaching problem solving have been explicit teaching of the processes involved and sufficient practice to master the strategies learned Fleischner, Nuzum, & Marzola, 1987; Marzola, 1985; Nuzum, 1982). Essential strategies for successful problem solving include analyzing available information and determining what part of that information is salient to the task, selecting appropriate actions in the sequence, monitoring performance as the solution process continues, and checking the answer for both accuracy and logic (Garnett & Fleischner, 1987).

Nuzum (1982) and Marzola (1985) used prompt cards and a script to help LD students structure their problem-solving strategies. They provided direct instruction in the information and procedures critical to solving arithmetic story problems. Rather than emphasizing isolated elements, their plans emphasized the total problem-solving process.

Nuzum's (1982) problem-solving plan was tested using a single subject design. Four LD students in a resource room were given individual instruction in the use of her plan. Marzola's (1985) study was conducted with small groups (3 to 5 students) who were also in a resource room setting. Both studies demonstrated that the use of explicit instruction coupled with mastery learning resulted in significant problem-solving gains for LD students. Practice alone was not sufficient for improving problem-solving performance.

Related Topics

Money

Even young children just entering school usually have some concept of the difference between common coins like pennies, nickels, dimes, and quarters. Formal instruction in money concepts usually begins with matching coins to their names, ascribing values to different coins, and determining the value of groups of similar coins. Most LD children who have problems with word retrieval, discrimination, and sequencing will experience difficulty learning these initial money concepts (Bley & Thornton, 1981).

Whenever possible, real money should be used during instructional activities. If money substitutes must be used, they should look as much like the real thing as possible. Coin stamps are particularly useful for children who have discrimination difficulties because they can be color-coded to aid in identification. Bley and Thornton (1981) suggested using color-coded coin stamps on a "coin line" to represent the relative values of coins.

After children have learned to identify the coins, match coins to their relative values, and count coins in groups, they are taught exchange. Young children can participate in many activities (particularly buying and selling simulations) to help them understand the equal value of different groups of coins. These simulations can be especially beneficial for LD students. (See Bley & Thornton, 1981, for a variety of game ideas.)

During second grade, children usually learn to determine the value of a group of mixed coins. Silbert, Carnine, and Stein (1981) recommend a two-step strategy for counting mixed coins. First, group like coins together. Then, identify which coin is worth the most and count all coins with that value. Proceed to the coin with the next highest value and repeat the procedure. A prerequisite skill for counting a group of unlike coins is understanding the addition of 1, 5, or 10 to a two-digit number ending in zero or 5.

Giving equivalent change and verifying change received are usually introduced at the third grade level. Students must be able to count groups of coins, a skill that should have been mastered earlier. Silbert, Carinine, and Stein (1981) provided examples to facilitate this process. Bley and Thornton (1981) suggested using coins on a money line to teach giving change.

Decimal notation to express money is generally taught during third grade. Students often have difficulty reading and writing amounts below 10¢ using decimal notation. Teachers usually save these more difficult tasks until students have mastered writing quantities above 10¢. Once this concept is established, students need to be reminded that when writing money amounts, there must always be two numbers written after the decimal point. Bley and Thornton (1981) recommended color coding to remind students to include a zero if necessary.

Time

With the advent of the digital clock, direct instruction in telling time on a conventional clock with minute, hour, and second hands may be neglected. But, as Bley and Thornton (1981) cautioned, the use of a digital clock does not communicate the same sense of time that a standard clock does. Use of a standard clock helps children to understand how long an activity will last.

Telling time accurately involves complex skills that can cause great difficulty for LD children. Silbert, Carnine, and Stein (1981) outlined the discrimination skills that are required when telling time: discriminating the direction clock hands move, discriminating the minute hand from the hour hand, discriminating minutes from hours on a clock (particularly difficult because minutes are not represented by numbers on a clock), and discriminating vocabulary (e.g., when to use the word *after* and when to use *before*).

Because of the complex discriminations required to tell time, Silbert, Carnine, and Stein (1981) suggested dividing instruction into three stages: expressing time as minutes after the hour; expressing time after the hour in different ways, such as using a colon (e.g., 3:10) and terms like quarter past and half past; and expressing time as minutes before the hour. These tasks are divided into small steps. (The first stage, for example, is divided into three separate steps: telling time as minutes after the hour with the minute hand pointing to a number, not pointing to a number, and with the hour stated first.)

Silbert, Carnine, and Stein (1981) advocated teaching time by analyzing the task into its smallest component parts, following a suggested script, and constantly measuring mastery. Bley and Thornton (1981) also divided skill acquisition into small steps but placed more emphasis on motivating activities, including games and color-cued models. All emphasized mastering prerequisite skills before progressing to the next level of complexity.

In second grade, children are taught to tell time by the hour, the half hour, and the quarter hour and by 5-minute intervals. In third grade, children are taught to tell time in 1-minute intervals. Use of a one-handed clock (with only the hour hand) may help children to tell time to the hour more easily. Bley and Thornton (1981) suggested color coding hours in green and minutes in red to make them easily distinguishable.

SUMMARY

LD students often have significant deficits in arithmetic. Although research in the remediation of arithmetic problems has been limited, basic principles of math instruction can be tailored to the needs of students with learning disabilities. Researchers have found that the use of manipulative devices and visual examples are important tools for teaching mathematical concepts to LD students.

CHAPTER 7

Social Skills Training

Jean B. Schumaker
J. Stephen Hazel

R emediation of social skills deficits has gained attention over the past
few years. In the LD field, attention has grown from occasional articles and chapters on social skills to whole journal issues exploring the
topic. Until recently a major emphasis on social skills instruction with LD
individuals appeared unwarranted because their academic deficits appeared
to be their most serious limitation. Nevertheless, empirical evidence is now
available indicating that: (a) LD children are less well liked than their
peers (e.g., Bruininks, 1978a, 1978b; T. Bryan, 1974b, 1976; Garrett &
Crump, 1980; Perlmutter, Crocker, Cordray, & Garstecki, 1983; Scranton &
Ryckman, 1979); (b) LD youths perform similarly to juvenile delinquents
on a role-playing test of social skills (Schumaker, Hazel, Sherman, &
Sheldon, 1982); (c) LD youths participate less in school activities than any
other group (Deshler & Schumaker, 1983); and (d) LD individuals' social
problems continue into adulthood (Blalock, 1982a; Vetter, 1983; White,
Schumaker, Warner, Alley, & Deshler, 1980).

These findings have led to concern about the social abilities of the
learning disabled, especially in light of other research findings that corre-

Portions of this chapter originally appeared in articles by **Jean B. Schumaker** and **J. Stephen
Hazel** which both appeared in the *Journal of Learning Disabilities* (Vol. 17 (2), 422–431, 1984,
and Vol. 17 (8), 492–499, 1984) and were adapted by permission of Grune & Stratton for inclusion in this *Handbook*.

late childhood social problems with serious problems in adolescent and adult life. For example, when compared to socially competent peers, children exhibiting social problems have been found to have a higher incidence of dropping out of school (Ullman, 1957), delinquency (Roff, Sells, & Golden, 1972), and mental health problems (Cowen, Pederson, Babigian, Izzo, & Trost, 1973; Kohn, 1977; Kohn & Rosman, 1972). The LD population's social deficits may be just as handicapping as their academic deficits. If LD individuals have no means of compensating for their academic deficits through social competence, they are likely to be underemployed and less satisfied than their peers (White et al., 1980). Therefore, interventions for LD individuals must include social skills training if they are to succeed
in a variety of academic and nonacademic settings despite their disabilities.

THEORETICAL PERSPECTIVES AND PROBLEMS

For the purposes of this chapter, a social skill will be defined as any cognitive function or overt behavior in which an individual engages while interacting with another person or persons. Cognitive functions include capacities such as emphathizing with or understanding other persons' feelings, discriminating and making inferences about social cues, and predicting and evaluating consequences of social behavior. Overt behaviors include the nonverbal (e.g. eye contact, facial expression) and verbal components of a social performance. Social competence involves generative use of a variety of cognitive and overt social skills that leads to positive consequences for the individual and for those interacting with the individual (Libet & Lewinsohn, 1973; Trower, Bryant, & Argyle, 1978). Thus, social competence is a composite of skills, such as discriminating situations in which social behavior is appropriate (e.g., determining when someone is ready to talk), determining which verbal and nonverbal social skills are appropriate for a given situation (e.g., choosing skills that are appropriate for the age and sex of the other person), performing those social skills fluently in appropriate combinations according to current social mores, accurately perceiving verbal and nonverbal cues, and flexibly adjusting to this feedback (Hazel, Sherman, Schumaker, & Sheldon, 1985).

Besides being proficient at using social skills, individuals must also be motivated to use such skills. They must understand that appropriate use of social skills can lead to positive consequences, and they must be interested in obtaining those consequences. Adelman and Taylor (1982) suggested that the limited generalization and maintenance of social skills exhibited by LD individuals who have participated in social skills training programs is due to a lack of emphasis on the motivational aspects of social skills usage. Consequently, interventions aimed at promoting LD individuals' social competence must not only teach them to fluently use and perform social skills but must also motivate them to do so in a variety of situations and circumstances (Meyen & Schumaker, 1981).

Gresham (1981) conceptualized social competence problems as occurring in three distinct categories. First, socially incompetent individuals may not have learned the cognitive and overt social skills they need to succeed in social interactions. For these individuals, the skills are not present in their cognitive and behavioral repertoires. Gresham called this type of problem a "skill deficit." Another type of problem, a "performance deficit," appears when skills are present in an individual's repertoire, but are simply not performed. A third problem, a "self-control deficit," involves the emission of high rates of aversive behaviors. Gresham suggested that the content of social skills intervention for disabled individuals should be based on the alleviation of these three kinds of problems and "should be selected empirically on the basis of which skills discriminate handicapped children" (Gresham, 1981, p. 167).

Since a large number of empirically based research studies have focused on identification of social skills that discriminate LD individuals from non-LD individuals, a review of these studies should help in the selection of skills for a social skills training program. However, most attempts at identifying LD individuals' social skills problems have involved a statistical comparison of the performance of some social skill(s) by LD individuals with the performance of the same social skill(s) by non-LD individuals, matched to the LD subjects on the basis of age, sex, and race. Research reports of differences between LD and non-LD populations often do not clarify whether all members of the LD group emitted a particular behavior, but at lower rates than their non-LD peers, or whether some members of the LD group did not emit the behavior at all. Such information is critical in selecting the content of social skills interventions. On the one hand, if all the LD children already emit a given behavior, social skills training should be focused on motivating them to emit more of that behavior. On the other hand, if some of the LD children do not emit a behavior at all, they may need to be taught the particular behavior.

The results of the few research studies that have included the additional steps required to depict individual differences provide support for the notion that the LD population is heterogeneous with regard to social skills. In fact, these studies have shown that some members of the LD samples perform as well as (e.g., Schumaker et al., 1982), and are as well liked as (e.g., Perlmutter et al., 1983; Prillaman, 1981) as their non-LD peers. Consequently, not all members of the LD population need training in social skills. Because of the heterogeneity of the LD population, the results of the studies reviewed in this chapter must be examined with caution. Aggregated findings are probably masking the "true" picture that a significant proportion (e.g., 26% as found by Schumaker et al., 1982) of the LD population has no social deficits when compared to their non-LD peers.

A second problem inherent in identifying the content of social skills programs relates to the presence of other types of subgroups within the LD population. The ways in which the defining variables of these subgroups (e.g., age, sex, and race) interact with the social competence of LD individuals may be critical. For example, all the studies in this area have focused on the social skills of LD individuals within a certain age bracket. Usually, the same social skills have not been addressed in other age brackets. Since some evidence suggests that LD individuals' social performance changes as they get older (e.g., Donahue, Pearl, & T. Bryan, 1980; Gerber & Zinkgraf, 1982), it is unclear whether the characteristics of social skills performance at one age apply at other ages. Some deficits may be ameliorated through maturation and, hence, not be in need of remediation.

Similar questions arise in regard to sex and race variables. For example, the results of several studies have indicated differences between the way LD girls and LD boys are rated by peers and adults (Bruck & Hebert, 1982; J. Bryan & Perlmutter, 1979; T. Bryan, 1974b; Scranton & Ryckman, 1979) and the ways in which they perform social skills (T. Bryan, Cosden, & Pearl, 1982; T. Bryan, Donahue, & Pearl, 1981). Most studies, however, have not fully addressed this phenomenon. Most of the studies reviewed here focus on subjects of one sex and one race only or, in cases where more than one sex or race are included, fail to analyze the data with regard to these variables. Often such analyses are not possible due to the limited numbers of girls or minority individuals included in the samples.

A third problem related to using the literature reviewed here as the basis for choosing the content of social skills programs is that, with the exception of a few observational studies conducted in the natural environment (T. Bryan, 1974a; T. Bryan & J. Bryan, 1978; T. Bryan & Wheeler, 1972; T. Bryan, Wheeler, Felcan, & Henek, 1976; McKinney, McClure, & Feagans, 1982; Schumaker, Sheldon-Wildgen, & Sherman, 1980), most of the results are based on data that have been collected through tests, surveys, and/or in contrived situations. Although some of the contrived situations are more "natural" than others, it is unclear how well the data collected under such conditions represent the social behaviors that LD individuals actually use in natural environments.

A fourth problem that limits our ability to specify the social skills content of interventions for LD individuals is that the conclusions of most studies reviewed here are based on simple statistical differences between LD and non-LD groups. Only a few studies have attempted to relate statistical differences to functional measures such as how well liked the children are by peers and adults. Thus, very little is known about whether statistical differences imply functional differences that lead to lower social status, social problems, and the like. Since the social validity of results in this area is frequently open to question, it is difficult to know whether training in any particular skill will have a positive impact on the participants' social success.

A final problem is the lack of consensus with regard to the specificity of definitions for social skills and the ways in which social skills have been measured. Some researchers, for example, have focused on a very specific social skill such as eye movement (Raskind, Drew, & Regan, 1983), whereas others have addressed complex combinations of as many as 17 different verbal and nonverbal behaviors (Schumaker et al., 1982). When complex combinations of behaviors have been measured, it is usually impossible to determine from mean scores what components of those combinations have been performed or not performed. Additionally, even when researchers focus on what appears to be the same behavior, they often measure it in different ways. Sometimes, they give the same behavior different names.

THE CONTENT OF SOCIAL SKILLS TRAINING PROGRAMS

The theoretical and methodological problems surrounding social skills makes it difficult to specify the ideal content for intervention packages. Yet, the content must be specified. One means of approaching the problem is to review relevant research describing the social skills deficits of LD students. With knowledge of what social skills LD students lack, it might be possible to specify what they need to learn.

Cognitive Social Skills

Twenty research articles were reviewed to identify cognitive social skills that should be taught to LD individuals. The cognitive social skills identified through this process are choosing socially acceptable behaviors, discriminating social cues, and role-taking skills. Table 7-1 summarizes the reviewed research.

Although LD individuals seem to understand what is acceptable behavior (Ackerman, Elardo, & Dykman, 1979; J. Bryan & Sonnefeld, 1981; Fincham, 1977), they have problems choosing appropriate social behaviors for their own use. For example, when asked to choose which of several behaviors they would *actually use,* LD individuals were significantly more likely than their peers to choose less socially acceptable responses (J. Bryan, Sonnefeld, & Greenberg, 1981; T. Bryan, Werner, & Pearl, 1982; Pearl, Donahue, & T. Bryan, 1983). Importantly, the children's choices of social behaviors were significantly correlated in one study with their sociometric status (J. Bryan, Sonnefeld, & Greenberg, 1981).

TABLE 7-1
Cognitive Social Skills

Significant Difference Found	No Significant Difference Found	Sample	Measure/Task	Additional Notes	References
	Moral reasoning Role-taking	60 males, 7-10 years old, 20 LD and 40 non-LD	Moral Judgment Interview Flavell 7 Picture Story Test		Ackerman, Elardo, & Dykman, 1979
	Moral reasoning	56 males, 8-9 years old, 28 LD and 28 non-LD	Competing stories task		Fincham, 1977
	Choice of which ingratition tactics are appropriate for particular situations	60 males, 9-13 years old, 22 LD and 38 non-LD	Questionnaire		J. Bryan & Sonnefeld, 1981
Choice of which ingratiation tactics they would use in particular situations (↓ F)		272 males and females,** grades 3-6	Questionnaire	Ingratiation responses significantly correlated with sociometric status	J. Bryan, Sonnefeld, & Greenberg, 1981
Choice of antisocial behavior when pressured by peers (↑)	Choice of prosocial behavior when pressured by peers	50 males & females,** grades 5-8 23 LD and 27 non-LD	Questionnaire		T. Bryan, Werner, & Pearl, 1982

Social problem solving (↓)	236 males & females,** 13-18 years old, 119 LD and 117 non-LD	Verbal problem-solving task		Schumaker, Hazel, Sherman, & Sheldon, 1982
Predicting consequences (↓) Making inferences from social cues (↓)	40 males, 9-11 years old, 20 LD and 20 non-LD	Test of Social Inference		Bruno, 1981
Making inferences from social cues (↓)	64 males and females,* 7-8 and 10-11 years old, 32 LD and 32 non-LD	Test of Social Inference	Showed LDs ability increases with age	Gerber & Zinkgraf, 1982
Making inferences from social cues (↓)	88 males & females,** grades 6-8, 43 LD and 45 non-LD	Answering questions in relation to T.V. soap opera segments	Differences maintained when IQ controlled	Pearl & Cosden, 1982

(continued)

KEY: ↑ Where LDs emitted significantly more of a behavior than peers. ↓ Where LDs emitted significantly less of a behavior than peers. NF Functional differences analyzed but not found. F. functional differences found. * Sex differences not analyzed. **Sex differences not found. *** Sex differences found. # Sex differences not related to group.

TABLE 7-1 (continued)

Significant Difference Found	No Significant Difference Found	Sample	Measure/Task	Additional Notes	References
Interpretation of nonverbal cues (↓)		34 males & females,* grades 3-5, 23 LD and 11 non-LD	Profile of Non-verbal Sensitivity (choose description of filmed scene)	No differences related to race	T. Bryan, 1977
Sensitivity to visual cues (↓) Sensitivity to auditory cues (spliced condition) (↓) Social perception on Four Factor Test (↓)	Sensitivity to auditory cues (filtered condition)	147 males & females,# grades 8-9 54 LD and 93 non-LD	Profile of Non-verbal Sensitivity Four Factor Tests of Social Intelligence		Axelrod, 1982
Identifying the emotions of others (↓)		50 males, 7-12 years old, 25 LD and 25 non-LD	Borke Scales for Empathy (identify the emotion of the main character in a story)		Bachara, 1976
Identification of facially expressed emotions (↓)		34 males and females,* 14-18 years old, 17 LD and 17 non-LD	Answering questions after watching videotaped scenes		Wiig & Harris, 1974

Behavior		Sample	Task	Findings	Reference
Responding to facial feedback (puzzled face) (↓ LD girls in grades 1 & 2; ↑ LD boys in grades 1 & 2)	Responding to facial feedback and verbal feedback (boys in grades 1 & 2 and all in grades 3-8)	127 males and females,*** grades 1-8, 67 LD and 60 non-LD	Referential Communication Task	Showed LD's ability increases with age	Pearl, Donahue, & T. Bryan, 1983
Role taking (↓) (cognitive, affective, & perceptual)		97 males and females,* 5-11 years old, 58 LD and 39 non-LD	Answering questions in relation to role-taking tasks	LDs' scores plateau at 8 years old	Dickstein & Warren, 1980
Role-taking (↓ NF) (cognitive & affective)		40 males and females,** 7-10 years old, 20 LD and 20 non-LD	Adapted from Dickstein & Warren's tasks		Bruck & Hebert, 1982
Role-taking (↓) Decentering (↓)		58 males and females,* grades 3-4, 29 LD and 29 non-LD	Feffer's Role-taking Task, Piaget's Mountain Task	When IQ was controlled for, differences did not maintain on role-taking	Horowitz, 1981

(continued)

KEY: ↓ Where LDs emitted significantly more of a behavior than peers. ↓ Where LDs emitted significantly less of a behavior than peers. NF Functional differences analyzed but not found. F Functional differences found. * Sex differences not analyzed. ** Sex differences not found. *** Sex differences not found. # Sex differences found. # Sex differences not related to group.

119

TABLE 7-1 (continued)

Significant Difference Found	No Significant Difference Found	Sample	Measure/Task	Additional Notes	References
Role-taking (↓)		64 males and females,# grades 3–4, 32 LD and 32 non-LD	Story-telling task in relation to cartoon series		B. Wong & R. Wong, 1980
Appraisal of message adequacy (↓ 1st and 2nd grade girls)	Appraisal of message adequacy (3rd, 4th, 5th, 6th, 7th, & 8th grade girls; all boys)	116 males and females,*** grades 1–8, 61 LD and 55 non-LD	Task of discriminating adequate from inadequate messages		Donahue, Pearl, & T. Bryan, 1980

KEY: ↑ Where LDs emitted significantly more of a behavior than peers. ↓ Where LDs emitted significantly less of a behavior than peers. NF Functional differences analyzed but not found. F Functional differences found. * Sex differences not analyzed. ** Sex differences not found. *** Sex differences found. # Sex differences not related to group.

In another related study, when LD adolescents were asked to specify how they would solve social problems and behave in particular situations (a task requiring them to name optional behaviors, identify consequences for each option, and specify how they would behave), they performed significantly fewer components of this problem-solving skill than their peers (Schumaker et al., 1982). Bruno (1981) also found LD children to be less capable of predicting consequences for behaviors than their peers.

These findings are cause for concern, especially in view of LD individuals' propensity to choose antisocial behaviors when pressured by peers (T. Bryan, Werner, & Pearl, 1982). Such a propensity may serve as a link between learning disabilities and juvenile delinquency. Additionally, these findings are cause for concern since the skill of choosing acceptable behavior appears to be related to popularity among peers.

Another cognitive social skill that LD individuals may need to learn is the skill of discriminating social cues. The results of several studies show that LD children's performance on social inference tasks is significantly worse than that of their non-LD peers. They are less able to interpret cues such as facial expressions, motor actions, and voice tone (Axelrod, 1982; Bachara, 1976; Bruno, 1981; T. Bryan, 1977; Gerber & Zinkgraf, 1982; Pearl & Cosden, 1982; Wiig & Harris, 1974). LD boys are less likely than non-LD peers to adjust their communication to the age of the listener (T. Bryan & Pflaum, 1978) and to the power of and intimacy with the listener (Donahue, 1981).

LD individuals may also need training in role-taking skills, which have been defined as the ability to "understand and take into account the thoughts (cognitive role-taking) and feelings (affective role-taking) of another individual as distinct from one's own" (Bruck & Hebert, 1982, p. 353). With one exception (Ackerman et al., 1979), all the role-taking studies reviewed here showed LD individuals perform significantly poorer than peers on role-taking tasks (Bruck & Hebert, 1982; Dickstein & Warren, 1980; Horowitz, 1981; Wong & Wong, 1980). The researchers (Bruck & Hebert, 1982) who tried to relate performance of role-taking skills to functional measures of social competence (parents' and teachers' ratings of children's social behavior) found no relationship. If parents and teachers are indeed good judges of children's social competence, these data indicate that role-taking skills as measured in these studies may not be related to social skills performance.

Clearly, additional research should be focused on the cognitive social skills deficits of the LD population. For example, studies are needed that focus on the skills of discriminating situations where social behavior, in general, is appropriate. LD individuals' ability to determine whether someone is willing to interact or whether a situation is "right" for interaction has not been determined. Also needed are additional studies that relate cognitive social skills deficits to actual social functioning and social problems and studies involving tasks that more closely approximate real use of cognitive skills in naturally occurring social situations (Maheady & Maitland, 1982).

Overt Social Behaviors

A review of 26 research studies that focused on the overt social skills performance of LD individuals revealed a number of overt social behaviors that could be targeted in training programs for LD individuals. The findings are summarized in Table 7-2. LD individuals appear to exhibit deficits in such nonverbal skills as smiling when talking (J. Bryan & Sherman, 1980; J. Bryan, Sherman, & Fisher, 1980), hand illustrations while talking (J. Bryan, Sherman, & Fisher, 1980), and forward body lean (Raskind, Drew, & Regan, 1983). Only the results of smiling while talking have been replicated, and both studies identifying this skill as a deficit included only boys in grades 3 and 5.

A wide variety of verbal behaviors are deficient in LD individuals, including many that can be classified as conversational skills. Such behaviors as asking questions in general (T. Bryan, Donahue, Pearl, & Sturm, 1981), asking process questions (T. Bryan et al., 1981; Donahue & T. Bryan, 1983), and making requests (Donahue, Pearl, & T. Bryan, 1980) are important conversational components that are deficient in the LD population. LD individuals seem to have difficulty accurately and fully communicating information to others (Banikowski, 1981; Noel, 1980; Spekman, 1981). Their statements are less complex than their peers' (T. Bryan & Pflaum, 1978; Donahue, Pearl, & T. Bryan, 1982). LD individuals often are deficient in making positive statements (Schumaker, Hazel, Sherman, & Sheldon, 1982; Smiley & T. Bryan, 1983a, 1983b). They make fewer conversational statements (Smiley & T. Bryan, 1983a), fewer self-disclosing statements (Smiley & T. Bryan, 1983b), and their overall conversational skills are poorer (Mathews, Whang, & Fawcett, 1982; Schumaker, Hazel, Sherman, & Sheldon, 1982).

LD individuals seem to have problems in conflictual situations. Researchers have found that they disagree and argue less than their non-LD peers (T. Bryan, Donahue, & Pearl, 1981). This may be because they lack the skills of persuasion (T. Bryan et al., 1981; Donahue, 1981), negotiation (Schumaker et al., 1982), resisting peer pressure (Schumaker et al., 1982), and explaining a problem (Mathews et al., 1982). LD individuals often have difficulty giving and accepting criticism (Mathews et al., 1982, Schumaker et al., 1982).

In addition to these deficits, some behavioral excesses appear to be present in LD individuals. They make significantly more negative comments (Smiley & T. Bryan, 1983a, 1983b) and competitive statements (T. Bryan,

Wheeler, Felcan, & Henek, 1976) than their non-LD peers. Although there is conflicting evidence on whether they make more rejection statements than peers (T. Bryan & J. Bryan, 1978; T. Bryan et al., 1976), there is some evidence that they receive more rejection statements than peers. Evidence suggests that rejection statements are negatively related to peer popularity (T. Bryan & J. Bryan, 1978). Research by Moore and Simpson (1984) high-lighted the reciprocal nature of rejection statements: individuals who make such statements are more likely to receive them. If LD individuals make more rejection statements than non-LD peers, they may cause themselves to become the recipients of rejection statements.

Unfortunately, few studies in this area have included the necessary steps to show that the apparent deficits and excesses named above are related to peer popularity and social success. Where functional differences have been found (J. Bryan & Sherman, 1981; T. Bryan & J. Bryan, 1978; Mathews, Whang, & Fawcett, 1980, 1982; Noel, 1980), the subjects' perform-ance of overt social skills was correlated either with sociometric ratings of peers or with judges' ratings of the subjects' social behavior, or was related to competent and incompetent individuals' performance of the same skills. Clearly, research is needed to socially validate deficits that are identified through statistical techniques.

Additional research is needed within natural settings to focus on devel-opmental changes, the presence of subgroups within the population, and contradictions within the literature. Comparisons between the social skills performance of LD individuals who have been identified as socially unskilled (or rejected) and the performance of individuals who have been identified as socially skilled (or accepted) are also needed. Hazel et al. (1985) have sugges-ted several research methods that are applicable to this problem.

Research is also needed to determine whether certain social skills are not part of LD individuals' repertoires (skill deficits) or whether such skills are present but not used (performance deficits). In one study, J. Bryan, Sherman, and Fisher (1980) addressed this issue by telling half of the sub-jects (the "ingratiation" group) to "make the lady like you" and the other half of the subjects (the "natural" group) to "act natural." The children in the "ingratiation" group were found to smile significantly more than their counterparts in the "natural" group. Since smiling is a behavior LD children are often deficient in (e.g., J. Bryan & Sherman, 1981; J. Bryan, Sherman, & Fisher, 1980), this study indicates that LD children may not be typically motivated to smile or to try to make people like them. Pearl, T. Bryan, and Donahue (1983) suggested that LD individuals' feelings of incompetence might cause them not to use social skills even though the skills are present in their repertoires. Another factor that may be related to the skill-deficit versus performance-deficit issue is the complexity of a

(text continued on page 134)

TABLE 7-2
Overt Social Behaviors

Significant Difference Found	No Significant Difference Found	Sample	Situation	Additional Notes	References
	Peer interactions	44 males and females,** grades 2 and 4 47 LD and 22 non-LD	Natural: Classroom		McKinney, McClure, & Feagans, 1982
	Peer interactions	94 males and females,* grades 7-9 47 LD and 33 non-LD	Natural: Classroom		Schumaker, Sheldon-Wildgen, & Sherman, 1980
	Time in social interactions	20 males, grades 1, 2, 4, 6 and kindergarten, 10 LD and 10 non-LD	Natural: Classroom		T. Bryan & Wheeler, 1972
	Time in social interactions	10 males, grade 3, 5 LD and 5 non-LD	Natural: Classroom		T. Bryan, 1974a
	Smiling Nonfunctional touching of self Face to face regards	20 males, grades 2 and 4, 10 LD and 10 non-LD	Contrived: T.V. talk show format	Duration of face to face regards correlated with social hostility ratings for non-LD children	J. Bryan, T. Bryan, & Sonnefeld, 1982

Face-to-face regards while talking (↓ F) Smiling while talking (↓)	Number of words spoken Face-to-face regards while listening Smiling while listening	27 males, grades 3 and 5, 13 LD and 14 non-LD	Contrived: Interview format	Used correlation of behaviors with judges' ratings	J. Bryan & Sherman, 1980
Hand illustrations while talking (↓ F) Smiling while talking (↓)	Number of words spoken Smiling while listening Face-to-face regards while talking and listening Pause filling Nonfunctional touching of self while listening	26 males, grades 3 and 5, 13 LD and 13 non-LD	Contrived: Interview format		J. Bryan, Sherman, & Fisher, 1980
Forward lean (↓)	30 other non-verbal behaviors	37 males, grades 3-5, 17 LD and 20 non-LD	Contrived: Interview format		Raskind, Drew, & Regan (1983)

KEY: ↑ Where LDs emitted significantly more of a behavior than peers. ↓ Where LDs emitted significantly less of a behavior than peers. NF Functional differences analyzed but not found. F Functional differences found. * Sex differences not analyzed. ** Sex differences not found. *** Sex differences found. # Sex differences not related to group.

(continued)

125

TABLE 7-2 *(continued)*

Significant Difference Found	No Significant Difference Found	Sample	Situation	Additional Notes	References
Amount of talk (↓) Process questions (↓) Eliciting elaborated responses to choice questions (↑)	Conversational devices Comments Contingent responses Use of modeled topics Eliciting elaborated responses to process questions	104 males, grades 2-8, 51 LD and 53 non-LD	Contrived: T.V. talk show format		Donahue & T. Bryan, 1983
Accurate description of task (↓)	Questioning Continuances Confirming statements Requests for clarification Feedback Relevant responses to questions Elaborative responses	69 males and females,* grades 7-8, 25 LD and 44 non-LD	Contrived: 8 interaction activities (e.g., interview on how to spend $1000)		Banikowski, 1981

Communication of information (↓)	Turn-taking Responding to requests for more information Following directions Question asking	48 males, 9-11 years old, 12 LD and 36 non-LD	Contrived: Referential communication task	Spekman, 1981
No. words per t-unit (↓) No. words per main clause (↓)	No. words in description No. of subordinate clauses per t-unit No. words per subordinate clause No. t-units	127 males and females,* grades 2, 4, 6, & 8 67 LD and 60 non-LD	Contrived: Referential communication task	Donahue, Pearl, & T. Bryan, 1982
T-units (↓) Complexities per t-unit (↓) Modifiers (↓) Adjusting communication to age of listener (↓) (LD boys only)	Bits of information communicated Incompetent communications	40 males and females,*** grades 4-5, 20 LD and 20 non-LD	Contrived: Teaching a lab game	T. Bryan & Pflaum, 1978

(continued)

KEY: ↑ Where LDs emitted significantly more of a behavior than peers. ↓ Where LDs emitted significantly less of a behavior than peers. NF Functional differences analyzed but not found. F Functional differences found. * Sex differences not analyzed. ** Sex differences not found. *** Sex differences found. # Sex differences not related to group.

TABLE 7-2 *(continued)*

Significant Difference Found	No Significant Difference Found	Sample	Situation	Additional Notes	References
Specific appeals (↓ boys) Total no. of types of appeals (↓ boys) Level of persuasive appeals (↓ boys) No of appeals (↓ boys, ↑ girls) Polite requests (↑ girls) Adjusting requests to intimacy with listener (↓ boys) Adjusting requests to power of listener (↑ boys)	Specific appeals (girls) Total no. of types of appeals (girls) Level of persuasive appeals (girls) Polite requests (boys) Adjusting requests to intimacy with listener (girls) Adjusting requests to power of listener (girls)	63 males and females,*** grades 2, 4, and 6, 33 LD and 30 non-LD	Contrived: Role-play situations		Donahue, 1981
Positive statements (↓) Self-disclosing statements (↓) Negative comments (↑)		20 males, junior high (mean age = 12-13 years old) 10 LD and 10 non-LD	Natural: Obstacle course activities		Smiley & T. Bryan, 1983b

Measures	Sample	Setting	Results	Reference
Question asking in general (↓) Asking process questions (↓) Eliciting elaborative responses (↓) Conversational devices: (↑ 2nd graders & girls) Non-functional self-touching (↑ 2nd graders, girls) Turn-taking Confirmations	40 males and females,*** grades 2 and 4, 20 LD and 20 non-LD	Contrived: Talk-show format	LDs were less able to maintain the role of host	T. Bryan, Donahue, Pearl, & Sturm, 1981
Requests for more information (↓) General requests (↓) Latency of responses Specific requests	116 males and females,** grades 1-8, 61 LD and 55 non-LD	Contrived: Referential communication task		Donahue, Pearl, & T. Bryan, 1980
Reference to general labels (↓ F) Reference to shape (↑ NF) No. of words used Reference to size Reference to major parts Reference to function Listening	80 males, 9-11 years old, 40 LD and 40 non-LD	Contrived: Referential communication task	Use of labels significantly related to listener's accuracy in choosing correct picture	Noel, 1980

(continued)

KEY: ↑ Where LDs emitted significantly more of a behavior than peers. ↓ Where LDs emitted significantly less of a behavior than peers. NF Functional differences analyzed but not found. F Functional differences found. * Sex differences not analyzed. ** Sex differences not found. *** Sex differences found. # Sex differences not related to group.

TABLE 7-2 *(continued)*

Significant Difference Found	No Significant Difference Found	Sample	Situation	Additional Notes	References
Disagreeing (↓) Monitoring statements (↓) Maintaining speaker role (↓) Arguing (↓) Persuading (↓) Laughing alone (↑ boys) Agreeing (↑) Responding to requests for clarification (↑)	Turn-taking Positive statements Negative statements Laughing with others Laughing alone (girls only)	100 males and females,*** grades 3-8, triads of 1 LD and 2 non-LD, 54 LD and 46 non-LD	Contrived: Group problem-solving task		T. Bryan, Donahue, & Pearl, 1981
Positive statements (↓) Conversational statements (↓) Negative statements (↑) Positive actions (↑)	Helping Organizational statements On-task statements Talking simultaneously Listening to strategies Evaluating strategies Non-productive behavior Negative actions	16 males, junior high (mean age = 14.9 for LD, 13.5 for non-LD) 8 LD and 8 non-LD	Natural: Group raft-building activity		Smiley & T. Bryan, 1983a

Behaviors	Setting	Sample	Source
Resisting cooperative initiations of partner (↑) (dyads with LD boys) Listening (↑) (dyads with LD girls) Working together (↑) (dyads with LD girls)	Contrived: Study task	108 males and females,*** grades 7-8, 26 LD and 82 non-LD	T. Bryan, Cosden, & Pearl, 1982
Resisting peer pressure (↓) Giving negative feedback (↓) Negotiation (↓) Accepting negative feedback (↓) Giving positive feedback (↓) Conversation (↓)	Following instructions Contrived: Role-play tests	236 males and females,*** 13-18 years old, 19 LD and 117 non-LD	Schumaker, Hazel, Sherman, & Sheldon, 1982

KEY: ↑ Where LDs emitted significantly more of a behavior than peers. ↓ Where LDs emitted significantly less of a behavior than peers. NF Functional differences analyzed but not found. F Functional differences found. * Sex differences not analyzed. ** Sex differences not found. *** Sex differences not found. # Sex differences not related to group.

(continued)

131

TABLE 7-2 *(continued)*

Significant Difference Found	No Significant Difference Found	Sample	Situation	Additional Notes	References
Participating in a job interview (↓ F) Accepting criticism from an employer (↓) Providing constructive criticism to co-worker (↓ F) Explaining a problem to a supervisor (↓ F)	Getting a job lead Telephoning potential employer for job interview Accepting suggestions from employer Complimenting a co-worker Accepting compliment from a co-worker	50 males and females,* 15-19 years old, 25 LD and 25 non-LD	Contrived: Role-playing situations		Mathews, Whang, & Fawcett, 1982 Mathews, Whang, & Fawcett, 1980
Rejection statements (↑ F)	Requests for information Self-image statements Helping behaviors Positive statements Self-talk	50 males and females,** grades 4-5, 25 LD and 25 non-LD	Natural: Classroom environment	LDs made more rejection statements and received fewer votes on sociometric measures	T. Bryan & J. Bryan, 1978

Competitive statements (↑) Rejection statements Consideration statements Intrusive statements Self-image enhancers Asking for information/ advice Cooperation statement Helping actions/ statements	34 males and females,* grades 3-5 17 LD and 17 non-LD	Natural: Classroom	T. Bryan, Wheeler, Felcan, & Henek, 1976
Communication of bad news (↓)	100 males and females,*** grades 1-4, 50 LD and 50 non-LD	Contrived: Role play	Pearl, Donahue, & T. Bryan, 1983

KEY: ↑ Where LDs emitted significantly more of a behavior than peers. ↓ Where LDs emitted significantly less of a behavior than peers. NF Functional differences analyzed but not found. F Functional differences found. * Sex differences not analyzed. ** Sex differences not found. *** Sex differences found. # Sex differences not related to group.

social skill. That is, the absence of a simple social skill like smiling might represent a performance deficit, whereas the absence of a complex social skill such as suggesting a compromise might represent a skill deficit. Clearly, more studies are needed to examine skill deficits and performance deficits.

In summary, on the average, LD children exhibit deficits in many of the variables constituting the definition of social competence given above: they tend to choose less socially acceptable behaviors for use in specifically named situations; they are less able to predict consequences for behaviors; they misinterpret social cues; they are less likely to adapt their behavior to the characteristics of their listener; they perform certain appropriate verbal and nonverbal skills at significantly lower levels than their peers; and they perform certain inappropriate skills at significantly higher levels than their peers. Whether or not LD individuals can discriminate when social behaviors, in general, are appropriate is unclear. To be effective, social skill training for LD individuals must, at a minimum, cover each of the areas in which problems have been identified. Such training must also incorporate methods for assessing the problems of the individuals they are designed to serve.

THE ASSESSMENT OF SOCIAL SKILLS

A critical component of social skills training programs for LD individuals is an assessment method that measures initial social skills levels and progress in skill acquisition and usage. Because LD individuals have heterogeneous social skills, an assessment system is required to determine the individual training needs of each person. Unfortunately, few psychometrically acceptable assessment procedures have been developed for these purposes (Arkowitz, 1981). No instrument has been developed that has been based specifically on the social skills problems exhibited by the LD population.

To measure social skills functioning adequately, a device must measure a person's behaviors and the consequences of those behaviors, overt behaviors and cognitive behaviors, the quality of behavioral responses (sequences, timing, content), the presence or absence of skills in a person's repertoire (revealing a performance deficit versus social skills deficits), a person's physical appearance, and the use of skills in situations of interest (Arkowitz, 1981). In order to be psychometrically acceptable, assessment devices must be reliable and valid, sensitive to changes in the subject, nonreactive, and capable of yielding diagnostic information specific to the skills that should be taught (Gresham, 1981). To be useful for teachers, a social skills assessment tool must be quick and easy to use and not require additional resources.

According to several detailed reviews (Arkowitz, 1981; Gresham, 1981), no available social skills assessment device approaches the above requirements. A single instrument may not be able to meet all the requirements. It is beyond the scope of this chapter to review in detail the advantages and disadvantages of the assessment devices that have been employed to measure social skills (for reviews on this topic see Arkowitz, 1981; Gresham, 1981; Hops, 1981; Michelson, Foster, & Ritchey, 1981). Instead, the purpose of this discussion is to briefly describe a number of assessment techniques and to provide directions for additional work in the area.

The general types of social skills assessment devices that have been used in the LD field are behavioral observation codes, behavioral checklists, sociometric devices, and behavioral rating scales. Each of these methods and the ways in which each has been used will be related to how well it meets the requirements specified above and whether it can be used by LD teachers as a useful and effective component of a social skills intervention program for LD individuals.

Behavioral Observation Codes

Behavioral observation codes have been used in studies to measure the social skills of LD children (e.g., Banikowski, 1981; J. Bryan, Sherman, & Fisher, 1980). Typically, subjects were asked to complete an interactive task (e.g., interview someone, teach someone a game), and their social behavior was observed while they completed the task. In a few studies, the children were observed in naturally occurring interactions. In some studies, durations of behaviors were averaged to obtain average duration measures.

This type of assessment system offers numerous advantages. When used in natural contexts, it reflects the behaviors a person would typically emit and reflects changes in behavior. It can be very reliable if efforts are made to train observers and to carry out adequate interobserver reliability checks (e.g., Harris & Lahey, 1978; Hartman, 1977). Behavioral observation codes can be used to assess actual behaviors and their consequences and can be used repeatedly in natural environments.

One of the problems associated with behavioral observation codes is that simple measures of social interactions (e.g. number of interactions, time in interactions) in general, do not have social validity or long-term predictive validity (Gresham, 1981). In addition, they do not differentiate LD from non-LD subjects (e.g., T. Bryan , 1974a; T. Bryan & Wheeler, 1972; McKinney, McClure, & Feagans, 1982; Schumaker, Sheldon-Wildgen, & Sherman, 1980). Thus, developers of this type of measure must carefully specify the overt behaviors to be observed *within* interactions. Additionally, such observation systems usually are not designed to account for the quality of a behavior; they merely indicate whether a behavior (e.g., a positive statement) occurred or did not occur within a given time. Since there is great variability in the degree to which a behavior is appropriate for a given set of circumstances, an assessment system should allow measurement of the quality of responses as well as quantities of responses. Although such measures could conceivably be included within observational systems, no one has demonstrated a method for doing this. Another problem with the use of behavioral assessment devices is that no observation code has been developed that specifically targets a wide range of the problems of LD individuals. A final problem is that normative cut-off levels for performance of social skills have not been determined to identify individuals who need training.

There are several other problems associated with the use of behavioral observation codes by LD teachers. First, behavioral observation systems are time-consuming and often difficult and exhausing to use. Teachers usually do not have the time and energy required to learn how to use the devices and to actually use them in regular classes. Asher and Hymel (1981) suggested that more than two hours of observation time per child are required to insure sufficient observation of low-frequency behaviors. Such a time expenditure appears exorbitant when LD teachers' other responsibilities are taken into account. Second, even if LD teachers had sufficient energy and time to use an observational code themselves or could train a paraprofessional or volunteer to use a behavioral observation system, opportunities for childrens' use of the social behaviors of interest cannot be guaranteed during scheduled observation sessions. In some instances, the most critical interactions may be those that are inaccessible to teachers and paraprofessionals (e.g., those interactions that take place on the playground, in the locker area, in hallways between classes, at the lunch table). It appears that behavioral observation codes may not be very practical for LD teachers.

Behavioral Checklists

Another behavioral observation system that has been used with LD individuals is the behavioral checklist (Hazel, Schumaker, Sherman, & Sheldon, 1982; Mathews, Whang, & Fawcett, 1982; Schumaker & Ellis, 1982). This system generally involves a list of behaviors that could occur in a specific kind of interaction. After watching an interaction, the teacher indicates, by using either a checkmark or a 3-point rating scale, whether or how well each behavior on the list was performed by the subject. The behavioral checklist has been used to measure overt social behaviors in role-play situations (Hazel et al., 1982; Mathews et al., 1982), naturally occurring situations (Whang, Fawcett, & Mathews, 1981), and contrived situations within the natural milieu (Schumaker & Ellis, 1982). One checklist has been used to measure cognitive behaviors exhibited while completing a problem-solving task (Hazel et al., 1982). The checklists that have been used were shown, in separate studies (Hazel, Schumaker, Sherman, & Sheldon-Wildgen, 1981; Mathews, Whang, & Fawcett, 1980), to be reliable and valid. The instrument developed by Hazel et al. (1981) includes 8 check-lists for recording complex social skills identified by professionals, parents, and youths as important for adolescents. The Mathews et al. (1980) instrument consists of 10 checklists for complex job-related social skills that were identified as important by experts in the field of employment.

The major advantage of checklists is that they are easy to use. Little time (2 hours) is required to train individuals to use checklists reliably (Hazel, Schumaker, & Sheldon, 1984) and little time (20–30 seconds) is required to record the behaviors that occur in an interaction.

Another advantage of behavioral checklists is that they allow the observer to record overt verbal and nonverbal behaviors, the circumstances surrounding the interaction, and the consequences of the behaviors. As mentioned, one checklist has been employed to measure the use of some cognitive behaviors (e.g., problem solving, Hazel et al., 1982). Other check-lists can conceivably be designed to measure the use of other cognitive skills. Checklists allow sequences and timing of behaviors to be easily recorded and they allow teachers to pinpoint specific behaviors to be taught. Furthermore, since a rating scale can be used in conjunction with behavioral checklists, they allow the recording of a gross level of quality within responses. Checklist recording systems have not previously incor-porated more specific measures of quality regarding the appropriateness of a given response for particular circumstances. However, this kind of sys-tem could be developed.

Checklists can be used repeatedly; the checklists themselves are not reactive. Checklists have been used in conjunction with role-play situ-ations, natural situations, and with contrived situations within the natural environment. The major advantage of role-play situations are that they are easy to generate and use and only require a few minutes to complete. Their major disadvantage is that behaviors exhibited in role-play situations do not necessarily represent behaviors that occur in natural situations (Schumaker & Ellis, 1982; Van Hassalt, Hersen, & Bellack, 1981).

Whenever possible, the observation of naturally occurring situations is optimal. Unfortunately, opportunities for targeted behaviors to occur are not often present during observation sessions or are inhibited by the pres-ence of observers (Whang, Fawcett, & Mathews, 1981). In addition, teachers are usually too busy to watch a student for an entire hour to see, for exam-ple, how she accepts a compliment from a peer.

Contrived situations programmed to occur without the advance knowledge of the subject can be a helpful compromise. They are easy to set up, they take very little time (2–3 minutes), and the teacher knows when they are going to occur and can focus on the subject at the optimal time.

Specific circumstances can be incorporated to measure cognitive skills, and contrived situations insure that a natural opportunity for the use of given social skills is presented to the subject.

One of the major problems associated with the use of behavioral checklists is that normative cut-off points have not been identified for discriminating LD individuals needing social skills training from those who do not. Although some data on non-LD individuals' performance of certain skills are available (Mathews et al., 1980; Schumaker et al., 1982), study samples were not large enough to provide stable norms.

Another problem with behavioral checklists as well as with behavioral codes is that behaviors not represented on the checklist are not recorded. Usually, only appropriate behaviors are listed on a checklist. Obviously, allowances should be made within the checklist format for recording behavioral excesses such as negative remarks and competitive statements.

Sociometric Assessment

Numerous researchers have utilized sociometric devices to determine whether, on the average, LD individuals are less well-liked than their non-LD classmates (Bruininks, 1978a, 1978b; T. Bryan, 1974b, 1976; T. Bryan & J. Bryan, 1978; Garrett & Crump, 1980; Prillaman, 1981; Scranton & Ryckman, 1979; Siperstein, Bopp, & Bak, 1978). In general, the subjects in these studies have been asked to identify three individuals in their class whom they consider to be friends and three classmates they would not choose to be friends. The votes for each child are tallied to determine the most socially accepted and rejected children. Bruininks (1978a, 1978b) used a more reliable and sensitive form of the sociometric device (see Gresham, 1981) that requires each child to rate every other child in the class using Likert-type scales. The ratings for each student are averaged to obtain a measure of social acceptance. To date, this technique has not been used to identify children for social skills intervention, yet it might be used to distinguish the most rejected children within a given group.

The advantages of the sociometric device (especially the rating-scale measure) are (a) its results reflect the feelings of the peer group about an individual's social competence (a form of social validity); (b) it has good predictive validity; (c) it is sensitive to changes in young children's social behavior; (d) it has acceptable test–retest reliability; and (e) it demonstrates concurrent validity with behavioral measures (Gresham, 1981). Since each child's score can be compared to other children's scores in a class, a type of normative data can be generated. Sociometric devices are also easy for a teacher to use and take relatively little time to implement.

One of the disadvantages of sociometric devices is that they tend to be insensitive to changes in the behavior of children above the ages of 9 and

10 years, when friendships are more stable than at younger ages (Oden & Asher, 1977). Also, results may vary according to the makeup of a class population. For example, Perlmutter et al. (1983) found that LD adolescents attending classes in which 25% or more of the students were LD received higher sociometric ratings than LD adolescents who attended classes with fewer LD students. This disadvantage is closely related to another practical problem at the secondary level: choosing a class within which to administer the sociometric device. Typically, LD students at the secondary level are mainstreamed in "low track" courses, whereas the students who are generally considered to be the most popular are enrolled in college preparation courses. For these reasons, the application of sociometric devices above age 10 may be considerably limited.

Another disadvantage of sociometric devices is that they provide no diagnostic information with regard to which social skills should be taught to an identified individual. Therefore, they must be used in combination with another assessment instrument.

Finally, sociometric measures cannot be used too often because they tend to be reactive (Gresham, 1981). Additionally, many individuals are opposed to their use (especially the peer-nomination type where negative nominations are made); they argue that such devices "teach" rejection or reinforce children for rejecting some of their peers (Asher & Hymel, 1981). This consideration is especially important when promoting acceptance of disabled children in mainstreamed classes.

Behavioral Rating Scales

Researchers have utilized behavioral rating scales to measure LD individuals' use of certain behaviors and the impressions they make on significant others (teachers, parents, peers). Usually, rating scales list several behaviors or descriptive items and the respondent (teacher, parent, or peer) is asked to indicate how well a specific person emits each behavior or fits each description. For example, an item might require a respondent to indicate on a scale from 1 to 7, "how well Johnny responds to criticism." Sometimes, rating scales are used to allow individuals to rate their own social skills. Using such a device, one research group (Hazel, Smalter, & Schumaker, 1983) asked LD adolescents to rate themselves. In addition, they had LD teachers rate the LD adolescents- social skills based on the assumption that the results of the teacher-rating scale combined with those from the youth-rating scale could serve as the basis for intervention decisions.

The major advantage of rating scales are that they provide a relatively quick and easy method for assessing skills and a measure of how individuals impact significant others in their lives. From responses to such a scale, target behaviors can be chosen for intervention. Conceivably, a rating scale could be developed that lists, objectively, all the empirically validated problems LD individuals demonstrate in the social realm, normative data could be collected, and criterion cut-off points could be identified. Since some behavioral rating scales for social behavior have been found to be reliable and sensitive to treatment effects (see Michelson, Foster, & Ritchey, 1981), instruments might also be developed for LD individuals that are psychometrically acceptable.

In spite of the numerous advantages of using behavioral rating scales, they do present several problems. For example, responses to items on them tend to be global indicators of a person's abilities. Thus, such cognitive skills as adjustments to subtle changes of circumstance cannot be measured by this method without making the device unreasonably long and time-consuming to complete.

Another problem related to rating scales is that correlations between behavioral ratings and behavioral observations are not high. Research by Hazel et al. (1983), indicated that, although behavioral teacher ratings were significantly correlated ($r = 0.64$) with behavioral checklist measures of LD adolescents' performance in role-play situations, they were not related to these adolescents' performance in contrived situations in the natural environment ($r = 0.00$). Surprisingly, LD adolescents' ratings of their own skills on the same rating scale correlated significantly with both their performance in role-play situations ($r = 0.76$) and in contrived situations in the natural environment ($r = 0.26$). Thus, behavioral rating assessments may be an inaccurate representation of actual behavior.

In summary, of the assessment devices employed to measure LD individuals' use of social skills, none seems ideal for serving as the foundation of a social skills intervention program for LD individuals. Although behavioral codes and checklists provide measures of actual behavior, they do not provide measures of social validity with regard to how others accept target children. Similarly, although sociometric devices and rating scales provide socially valid measures, they do not measure specific social behaviors. An acceptable compromise may require the development of two instruments: one to be used as a global screening device, the other to be used to pinpoint particular problem behaviors. Sociometric devices (the rating-scale type) and/or behavioral rating scales appear appropriate for screening younger children. Behavioral rating scales are recommended for screening older individuals. Behavioral checklists seem to be the most practical instruments for teachers to use for pinpointing target behaviors. Preferably, they should be used in conjunction with contrived situations in the natural environment.

INTERVENTION APPROACHES

Although a number of social skills deficits and excesses have been identified for the LD population, the ideal content of social skills programs cannot be specified with confidence. Nevertheless, a tentative profile has been compiled that will enable the development of preliminary social skills interventions. One prerequisite for these interventions is that they contain adequate assessment devices for selecting those individuals most in need of training and for specifying what skills they need to learn. Teaching procedures should enable instructors to rapidly teach the requisite skills and to promote generalization and maintenance of skill use in natural environments.

The remainder of this chapter will focus on the procedures that have been used to change LD individuals' social skills performance and to help them generalize their use of social skills.

Methodological Issues

To provide a framework within which social skills training procedures can be evaluated, several methodological issues must be explored. First, the descriptions of intervention procedures evaluated in different studies must be adequate. In many studies, for example, the training procedures are named without being specified. Without adequate specification, it is unclear whether one author's use of the term "practice" is equivalent to another author's use of the term "rehearsal." Thus, it is often difficult to determine the specific procedures employed during an intervention study.

A second methodological issue relates to the use of "packages" of procedures. In the majority of studies reviewed, intervention consisted of the application of a variety of procedures in combination without a component analysis of the relative contributions of each procedure to changes in subjects' use of a given skill. This "package" approach appears to be valid. However, it is currently impossible to determine whether each procedure in the package is necessary. This is an important consideration since instructional time is often limited for social skills training.

Related to the difficulty of identifying specific procedures important for social skills training, is the determination of training procedures most effective for ameliorating different types of social skills deficits. It is unclear, for example, whether the remediation of overt social skills deficits requires different training procedures than the remediation of cognitive social skills deficits. Few studies have explored the relationship between training procedures and types of social skills deficits. To date, training of cognitive social skills in isolation from overt social skills has received little research attention.

A final methodological issue related to the social skills training literature in the LD field concerns the measures used to show changes in LD individuals' social skills performance. Typically, changes in LD individuals' overt behavior have been assessed in contrived situations by means of quantitative measures taken immediately before and after training. Rarely have changes been shown in naturally occurring interactions in the natural interactions in the natural environment after training. In addition, changes in overt behaviors have rarely been related to improved social relationships, social standing, social confidence, and the individual's satisfaction with his or her own life. Thus, it is difficult to determine whether or not the social skills training procedures have produced changes in social competence that have a positive impact on everyday lives.

In summary, the methodological problems in the LD social skills training literature include inadequate procedural descriptions, lack of component analysis, lack of studies of the relationship between instructional procedures and remediation of specific types of skill deficits, and inadequate measurement procedures. Although these methodological problems are significant, a number of studies have provided a foundation for future research. Such studies have identified instructional procedures that appear to improve the social skills performance of LD children and adolescents and to insure generalization of the skills. These procedures and studies are reviewed in the following two sections. Occasionally, for illustrative purposes, studies employing subjects representing disabling conditions other than LD have been included.

Techniques for Improving Social Skills

A variety of techniques have been used to improve the social skills performance of LD individuals. Usually, the choice of procedure is based on assumptions about the nature of the social skills deficit. The lack of appropriate social skills may stem from one of three problems: performance deficit, skill deficit, or behavioral excess. A *performance deficit* is typically thought to be due to either a paucity of discriminative cues within the environment for performing a given skill or a lack of motivation to perform the skill, even though the skill is present in the repertoire. The procedures chosen to remediate this kind of skill deficit usually focus on increasing the salience or frequency of discriminative cues within the environment or on increasing the individual's motivation to perform a social skill. In the case of a *skill deficit,* the individual, although motivated to perform the skill, lacks the ability and knowledge to perform the skill. Remediation of this kind of deficit usually focuses on teaching the individual to perform certain social skills. Finally, *behavioral excesses* refer to the performance of inappropriate social behaviors at excessively high rates. Remediation in this area can focus on teaching individuals to stop using inappropriate behaviors and/or teaching them to use behaviors that are incompatible with the inappropriate behaviors. Incompatible social behaviors may be exemplified as follows: a person using a calm voice and negotiating rationally cannot simultaneously be screaming and making negative statements.

The procedures that can be used to improve the social competence of LD individuals tend to fall into three categories: (a) those that involve the manipulation of antecedent and consequent events to eliminate performance deficits and behavioral excesses; (b) those that focus on improving control over social behavior; and (c) those that involve the teaching of new skills to ameliorate skill deficits or to provide incompatible responses to replace behavioral excesses.

Manipulation of Environmental Events

One technique that can be useful for eliminating performance deficits and behavioral excesses is the manipulation of antecedent and consequent events associated with the target social behavior. This technique focuses on changing environmental events in an attempt to increase the probability of future occurrence of appropriate social behaviors while decreasing the probability of occurrence of inappropriate behaviors. A number of different procedures can be used to alter antecedent conditions. For example, the manipulation of antecedent events may involve restructuring the individual's environment to increase the salience of the discriminative cues for emitting the appropriate social behavior. In two studies (Strain, 1977; Strain, Shores, & Timm, 1977) in which this technique was applied, peers were asked to encourage behaviorally disabled preschoolers to engage in social interactions. Strain and his colleagues showed that subjects' positive social behaviors (motor-gestural and vocal-verbal) increased in the training setting when peers were asked to initiate social interactions with the target children. During these conditions, the target children initiated more interactions than in the baseline condition and generalized their use of positive social behaviors to free-play situations.

Another approach to modifying antecedent conditions involves the use of cooperative goal structures that promote the use of social behavior. For example, T. Bryan, Cosden, and Pearl (1982) found that pairs of LD and non-LD youths whose incentives for doing well academically were based on the pair's performance displayed significantly more positive social behaviors (e.g., listening, questioning, working together) than youths whose performance was based on individual incentives. Similarly, Martino and Johnson (1979) showed that a cooperative swimming assignment during instructional time led to more friendly interactions during a free swim period than did individual assignments for pairs of LD and non-LD elementary-age boys. Thus, cooperative goal structures may be useful for increasing the occurrence of positive social behaviors already in youths' repertoires.

Other techniques that have been employed to increase the use of appropriate social skills and decrease the use of inappropriate social behaviors are the delivery or withholding of particular consequences contingent upon the occurrence of social responses. If an appropriate social behavior occurs, reinforcement is delivered. In contrast, if an inappropriate behavior occurs, reinforcement is withheld or punishment is applied. A token system may be used to deliver or withdraw tokens (or points) contingent upon the occurrence of certain social behaviors. Tokens can be exchanged later for a desired reward. Broden, Hall, Dunlap, and Clark (1970) used a token system in a special education classroom with junior high students who were several years behind in academic achievement. Results showed that reinforcement for appropriate behavior decreased the incidence of disruptive social behavior in the classroom. Iwata and Bailey (1974) found equivalent decreases in classroom rule violations (e.g., speaking out of turn) with elementary special education students using both reward and cost token procedures.

Another type of contingency management approach involves the application of group contingencies to modify the social behavior of one or all members of a group. Using this approach, rewards for the whole group are contingent upon a specific level of social skill performance by certain members of the group or by all members. Rosen, O'Leary, and Conway (1983) reported significant treatment effects, as indicated by teacher ratings of the hyperactive and problem behaviors of a hyperactive elementary child when the entire class received rewards based on the subject's appropriate social behavior. These effects appeared to maintain for one month after treatment was terminated.

Home-based contingency management systems have also been applied to special education students to change their social behavior. Typically, such an approach involves some type of home-school communication requiring the teacher(s) to record the child's social behavior during the day. The child carries this record home and receives reinforcement at home dependent on the recorded behavior at school. Schumaker, Hovell, and Sherman (1977a) showed increases in junior high students' appropriate social behavior (e.g., speaking courteously to the teacher, raising hand before speaking) in regular and special education classes following the introduction of a home-based contingency management system. Teacher satisfaction with the students' behavior also increased. Schumaker, Hovell, and Sherman (1977b) indicated that the system could be faded out while maintaining the same levels of social behavior in some students, but not in others.

In summary, antecedents and consequences can be arranged to increase the occurrence of desirable social behaviors while decreasing the use of undesirable social behaviors. Unfortunately, only a limited number of studies have been conducted in this area, and few have focused on the behavioral deficits and excesses identified for LD individuals. Additionally, little is known about the lasting effects of identified interventions. Finally, according to some authors, the critical feature behind LD individuals' social competence is whether they become *internally* motivated to use and avoid certain social behaviors (Adelman & Taylor, 1982; Deshler, Schumaker, & Lenz, 1984). It is unclear whether the application of external contingencies or the arrangement of antecedent events can change LD individuals' internal motivation to perform social behaviors over long periods of time. Additional research is needed to examine these issues.

Self-control Techniques

Another technique that has been used to reduce the rate of inappropriate social behaviors (behavioral excesses) is cognitive training aimed at teaching self-control of personal behaviors. Although the results of some studies have shown that self-recording of behaviors (e.g., Broden, Hall, & Mitts, 1971) and self-evaluation of behaviors (e.g., Kaufman & O'Leary, 1972) can decrease classroom disruptiveness (e.g., talking-out behaviors, out-of-seat behaviors), none of the studies has focused on LD individuals and the behavioral excesses specifically identified for LD individuals within social interactions (e.g., negative statements). Some evidence suggests that LD individuals can learn to use self-control procedures (e.g., Hallahan, Lloyd, Kosiewicz, Kauffman, & Graves, 1979; Seabaugh & Schumaker, 1981). However, empirical research needs to be conducted before more definitive conclusions can be drawn.

Instructional Approaches

The instructional interventions that have been used to facilitate social skill acquisition for skill-deficient individuals include four types of instructional procedures: descriptive procedures, modeling procedures, rehearsal procedures, and feedback procedures.

Descriptive procedures are primarily oral techniques whereby a teacher describes how to perform a skill appropriately. Descriptions may include one or more of the following: a definition of the skill, rationales (motivational reasons) for using the skill, the general characteristics of situations and examples of specific situations where a skill can be used, descriptions of the behavioral steps involved in using the skill, and a presentation of the societal rules regulating use of the skill (Hazel et al., 1985).

Modeling procedures involve a demonstration of a social skill. Skill performance can be illustrated live or by film, audiotape, or pictoral models. The purpose of modeling is to give the learner an accurate sequential representation of all the behavioral components. Modeling may also include a representation of the cognitive processes involved in a skill if the person giving the demonstration "thinks aloud" while performing the skill (Deshler, Alley, Warner, & Schumaker, 1981).

Rehearsal and feedback procedures have typically been used together. Rehearsal may include verbal rehearsal of required skill steps to ensure that the individual has memorized the steps in sequence and knows what to do next. It can also include structured practice (e.g., role-play activities) of the skill. Following either type of rehearsal, the learner typically receives feedback about performance from the instructor or other learners. Such feedback informs the learner which steps were performed well and which behaviors need improvement. Verbal feedback can be supplemented by video-taped replays of an individual's performance. Sometimes, a mastery criterion requiring a specified performance level by each learner is integrated with the rehearsal and feedback procedures. Thus, learners must master the skill at this level before being allowed to proceed to another skill.

The majority of interventions evaluated in social skills training studies have included combinations of these teaching procedures. However, in spite of such combination approaches, some authors have emphasized one procedure over others. An example of a primarily descriptive approach to social skills training was conducted with "low-accepted" elementary-aged children (identified with sociometric measures) by Oden and Asher (1977). Through an instructional procedure called "coaching," the children (a) were provided with oral descriptions of the importance of each skill, (b) were asked to name example situations in which the skill could be used, and (c) were told to use the skill in a play session immediately following the instruction. After the play session, a review session was held during which the children were asked to evaluate what happened during the play session. No instruction or supervision was provided during the play session. Skills taught included participation, cooperation, communication, and validation support. Although Oden and Asher's data showed no gains in behavioral measures, they found significant improvement in sociometric ratings of the target children's play behavior following training. Even more sociometric gains were shown one year after training had terminated for the children who had received the coaching procedure.

Donahue and Bryan (1983) primarily used a modeling approach to teach conversational skills to LD boys. Their results showed that LD boys who listened to an audiotaped performance of interviewing skills used significantly more open-ended questions and comments in a subsequent "TV talk show" than did LD boys who did not hear the audiotape.

Other researchers have emphasized instructional procedures in combination. For example, Cooke and Apolloni (1976) combined descriptive procedures with modeling, prompting during supervised play periods, and praise to teach social skills to elementary-age LD children. The skills targeted for training included smiling, sharing, positive physical contact, and complimenting. These authors found that the subjects' use of the four skills increased substantially in training sessions, and that their use of three of the four skills increased in unsupervised play sessions conducted in the training setting after each training session. Additionally, untrained children's use of the targeted skills increased when they were brought into the unsupervised play sessions with the trained children. Cooke and Apolloni also showed that the children's use of the skills maintained after training was terminated.

In another study utilizing the "package" approach to social skills training, Hazel, Schumaker, Sherman, and Sheldon (1982) used description, modeling, rehearsal, and feedback procedures to train groups of LD and non-LD adolescents to use five overt and one cognitive social skill. The descriptive procedures included explanations, rationales, example situations, and descriptions of the skill steps. The modeling procedure consisted of a live demonstration of the skill by a group leader. The rehearsal procedures consisted of both verbal rehearsal of the skill steps and behavioral rehearsal of the skill by the learners in role-play situations. Finally, following each role-play rehearsal, the learners received feedback on their performance. The youths continued to practice until they had met the criterion of 100% accuracy in performing the skill. The LD youths in this study showed substantial gains in their performance of the six trained skills (giving positive feedback, giving negative feedback, accepting negative feedback, resisting peer pressure, problem solving, and negotiation) in novel role-play tests. Following training, the LD youths performed most of the skills at levels comparable to those of non-LD youths.

Using a similar package of instructional procedures, Whang, Fawcett, and Mathews (1981) taught LD adolescents six social skills relevant to occupational situations. The skills included accepting a compliment, complimenting a co-worker, accepting an instruction from a supervisor, accepting criticism from a supervisor, providing constructive criticism to a co-worker, and explaining a problem to a supervisor. The teaching procedures consisted of written descriptions of the skills, rationales for using the skills, examples of appropriate performance of the skills, study questions about the skills, and live rehearsal and feedback. Following training, the youths showed substantial increases in their social skills performance in novel role-play situations in the training setting.

Gorney-Krupsaw, Atwater, Powell, and Morris (1981) trained LD students in social skills for interacting with teachers. The specific skills included initiating positive interactions, responding to requests, and recruiting attention for help. The training included description, modeling, rehearsal, and feedback procedures. Results showed substantial improvements in the skill performance in novel role-play situations in the training setting following training.

In another study that combined the four instructional procedures, LaGreca and Mesibov (1981) taught initiation of social interactions and commmunication-conversation skills to LD adolescent boys. Results showed substantial increases in subjects' performance of targeted skills in role-play situations following training. Their peformances more closely approximated those of non-LD adolescents after training than prior to training. Additionally, adult "judges" rated the LD boys as more socially skilled after training than before training. Finally, the LD boys reported a higher frequency of interactions after training than before training.

In a slightly different version of the "package" intervention, Hazel, Smalter, and Schumaker (1983) utilized workbook and comic book formats (Schumaker, Hazel, & Pederson, 1988) to present descriptions, rationales, rules, skill steps, models, discrimination training, and verbal rehearsal training to LD and other mildly disabled secondary students. This initial training was followed by live practice and feedback. Example skills included how to give and accept criticism, join activities, make friends, and negotiate conflicts. Results showed substantial increases in social skills performance in novel role-play situations following training.

The majority of the studies reviewed here have focused on teaching overt social skills. Whether or not the same procedures are useful for teaching cognitive social skills remains unclear. In some of the studies, attempts were made to teach cognitive skills such as the discrimination of situations in which to use certain social skills. Unfortunately, improvements in cognitive social skills have rarely been directly measured. In one study in which the use of cognitive social skills was directly measured, Hazel et al. (1982) measured LD adolescents' performance of social problem-solving skills before and after training. Although the subjects showed some improvement in their use of these skills, their performance after training did not equal that of non-LD adolescents. When measures of cognitive skills have been gathered indirectly, they have typically been collected in role-play situations. For example, Hazel et al. (1982) presented each youth with a series of role-play situations without telling the youths what skills to use in each situation. Thus, the youths were required to make inferences from available cues, discriminate what skills to use, and use them correctly to receive a high score on their role-play performance. Since the subjects' performance improved after training, it may be safe to assume that they were using some of the appropriate cognitive skills. Additional research is needed to determine whether the procedures that are effective in teaching overt social skills are equally effective for teaching cognitive social skills.

In summary, results of the reviewed studies show that LD individuals' overt social skills performance in contrived situations can be substantially increased through the use of such instructional procedures as description, modeling, rehearsal, and feedback. These procedures appear to be effective for helping LD individuals perform social skills at levels comparable to those of non-LD individuals in novel role-play situations (Hazel et al.,

1982; LaGreca & Mesibov, 1981). Additional studies are needed to explore the contribution and effectiveness of each of these procedures when used alone. Furthermore, research must be conducted to determine the most effective procedures for teaching cognitive social skills.

Techniques for Promoting Generalized Social Skills Usage

Results of several studies have indicated that instructional procedures such as description, modeling, rehearsal, and feedback are often insufficient for producing generalized use of newly learned social skills by LD individuals in social interactions in the natural environment. For example, Whang et al. (1981) measured LD adolescents' use of newly learned social skills in job settings after they had met criterion in role-playing situations. These authors found that although the youths showed some improvement in their use of the target skills in job settings, they often did not use those skills at levels comparable to levels achieved in training. Gorney-Krupsaw et al. (1981) arrived at similar results with regard to LD adolescents' use of social skills in the regular classroom. The adolescents tended either to use an entire skill infrequently or to use only a small percentage of a skill's components. Whang et al. and Gorney-Krupsaw et al. noted that natural opportunities for use of the skills occurred infrequently and were thus difficult to "catch" in scheduled observation sessions.

As a follow-up to these two studies, Schumaker and Ellis (1982) conducted an investigation in which opportunities for use of a newly learned skill were programmed into naturally occurring activities in a resource room to insure that the youths had opportunities to demonstrate generalized use of the skills. Again, although improvement was seen in the use of some skills in the natural environment, the youths showed little improvement of several other skills for which they had received training. Consequently, the authors concluded (a) criterion performance in role-play situations does not necessarily indicate how a youth will act in the natural environment; (b) the final measure of the effectiveness of a social skills program must be taken in the natural environment; and (c) LD adolescents need generalization training in addition to traditional instruction if generalized use of the skills is to be assured.

Two groups of researchers systematically tried to validate generalization training procedures for social skills training programs for LD individuals. Berler, Gross, and Drabman (1982) combined several generalization procedures suggested by Stokes and Baer (1977) with the instructional procedures of description, rationales, modeling, practice, videotaped replays, and feedback. In their study, three elementary-age LD children were trained in five social skills: eye contact, responding to unfair criticism, initiating social interactions, giving compliments, and requesting new behavior. The generalization procedures included multiple exemplars, stimuli common to both the training and the natural environments (e.g., peers and teacher), and the rehearsal of scenes spontaneously developed by the children. Berler et al. reported that although the children showed improved use of the targeted skills in trained and untrained role-play test situations, no improvements were found in verbalization rates in free-play activities and in sociometric measures that could be related to the training. Since these researchers measured general verbalization rate in free-play sessions without measuring the target behaviors, they may have missed improvements in the target behaviors. Nevertheless, results of this study seem to indicate that generalization procedures used only in the training setting may not be powerful enough to produce generalized use of newly learned social skills in the natural environment by LD children.

A more recent study, Schumaker, Hazel, Pederson, and Nolan (in preparation) used generalization procedures in the training setting and in the natural milieu to promote generalized use of LD adolescents' newly learned social skills. In addition to the instructional procedures described above for the Hazel et al. (1982) study, which also incorporated several generalization techniques recommended by Stokes and Baer (1977), these researchers utilized non-cued opportunities for use of the skills in the natural environment (the classroom) to facilitate generalization. Once the youths met criterion on a skill in role-play situations in the training setting, they were instructed to look for opportunities to use the skills in everyday interactions. Each time a non-cued opportunity for use of the skill was presented within naturally occurring activities, the youths were observed to determine which skill components they used, and they were given feedback on their performance. Schumaker et al. found that after the youths met criterion in non-cued situations, they exhibited generalized use of the skills in settings around the school (e.g., in the office, classrooms, hallways) when other non-cued opportunities to use the skills were provided by individuals not involved in the training.

These results indicate that generalization training (including opportunities to use the skills and feedback) must be extended to the natural environment if LD individuals are to generalize their use of newly learned skills.

Additional research is needed to validate the most effective and practical methods for promoting generalized use of social skills and to determine whether generalized use across settings and time results in improved social standing for individuals who have received training. Unfortunately, it is beyond the scope of this chapter to suggest specific generalization techniques that should be experimentally evaluated. (For a detailed discussion of this topic, see Hazel et al., in press.)

Ethical Concerns

Although only a limited number of studies have reported that social skills training has a positive impact on LD individuals' social lives, the absence of evidence does not mean that social skills training is unnecessary. Indeed, we have noted countless instances (reported by teachers and youths) of improvement in LD individuals' lives after social skills training. Training of social skills in LD individuals appears to be worthwhile if (a) empirically validated teaching procedures are used (see Schumaker, Pederson, Hazel, & Meyen, 1983, for a review of social skills training programs), (b) generalized use of the skills is actively programmed within the natural environment, and (c) the following issues are taken into consideration.

First, since there is little empirical evidence that social skills training positively impacts LD individuals' lives, since some LD individuals may not need social skills training (Schumaker et al., 1982), and since LD individuals have other deficits in need of remediation, social skills training should not be considered a panacea for all LD individuals. Appropriate assessment techniques should be utilized to determine which LD individuals need social skills training and which skills must be trained in order to maximize the most cost-efficient use of the small amounts of instructional time available within most special education programs.

Second, because of the uncertainty of the long-term outcome of social skills training, parents and LD individuals must be carefully informed about the information available on the benefits of social skills training. Other skill deficits must be carefuly weighed against social skills deficits, and instructional time should be assigned accordingly through the IEP process with active involvement of the parents and child (Van Reusen, 1984; Bos, Schumaker, & Deshler, 1987).

Third, parents and significant others in the student's environment (e.g., teachers) should be informed of the social skills being taught. At a minimum, parents and others must be told how the student may be expected to behave in certain kinds of situations in the future and how they can encourage the use of newly learned social skills. Such communication will prevent the youth from being punished for "acting differently" and may promote reinforcement of social skills use in the natural environment. Parents and others can also become more directly involved in training. Research (Serna, Schumaker, Hazel, & Sheldon, 1986) has shown that youths whose parents learned skills reciprocal to those the youths learned (e.g., when the youths learned to accept criticism, the parent learned to give criticism) maintained their use of the skills at post-training levels longer than youths whose parents were not involved in the training. Thus, others' involvement in social skills training can be beneficial.

Fourth, social skills trainers must be properly prepared. Research in progress has indicated that individuals who simply read a social skills training manual and conduct social skills training sessions do not promote change in the subjects' use of social skills in novel role-play situations (G. DeFalco, personal communication, March, 30, 1984). Such results reflect a need for the training of individuals expected to teach social skills. Social skills training is complex and requires study and practice. Fortunately, individuals can be trained to teach social skills effectively in a relatively short period of time (Hazel, Schumaker, and Sheldon, 1984). Because the most effective methods for teaching social skills may not yet be known, a commitment to become a social skills trainer also requires a commitment to continued monitoring of recent developments in the broad field of social skills training.

Fifth, social skills training involves the training of skills that some individuals consider "value laden." That is, teaching an individual to make friends or get along with others places a positive value on such activities. Some cultures value certain social skills more than others. Some social skills mean different things in different cultures. Consequently, anyone involved in social skills training must take such considerations into account when designing skills to teach and in responding to feedback about the skills. Social skills training should be presented as a way of increasing an individual's options in social situations. Skills should not be presented as the "only" way to behave.

Sixth, participants should be fully informed about what to expect when they use newly learned skills. For example, they must be prepared to encounter many individuals who are not socially skilled and who may be unreasonable. Thus, along with learning how to negotiate, they need to know how to recognize a situation where an issue is not negotiable; along with learning how to avoid a fight, they need to know when it is appropriate to defend themselves; and along with learning how to make friends, they need to know how to discriminate individuals who are not open to friendships with them.

To conclude, although social skills training holds promise for special educators, it is associated with ethical issues that must be carefully considered and acted upon. Only if care is taken can the promise of social skills training be fulfilled.

SUMMARY

Social skills training has become an important component in LD intervention packages. Many LD students require intervention directed at improving their social skills and research findings have generally supported these efforts. Several social skills have been identified as deficits or excesses for LD individuals. Social skills assessment systems have been developed and procedures have been tested for increasing the use of appropriate behaviors, decreasing the use of inappropriate behaviors, training new social skills to mastery, and promoting generalized use of newly learned social skills. Additional work is needed to specify those social skills that are functionally related to social competence and social standing for LD individuals, to develop practical assessment devices for use by educators to measure application of these skills, and to further investigate procedures that promote acquisition and generalization of newly learned social skills. Finally, research needs to focus on documenting the impact of social skills training on the lives of LD individuals. Only this kind of documentation can illustrate whether investments in social skills training are paying off in the intended manner.

Adjunct and Alternative Methods

The previous section dealt with primary intervention practices for academic and social areas. At times, besides efforts directed at academic and social deficits, LD interventions may emphasize what might be termed adjunct and alternative methods. Depending upon the particular needs of the LD student, these interventions may be added to the primary interventions in an effort to obtain a comprehensive treatment package. This section explores the forms adjunct and alternative programs may take.

Chapter 8 discusses a variety of intervention practices that may be termed "controversial." The use of these interventions (e.g., psycholinguistic training or perceptual motor training) is widely debated in the LD field. It is important to assess their efficacy in a systematic and objective manner so that realistic conclusions can be drawn about their proper place in the spectrum of LD interventions.

The use of drugs to treat learning disabilities is another practice that engenders strong emotion. Chapter 9 focuses on the effects of drugs on academic performance. Short- and long-term studies are reviewed with respect to methodological issues that may limit individual study findings. Although there is some indication that drugs may have a positive influence on achievement, gains must be interpreted in light of the availability and practicality of an alternative educational intervention that may be equally effective.

The problems of LD students are not restricted solely to the individual student, but also include the immediate family. The presence of an LD child introduces stress into a family and uncertainty about the future. Chapter 10 discusses the difficulties encountered by a family with an LD child and presents a framework for measuring the life cycle needs and psychosocial tasks of LD children and their families that are necessary for continued family functioning, stability, and growth.

Part III includes a wide assortment of activities that serve as adjunct and alternative programming. These interventions may or may not be appropriate for particular LD students, but it is important to be aware of how these practices, beyond strict academic interventions, allow for more comprehensive treatment packages.

CHAPTER 8

Controversial Practices

G. V. Glass

The LD field has developed non-traditional procedures that, although common to the repertoire of LD specialists are also controversial. Some of these methods have been the basis for acrimonious debate that has defied resolution. The ideological issues involved have kept these issues controversial and have led to political squabbling that prevents consensus regarding the status of these unique practices.

One example will illustrate the nature of the problem and the tenor of debate. The Illinois Test of Psycholinguistic Abilities (ITPA) has served as the clinical model for a variety of remedial and developmental language programs. These programs are based on the assumption that language is composed of discrete components and that these components can be taught. This last assumption has precipitated debate over the efficacy of psycholinguistic training. For example, Hammill and Larsen (1974) reviewed 39 studies of ITPA total scores and subtests and concluded that ". . . researchers have been unsuccessful in developing those skills which would enable their subjects to do well in the ITPA . . . [and] . . . the idea that psycholinquistic

Portions of this chapter appeared previously in **K. A. Kavale** and **G. V. Glass** (1982). The efficacy of special education interventions and practices: A compendium of meta-analysis findings. *Focus on Exceptional Children 15*(4), 1–14 and in Kavale, K. A., and Glass, G. V. (1984). Meta-analysis and policy decisions in special education. In B. K. Keogh (Ed.), *Advances in special education: Vol. 4* (pp. 195–247). Greenwich, CT: JAI Press.

constructs, as measured by the ITPA, can be trained by existing techniques remains nonvalidated" (p. 10–11).

Minskoff (1975) offered a critique of Hammill and Larsen's (1974) review that stated, "Because of Hammill and Larsen's oversimplified approach, 39 studies with noncomparable subjects and treatments were grouped together. Moreover, for the most part, they reviewed methodologically inadequate studies in which there was short-term training using general approaches to treatment primarily with mentally retarded or disadvantaged subjects having no diagnosed learning disabilities" (p. 137). In effect, Minskoff suggested that Hammill and Larsen had compared "apples and oranges." Ten specific methodological errors were described that limited conclusions drawn from the studies. Minskoff provided guidelines for research on psycholinguistic training. Specifically, 15 criteria were established for evaluating psycholinguistic remediation. It was suggested that psycholinguistic disabilities can be treated, and a major criterion for evaluating effectiveness should be its relationship to various academic and social demands made on a child at a particular age. Minskoff concluded by decrying the skepticism surrounding psycholinguistic training since, "it can be dangerous if it leads to the abolition of training methods that may be beneficial to some children with psycholinguistic disabilities" (p. 143).

Newcomer, Larsen, and Hammill (1975) contested Minskoff's (1975) major points. Suffice it to say that the rhetoric became increasingly confusing and enmeshed in trivial controversy. Nevertheless, Newcomer et al. contented that, "the reported literature raises doubts regarding the efficacy of... available Kirk–Osgood psycholinguistic training programs..." (p. 147).

The debate lay dormant for 3 years until Lund, Foster, and McCall–Perez (1978) offered a reevaluation of the 39 studies reviewed by Hammill and Larsen (1974). The studies were reexamined individually to determine the validity of negative conclusions regarding the effectiveness of psycholinguistic training. Six of the 24 studies clearly showed positive results for psycholinguistic training and "... contraindicate the conclusions that such training is nonvalidated" (p. 317). Of 10 studies showing negative results, only 2 were reported accurately. The remaining 8 were either equivocal or showed positive results. Specifically, 4 of the 10 studies were inaccurately reported since the original data showed positive results; 2 of the 10 studies compared groups under different training programs, making the negative results reported inaccurate since both groups made substantial progress; and 2 of the 10 studies contained insufficient data on which to base judgments. The eight studies that showed some positive results (less than six subtests) actually included three studies that attempted to improve abilities only in one or more specific areas; one study that compared treatment groups instead of trained versus nontrained subjects; and four studies that had only varying degrees of relevance to the primary question. Lund et al.

(1978) reached conclusions markedly at variance with the statement that psycholinguistic training is nonvalidated.

> Our analysis indicates that some studies show significant positive results as measured by the ITPA, some studies show positive results in the areas remediated, and some do not show results from which any conclusions can be drawn. It is, therefore, not logical to conclude either that all studies in psycholinguistic training are effective or that all studies in psycholinguistic training are not effective (p. 317).

The special education community did not wait long for the debate to continue. Hammill and Larsen (1978) reaffirmed their original position. The point-by-point rebuttal of the Lund et al. (1978) reevaluation was presumed to show that, in fact, the original report did not inaccurately report, inappropriately categorize, or misinterpret the original 39 studies. The rebuttal concluded with the statement that

> the cumulative results of the pertinent research have failed to demonstrate that psycholinguistic training has value, at least with the ITPA as the criterion for successful training. It is important to note that, regardless of the reevaluations by propsycholinguistic educators, the current state of the research strongly questions the efficacy of psycholinguistic training and suggests that programs designed to improve psycholinguistic functioning need to be viewed cautiously and monitored with great care (Hammill & Larsen, 1978, p. 413).

After five years of feckless debate, a nagging question remained: What is really known about the efficacy of psycholinguistic training? Increasingly, the principal issue had become entangled in a maze of extraneous detail only tangentially related to the major question: Should psycholinguistic training be included in the remedial curriculum for LD?

The problem is not a lack of research in these controversial areas. The problem is that research findings have proved to be conflicting, variable, and sometimes paradoxical. What is required is a way to synthesize study findings to provide general and accurate conclusions. Research synthesis has long been neglected and that neglect has contributed to the difficulties in resolving disputes.

METHODS OF RESEARCH SYNTHESIS

In the past, research synthesis was shaped by the size of the research literature. For example, the question of the efficacy of special versus regular class placement was probably answered by a narrative, rhetorical integration during the 1940s (Shattuck, 1946), but the burgeoning literature became increasingly difficult to harness (Guskin & Spicker, 1968; Johnson,

1962; Kirk, 1964; Meyers, MacMillan, & Yoshida, 1980). An unwieldy literature generates methods of integration that are unsystematic and fall short of meeting rigorous scientific standards. The standards of objectivity, verifiability, and replicability are often overlooked in an effort to reach a conclusion.

The most common method of research integration is the narrative review, which attempts to reach a conclusion through a verbal report of individual studies. Complications arise, however, when individual study findings do not agree, since the review process is based on inference. Typically, conclusions are qualified either by criticizing the research design of an individual study or by discounting the findings of a study that do not fit stipulative parameters for sampling, measurement, or analysis (Jackson, 1980). Such qualifications, although eliminating conflicting results, are subjective and inject the possibility of bias and prejudice. The literature base is reduced and the remaining studies reveal a consistency, but this consonance is achieved for the wrong reasons (Feldman, 1971).

The inability to chronologically arranged verbal descriptions to portray the accumulated knowledge led to the development of methods based on classifications and measurements of conditions and results of studies. Typically, these studies are classified in contingency tables with respect to the significance or nonsignificance of the test of a statistical hypothesis. This "box-score" integration is based on a "voting method" (Light & Smith, 1971) wherein the number of studies falling into each category is tallied and the category containing the most studies is declared the "winner." The winning category is used as the basis for conclusions about the topic studied.

One primary difficulty with box-score integrations is the disregard of sample size. Since large samples produce more statistically significant findings than do small samples, the box-score method is biased against studies with small samples (Carver, 1978).

A second difficulty with the box-score method is the discarding of good descriptive information. Is anything known if 40 of 50 studies reveal mainstreaming to be more efficacious than segregation for exceptional children? The real question is the magnitude of the experimental relationship: Does mainstreaming win by a nose or in a walk-away? Tallies of statistical significance or nonsignificance reveal little about either the strength or importance of a relationship. Unfortunately, tests of statistical significance are strongly believed to be more informative than they actually are. The mathematical properties of the box-score method of integration were evaluated by Hedges and Olkin (1980), and their findings cast the method in an unfavorable light. Clearly, research synthesis by means of box-score methods is not entirely acceptable.

The failure of common methods of research synthesis to provide reliable conclusions undermines confidence in a discipline such as learning disabilities. It is little wonder that resolution is not achieved and debate becomes entangled in a maze of detail only tangentially related to the major question. The outcome is usually a conclusion that is idiosyncratic, authoritarian, and subjective.

To overcome the difficulties associated with traditional methods of research integration, quantitative methods, commonly referred to as *meta-analysis*, have been proposed (Glass, McGaw, & Smith, 1981). As a statistical analysis of empirical studies, meta-analysis satisfies the following basic requirements: (1) it is quantitative and uses statistical methods for organizing and extracting information from large data bases; (2) it eliminates bias in study selection by not prejudging research quality; (3) it makes use of all information by transforming study findings into commensurable expressions of magnitude of experimental effect; (4) it detects statistical interactions by analyzing study characteristics that mediate findings; and (5) it seeks general conclusions. The demand for policy implications requires practical simplicity that does not do violence to more interactive conclusions.

Meta-analysis is based on a statistic that represents the magnitude of experiemental effect or relationship. The basic effect size (*ES*) statistic for experimental treatment or programs is $ES = (\overline{X}_e - \overline{X}_c) / SD_c$ where $\overline{X}_e$ = average score for the experimental group on the outcome measure, $\overline{X}_c$ = average score for the control group on the outcome measure, and SD_c = standard deviation of the control group. In the case of correlational research, where the magnitude of the relationship between two variables is investigated, the basic effect size is $ES = r_{xy}$ where r_{xy} = Pearson product-moment correlation coefficient.

Effect size may be interpreted as a z-score and translated into notions of overlapping distributions of groups and comparable percentiles. For example, suppose a hypothetical study investigating the efficacy of temporal centripetal therapy revealed an effect size of $+1.00$. This would indicate that a subject at the 50th percentile of the control group would be expected to rise to the 84th percentile of the control group after therapy. The obtained effect size of $+1.00$ indicates a superioity of one standard deviation for the treatment group. If two separate distributions are drawn for those receiving therapy and those in the control condition, the distribution will be separated by one standard deviation at their means, as shown in Figure 8–1. The average of the therapy curve is located above 84% of the area under the control group curve. This relationship suggests that the average child receiving therapy was better off than 84% of the control group, whereas only 16% of the control group was better off at the end than the average child receiving therapy. The interpretation of effect size may be further clarified by comparisons (1) to other known interventions (e.g., *ES* $= +1.00 >$ for one year's instruction in elementary school achievement), (2) within a meta-analysis (e.g., method X [mean $ES = +1.00$] is half again more beneficial than method Y [mean $ES = +.50$]), or (3) to the aggre-

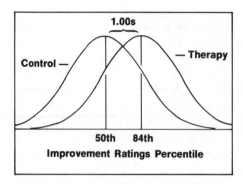

Figure 8-1
Illustration of the findings from a hypothetical study assessing the efficacy of
temporal centripetal therapy.

gated findings of other meta-analyses (e.g., treatment A [mean *ES* = .60] is
approximately five times as effective as treatment B [mean *ES* = .12]).
Meta-analysis adds clarity and explicitness to the review process and provides conclusions that are objective, verifiable, and replicable (Kavale &
Glass, 1981).

CONTROVERSIAL PRACTICES IN LEARNING DISABILITIES

By summarizing the findings from several meta-analyses, it is possible
to delineate the efficacy of particular LD practices and to place the question of their validity into a different context.

Psycholinguistic Training

For example, previous reviews could not settle the long-standing
debate over the efficacy of psycholinguistic training. It remained unclear
whether psycholinguistic training was a viable treatment alternative until
Kavale (1981a) performed a meta-analysis of 34 studies investigating the
effectiveness of psycholinguistic training. The 34 studies produced an overall effect size of .39. This finding was based on data representing approximately 1,850 subjects, averaging 7.5 years of age with a mean IQ of 82,
who received an average of 50 hours of psycholinguistic training. Thus, the
average subject receiving psycholinguistic training stood at approximately
the 65th percentile of subjects receiving no special psycholinguistic training; the latter remained at the 50th percentile.

Table 8-1 presents effect size classified by ITPA subtest. If subtests
with "thin" data (i.e., 5 or fewer effect size measurements) are eliminated,
then five of the nine subtests show modest, albeit positive, effects. It is
questionable whether these psycholinguistic abilities respond to training at
a level that would warrant continuation of training. The case is different for

TABLE 8-1
Average Effect Sizes for ITPA Subtests

ITPA Subtest	Mean Effect Size	No. of Effect Sizes
Auditory reception	.21	20
Visual reception	.21	20
Auditory association	.44	24
Visual association	.39	21
Verbal expression	.63	24
Manual expression	.54	23
Grammatic closure	.30	21
Visual closure	.48	5
Auditory sequential memory	.32	21
Visual sequential memory	.27	21
Auditory closure	−.05	3
Sound blending	.38	3

four abilities: auditory and visual association, and verbal and manual expression. For these psycholinguistic abilities, training improves functioning from 15 to 23 percentile ranks at the center of the distribution. Thus, the average trained subject would be better off than approximately 65% to 73% of untrained subjects on associative or expressive abilities.

Subtests of the ITPA were patterned on psycholinguistic constructs derived from a semantic model of communication. Table 8-2 presents an analysis of the effects of training on theoretical psycholinguistic dimensions underlying the ITPA. The box-score analysis offered by Hammill and Larsen (1974) suggested that both representational level and the visual-motor modality were not particularly responsive to training. The effect sizes of .40 and .38, respectively, for these abilities belie such an interpretation since the 15 and 14 percentile rank improvement shown by

TABLE 8-2
Average Effect Size for ITPA Psycholinguistic Constructs

Dimension	Construct	Mean Effect Size
Level	Representational	.40
	Automatic	.21
Processes	Reception	.21
	Organization	.32
	Expression	.59
Modalities	Auditory-verbal	.32
	Visual-motor	.38

trained subjects in representational level and visual-motor modalities subtests cannot be easily dismissed.

The effect size data were next integrated for important study features, and the findings are shown in Table 8-3. Not surprisingly, prescriptive, individualized approaches were found to be superior to generalized, nonindividualized methods. As with many other educational approaches, individualized instruction proved superior. The next finding was surprising; the Peabody Language Development Kits (PLDK) demonstrated the largest effect size when compared to both ITPA-related activities and sensory, perceptual, or motor training activities.

On the surface, the superiority of the PLDK appears contrary to expectation since ITPA-type activities should be most closely related to the criterion measure, the ITPA itself. Upon reflection, these findings are not surprising if viewed in terms of program structure. The PLDK represents a highly structured sequence of lessons designed to increase general verbal ability, whereas ITPA training procedures; (Kirk & Kirk, 1971) are only suggestions and guidelines for training activities. Consequently, they do not represent a comprehensive training package but merely examples for psycholinguistic training activities that must be structured and planned by individual teachers (Kavale, 1981a).

This meta-analysis appears to provide an affirmative answer to the question of the effectiveness of psycholinguistic training. Serious doubt must be cast on previous conclusions such as "the overwhelming consensus of research evidence concerning the effectiveness of psycholinguistic training is that it remains essentially nonvalidated...." (Hammill & Larsen, 1978, p. 412).

Findings for ITPA total score and subtest scores provided validation for the benefits of psycholinguistic training. Hammill and Larsen (1974) probably overstated their case when they concluded their review of the same literature with the statement that "... neither the ITPA subtests nor their theoretical constructs are particularly ameliorative" (p. 12). Clearly,

TABLE 8-3

Average Effect Size for Study Features

Feature	Mean Effect Size	No. of Effect Sizes
Approach		
General	.37	38
Prescriptive	9	6
Method		
ITPA	.30	12
PLDK	.49	14
Other	.35	9

the findings regarding the receptiveness to intervention of the expressive constructs, particularly verbal expression, and the representational level subtests are encouraging since they embody the language aspects of the ITPA and, ultimately, productive language behavior.

For a basic area like language, the average elementary school pupil gains about one standard deviation ($\overline{ES}$ = 1.00) over the school year and exceeds about 84% of the pupils' scores made on a language achievement measure at the beginning of the school year. The approximately 60% success rate for training verbal expression is substantial and is particularly important for children who are likely to manifest difficulties in this area. In fact, roughly 50 hours of psycholinguistic training produce benefits on the verbal expression subtest ($\overline{ES}$ = .63), exceeding that which would be expected from one-half year of schooling in language achievement ($\overline{ES}$ = .50).

In concrete terms, improvement of this magnitude translates into perhaps an additional half-dozen correct responses on a test like the ITPA. If these six items are considered proxies for hundreds of skills, abilities, and bits of information, then an improvement in these seemingly few items is significant. Consider an analogous situation: a child with IQ 130 answers perhaps nine more information questions or nine more vocabulary items on the WISC-R than a child with IQ 100. Does this suggest that the difference between IQ 100 and IQ 130 is nine bits of knowledge? Certainly the abilities involved transcend nine pieces of information. Likewise, improvement on a test of verbal expression represents more than the expected increase of six items since it comprises a complex amalgam of language abilities. Thus, for a child deficient in the areas enhanced by psycholinguistic training, remedial programs are likely to provide salutary effects and advantages that probably surpass the abilities themselves.

The methodology of meta-analysis has brought the multiple findings in the psycholinguistic training literature into clearer focus. A "box score" analysis of the same findings would have resulted in more equivocal conclusions since over half the reported outcomes were not statistically significant. The selected benefits of psycholinguistic training must be considered in policy judgments. It is not an all-or-none proposition. Caution must be exercised since specific situations exist in which psycholinguistic training is effective and should be included within a total remedial program.

The methods of meta-analysis were used to investigate the effectiveness of other LD practices. The findings are summarized in Table 8-4.

Perceptual-Motor Training

Two other process training strategies were investigated and the findings were not optimistic. Perceptual-motor training activities have a long history in special education (since the days of Itard and Seguin) and widely disseminated clinical evidence has acknowledged its efficacy.

TABLE 8-4
Effectiveness of LD Practices

Practice	Studies	Effect Size	% Rank
Psycholinguistic Training	34		
Reception		.21	58
Association		.44	67
Expression		.63	74
Perceptual-Motor Training	180		
Perceptual		.17	57
Achievement		.01	50
Cognitive		.03	51
Modality Model	39		
Assessment		.51	70
Teaching		.14	56
Special Versus Regular Class	50		
EMR		−.14	44
LD/BD		.29	61
Stimulant Medication	135		
Behavioral		.80	79
Intelligence		.39	65
Achievement		.38	65
Feingold Diet	23		
Behavioral		.29	61
Attention		.02	51
Achievement		−.05	48

Kavale and Mattson (1983) found 180 experiments assessing the efficacy of perceptual-motor training. A total 637 effect size measurements were obtained, representing about 13,000 subjects who averaged 8 years of age with an average IQ of 89 and an average of 65 hours of perceptual-motor training. The overall effect size across 637 measurements was .082, which in relative terms, indicates that a child who is no better off than average (i.e., at the 50th percentile), rises to the 53rd percentile as a result of perceptual-motor interventions. At the end of treatment, the average trained subject was better off than 53% of control subjects, a gain only slightly better than no treatment at all. Additionally, of 637 effect size measurements, 48% were negative, suggesting that the probability of obtaining a positive response to training is only slightly better than chance.

Examination of Table 8-4 reveals perceptual-motor training has essentially no effect on achievement and cognitive outcomes and only a very modest effect on the areas to which training is directed, perceptual-motor processes.

The overall effect of perceptual-motor training appears negligible. A single index may mask an important subset where perceptual-motor might possibly be more effective. The effect size data were consequently aggregated into increasingly differentiated groupings with the findings shown in Table 8–5 and 8–6. These findings speak for themselves. Regardless of how global or discrete the aggregation, the effects of perceptual-motor training present an unbroken vista of disappointment. There are no positive effects and nothing indicative of an effective intervention.

Table 8–7 and 8–8 provide aggregrated effect size data for two study features: diagnostic category and grade level. Interpretation is unclouded: essentially no effects are seen in all groups and at all grades. Nothing in these data suggests any selected benefits for perceptual-motor training. In no instance was perceptual-motor intervention effective. In fact, some of the lowest effect size measurements were found for learning and reading-disabled children for whom perceptual-motor training is a favored treatment approach.

Perceptual-motor training programs have taken a variety of forms and the names associated with these programs read like the roster from the

TABLE 8–5

Average Effect Sizes for Perceptual-Motor General Outcome Categories

General Outcome Categories	Mean Effect Size	No. of Effect Sizes
Perceptual/Sensory Motor		
Gross motor	.214	44
Fine motor	.178	28
Visual perception	.149	146
Auditory perception	.122	16
Academic Achievement		
Readiness	.076	69
Reading	−.039	142
Arithmetic	.095	26
Language	.031	18
Spelling	.021	16
Handwriting	.053	12
Cognitive/Aptitude		
Verbal IQ	−.007	53
Performance IQ	.068	54

TABLE 8-6

Average Effect Sizes for Perceptual-Motor Specific Outcome Categories

General Outcome Categories	Mean Effect Size	No. of Effect Sizes
Gross Motor Skills		
Body awareness/image	.256	22
Balance/posture	.263	14
Locomotor skills	−.017	8
Visual Perceptual Skills		
Visual discrimination	.146	31
Figure-ground discrimination	.173	28
Visual-motor ability	.222	26
Visual integration	.086	17
Visual-spatial perception	.144	16
Visual memory	.062	15
Reading Achievement		
Word recognition	−.016	36
Comprehension	−.055	33
Oral reading	−.037	17
Vocabulary	−.012	25
Speed/rate	−.038	8

TABLE 8-7

Average Effect Size for Subject Groups

Subject	Mean Effect Size	No. of Effect Sizes
Normal	.054	58
Educable mentally retarded (IQ = 50–75)	.132	143
Trainable mentally retarded (IQ = 25–50)	.147	66
Slow learner (IQ = 75–90)	.098	14
Culturally disadvantaged	.045	85
Learning disabled	.018	77
Reading disabled	−.007	74
Motor disabled	.121	118

TABLE 8-8
Average Effect Size for Grade Level

Level	Mean Effect Size	No. of Effect Sizes
Preschool	.053	47
Kindergarten	.099	129
Primary (gr. 1–3)	.079	226
Middle (gr. 4–6)	.066	74
Junior high school	.085	94
High school	.088	67

Special Education Hall of Fame. The effect sizes for various training methods are shown in Table 8-9. Again the findings offer a bleak picture; there is nothing even hinting at positive effects. The studies investigating the efficacy of individual programs included studies performed by program advocates and by independent investigators. A single example will reveal the fragility of such empirical findings. The Delacato program, based on the concept of neurological patterning, was assessed by both Delacato disciples and by more critical investigators. The Delacato sources produced an effect size of .723, whereas the non-Delacato sources revealed an effect size of −.242.

Contrary to the suggestions that the available evidence does not allow either a positive or negative evaluation of perceptual-motor training (Hallahan & Cruickshank, 1973), meta-analysis indicates that the necessary empirical evidence is available. It is not premature to draw definitive conclusions regarding the efficacy of perceptual-motor interventions since the available research offers the negative evidence necessary for questioning

TABLE 8-9
Average Effect Sizes for Perceptual-Motor Training Programs

Training Program	Mean Effect Size	No. of Effect Sizes
Barsch	.157	18
Cratty	.113	27
Delacato	.161	79
Frostig	.096	173
Getman	.124	48
Kephart	.064	132
Combination	.057	78
Other	−.021	82

the value of perceptual-motor training. However, deep historical roots and strong clinical tradition will hinder the removal of perceptual-motor training from its prominent position as a treatment technique. Meta-analysis suggests that serious discussion about the viability of perceptual-motor training is warranted.

Modality Instruction

Modality instruction is another popular process strategy in LD (see Kavale & Forness, 1987). Based on the search for aptitude and treatment interactions, the modality model evaluates modal preferences (visual or auditory) to determine particular learning styles that are used in differential programming emphasizing the use of visual or auditory materials. The findings summarized in Tables 8-10 and 8-11 do not offer support for the modality model.

In terms of modality assessments (Table 8-10), the original effect size was .93, which approached the one standard difference typically used for establishing groups. When corrected for measurement effort in tests used for assessing modality preferences (average $r = .56$), however, the level of group differentiation is reduced. Instead of differentiating more than 8 out of 10 cases, group differentiation was no better than 7 out of 10 cases. Thus, only 70% of the subjects could be clearly differentiated, which suggests considerable overlap between subjects exhibiting a modality preference and those not exhibiting a preference.

With respect to modality teaching (Table 8-11), the effect size of .14 translates into only a 6 percentile rank improvement. This indicates a 56% level of improvement, which is only slightly above chance (50%) and suggests, conversely, that 44% of the subjects did not reveal any gain with modality teaching. Furthermore, 35% of the effect size measurements were negative, indicating that in more than one-third of cases, subjects receiving instruction matched to their preferred learning modality actually did less

TABLE 8-10
Effects of Modality Assessments

Modality	Number of Effect Sizes	Mean Effect Size (Uncorrected)	Mean Effect Size (Corrected)	Subjects Differentiated from Comparison Group
Auditory	47	.925	.552	71%
Visual	46	.899	.506	70%
Kinesthetic	20	.970	.430	67%

TABLE 8-11
Effects of Modality Matched Instruction

Method	Number of Effect Sizes	Mean Effect Size	Standard Error of Effect Size	Percentile Status of Experimental Subject in Control Group
Auditory	80	.184	.028	57
Visual	81	.086	.037	54
Kinesthetic	44	.175	.045	57

well than control subjects receiving no specially modified instruction. These findings were similar across modalities (auditory, visual, and kinesthetic), across standardized achievement measures, and across reading skills.

Although intuitively appealing, the modality model has little empirical support. Groups seemingly differentiated on the basis of modality preferences actually revealed considerable overlap, and it was problematic whether any of the presumed differences could be deemed preferences. Little or no gain in reading achievement was found when instructional methods were matched to preferred learning modality. Only modest improvement was demonstrated for auditory, visual, or kinesthetic teaching methods.

A possible explanation for the ineffectiveness of modality teaching is the difficulty in isolating primarily auditory or visual instructional practices and materials. All modalities appear to strongly influence the learning process, and only in extreme cases (e.g., sensory deficits) can instruction by differentiated on the basis of modality. Quite possibly, modality factors per se make only a minor contribution to the constellation of factors producing individual differences in learning.

The remainder of the effect size measurements in Table 8-11 reveal that a majority are below .50, suggesting that the aggregate findings across a variety of special education practices represent less than one-half standard deviation advantage for the treated groups. An exception is the finding for special class placement.

Special Versus Regular Class Placement

The mainstreaming movement has brought profound changes to long-established policies in special education. PL 94-142 demanded placement in the "least restrictive environment," which, for many exceptional children, meant placment in the regular class instead of the previously favored special segregated class. Justification for the mandate was found in a series of efficacy studies suggesting that the special class may be inappropriate for the education of exceptional children. In the 1960s, there was an increased call for the abandonment of segregated self-contained classes (Dunn, 1968; Johnson, 1962; Kirk, 1964). Nevertheless, a nagging question remained: "Was the mainstreaming movement justified?" The most vocal advocates of mainstreaming (e.g., Christopolos & Renz, 1969) have built their arguments on a philosophical rather than empirical foundation. The philosophical commitment to mainstreaming, however, appears to be more steadfast than warranted by the empirical evidence: the research literature has been criticized for a number of serious methodological flaws that confound interpretation (Guskin & Spicker, 1968; MacMillan, 1971). Consequently, research has provided little convincing evidence that either supports or disputes the efficacy of special or regular class placement for exceptional children. Under these circumstances, it is difficult to formulate a persuasive policy.

Carlberg and Kavale (1980) performed a meta-analysis on 50 studies examining the efficacy question. In this case, the basic effect size statistic took the following form:

$$ES = \frac{\overline{X} \text{ special} - \overline{X} \text{ regular}}{SD \text{ regular}}$$

The special class was treated as the experimental group, which means a positive effect size favors the special class and a negative effect size favors the regular or mainstream class. The 50 studies produced 322 effect size measurements and, at the highest level of aggregation, yielded an effect size of −.12. These data represented approximately 27,000 students, who averaged 11 years of age, with a mean IQ of 74, and who remained in the special class for a little under two years. Approximately 58% of the effect size measurements were negative. In more than half the cases, special classes were less effective than regular classes. Since the average comparison regular class subject would be at the 50th percentile, the effect of approximately two years of special class placement was to reduce the relative standing of the average special class subject by 5 percentile ranks. In real terms, this reduction represents about 2 months credit on most elementary achievement tests. Thus, special class students were worse off than if they had remained in regular classes.

Efficacy studies generally measure two outcomes. In the Carlberg and Kavale (1980) analysis, achievement and social/personality variables revealed effect sizes of −.15 and −.11 respectively. Thus, special class placement was inferior to regular class placement regardless of outcome measures. Special class subjects declined by 6 and 4 percentile ranks on achievement and social/personality measures respectively.

These findings predict a significant, albeit small, negative effect for special class placement. The critics were apparently correct; special education placement produced no tangible benefits. When the effect size measurements were classified and averaged in different ways and were correlated with important study features, the primary finding was not challenged. Regardless of age, IQ, and length of special class placement, the fact remained that the special class was an inferior placement option.

This meta-analysis brought to light, however, a surprising finding related to diagnosis. Effect size measurements were classified into three categories: educable mentally retarded (IQ 50–75), slow learner (IQ 75–90), and LD or BD/ED. The findings are shown in Table 8–12. Special class placement was most disadvantageous for exceptional children whose primary problem was lower IQ levels (EMR and SL). In comparison to regular class counterparts, SL students lost 13 percentile ranks whereas EMR students declined by 6 percentile ranks. For LD and BD/ED children in special classes, however, an improvement of 11 percentile ranks resulted from the placement. The average LD or BD/ED pupil in a special class was better off than 61% of those placed in a regular class. Thus, unconditional judgments about mainstreaming must be tempered.

This appears to be a significant finding. Yet, the disturbing question of why some pupils placed in special classes are slightly worse off (in terms of achievement and social and personality adjustment) than they would have been had they been left in regular classrooms remains. We may speculate that the significant variable appears to be intelligence. If a child is placed in a special class because of a low IQ, it may lower teacher expectations for performance, which results in less effort on the teachers' part and less learning on the child's (Braun, 1976; Rosenthal & Jacobson, 1968; Rosenthal & Rubin, 1978). Lowered expectancy, whether conscious or unconscious, may divert instructional efforts away from academic pursuits and toward a maintenance function. As such, the special class may become an instrument for preserving social order and not necessarily an arrangement for providing a better education.

On the other hand, the normal intelligence of LD and BD/ED pupils (at least, by definition) apparently does not dampen teacher expectation. Special class teachers apparently take an optimistic view and attempt to improve academic functioning. Perhaps this effort represents the "real"

TABLE 8-12
Average Effect Size by Special Education Diagnosis

Diagnosis	Average Effect of Special vs. Regular Placement	No. of Effect Sizes
EMR (IQ 50–75)	−.14	249
SL (IQ 75–90)	−.34	38
LD and BD/ED	.29	35

special education, not a system seeking the status quo but a system focusing on individual learning needs and abilities to design an effective program of academic remediation to overcome academic deficits.

Carlberg and Kavale's (1980) research suggests that special education must become more than special methods and materials. If not combined with a shift toward more positive attitudes, its "specialness" is lost and no tangible benefits accure to pupils. The 50 studies surveyed included a multitude of different service delivery models under the general rubric of special education placement. Since no service arrangement proved more effective, it appears that the differences are related to indeterminate and imperceptible variables not easily assessed or controlled. Consequently, special educators must seek a frame of reference emphasizing the potential for growth in all its clientele.

Stimulant Drugs and Hyperactivity

From its inception, special education has shown a fascination for medicine. Conversely, at times, medicine has shown a fascination for schools. The interface of this relationship has resulted in medically oriented interventions becoming an integral part of the special education repertoire of remedial techniques. Two meta-analyses have investigated medical treatments and provide information for deciding policy about the inclusion of medical treatment in remedial programs.

The practice of treating hyperactive children with stimulant drugs is among the most controversial and emotionally loaded issues in special education. The medical community considers stimulant drugs to be the most efficacious treatment for hyperactivity. This conclusion has been challenged, first in the form of critical reviews suggesting no positive interpretation could be drawn from extant literature because of numerous methodological flaws and, second, in the form of ideological, political, and moral attacks on stimulant drug treatment. The question of the efficacy of stimulant drug treatment requires examination.

Kavale (1982a) found 135 studies assessing the effectiveness of stimulant drug treatment for hyperactivity. The studies represented approximately 5,300 subjects averaging 8.75 years of age with an average IQ of 102. Subjects received medication for an average of 10 weeks. The effect size of 984 measurements was .578, which indicates that the average drug-treated child moved from the 50th to the 72nd percentile as a result of drug intervention. This 22 percentile rank gain suggests that an average drug-treated child would be expected to be better off than 72% of untreated control children.

The diverse assortment of outcomes measured in drug research makes it difficult to interpret a single index of drug efficacy. Three major outcome classes were identified: behavioral, cognitive, and physiological. The findings are illustrated in Figure 8-2 in the form of normal distributions comparing hypothetical drug-treated and control populations. This more refined analysis revealed substantial positive effects on behavioral and cognitive outcomes. The negative effect of physiological outcomes indicated that drug intervention produced some negative consequences. The physiological findings are generally difficult to interpret and are outside the province of this chapter. Further refinement of the data in each outcome class is presented in Table 8-13.

Note (with the exception of anxiety) the impressive gains on behavioral outcomes. Substantial benefits were found in ratings of behavioral functioning, lowered activity levels, and improved attending skills. Although not of the same magnitude as behavioral improvements, cognitive functioning also exhibited consequential improvement. An intriguing question arises as to whether these cognitive improvements are a direct result of drug treatment or a manifestation of improved behavioral functioning, particularly attention and concentration. Regardless of the answer, the special education practitioner can expect improved functioning in the cognitive area. For example, the effect sizes for achievement measures are shown in Table 8-14. With the exception of arithmetic, the gains in academic achievement represent a level of improvement equal to approximately a half-year's worth of schooling ($\overline{ES}$ = .50). The effects of drug treatment exhibit a similar gain in achievement in only 10 weeks. From a perspective of effi-

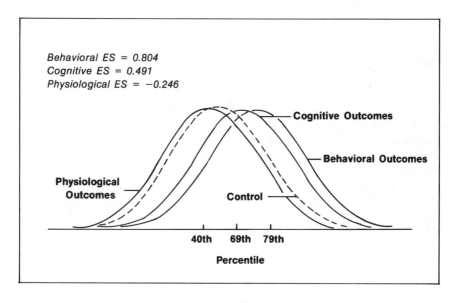

Figure 8-2
Effect of stimulant drug therapy on behavioral,
cognitive, and physiological outcome classes.

TABLE 8–13

Average Effect Sizes for Outcome Categories

Category	Mean Effect Size	No. of Effect Sizes
Behavioral		
Global improvement ratings	.886	192
Rating scales & checklists	.837	113
Activity level	.846	127
Attention & concentration	.782	119
Behavior (social & classroom)	.634	92
Anxiety	.118	12
Cognitive		
Intelligence	.391	54
Achievement	.383	47
Drawing & copying	.467	38
Perceptual, memory & motor	.412	91
Learning characteristics	.367	41
Physiological		
Biochemical	.558	7
Psychophysiological	−.275	51

TABLE 8–14

Average Effect Sizes for Achievement Measures

Measures	Mean Effect Size	No. of Effect Sizes
Wide Range Achievement Test		
Reading	.322	11
Arithmetic	.094	10
Spelling	.365	7
Iowa Test of Basic Skills	.628	6
Gray Oral Reading	.424	3
Language	.500	6
Handwriting	.437	4

cacy and efficiency, drug treatment represents an advantageous intervention for special education.The overall effect size of .578 for stimulant drugs
was obtained from six major drugs as shown in Table 8–15. All major
drugs with the exception of caffeine appear to be effective in the treatment
of hyperactivity. The findings provide support for stimulants being the most
popular treatment for hyperactivity.

Diet Treatment and Hyperactivity

In 1975, Dr. Benjamin Feingold suggested that the ingestion of artifical
(synthetic) food additives (colors and flavors) results in hyperactivity in
children (Feingold, 1976). The suggested treatment was based on the Feingold Kaiser–Permanente (K-P) diet, designed to eliminate all foods containing artifical food additives from the diet (Feingold, 1976).

Feingold (1976) reported that between 40% to 70% of hyperactive children who strictly adhered to the Feingold K-P diet demonstrated a marked
reduction in hyperactive behavior. Although the available evidence, based
on uncontrolled clinical trials and anecdotal accounts, was challenged, the
diet received widespread media attention and a favorable and enthusiastic
response from the general public. Two interdisciplinary panels were formed
and called for empirical, controlled evaluations of the Feingold K-P diet.
Empirical studies were initiated by the findings did not clarify the effects
of the Feingold K-P diet. The question remained: Is there any justification
for the major dietary changes required by the Feingold K-P diet to reduce hyperactivity?

Kavale and Forness (1983) examined 23 studies assessing the efficacy of
the Feingold K-P diet in treating hyperactivity. The 23 studies produced 125
effect size measurements and yielded an overall effect size of .118. A median
effect size of .045 suggested a skewed distribution with the ES probably
overestimating the treatment effect. The average subject was 8.3 years of age,
had an IQ of 99, and remained on the Feingold K-P diet for 39 weeks.

TABLE 8–15
Average Effect Sizes for Stimulant Drugs

Drug	Mean Effect Size	No. of Effect Sizes
Methylphenidate (Ritalin)	.634	540
Dextroamphetamine (Dexedrine)	.585	276
Magnesium Pemoline (Cylert)	.540	61
Levoamphetamine	.447	29
Amphetamine (Benzedrine)	.438	33
Caffeine	.111	45

In relative terms, the effect size measurement of .118 indicates that a child no better off than average (i.e., at the 50th percentile), would rise to the 55th percentile as a result of the Feingold K-P diet. When compared to the 22 percentile rank gain for stimulant drug treatment, the 5 percentile rank improvement for diet intervention is less than one-fourth as large. Drug-treated subjects were better off than almost three-quarters of control subjects, whereas just over one-half of diet-treated subjects were better off than controls (50% level). Although the average age and IQ were similar for drug-treated and diet-treated subjects, the average duration of treatment differed: 39 weeks in a diet study and 10 weeks in a drug study. In relation to overall effect size (.118 vs. .587), these comparisons suggest that when compared to Feingold K-P diet treatment, drug treatment is approximately five times as effective in about one-fourth the time. Thus, the Feingold K-P diet is cast in an unfavorable light since it produces a substantially lower treatment effect than stimulant drug treatment and approximates the negligible effects ($\overline{ES}$ = .082) of perceptual-motor training.

The effect size data were aggregated into descriptive outcome categories. The findings are shown in Table 8-16. The effects of the Feingold K-P diet ranged from a loss of 2 percentile ranks (learning ability) to a gain of 11 percentile ranks (Conners Scale–Teachers and hyperkinesis ratings). Thus, the only obvious effect of diet treatment is on overt behavior, specifically, a reduction in hyperactivity, with little influence on more cognitive aspects of behavior. This conclusion, however, must be tempered. Global ratings of improvement possess two major problems: objectively defining improvement and psychometric deficiencies (reliability and validity). These problems influence the reactivity or subjectivity of outcome measures. Reactive measures are those that are under the control of observers who have an interest in achieving predetermined outcomes (e.g., "improvement"). Nonreactive measures, on the other hand, are not easily influenced by observers. The correlation of effect size and ratings of reactivity was

TABLE 8-16
Average Effect Size for Outcome Categories

Category	Mean Effect Size	No. of Effect Sizes
Conners Scale — Parents	.156	26
Conners Scale — Teachers	.268	9
Global improvement	.128	23
Hyperkinesis rating	.293	15
Attention	.015	36
Disruptive behavior	.052	6
Impulsivity	.153	5
Learning ability	−.055	10

significant (r = .181) suggesting that larger treatment effects were associated with more reactive measures. Additionally, aggregations of reactive versus nonreactive measures found overall effect size measurements of .179 and .001 respectively, suggesting that in those instances where instruments paralleled the valued outcomes of observers, there was a tendency to view more improvement as revealed in larger treatment effects.

The initial evaluations of diet treatment by Dr. Feingold and associates were based on clinical trial and observation: treatment A is given and effect B is measured. The findings from such quasi-experimental designs are at variance with results from studies with more rigorous experimental control. Of the 23 studies, 6 were uncontrolled clinical trails ($\overline{ES}$ = .337) and 17 were controlled studies ($\overline{ES}$ = .089). There was, however, a significant relationship (r = .193) between effect size and ratings of design quality, which indicates that larger effect size measurements were associated with studies rated low on internal validity. Thus, findings from uncontrolled studies cannot be taken as evidence for the efficacy of the Feingold K-P diet because the lack of control makes it difficult to attribute improvement to the treatment rather than to artifacts of the study conditions.

The controlled studies used two primary experimental designs. A diet crossover study placed groups of hyperactive children on two experimental diets; one followed the Feingold K-P diet strictly while the other was disguised as the Feingold K-P diet but actually contained the substances supposedly eliminated. A challenge study selected groups of children who appeared to respond to the Feingold K-P diet who were then divided into experimental and control conditions. Both groups were given a strict Feingold K-P diet, but the experimental group was also given a challenge food (usually a cookie or drink) that appeared to meet the diet guidelines but acutally contained supposedly eliminated substances.

Of the 17 controlled studies, 7 used a diet crossover design and 10 were challenge studies. The diet crossover studies exhibited an overall effect size of .196 whereas challenge studies revealed an overall effect size of .045. Diet crossover studies, however, although an improvement over uncontrolled clinical studies, still possess methodological difficulties that suggest caution in interpretation. Challenge studies, on the other hand, offer a methodology that permits the attribution of behavioral change to the substances eliminated in the Feingold K-P diet. Challenge studies can be considered the "best" studies in terms of design and control and provide the strongest evidence for the efficacy of the Feingold K-P diet. The weight of this evidence is decidedly negative ($\overline{ES}$ = .045) since at the end of diet treatment the average treated subject was better off than 52% of control subjects, a gain only slightly better than no treatment at all.

These findings offer little support for the Feingold hypothesis. The modest and limited gains suggest a more temperate view of the efficacy of the Feingold K-P diet than that asserted by the diet's proponents. The slight improvement shown by some children should not interfere with the critical examinations of the Feingold K-P diet, which may postpone more appropriate medical, psychological, or educational intervention (Wender, 1977).

Although the Feingold diet offers an appealing treatment approach for hyperactivity since it offers an alternative to stimulant medication and is consonant with attitudes labeling natural foods as "good" and artificial/synthetic ingredients as "bad," it is not without pragmatic difficulties. The implementation of the Feingold K-P diet requires an abrupt lifestyle change. Since increased vigilance is necessary in grocery shopping and food preparation, families generally cannot eat at restaurants, and the child cannot eat school lunches (Sheridan & Meister, 1982). Lew (1977) conducted a 4-week trial of the Feingold K-P diet on her family and concluded that "the Feingold Diet is indeed a very different and very difficult diet to maintain in practice. the deprivations to the participants are real and is not the hyperactive child already set apart from his peers and family enough?" (p. 190). The available evidence suggests that the Feingold K-P diet is not an effective intervention approach for hyperactive children. The negative empirical findings call into question the validity of the Feingold K-P diet as a treatment for hyperactivity and suggest a cautious policy toward accepting the Feingold hypothesis.

Assessment

Besides the question of treatment efficacy, other LD practices are controversial. One such area is assessment. The meta-analytic findings investigating the validity of several practices are presented in the following section.

Auditory and Visual Perception

Auditory and visual perceptual skills have been assumed to be related to reading ability and have often been used in assessments to predict reading achievement. But the research investigating the nature of the relationships has produced mixed results that have been interpreted both positively and negatively.

Kavale (1981b, 1982b) performed meta-analyses on 267 studies investigating the relationship between auditory (n = 106) and visual (n = 161) perception and reading ability. A total of 2,294 effect size measurements were collected with 1,509 descriptive of the relationship of auditory (n = 447) and visual (n = 1062) perception to reading achievement. The remainder (785) were descriptive of the relationships among perceptual skills and intelligence, intelligence and reading, and reading skills. These data represented approximately 50,000 subjects whose average age was 7.87 years, in grade 3.3, and whose average IQ was 104.55.

For auditory perception and reading, the overall effect size was .369. The average correlation was .387 for visual perception and reading. The usual method for interpreting the importance of a correlation in terms of a coefficient of determination (r^2) that reflects the percent of variance explained underestimated the importance of relationships. Rosenthal and Rubin (1982) suggested an alternative in the binomial effect size display (BESD) that indicates the change in predictive accuracy attributable to a certain assessment variable and is computed by .50 $\pm$ $r/2$. Suppose a particular relationship reveals an r of .32, it is said to account for "only 10% of the variance," but the BESD shows that this proportion of variance is equivalent to increasing the predictive accuracy from 34% to 66%, which would mean reducing the number of incorrect predictions from 66% to 34%. With a BESD interpretation, auditory perception increases predictive accuracy from 32% to 68% and visual perception produces an increase from 31% to 69%.

The findings for the relationship of five auditory perceptual skills and eigth visual perceptual skills to reading ability are displayed in Table 8-17. On average, each auditory and each visual perceptual skill increased the accuracy of predicting reading ability by 40%. Little variability emerged among auditory perceptual skills. Visual perceptual skills exhibited greater

TABLE 8-17
Relationship of Auditory and Visual Perceptual Skills to Reading Achievement

Skill	N	M	Predictive Accuracy Increased From	To	Difference in Predictive Accuracy
Auditory					
Auditory discrimination (AD)	183	.371	31%	69%	37%
Auditory blending (AB)	67	.377	33%	71%	38%
Auditory memory (AM)	99	.383	29%	67%	38%
Auditory comprehension (AC)	26	.402	30%	70%	40%
Auditory-visual integration (A-V)	72	.324	34%	66%	32%
Visual					
Visual discrimination (VD)	291	.385	33%	71%	38%
Visual memory (VMem)	139	.472	28%	76%	48%
Visual-motor integration (VMot)	305	.361	28%	64%	36%
Visual closure (VC)	77	.427	24%	66%	42%
Visual spatial (VS)	64	.326	34%	66%	32%
Visual association (VA)	95	.377	31%	69%	38%
Figure ground discrimination (FG)	46	.251	39%	65%	26%
Visual-auditory integration (V-A)	45	.338	33%	67%	34%

divergence, which was accounted for primarily by the small increase (26%) for figure ground discrimination, compared to the large increase in predictive accuracy for visual memory (48%). Although, on average, prediction of reading ability was approximately equal to that of auditory perceptual skills (68%), visual memory emerged as the best predictor, with successful predictions increased from 28% to 76%.

The perceptual skills data were aggregated across individual reading skills as shown in Table 8-18. For general reading, auditory perceptual skills increased predictive accuracy by 38%, on average, which was almost the same as the average 39% increase in predictive accuracy for visual perceptual skills. The skills of auditory discrimination, auditory blending, and auditory memory increased predictive accuracy for word recognition to 69%, whereas visual spatial, visual memory, and visual association increased predictive accuracy to approximately 73%. Measures of reading comprehension found approximately equal percentage increases (to about 69%) for all auditory perceptual skills. Greater variability was found among visual skills. Auditory memory was by far the best predictor of vocabulary skills, increasing predictive accuracy by 60%.

Several popular tests of auditory and visual perceptual functioning were used frequently enough to allow for meaningful integration with the results shown in Table 8-19. The auditory discrimination (Wepman, Murphy-Durrell) and visual-motor integration (Bender) measures were less effective, by an average 4%, in increasing predictive accuracy when compared to the averages across all auditory discrimination (.371) and visual-motor integration (.361) measures. The two most popular auditory memory instruments (WISC-Digit Span, ITPA-ASM) increased predictive accuracy to levels greater than the average 67% across all auditory memory measures. The most often used auditory blending measures (Roswell-Chall, ITPA-SB) were also more effective than the average percentage increase (38%) for all auditory blending measures. The Frostig test was significantly less effective in increasing predictive accuracy than the average coefficient for visual perception measures (.387). The ITPA subtests increased predictive accuracy by percentages ranging from 34% to 60%, with an average increase of 41%. The best predictor was sound blending, which increased successful prediction of reading achievement from 22% to 82%.

To complete the description of the relationship between auditory and visual perceptual skills and reading, the role of intelligence (IQ) was assessed. Partial correlations with IQ constant were calculated, which produced a decrease in the magnitude of the relationships. Auditory perceptual skills declined in predictive accuracy by an average 13%, and visual perceptual skills declined by an average 23%. The greatest suppression in predictive accuracy was found for memory skills, whereas discrimination abilities exhibited the most independence from IQ. The accuracy of predicting word recognition skills was least affected, whereas the predictive accuracy for

TABLE 8-18

Relationship of Auditory and Visual Perceptual Skills to Reading Skills

Skill	General Reading Ability (GR)				Word Recognition (WR)				Reading Comprehension (RC)				Vocabulary (VO)			
			PAI				PAI				PAI				PAI	
	N	M	From	To	N	M	From	To	N	M	From	To	N	M	From	To
Auditory																
AD	59	.382	31%	69%	46	.342	35%	69%	32	.361	32%	68%	19	.399	30%	70%
AB	22	.413	31%	73%	12	.307	39%	69%	14	.336	33%	67%	5	.242	35%	59%
AM	33	.368	32%	68%	24	.413	27%	69%	23	.404	30%	70%	9	.603	22%	82%
AC	11	.394	28%	68%	5	.277	34%	62%	6	.381	31%	69%	4	.267	39%	65%
A-V	24	.318	34%	66%	27	.332	33%	63%	15	.355	34%	70%	5	.161	42%	58%
Visual																
VD	143	.418	29%	71%	18	.477	26%	74%	25	.372	31%	69%	14	.315	34%	66%
VMem	52	.472	29%	77%	45	.463	27%	73%	49	.463	31%	77%	21	.488	28%	76%
VMot	164	.409	28%	68%	16	.398	28%	68%	13	.361	30%	66%	14	.342	31%	65%
VC	23	.376	29%	67%	18	.272	36%	64%	16	.363	32%	68%	9	.297	33%	63%
VS	11	.367	32%	68%	23	.348	31%	65%	20	.345	31%	65%	17	.401	28%	68%
VA	17	.410	29%	71%	24	.356	32%	68%	26	.301	35%	65%	20	.355	30%	66%
FG	13	.262	37%	63%	6	.266	37%	63%	9	.244	38%	62%	8	.225	37%	59%
V-A	15	.416	29%	71%	8	.441	28%	72%	5	.273	39%	61%	6	.199	40%	60%

PAI = Predictive accuracy increased.

TABLE 8-19
Relationship of Auditory and Visual Perceptual Measures to Reading Ability

Measure	N	M	Predictive Accuracy Increased From	To	Difference In Predictive Accuracy
Bender [1]	81	.318	34%	66%	32%
Wepman [2]	59	.352	32%	68%	36%
Roswell–Chall [3]	29	.465	27%	73%	46%
Murphy–Durrell [4]	35	.313	32%	64%	32%
WISC–Digit span [5]	34	.329	36%	68%	32%
Frostig [6]					
Eye motor	31	.237	36%	60%	24%
Figure ground	32	.226	39%	61%	22%
Form constancy	31	.292	33%	63%	30%
Position in space	37	.268	37%	63%	26%
Spatial relations	37	.274	36%	64%	28%
Total	36	.253	36%	62%	26%
ITPA [7]					
Visual reception	24	.337	33%	67%	34%
Auditory association	15	.389	31%	69%	38%
Visual association	19	.347	33%	67%	34%
Auditory sequential memory	27	.388	33%	71%	38%
Visual sequential memory	57	.412	29%	71%	42%
Visual closure	17	.375	29%	67%	38%
Sound blending	16	.597	22%	82%	60%

[1] Bender visual motor gestalt
[2] Wepman auditory discrimination test
[3] Roswell–Chall auditory blending test
[4] Murphy–Durrell diagnostic reading readiness test
[5] Wechsler intelligence scale for children
[6] Marianne Frostig development test of visual perception
[7] Illinois Test of Psycholinguistic Abilities

reading comprehension and vocabulary skills was most attenuated with IQ constant.

A step-wise multiple regression analysis was used to determine the extent and significance as well as the best combination of variables for predicting reading achievement (Table 8-20). With IQ entered, it was the first variable for three reading skills (general reading ability, reading comprehension, and vocabulary) but only a minimal factor for word recognition. When IQ was not entered, visual memory was the initial variable and

TABLE 8–20
Step-Wise Multiple Regression of Auditory Perceptual Skills and Visual Perceptual Skills in Predicting Reading Abilities With and Without Intelligence as a Variable

GR		WR		RC		VO	
Variable	**R^2**	**Variable**	**R^2**	**Variable**	**R^2**	**Variable**	**R^2**
IQ	.580	VMem	.212	IQ	.578	IQ	.449
VD	.612	AM	.314	AC	.657	AC	.508
VC	.634	VD	.365	VD	.693	AD	.558
VMem	.646	VC	.398	AD	.707	VMem	.586
AB	.658	AC	.427	A-V	.715	A-V	.616
VMot	.666	AB	.461	VC	.717	VMot	.634
AD	.670	VMot	.483	VA	.720	VA	.648
AC	.675	AD	.497	AM	.722	AM	.661
VA	.676	A-V	.502	VMot	.723	AB	.661
AM	.676	IQ	.504	AB	.724	VD	.662
A-V	.676	VA	.504	VMem	.724	VC	.662
VMem	.203	VMem	.212	VMem	.212	VMem	.240
AB	.317	AM	.314	AM	.314	AM	.360
VC	.373	VD	.365	VD	.351	AD	.396
VD	.400	VC	.399	AB	.373	A-V	.447
VMot	.419	AB	.427	AC	.395	VMot	.493
AD	.431	AB	.461	VC	.420	VA	.520
AM	.434	VMot	.483	AD	.437	AC	.539
AC	.437	AD	.497	VMot	.446	AB	.547
VA	.439	A-V	.502	A-V	.451	VC	.547
A-V	.440	VA	Not Entered	VA	.452	VD	.548

the second step in each case was an auditory variable. The remaining variables did not add significantly to the proportion of predicted variance.

The magnitude and nature of the relationship of auditory and visual perception to reading indicated that they successfully increased the accuracy of predicting reading skills. The magnitude of that increase, however, was either amplified or attenuated by the particular subset of perceptual and reading variables considered.

Wechsler Profiles

The *Wechsler Intelligence Scales* (WISC, WISC-R, and WPPSI), with their separate verbal and performance scales composed of 10 or 12 subtests, seem particularly attractive for attempting to identify a set of characteristics that might be useful for differential diagnosis. Research has suggested that LD children may differ from non-LD children with respect to verbal-performance discrepancies and patterns of subtest scatter, evidenced in recategorizations and profiles based on factor scores or theoretical models of cognitive abilities.

Kavale and Forness (1984) performed a meta-analysis on 94 studies investigating WISC differences between non-LD and LD children. The average study included subjects in grade 6.2 whose average age was 11.47 years, and was published in 1973 with a sample size of 105 (total N = 9372) that was 63% male. The obtained effect size measurements for Full Scale (−.199) Verbal Scale (−.391), and Performance Scale (−.160) suggest that approximately 58%, 65%, and 54%, respectively, of non-LD children would score above the LD group and indicates considerable overlap between the distributions of non-LD and LD populations. When translated into IQ scores, the LD group revealed full scale IQ, verbal scale IQ, and performance scale IQ scores of 97, 94, and 98, respectively, which fall within the average classification. Traditional thinking has suggested that LD children are characterized by VSIQ and PSIQ (V − P) differences. The V − P discrepancy (PSIQ > VSIQ) exhibited an effect size of .231 that translates into a 3.46 IQ point difference, which fails to meet the 11 IQ point difference required for significance (.05).

The findings for WISC verbal and performance subtests are presented in Table 8-21. The verbal subtests revealed greater suppression than the performance subtests. The verbal effect size data indicate that anywhere

TABLE 8-21
Average Effect Size for WISC Verbal and Performance Subtests

	Number of Effect Sizes	Mean Effect Size	Scaled Score Equivalent	Percentile Rank
Verbal Subtest				
Information (I)	62	−.377	8.87	37
Similarities (S)	62	−.001	10.00	50
Arithmetic (A)	63	−.436	8.69	37
Vocabulary (V)	63	−.210	9.37	37
Comprehension (C)	61	+.044	10.13	50
Digit span (DS)	43	−.610	8.17	25
Performance Subtests				
Picture completion (PC)	60	+.234	10.70	63
Picture arrangement (PA)	60	+.105	10.32	50
Block design (BD)	60	+.038	10.11	50
Object assembly (OA)	58	+.092	10.28	50
Coding (CO)	57	−.410	8.77	37
Mazes (M)	6	−.355	8.93	37

from 48% to 73% of the general population may exhibit higher scores than the LD group in verbal subtests. When translated into scaled score equivalents, the average value for the five regular tests (M = 9.41) was only about one-half point below the mean (10), with all percentile rankings within the average classification. The performance subtests revealed four instances when the LD group performed better than the non-LD comparison group. The findings suggest that anywhere from 41% to 66% of the total population would be expected to score at a higher level than LD subjects, which again reveals considerable overlap between the populations. The five performance subtests produced an average value (10.04) practically equal to the mean-scaled score (10).

Differentiation between non-LD and LD groups has been suggested on the basis of intersubtest variability or scatter. Although several approaches to scatter have been suggested, each approach revealed the same finding: the LD group actually exhibited less variability than the non-LD group, which results in little uniqueness or diagnostic value in WISC subtest scatter and a relatively flat profile.

The WISC subtests were recategorized into groupings based on hypotheses about cognitive abilities (Table 8–22). Although effect size data indicated some pattern of strength and weakness, translation into scaled-score equivalents found the LD group only about a half point above the mean (10) in the areas of strength and only approximately a point and one-half below the mean in weaker areas. When compared to the required deviation (±3) for significance, none of the recategorized scores revealed any area to be a significant strength or weakness for the LD group, and all scaled scores place the LD group within the average range. Similar findings were found for WISC profiles (either a specification of subtests as low versus high, or only an indication of subtests where the LD group scores low), WISC factor scores (based on factor analytic studies assessing construct validity), and WISC patterns (based on descriptions of cognitive abilities and operations). Thus, in each instance, the regroupings failed to demonstrate distinctive ability clusterings that might be useful for clinical differentiation of LD and non-LD children.

The differential diagnosis of LD with the WISC, although intuitively appealing, appears unwarranted. Although the structure of the WISC leads to the assumption that there ought to be subtest patterns, and established clinical practice operates as if these patterns were fact, the meta-analysis performed by Kavale and Forness (1984) found no distinctive characteristics that would be useful for LD diagnosis. Regardless of the manner in which WISC subtests were grouped and regrouped, no recategorization, profile, pattern, or factor cluster emerged as a clinically significant indicator of learning disabilities. In fact, the average WISC profile for LD does not reveal anything extraordinary and appears not unlike that found for the average normal child, illustrated by a composite rendering of findings as shown in Figure 8–3.

TABLE 8-22
Average Effect Sizes for WISC Recategorized Scores

Recategorization	Subtests	Number of Effect Sizes	Mean Effect Size	Scaled Score Equivalent
Bannatyne I				
Spatial	PC, BD, OA	178	+.122	10.37
Conceptual	S, V, C	186	−.057	9.83
Sequential	DS, PA, CO	160	−.271	9.19
Bannatyne II				
Spatial	PC, BD, OA	178	+.122	10.37
Conceptual	S, V, C	186	−.057	9.83
Sequential	A, DS, CO	163	−.473	8.58
Acquired knowledge	I, A, V	188	−.341	8.98
Keogh & Hall				
Verbal comprehension	I, V, C	186	−.182	9.45
Attention–concentration	A, DS, CO	163	−.473	8.58
Analytical field approach	PC, BD, OA	178	+.122	10.37
Bush & Waugh				
Spatial	PC, BD, OA	178	+.122	10.37
Conceptual	S, V, C	186	−.057	9.83
Perceptual organization	BD, OA	118	−.065	9.81
Verbal comprehension	I, S, V, C	248	−.137	9.59
Concentration	DS, A, CO	163	−.473	8.58
Vance & Singer				
Spatial	PC, BD, OA	178	+.122	10.37
Conceptual	S, V, C	186	−.057	9.83
Sequential	A, DS, CO	163	−.473	8.58
Acquired knowledge	I, A, V	188	−.341	8.98
Distractibility	A, DS, CO, M	169	−.469	8.59

A PERSPECTIVE ON CONTROVERSIAL PRACTICES

The results of the meta-analyses reported in this chapter paint a mixed picture of the efficacy of LD interventions and practices, which were shown to be both effective and not effective. This conclusion is further complicated by Swanson's (1984b) finding that theory tends not to guide teaching practice. Swanson reported a significant discrepancy between what teachers say and what they do, which makes it likely that teacher's are most comfortable with what is familiar and what has intuitive appeal. Regardless of how exciting teachers may find new theoretically based strategies, existing interventions are usually favored. However these favored interventions are not always effective.

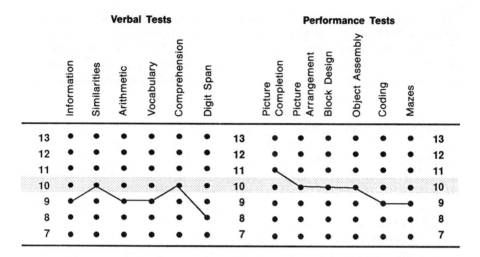

Figure 8–3
The WISC scaled score profile of the average learning disabled child.

An efficacy summary is shown in Table 8–23. Two observations about this table are important. One is that most of the effect size measurements are below .50 and represent less advantage than one-half year of schooling. It may be that special education has taken its *special* adjective too seriously and placed too much faith in its unique interventions. There has always been a demand for instant and simple solutions in special education. However, the LD field has never been able to provide *the* solution and meta-analytic findings cast doubt about any of the interventions reviewed here laying claim to being the only answer.

The fundamental concepts of the LD field have also been questioned. Consider, for example, the cornerstone of most LD intervention models: individualized instruction and its mandate, the Individualized Educational

TABLE 8-23
Learning Disability Efficacy Summary

Practice	Mean Effect Size	Standard Deviation
Psycholinguistic training	.39	.54
Perceptual-motor training	.08	.27
Modality model	.28	.34
Special class placement	−.12	.65
Stimulant drugs	−.59	.61
Feingold diet	.12	.42

Program (Schenck, 1980). Lloyd (1984) questioned the validity of the assumption that certain kinds of instruction are better for some students and other kinds are better for other students. Based on Salomon's (1972) three models of individualization — remedial, compensatory, and preferential — little evidence was found to support any aptitude × treatment interaction hypotheses. Instead Lloyd (1984) suggested that instruction be based on "skills students need to be taught."

Fuchs and Fuchs (1986) followed this suggestion with a call for systematic formative evaluation as the basis for individualization. Systematic formative evaluation focuses on ongoing evaluation and modification of proposed programs to provide a data base from which individualized programs may be developed. The advantages of systematic formative evaluation include the fact that (1) it is an inductive, rather than deductive, approach to individualization, which avoids the pitfalls of formulating a diagnosis before the relationship between learner characteristics and educational intervention is fully established, (2) it is based on psychometrically acceptable measurement procedures, and (3) it is ecologically valid because of repeated measurement in the classroom setting. Thus, even a fundamental concept such as individualization is subject to varying interpretation and, depending on its conceptualization, may or may not possess utility for special education practice.

The second observation about Table 8–23 relates to the column illustrating the standard deviation (SD) associated with each effect size measurement. The two statistics may be used to represent a form of expectation about an intervention. But the standard deviation column reveals a disconcerting fact: the standard deviation measurements reveal magnitudes two to three times greater than the effect size measurements. In each case, the treatment exhibited greater variability than it did average effectiveness. This means that from one study to the next, the effect of an intervention can vary over a wide range, from negative to zero to positive. Thus LD treatments are more variable than beneficial in their effects.

Variability makes LD treatments essentially unpredictable. In an effort to harness some of the variability, meta-analysis techniques attempt to determine if some features of studies (e.g., age, sex, treatment duration, setting, IQ, severity) might correlate substantially with effect size. If some correlations were significant, then it would be possible to predict, for example, when psycholinguistic training or stimulant drug treatment would be effective. Unfortunately, correlations were never of a magnitude that permitted useful predictions. Thus LD interventions may produce benefits, but they do so in a manner that is essentially unpredictable.

The variability and unpredictability of LD treatments suggest that the system does not represent "perfect" knowledge (Brodbeck, 1962). This implies that LD practice cannot operate on the basis of prescriptive action, that is, a single course of action under a wide range of circumstances. A treatment plan for learning disabilities must be viewed as an enterprise that is unlawful, unpredictable, and unknowable in a purely scientific sense.

The tacit acknowledgment of this view of learning disabilities can be seen in debates over the philosophical underpinnings of practice. Heshusius (1982) suggested that the foundation provided by a predominantly mechanistic (i.e., behavioral) approach serves only to reduce teaching and learning to the subordinate level of rules and instrumentality. The required measurement and quantification of instruction and student learning tend not to operate at levels that are meaningful or worthwhile for the child. Heshusius (1982) warned that the mechanistic assumptions of current LD practices are too narrow or simplistic, and that inadequate descriptions of student behavior and behavior change are the ultimate consequences. Although recognizing that no one model holds ultimate truth or reality, Heshusius (1982) contended that LD practitioners have been trying to do the impossible — "to force the innately unpredictable into the predictable, the unmeasurable into the measureable, and wholeness into fragmentation" (p. 12). Furthermore, the current predominant paradigm in learning disabilities demands that teachers become behavioral engineers or technicians, a transformation that serves to promote the reduction of complex reality into quantifiable triviality. A more holistic approach could allow for an understanding of "complexity in its own right and the relationship of the whole to its parts, rather than trying to understand complexity by fragmenting it and reducing it to small, statistically measurable units over which one has control" (Heshusius, 1986, p. 463). This view did not go unchallenged (Ulman & Rosenberg, 1986) and mechanistic approaches have been credited with being the primary agents for the efficient evaluation and modification of interventions (Polloway et al., 1985).

In a similar manner, Iano (1986) suggested that the natural science-technical model fails to capture the complexity of the teaching-learning process and has created an artifical distinction between researchers and practitioners. Researchers tend to reduce classroom behavior to controlled or defensible variables that fail to recognize classroom reality, whereas teachers view these variables as minor contributors and have little confidence in the applicability of research. Iano's (1986) view was followed by commentary (Carnine, 1987; Forness & Kavale, 1987; Lloyd, 1987) criticizing, expanding, or clarifying specific points.

These debates have focused on the increased attention directed at model-based practice in learning disabilities. Currently, the validity and worth of any particular model is practically impossible to determine. It may be that LD personnel must accept the fact that multiple models can be equally productive for studying the efficacy of special education (Labouvie, 1975). Although different models would lead to different interpretations of observed intervention effects, all would be retained for utilization in classroom situations. This relativism, or belief that judgments concerning the adequacy of conflicting models cannot be made, has been challenged (Phillips, 1983). For example, Soltis (1984), although encouraging tolerance for all educational perspectives within an "associated community," emphasized that open-mindedness must not be viewed as being synonymous with empty-mindedness; special educators must exercise judgment when evaluating interventions. Donmoyer (1985) asserted that relativism has contributed to the LD field being a "solipsistic morass," where any conclusion regarding the effectiveness of an intervention could be judged as positive as any other intervention, even when conflicting findings exist.

SUMMARY

The variability inherent in LD models is also apparent in general education models (i.e., programs of what to teach, when, and how). These models show success is highly variable (e.g., Dunkin & Biddle, 1974; Joyce & Weil, 1972; Peterson & Walberg, 1979). What works in one place does not necessarily work someplace else. Consequently, LD practice must be viewed with uncertainty, which introduces "risk" (Kaplan, 1964) since an intervention may or may not work.

The uncertainty and risk in the LD field does not preclude rational program planning. Glass (1979) commented on the general principles necessary to cope sensibly with uncertainty: "Such systems must be monitored diligently; the actors within them must remain versatile and flexible, and the services must be highly decentralized. Persons must command options instead of eternal truths" (p. 14).

Where does the LD practitioner find these options? it is apparent that no model or special intervention is the answer. A wide assortment of intervening variables influences the teaching–learning process. Studies of these variables has been commonly referred to as "effective schooling" research (e.g., Mackenzie, 1983; Purkey & Smith, 1983; Squires, 1983).

Effective schooling research has identified practices and characteristics associated with improvement in student achievement and student behavior. These include (1) a clearly defined curriculum, (2) focused classroom instruction and management, (3) firm, consistent discipline, (4) close monitoring of student performance, and (5) strong instructional leadership.

The implications of effective schooling research for LD practice have been discussed (Bickel & Bickel, 1986; Samuels, 1986) and suggest the necessity of reconceptualizing how instructional services should be conceived and delivered. One point seems clear: when the success or failure of an LD intervention is contingent on relatively uncontrolled (and unknown) factors, the key player becomes the teacher, whose own skills and abilities must interpose between the intricate events involved in the special education teaching–learning process. This will best be achieved, not by a dogmatic belief system, but by an array of rational choices gleaned from the effective schooling literature.

Stevens and Rosenshine (1981) suggested characteristics of effective teaching, which included instruction that is (1) teacher directed, (2) group based, (3) academically focused, and (4) individualized. However, discrepancies exist between these suggestions for effective teaching and the observation of actual teaching practice (Morsink, Soar, Soar, & Thomas, 1986). Specifically, only a small amount of time was spent on activities that could be considered direct instruction, with active learner involvement and teacher feedback (Englert, 1983). Students did not appear to receive frequent teacher attention (Gable, Hendrickson, Young, Shores, & Stowitschek, 1983). Apparently, effective schooling research needs to be better integrated into practice. It must be communicated clearly that schooling does make a difference and that teachers can substantially influence student outcomes.

The effectiveness of LD interventions must include elements of both art and science, because science (research) does not automatically apply in the real world. Phillips (1980) termed this distinction the "is/ought dichotomy"; research findings take an *is* form (X is Y) whereas practical implications take an *ought* form (A ought to do B). Effective schooling literature can insure that the "art" of intervention (i.e., the individual teacher's interpretation of what is best practice) possesses a rational basis. The outcome will be an enhanced quality of education for LD students based on the artful application of science.

CHAPTER 9

Pharmacotherapy

Kenneth D. Gadow

R esearch on pharmacotherapy for learning disabilities consists primarily of investigations into the effects of stimulant drugs on hyperactive children. Because the majority of the subjects in these studies experienced school achievement problems, it is accurate to say that over the past five decades we have acquired a considerable body of information about stimulant drugs and learning disabilities. However, there are only three published studies of drug research with nonhyperactive LD children (Aman & Werry, 1982; Gittelman-Klein & Klein, 1976; Gittleman, Klein, & Feingold, 1983). In general, researchers in the hyperactivity area have done a relatively poor job of describing learning disabilities in their treatment samples, and studies of LD children have generally omitted an assessment of hyperactivity. The most serious and extensive inquiry into differences among groups of hyperactive, LD, and hyperactive LD children has been made by Dykman and his colleagues (see, for example, Dykman, Ackerman, & McCray, 1980).

Academic underachievement is a common problem in clinic-identified samples of hyperactive children. Comparisons between hyperactive and nonlabeled peers have repeatedly shown higher rates of academic failure (e.g., failed grades, retentions, special class placement) in the former

This chapter originally appeared as an article by **Kenneth D. Gadow** in *Learning Disabilities: An Interdisciplinary Journal* (Vol. II (10), 127–140, 1983) and was adapted by permission of Grune & Stratton for inclusion in this *Handbook*.

group (e.g., Borland & Heckman, 1976; Cantwell & Satterfield, 1978; Minde, Lewin, Weiss, Lavigueur, Douglas, & Sykes, 1971). Although academic deficits are common in hyperactive samples, figures vary greatly from one study to the next, few investigators have documented the prevalence of learning disabilities per se (Lambert & Sandoval, 1980), and the percentage who are labeled learning disabled and scheduled for special education services is generally not reported. Minimum IQ scores for inclusion in most treatment studies range from 70 to 85, ruling out a diagnosis of mental retardation.

Treatment prevalence studies indicate that approximately 1% to 2% of the children attending elementary schools are currently receiving psychotropic drugs (usually stimulants) for hyperactivity, which, on a national level involves an estimated 300,000 to 600,000 children (Gadow, 1981). Although the presence of a learning disability no doubt increases the probability of medical referral and subsequent treatment with medication in hyperactive children, learning disabilities as defined by federal law are not generally considered to be an indication for drug therapy. Therefore, even though the extent of pharmacotherapy for nonhyperactive LD children is not known, it is probably quite limited. This should not be interpreted to suggest that psychotropic drug use is uncommon in special education programs for LD youngsters. Surveys have found drug treatment prevalence rates for hyperactivity to be at least 7% for LD children and adolescents in a variety of special education settings (Cullinan, Gadow, & Epstein, in press) and as high as 23% for self-contained special education classes for elementary school-age children (Safer & Krager, 1984).

This chapter discusses the research literature on the effects of stimulant drugs on the academic performance of hyperactive and LD children. In that there are several reviews of short-term drug studies (e.g., Aman, 1978, 1980; Barkley & Cunningham, 1978; Gadow, 1983, 1986; Pelham, 1985; Pelham & Murphy, 1985), only a brief summary of these prior efforts is presented. This is followed by a discussion of the findings from 11 long-term investigations of drug- versus nondrug- or minimally drug-treated hyperactive children. These long-term studies are of particular interest because they address some of the most important questions regarding the efficacy of treatment; namely, its impact on adolescent and adult status. They are discussed here in some detail to provide insight into the nature of the data base on which our clinical decisions are currently being made.

SHORT-TERM STUDIES

In their oft-cited review of stimulant drugs and academic achievement, Barkley and Cunningham (1978) reported that 83% of the academic dependent measures employed in 17 short-term stimulant drug studies failed to demonstrate improvement with medication. This was true for all academic skills, including reading, arithmetic, and spelling. Similarly, Aman (1982) reviewed 10 drug studies of children who were selected on the basis of a learning problem and found no justification for the use of stimulants in the treatment of reading disorders. Although it is a widely held belief that stimulant drugs do not enhance academic achievement, this is still a matter of debate. Some, for example, maintain that the number of pertinent variables and methodological issues is so great that a definitive study has yet to be conducted (e.g., Cantwell & Carson, 1978; Gadow, 1983; Sprague & Berger, 1980). Moreover, some recent studies of hyperactive children do support a treatment effect (see Gadow, 1983) on measures of academic productivity.

In the areas of reading, arithmetic, and spelling, stimulant drugs may enhance academic productivity. Methylphenidate (Ritalin), for example, was shown to improve performance on reading comprehension workbook assignments (Pelham, Bender, Caddell, Booth, & Moorer, 1985) and phonics workbook activities (Rapport, Murphy, & Bailey, 1982; Rapport, Stoner, Du Paul, Birmingham, & Tucker, 1985). Similarly, both methylphenidate (Pelham et al., 1985; Rapport et al., 1982, 1985; Sprague & Berger, 1980) and pemoline (Cylert) (Pelham, Swanson, Bender, & Wilson, 1980) improved performance on classroom arithmetic activities. The findings for spelling productivity are somewhat inconsistent. Pelham and his colleagues found that methylphenidate (Pelham et al., 1985) enhanced performance on weekly spelling tests but pemoline did not (Pelham et al., 1980). Both drugs did reduce spelling errors on a task involving nonsense words (Stephens, Pelham, & Skinner, 1984).

There is no doubt that stimulant drugs can improve handwriting in hyperactive children (e.g., Whalen, Henker, & Finck, 1981) and adolescents (Yellin, Hopwood, & Greenberg, 1982) and in children specifically selected on the basis of poor handwriting ability (Lerer, Lerer, & Artner, 1977). A number of published handwriting samples demonstrate the extraordinary effect that can be achieved in some cases (e.g., Gadow, 1986; Levy, 1973; Schain & Reynard, 1975; Taylor, 1979).

Relatively little pharmacotherapy research has been conducted on verbal communication disorders (Gadow, 1986). In highly structured settings with tasks designed to elicit verbal responses, methylphenidate has increased verbal productivity in hyperactive boys (Ludlow, Rapoport, Brown, & Mikkelson, 1979) and in children with cerebral dysfunction (Creager & Van Riper, 1967). In the former study, children with language impairments also showed improvement in language complexity. In hyperactive children who did not exhibit deficits in language complexity (Barkley, Cunningham, & Karlsson, 1983), methylphenidate reduced the number of verbalizations in both free and structured settings, with no concurrent change in complexity. Whalen, Collins, Henker, Alkus, Adams, and Stapp (1983) also found that methylphenidate significantly reduced task-irrelevant speech and reduced verbal productivity to a more normal level. Collectively, although these studies provide us with information about stimulants and hyperactive children, they tell us relatively little about the usefulness of stimulant medication for the treatment of communication disorders.

To date, there are only two large-scale studies of stimulant drug therapy for nonhyperactive LD children (Gittelman-Klein & Klein, 1976; Gittelman et al., 1983). In their earlier study, Gittelman-Klein and Klein (1976) randomly assigned 61 children to either methylphenidate or placebo conditions. All subjects were selected on the basis of being 2 years below reading grade level despite average intelligence, and most were receiving academic remediation in school. The research protocol called for the dosage to be increased from week 1 (10 mg, twice daily) to week 3 (30 mg, twice daily). For weeks 4 through 12, the best-tolerated dose was employed, which ranged from 20 to 60 mg. At the end of 4 weeks, the only statistically significant drug effect was for the WRAT arithmetic score (6 month superiority of the medicated over the placebo group). At the end of 12 weeks, however, arithmetic differences were trivial (2 months), but the WRAT reading score difference approached significance ($p = .06$). This is noteworthy because the WRAT is not particularly sensitive to short-term drug effects. The WRAT spelling scores were unaffected by medication. At the end of 12 weeks, teacher global ratings of reading and arithmetic performance did not discriminate between the two treatment groups. Based on these and other findings, Gittelman-Klein and Klein concluded that methylphenidate was not an effective agent for the remediation of reading deficits in nonhyperactive LD children. However, they also noted that treatment effects may be manifested only in the presence of a specialized academic intervention.

To test this hypothesis, Gittelman et al. (1983) randomly assigned nonhyperactive reading retarded children to one of three groups: (a) reading remediation (phonics program) and placebo, (b) academic tutoring (without reading instruction) and placebo, and (c) reading remediation and methylphenidate (60 mg/day contingent on the absence of side effects). The duration of intervention was 18 weeks. The results indicated that although medication did enhance cognitive task performance, it did not facilitate academic achievement (as measured by the WRAT and Gray Oral Reading Test). However, some additional achievement measures did show drug effects or trends favoring the medication-treated group, suggesting that the effect of methylphenidate on reading instruction was not a strong one. Quite unexpectedly, medication did enhance other areas of academic skill performance, namely arithmetic and social studies, which were not part of the reading program. However, a retest of these academic skills 8 months after the termination of treatment failed to show residual drug effects.

It is difficult to draw conclusions about the role of stimulant drugs in the treatment of learning disabilities because many findings are contradictory, and many issues are only partially explored. The most encouraging results are from studies that have employed measures of academic productivity, such as number of items completed or percentage correct (e.g., Bradley & Bowen, 1940; Pelham et al., 1980; Pelham et al., 1985; Rapport et al., 1982, 1985; Sprague & Berger, 1980; Stephens et al., 1984; Sulzbacher, 1972), although there are negative findings as well (Ayllon, Layman, & Kandel, 1975; Rapport, Murphy, & Bailey, 1980; Wolraich, Drummond, Salomon, O'Brien, & Sivage, 1978). The most discouraging results appear in research with standardized achievement test scores as the dependent variable (see Barkley & Cunningham, 1978). The extent to which drug response on these two groups of dependent measures correlate is not currently known.

Most of our existing knowledge is based on group comparisons, and very little research has been done with treatment (i.e., academic performance) responders selected a priori on the basis of a short-term, drug-placebo crossover. The fact that some children do react to medication with academic improvement has been demonstrated; that responders may share other common characteristics such as favorable clinical response (Loney, Kramer, & Milich, 1981), absence of severe learning disability, or above average IQ, is certainly worthy of investigation.

Little can be said about the configuration of subject, treatment (e.g., dosage), task, and setting (e.g., type of educational intervention) variables that produce short-term therapeutic improvement. Moreover, one would predict that if medication increased on-task behavior and academic productivity, over a period of time this would lead to enhanced skill acquisition and retention. Unfortunately, the follow-up treatment literature does not support this hypothesis.

LONG-TERM STUDIES

Drug studies that involve protracted treatment periods are commonly referred to as being long term. The actual time frame is arbitrary, but most investigators would probably accept treatment periods of somewhere between 6 to 12 months as a minimum criterion. There are really two subgroups of long-term studies, and they differ with regard to whether or not treatment has been administered on a continuous basis up to the point of assessment. If it has, the primary objective is efficacy, and in this sense, the long-term study is comparable to the short-term clinical trials. Nevertheless, short- and long-term drug studies of academic achievement differ in some very important ways as well. For example, none of the long-term studies have used placebo controls. If medication has been discontinued for a substantial period of time prior to assessment, the investigation is really addressing the residual benefits of treatment and may be more appropriately referred to as an outcome or follow-up study. In actual practice, however, the medication group may consist of youngsters who are in various stages of treatment, which makes classification impossible. For these and other reasons, all investigations that involve treatment periods of at least 1 year in duration are referred to here as long-term studies.

There are several different types of long-term studies of hyperactive children that attempt to assess the impact of treatment on academic performance. One type of study compares a treated hyperactive sample with a normal comparison group (e.g., Blouin, Bornstein, & Trites, 1978; Hechtman, Weiss, & Perlman, 1984; Riddle & Rapoport, 1976; Weiss, Kruger, Danielson, & Elman, 1975). Collectively, these studies show that stimulant drug therapy does not normalize the academic achievement of hyperactive children.

A second type of investigation, which does not contain a comparison group as such, looks to see if the treated group improves over the course of time (e.g., Huessy, Metoyer, & Townsend, 1974; Mendelson, Johnson & Stewart 1971; Minde, Weiss, & Mendelson, 1972). In general, the findings from these investigations are discouraging in that academic deficits persist, even with pharmacotherapy.

Studies that compare medication-treated subjects with a variously treated hyperactive contrast group constitute a third category. The latter includes children who received (a) medication for a brief period (Hechtman et al., 1984; Weiss et al., 1975), (b) medication or placebo for a moderately short period and are essentially treatment dropouts (Charles & Schain, 1981; Quinn & Rapoport, 1975; Riddle & Rapoport, 1976; Satterfield, Satterfield, & Cantwell, 1981), and (c) no medication at all (Blouin et al., 1978; Loney, Kramer, & Kosier, 1981). Ideally, a randomly assigned placebo control group comprised of drug responders should serve as a comparison group in outcome research. However, for a number of practical and ethical reasons, the formulation of such a group is probably an impossibility.

There are at least 11 published long-term (1 year of treatment or more) studies in which drug- and nondrug- (or minimally) treated hyperactive individuals were compared during childhood, adolescence, or adulthood with regard to academic performance. These studies represent six treatment samples, several of which were the subject of two or more research reports.

Montreal Children's Hospital

Weiss et al. (1975) followed three groups of hyperactive children for 5 years after initial evaluation. One group (N = 24) was treated with methylphenidate; mean age at initial evaluation was 8.0 years, dosage ranged from 20 mg/day, in two divided doses, to 50 mg/day, in three divided doses (mean = 30 mg/day), and the duration of treatment ranged from 3 to 6 years (mean = 4.3 years). Dosage was titrated according to behavioral response and was reevaluated (drug-free periods) on a periodic basis; compliance was calculated to be at 80%; and all outcome testing was conducted off medication, which required the withdrawal of medication in 12 cases 2 weeks prior to evaluation. The methylphenidate group originally consisted of 50 subjects. Children who had received medication for less than 3 years were excluded from the follow-up. In general, the omitted cases were considered "poor responders," and their inclusion would have negatively biased this treatment condition. The second group (N = 22) was treated with chlorpromazine (Thorazine); mean age at initial evaluation was 8.2 years, dosage ranged from 50 mg/day, in three divided doses, to 200 mg/day, in three divided doses (mean = 75 mg/day), and the duration of treatment ranged from 18 months to 5 years (mean = 30 months). However, in only a few cases did the treatment regimen extend beyond 2 years. Dosage was reevaluated (drug-free periods) on a periodic basis; compliance (ascertained from parent and patient reports) was calculated to be more than 80%; and all outcome testing was conducted off medication, which required the withdrawal of treatment in two cases. The third group consisted of children (N = 20) who had not received medication (usually chlorpromazine) for more than 4 months. Mean age at initial assessment was 8.2 years. All three groups were matched with regard to age. IQ, socioeconomic class, and sex.

Because all subjects in each group were initially assessed sometime between 1962 and 1967, a diagnosis of learning disability was not rendered in appropriate cases. Therefore, the prevalence of learning disabilities in these samples is unknown. However, Weiss and her colleagues did conduct a 5-year follow-up study of 37 children who were diagnosed in 1965 as being hyperactive and evaluated their academic progress (Minde et al., 1971). Twenty percent of the sample had received medication (either chlorpromazine or dextroamphetamine [Dexedrine]) for a period of 6 months to 4 years. A comparison group (N = 37) was formulated by pairing the hyperactive child with a classmate. The mean ages of the hyperactive and comparison groups were 11.0 years and 12.0 years, respectively. All hyperactive children had a WISC IQ score of at least 85 and were enrolled in regular classes. The results showed that the hyperactive group, compared with the control group, was more apt to have repeated one or more grades

(57% versus 16%), received significantly lower academic ratings (report cards) in all academic subjects, and scored lower on group administered intelligence tests (IQ 102 versus IQ 112, $p < .001$). Moreover, the majority of the hyperactive sample seemed to perform more poorly in school than would be predicted on the basis of their WISC IQ score. Interestingly, teacher ratings of academic performance were unrelated to teacher ratings of the severity of the child's behavior problems. Although comparison between subgroups from each sample matched on the basis of IQ did not reveal statistically significant differences in grade retentions, the hyperactive sample was clearly inferior with regard to academic performance. Investigations into the report card record of the hyperactive subjects in the 3 years prior to the outcome analysis revealed a consistent pattern of academic performance.

Weiss et al. (1975) compared the three groups with regard to the number of children who had been retained one or more grades and reported the following: methylphenidate (46%), chlorpromazine (55%), and "untreated" (70%). The performance discrepancies were not statistically significant. A more in-depth analysis of academic achievement was conducted by comparing the difference between the methylphenidate group and an individually matched group of classroom controls with the difference between Minde et al.'s (1971) group and their individually matched classroom controls. The methylphenidate group ($N = 24$) and Minde's therapeutically mixed (none had received stimulants for more than 6 months) group ($N = 37$) were matched by age at follow-up, WISC IQ, socioeconomic status, sex, and degree of hyperactivity at initial assessment. The dependent measure was report card grades that had been converted to a 3-point scale. The results indicated that there were no significant differences between the two groups of matched pairs on academic grades in reading, language, arithmetic, French, or spelling. In the methylphenidate group, the only predictor (initial assessment variable) for a favorable outcome (e.g., academic achievement) was a good family situation.

In discussing these findings, Weiss et al. noted that an acquired tolerance for the therapeutic effects of stimulant medication was not a satisfactory explanation for their findings. They noted, however, that there were some intergroup differences. For example, the methylphenidate-treated subjects did evidence more serious cognitive deficits than the other two groups. More important was their disclaimer pertaining to the possible insensitivity of the dependent measures to drug effects.

Hechtman et al. (1984) conducted a 10- to 12-year follow-up of hyperactive children ($N = 20$; mean age $= 21.8$ years) who were originally diagnosed in 1967, and who received continuous treatment with stimulant drugs for a minimum of 3 years. Twenty-five of the children in the initial patient group were the subject of a 5-year follow-up during adolescence

(Weiss et al., 1975). A comparison sample (N = 20) who were free of behavior and academic problems when in school was identified by mailing letters to former classmates of the hyperactive youths. A second group of hyperactive individuals (N = 68; mean age = 19.6 years) whose adult status was described in earlier reports (Hechtman, Weiss, Perlman, Hopkins, & Wener, 1979; Weiss, Hechtman, Perlman, Hopkins, & Wener, 1979), served as an "untreated" control group. However, this latter group was initially diagnosed 5 years prior to the medicated sample and subsequently entered adulthood at an earlier period of time. All three groups were matched on IQ and socioeconomic class, but due to differences in subject selection procedures, the stimulant-treated group was 2.2 years older than the untreated group. The results showed that the drug-treated group had completed slightly more years of education (11.0 years) than the untreated sample (10.4 years). The two groups were also very similar in the number of grades failed in high school (drug = 50%; untreated = 46%). Interestingly, even though the untreated group was younger than the drug-treated group at follow-up assessment, more members of the former (29%) were enrolled in postsecondary education than the latter (15%).

Georgetown University Hospital

In 1974, Rapoport, Quinn, Bradbard, Riddle, and Brooks reported the results of a study of 76 hyperactive grade-school boys from middle-class families who were treated with either methylphenidate (N = 29), imipramine (N = 29), or placebo (N = 18). The maximum dose of methylphenidate was 30 mg (mean = 20 mg) administered in the morning, and the maximum dose of imipramine was 150 mg (mean = 80 mg) administered in two divided doses. Although teacher global ratings of academic achievement indicated a methylphenidate-enhancing effect, comparisons between WRAT reading, spelling, and math scores at baseline (off medication) and at 6 weeks (on treatment) were not statistically significant (see also Barcley & Cunningham, 1978). No descriptive data were provided about academic performance or a diagnosis of learning disability. Following the 6-week drug evaluation, patients were returned to the care of their family physician.

The 1-year follow-up of this group of patients also failed to demonstrate a drug effect on academic achievement (Quinn & Rapoport, 1975). Of the 76 original subjects, 36 received medication (methylphenidate [N = 23] and imipramine [N = 13]) for a full year. A comparison group (N = 12) consisted of subjects who had shown a clinical response but whose treatment regimens were terminated for various reasons. The median daily doses of methylphenidate and imipramine were 20.7 mg ± 8.6 mg and 64.5 mg ± 19.2 mg, respectively, and they were usually administered in divided doses. No data were provided on compliance. The results yielded no statistically significant differences between the three groups on WRAT standard scores at baseline (off medication) and at the end of 1 year (on medication for drug groups and off medicaton for "no treatment" group). Quinn and Rapoport noted that the "no treatment" group composed of treatment dropouts could have biased the results, although they did not appear to differ from the treated groups. "Adverse home or school influences as well as the constitutional endowment of the child might have been confounded with the discontinuation of treatment" (p. 244).

Riddle and Rapoport (1976) also conducted a 2-year follow-up study of this same patient group (N = 72; mean age = 10.2 years). At the end of 2 years, 47 boys were still receiving medication, which was withdrawn for experimental purposes at least 3 weeks prior to the outcome assessment. Of the 47 on medication, 40 were receiving stimulants (mean dose = 32.8 mg/day) and 7 were receiving imipramine (mean dose = 100 mg/day). When the on-medication group was withdrawn from treatment, 50% of the teachers and 30% of the parents reported a deterioration in behavior, which suggests a pattern of limited efficacy in a number of cases. More than half of the entire sample had received special education or psychiatric help. Many of the children were probably learning-disabled considering the fact that "15 children had repeated one or more grades, 14 were attending special schools, and 12 others received special tutorial assistance" (p. 128). Riddle and Rapoport found no change in WRAT reading scores over the 2-year period for the entire sample (N = 72) and a significant decrease in math scores. (There was a statistically significant negative correlation between age and mathematics scale scores [r = .53]). Of the boys who had been maintained on stimulants for the entire 2-year period (i.e., no placebo trial or crossover to imipramine), their WRAT scores were virtually identical to the test scores for the entire sample. No academic performance data were provided on the difference between the continuous treatment group (N = 20) and the dropouts (off medication for 1 or more years; N = 25), but presumably it was slight. Riddle and Rapoport noted that the fact the active treatment group was tested off medication was a major methodological problem with regard to interpeting the academic performance findings. However, if outcome testing had been conducted on medication, any improvement in WRAT scores could be attributed to the attention-enhancing characteristics of the drug (baseline measures were obtained off medication).

Royal Ottawa Hospital

Blouin et al. (1978) conducted a 5-year follow-up of cases selected from clinic files that were retrospectively diagnosed and classified by the investigators. Of the 119 cases available for follow-up contact, 42 were

were diagnosed as hyperactive, 49 had school difficulty, and 28 were originally referred to the clinic for other reasons. In the hyperactive group, 27 had been treated with methylphenidate and the remaining 15 subjects had not received pharmacotherapy. Information about the drug regimen was obtained retrospectively from parent reports at outcome assessment. Data on dosage, schedule, duration of treatment, noncompliance, and monitoring procedures were either incomplete or unavailable. Mean duration of treatment ($N = 25$) was 1.9 years, and the mean daily dose ($N = 15$) was 20 mg. Although descriptive information on the academic performance of the drug group was limited, it is noteworthy that at initial assessment and follow-up, differences between the hyperactive group and the school difficulty (learning or reading disabilities) group on WRAT scores were not statistically significant. In other words, many of the children in the hyperactive group were learning-disabled. All initial assessments were made off medication, but some hyperactive children (number not specified) were evaluated at follow-up on medication. A comparison between drug- and nondrug-treated hyperactive subjects revealed no significant differences in academic achievement (WRAT) either at initial assessment or at follow-up. However, there were significant ($p = .094$) differences between these two groups on the Hyperactivity factor of the Teacher Rating Scale (Conners, 1970). Similarly, a comparison between good ($N = 15$) and poor ($N = 12$) responders, according to parent judgments revealed no statistically significant differences in academic achievement either at initial assessment or at follow-up.

UCLA Department of Pediatrics

Charles and Schain (1981) reevaluated a group of 98 hyperactive children who, 4 years previously, had participated in a 16-week drug study (see Schain & Reynard, 1975). In the initial treatment study, children were randomly assigned to either methylphenidate or placebo. The final average daily dose of methylphenidate ranged from 0.2 mg/kg to 1.9 mg/kg (with an average morning dose of 0.6 mg/kg) administered in two divided doses if necessary. (The exact number who received divided doses was not specified.) No data were presented on academic performance or the presence of learning disabilities in the sample.

The follow-up investigation located 70 children, of whom 62 participated in the study; age (mean = 12.3 years), male ($N = 49$), WISC IQ (mean = 104; range = 78 to 138), socioeconomic class (middle income), and initial positive therapeutic drug response ($N = 52$). Twelve children were still receiving medication at follow-up. Information pertaining to monitoring the treatment regimen, compliance, and dosage of medication was not provided. Academic performance at follow-up was as follows:

teachers judged 74% and 69% to be below grade level in reading and mathematics, respectively; 34% repeated one or more grades; 42% were in special education classes; and 24% were being tutored. Only one third of the children were in regular classes and at the expected grade level without support services. In order to determine if longer treatment with stimulants was associated with a more favorable outcome, the subjects were separated into five categories: (a) drug failures and placebo successes (none treated for more than 5 months; $N = 13$), (b) treated 7 to 23 months ($N = 10$), (c) treated 2 to 3 years ($N = 14$), (d) treated 3 to 4 years ($N = 13$), and (e) still receiving medication at follow-up ($N = 12$). Only the last group was evaluated on medication at the follow-up assessment. There were no statistically significant differences among the five groups with regard to sex, age, IQ, or initial severity of symptoms. Nevertheless, the fact that the on-medication group received a relatively high level of education support services suggests that the duration of treatment may be related to the severity of educational disability. There were no statistically significant differences (Chi-square tests) among the group in teacher judgments of academic performance, repeated grades, or special education services. However, on the basis of sample size alone, it is questionable whether less than 20% of the expected cell frequencies were below 5 (see Siegel, 1956). Charles and Schain also calculated the differences between (a) expected grade level and WRAT math, reading recognition, and spelling scores and (b) chronological age and several PIAT achievement scores. Seventy-seven percent of the youngsters were 2 or more years below grade level on one or more of the PIAT or WRAT subtests. However, there were no statistically significant differences between groups on any of these standardized achievement test scores.

University of Iowa

Loney, Kramer, and Kosier (1981) evaluated the adolescent status of 51 boys (mean age = 15.2 years) who met the diagnostic criteria for hyperkinesis/minimal brain dysfunction. Each child was initially assigned to one of two staff psychiatrists, each of whom preferred a different therapeutic modality, resulting in two treatment groups: stimulant medication ($N = 26$) and behavioral counseling ($N = 25$). Although group assignment was not random, it was not systematically made according to a child's IQ, socioeconomic status, or symptoms. All but one of the drug-treated subjects received medication for at least 6 months (mean maintenance dosage of methylphenidate = 37.8 mg/day, mean duration of treatment = 24.7 months, 63% received no drug-free periods). Information about noncompliance and verification of treatment response was not provided. Approximately 80% of the children in each group received school remediation. In addition, a majority of the children and/or their families received psychotherapy and/or counseling. Loney et al. used conventional stepwise regression analysis with academic achievement (WRAT scores) as the dependent measure, and eight referral variables as predictors. Treatment status (i.e., medication versus no medication) was entered as the final predictor. With this procedure, relevant referral characteristics were controlled before assessing the relationship between treatment status and academic achievement, which unfortunately, was not statistically significant.

Gateways Hospital (Los Angeles)

Satterfield and his colleagues reported on a 1-year (Satterfield, Cantwell, & Satterfield, 1979), 2-year (Satterfield, Satterfield, & Cantwell, 1980), and a 3-year (Satterfield et al., 1981) follow-up of a clinic population of 117 hyperactive children who were originally diagnosed between 1973 and 1974. At intake, all subjects were between 6 and 12 years old. At the end of 1 year, the average daily dosage of methylphenidate was 25 mg, typically administered in two divided doses. Compliance was routinely assessed (urinalysis) and behavioral procedures were employed to ensure compliance. Drug-free periods were generally scheduled for weekends and summers, and treatment efficacy was routinely monitored. On the basis of predicted grade-level scores (PIAT), the group was one-half to one grade level behind academically in all subjects (despite normal intelligence) before the onset of therapy, and 39% were receiving special-education services at the end of 1 year of treatment. The treatment clinic provided each child-family dyad with an individualized multimodality treatment package that included pharmacological, educational, and psychological interventions.

The 3-year follow-up evaluation compared the outcome of a treatment dropout group (less treatment) that received medication for less than 2 years ($N = 44$; mean duration of treatment = 9 months) and maximum treatment group (more treatment) that was treated from 2 to 3 years ($N = 56$; mean duration of treatment = 35 months). The two groups were comparable on a host of initial assessment measures, all of which were made off medication. At follow-up, 36 subjects were evaluated on medication, but group status was not specified. Satterfield et al. calculated PIAT lag scores by subtracting each child's observed PIAT score from the predicted PIAT score. Although the differences between the lag scores for the two groups were not statistically significant at initial assessment, the more-treatment group had significantly lower lag scores for mathematics, reading recognition, reading comprehension, general information, and total test performance. The general pattern of results was a marked deterioration in academic achievement in the group that received less treatment and improved performance in the group that received more treatment. Because the children and their families received multiple treatments, the contribution of medication to this favorable outcome cannot be determined.

Evidence for Residual Benefits

Eleven long-term studies of drug versus nondrug- or minimally drug-treated hyperactive children, many of whom experienced marked achievement problems, have been published. With the exception of one study (Satterfield et al., 1981), their findings uniformly support the conclusion that stimulant drug therapy does not enhance academic achievement, at least in terms of altering adolescent or adult outcome. Nevertheless, due to a number of methodological problems, the issue is not yet resolved. Moreover, there may very well be a subgroup of children in this treatment population for which medication does play a role in academic skill acquisition.

A much more difficult question is whether stimulant drugs alter school performance by enhancing some other important outcome variable. For example, the well-documented fact that stimulant drugs increase on-task behavior (Whalen, Henker, Collins, Finck, & Dotemoto, 1979), increase tolerance for overlearning (Ackerman & Dykman, 1982), and improve academic productivity suggests a possible mechanism for the higher level of self-esteen reported in some studies (e.g., Hechtman et al., 1984; Loney, Kramer, & Kosier, 1981). Unquestionably, our greatest interest in academic achievement stems from the belief that it is the key to socioeconomic success. Although the parameters of socioeconomic success (e.g., personal or family income, job satisfaction) have yet to demonstrate treatment reactivity (see, for example, Hechtman et al., 1984), it is purely speculation that academic performance deficits contribute markedly to these findings.

METHODOLOGICAL ISSUES

The oft-cited methodological difficulties associated with long-term studies include the impracticality of random assignment of subjects to treatment conditions, the ethical dilemma of protracted placebo controls, uncertainty over the ideal yardstick for dosage titration, pre- and post-assessments under different conditions (off medication and on medication), subject attrition, and the potential for bias by formulating "no treatment" comparison groups from nonresponders, adverse responders, and/or treatment rejectors. Additional problems are patient noncompliance (Sleator, 1985), potential inaccuracies of retrospective diagnoses, incomplete data base at initial assessment, inadequate dependent measures, poor monitoring of the treatment regimen (e.g., failure to use drug-free periods to reevaluate efficacy of treatment), sample size too small for the number of dependent measures or for complex statistical analyses, counterproductive treatment-generated patient attributions (Whalen & Henker, 1976), failure to exclude potential placebo responders from the drug responder group (noncrossed designs) or to administer medication in divided doses to prolong the therapeutic effect (Swanson & Kinsbourne, 1978; Swanson, Kinsbourne, Roberts, & Zucker, 1978), general failure to administer medication in contexts that maximize drug effects (Pelham, 1983), concurrent therapies that may either confound the interpretation of results or interact with the response to medication (Pelham, 1983), less-than-adquate description of learning disabilities, and the initation of treatment too long after the course of academic failure has already been established (Weiss, 1979). Interestingly, the disenchantment with the negative findings for academic achievement on the basis of methodological flaws does not come anywhere near the clamor that is often raised for positive findings (i.e., therapeutic benefit).

Perhaps the most important methodological issue concerning the evaluation of psychotropic drug effects on academic performance center on the selection of appropriate dependent measures (see Gadow & Swanson, 1985). Assessment procedures employed in both short- and long-term drug studies have changed very little since Bradley and Bowen's (1940) and Molitch and Sullivan's (1937) early studies, which employed measures of academic productivity and standardized achievement tests, respectively. Clearly, there should be more discussion about the way in which academic performance should be assessed in drug studies and the applicability of newer methods.

Although the methodological flaws inherent in long-term studies of hyperactive children preclude an adequate empirical test of drug effect, they are generally of much less relevance for the evaluation of typical treatment practices (Lasagna, 1974). In other words, whereas short-term studies are designed to assess drug *effects*, follow-up studies typically evaluate drug *therapy* in natural settings. In this sense, the existing literature probably provides a fairly accurate picture of the kinds of treatment effects that the clinician can generally expect.

PATIENT'S PERSPECTIVE

Very little information is currently available about the child's perception of drug-induced changes in academic performance. As part of one follow-up evaluation (Gadow & Sprague, 1980) of 24 male adolescents who were diagnosed as being hyperactive during their elementary school years and subsequently treated with stimulant drugs (see also Sleator, von Neumann, & Sprague, 1974), the subjects ($N = 22$) participated in an extended interview about their perception of the pharmacotherapy experience. When asked, "Did the medication make a difference in your schoolwork," only one youth responded negatively. In specifying the nature of the change (many subjects noted multiple improvements), three-fourths cited increased productivity (52%) and/or improved quality (48%) of school assignments. Sample comments were "I usually got more accomplished," "got better grades," and "got into it more." One third noted enhanced mental abilities such as improved concentration and longer attention span. The following excerpt from an interview with a 14-year-old male (duration of treatment: 4 to 5 years; current status: on medication) is an example of a positive attribution:

Interviewer: Why did you take the medicine?
Youth: I think to calm me down.

Interviewer: You think?
Youth: It really did because since I've been taking it my grades used to be C's and now they're up to A's and B's.

[Later]

Interviewer: What was your most important reason for taking the medicine?
Youth: If I got low grades all the way through school, I wouldn't be able to get into a college or something of my choice. That was the reason I had.

A number of adolescents commented on the drug's effect on motivation. One 15 year old (duration of treatment: over 6 years; current status: on medication), for example, said:

Interviewer: Did you feel any different?
Youth: It makes me feel kind of different.

Interviewer: Can you describe that at all?
Youth: It made me do my school work, but I didn't want to do it. I took control of me and made me do it anyway.

Another youth (age: 16 years; duration of treatment: 2 years; current status: off medication) commented as follows:

Interviewer: Can you explain the feeling [of the medication]?
Youth: I felt, at first when I started taking it, that I always wanted to read a book or something; but it would wear off or something, and I would be like normal.

Interviewer: When you took it you would feel like reading a book?
Youth: Yes. I wanted to read something all the time. I don't know why; it would just always affect me like that, and I hate reading.

These comments are most interesting because over four decades ago in his pioneering paper on amphetamine sulfate (Benzedrine) in children with behavior disorders, Bradley (1937) explained the increases in academic productivity, comprehension, and accuracy in the medicated children that he observed as a "drive' to accomplish as much work as possible during the school period" (p. 578).

Some students expressed concerns about the consequences of not taking medicine as seen in the following excerpt from an interview with a 14 year old (duration of treatment: 7 to 8 years; current status: on medication):

> Interviewer: Did you notice anything when you would forget?
> Youth: Yes, because I would get to school and I wouldn't be able to concentrate . . . . and sometimes when I knew I was going to have a test and say "Oh, no, I didn't take my pill! I'll flunk it. Oh, my god!" That was the worst thing in the world to flunk a test back then [elementary school] because I thought you flunk a test and you never will succeed in life!

It is true that the subjective impressions of these youths simply may reflect the explanations or perceptions (and even misperceptions) of their caregivers. It is equally plausible, however, that some of the children actually noticed drug-induced changes in their academic performance. Bradley (1937), for example, observed that "insight into school improvement was generally present, though few of the children attributed it to the medication they had received earlier in the day" (p. 578). (It should be noted that Bradley took precautions to prevent the staff from influencing the children's responses.) Moreover, although a compelling demonstration of drug-induced improvement in standardized achievement test performance is lacking, there is substantial evidence that stimulants do increase on-task behavior and academic productivity, at least in some cases. For some children, this is a pleasant experience. "Medication is at best a crutch, but if in the long run it enables the child to experience success and a sense of being loved and appreciated, it is well justified" (Bradley, 1957, p. 1056). One of our interviewees described this feeling as follows:

> Interviewer: Would you say the medication made you feel good?
> Youth: Not make me feel happy. But it made me feel better that I was doing better in school.

Some attention has been focused on the possibility that children's attributions concerning pharmacotherapy may undermine therapeutic progress by leading patients to believe that they cannot facilitate their own improvement (Whalen & Henker, 1976). However, the extent to which this is a serious clinical problem has been questioned (Rapoport, 1980; Sleator, Ullmann, & von Neumann, 1982; Weiss, 1981). The following excerpt from an interview with a 16-year-old youth (duration of treatment: 1 to 2 years; current status: off medication) who evaluated medication very favorably indicates that some children, in fact many (see Sleator et al., 1982), are eager to take charge of their problems:

> Interviewer: How did it [medication] do that [learn more]?
> Youth: I didn't used to listen to the teacher to what she was talking about

*and then I did and I learned more, studied a little bit and got bet-
ter grades.*

[Later]

Interviewer: How were you feeling at the time you made that decision
[to terminate treatment]?
*Youth: I felt like I was doing a lot more in my studies in school and all. I
thought I could do it myself without something helping me all the time.*

At first blush, the causal attributions generated by drug treatment
would appear to pale in comparison with a powerful drug response, and
the notation that they play a clinically significant role in altering the magnitude of the drug's effect on adolescent and adult outcome seems highly
speculative. Nevertheless, Rosen, O'Leary, and Conway (1983) described a
case study that, even with its acknowledged limitations, provides some insight into the importance of attribution in at least some cases over a short
term. They described the case of a 9-year-old hyperactive boy receiving
methylphenidate (dose = 5 mg/b.i.d.; duration of treatment = 18 months)
who had enrolled in a behavior therapy-oriented laboratory school for
hyperactive children. During the first 2 weeks of school, the dosage was reduced to 2.5 mg/b.i.d., after which the parents ran out of medication for 4
days. During this time, the child volunteered comments such as, "My pills
make me get done with work." The off-medication period was followed by
the administration of a placebo, twice a day, for 4 weeks. The percentage of
time on-task and academic work assignments completed were as follows: 2.5
mg/b.i.d. (on-task = 57%; academic = 83%), off medication (on-task = 15%;
academic = 52%), and placebo (on-task = 64%; academic = 87%). A brief
attribution training exercise led to the successful withdrawal of placebo.

SUMMARY

At the present time, any statement pertaining to the role of stimulant
drugs in the amelioration of learning disabilities must be qualified. The
findings from short-term investigations using standardized achievement
test scores suggest that if an achievement-enhancing effect exists, it is not
robust, and the results of long-term studies are uniformly negative. Nevertheless, there is a growing number of short-term studies of hyperactive
children that clearly show a marked treatment effect on measures of academic productivity. The significance of these findings is a matter of debate.
It would be premature to conclude that stimulants do not enhance
academic skill acquisition and retention or that clinical experimentation is
unwarranted. However, in each and every instance when academic deficits
are identified as a target of pharmacological intervention, treatment should

be faithfully monitored to include periodic assessment of treatment effects. The clinician would be well advised to employ a placebo crossover, periodic drug-free treatment assessment, and, of course, measures of academic productivity. The latter can consist of weekly evaluations of classroom assignment completion or any one of a number of automated or computerized learning machines in wide use in our public schools that provide both frequency and accuracy data.

Enthusiasm for medication-induced achievement gains must be balanced against the efficacy, practicality, and availability of alternative therapies. There are no data to suggest that stimulant drug treatment is superior to an *effective* educational intervention and there is only very limited support for the notion that it even enhances one (see Gadow, 1985; Gadow, Torgesen, Greenstein, & Schell, 1985). However, Pelham, Milich, and Walker (1986) completed a study that did show an additive effect when medication and contingent reward were used in combination. Pelham (1983, 1985) has also noted that (a) research in this area is limited; (b) there are some data to suggest that there is an interaction between the dose of methylphenidate and the efficacy or presence of concurrent interventions; and (c) the superiority of behavioral therapies is generally based on the results of studies that have employed measures of academic productivity, when these very measures are often disregarded as proof of a drug effect. Moreover, neither the efficacy of longer-term academically-oriented behavior therapy nor the long-term residual benefits of educational interventions has received much empirical scrutiny. Surprisingly, although there is a host of purported treatments for hyperactivity (only some of which have been compared with medication), few have been evaluated for their effect on academic performance (see Gadow, 1985).

Bradley's (1937) astute clinical observations regarding stimulants and academic performance still point the direction for future scientific inquiry: namely, the identification of treatment sensitive tasks and a descriptive analysis of drug responders. These goals may best be achieved by interdisciplinary, and possibly multicenter (see O'Leary, 1980) research teams. However, at this juncture, intensive (Chassan, 1979) single-subject analysis designs may be more prudent than traditional group comparison studies. At the very least, the former could be used as pre-placement procedures for the latter. As an aside, when group comparisons are employed, careful consideration should be given to multivariate designs and analyses (see Loney, Kramer, & Kosier, 1981). Researchers should also consider the feasibility of including academic performance measures in intervention studies with hyperactive and/or LD children, even when the expressed symptomatologic target of therapy is not academic skill acquisition or retention. In addition to the obvious cost benefits of such a proposal, it would permit a determination of the generalization of treatment effects to academic behaviors.

ACKNOWLEDGMENT

The author gratefully acknowledges the assistance of the following people for their comments and suggestions on a preliminary draft of this paper: Jan Loney, Susan O'Leary, Mark Rapport, Lee Rosen, and James Satterfield. The preparation of this paper was supported, in part, by grant MH 18909 from the National Institute of Mental Health.

CHAPTER 10

Family Intervention

David M. O'Hara
Judith M. Levy

Although the subject of family adaptation to a child having a learning disability has certainly been approached before, an extensive review of the literature has not been undertaken. Learning disability falls within the general classification of developmental disabilities. As such, both the learning disability and a family's ability to cope with a child having the disability have much in common with other disorders within this group. These include cerebral palsy, mental retardation, and autism. On the other hand, each of these disabilities has specific qualities that distinguish it from others in its functional and emotional impact on the child and family. The frameworks that will be discussed have been developed to enable professionals to better understand the individual and family dynamics associated with the impact of having a developmentally disabled child. Although for the most part, these theories have been developed by authors working with more seriously physically and mentally disabled children, they are relevant and useful to our understanding of LD children and their families. This chapter first reviews the literature pertaining to the general effect of a developmentally disabled child on a family (see Crnic, Friedrick, &

This chapter originally appeared as an article by **David M. O'Hara** and **Judith M. Levy** in *Learning Disabilities: An Interdisciplinary Journal* (Vol. III (6) 63–77), 1984) and was adapted by permission of Grune & Stratton for inclusion in this *Handbook*.

Greenberg, 1983, for a comprehensive review), and then discusses the specific case of learning disability.

THEORETICAL PERSPECTIVES

Miller (1968) suggested that parents normally progress through three stages of adjustment after hearing the news that they have a disabled child. The first of these stages is one of shock and disorganization and is characterized by individuals as "falling apart." Denial of the problem is seen as the hallmark of this stage and is necessary to avoid the emotional impact of facing reality. After the first stage, adjustment to the reality of the disability begins. During the second stage parents experience sorrow or grief, but the characteristic theme of this period seems to be the ambivalence parents experience as they partly accept and partly deny the disability. Equally characteristic is the apparent anger parents feel and the manifestation of this anger in their efforts to blame others, particularly professionals, for their child's disability. During this period, professionals describe parents as being egocentric and particularly difficult to work with. The final stage of adjustment Miller calls *reintegration*. After a period of time, people appear to be able to pull themselves together and to function more effectively and with some basis in reality. The family is able to find a place for the disabled child within their family structure. Parents appear able to go on meeting their own needs as well as those of other children within the family unit.

It is apparent from this description that Miller's framework is similar to that discussed by Kubler–Ross (1969) in describing the stages experienced by persons grieving the death or loss of a loved one. In fact, the concept of loss is pertinent to the emotional experience of parents learning that they have a disabled child, rather than the child they had expected. During a pregnancy, parents fantasize about, and consciously plan for, the birth of the baby who will meet their desire for the perfect child. This child will not only have the correct number of fingers and toes, but will also have the ambition and ability to carry out the dreams of the parent. This idealized child is the one that is lost and grieved over after the diagnosis of a developmental disability is made (Olshansky, 1962). For parents of the LD child, the impact of a diagnosis may not be shock and disorganization, because the diagnosis is often made much later, perhaps after school age. By this time, parents may be only too happy to hear a diagnosis that confirms their own suspicions and gives them an explanation for a set of previously undefined behaviors.

The drawback to theories outlining stages is, of course, that despite professionals' efforts to pigeonhole individuals and families, rarely is it so simple. The progression is not always in the proper order, regressions occur, and symptoms from one stage appear in another. The value of describing behaviors and emotions such as these is that it generates a range of what is expectable and suggests interventions that emphasize normalcy rather than pathology and that supports families.

The concept of normalcy is important in understanding families dealing with disability. Parents expect that children will develop according to predictable, cognitive, physical, and emotional norms. There will be good times and bad, satisfactions and dissatisfactions, but ultimately children grow up, become independent, and leave the nest to form their own families. In the case of a child with a learning disability, as with other disabilities, these expectations may be in jeopardy after the initial diagnosis. This lack of predictable milestones means that parents must learn to live with uncertainty.

Parents experience an assault to their ego integrity when they realize that they have produced a disabled child. This child, who is a direct extension of themselves, is imperfect, and may not meet usual standards for success. The normal response of parents may well be a period of denial in order to avoid being emotionally overwhelmed while they gradually adapt to reality. According to Wolfensberger (1967), families with disabled members have needs arising from three major sources: novelty shock, value crisis, and reality stress. Novelty shock normally occurs when parents learn that the child they had expected has not been born, and that, instead they are faced with a disabled child. Value crisis results from having been reared in a particular family in a particular culture having particular values. American culture values perfection, beauty, efficiency, intelligence, and self-sufficiency. Parents giving birth to a disabled child must find a niche in their value systems where this child can fit comfortably, with the least tension. Children with special needs require additional time, and place additional emotional and situational demands on parents and other family members. Wolfensberger calls this *reality stress* and offers suggestions for intervention to alleviate the overwhelming burden of care that some of these children present. However, this support usually is not offered until a diagnosis has been made, which for the family of the LD child may lead to a prolonged period of reality stress.

Olshansky (1962) identified the phenomenon of chronic sorrow that he suggested occurs in the lives of most parents having a disabled child. The initial grief felt by parents over the loss of the fantasized child becomes a recurring feature of their lives. Normally happy rituals, such as birthdays, holidays, family reunions, and weddings, serve to reawaken a sense of loss and grief. At each successive point, the family experiences a renewed emotional upheaval and needs to reactivate coping mechanisms to reestablish family functioning (Wikler, 1980). No one has explored the phenomenon of chronic sorrow in the lives of families of LD children. It probably is less acute but nonetheless present. Olshansky noted that chronic sorrow is present whether or not the child is cared for at home or is placed in residential care. Chronic sorrow is influenced by many factors, including personality, ethnic group, religion, and social class. Wikler, Wasow, and Hatfield (1981) noted that it occurs when the "culturally assumed enactment of roles does not occur," and when the child's abnormality is highlighted by deviance from normal developmental milestones. Simply put, stress occurs at those times when there is the greatest discrepancy between the parents expectations of parenting and reality. They added that professionals have underestimated the effect of chronic sorrow on the lives of families having older or adult disabled members. Based on the testimony of parents, Wikler has identified critical periods that have the potential to create crisis in family functioning.

The first of these occurs at the time the disability is initially diagnosed. The second may rise when the difficulties of parenting the disabled child require support from others. There may be actual crises of managing medication and school-related problems that are unique to the LD child. These events often bring helping professionals into the privacy of family life for the purpose of support and advice-giving, a disruption not ordinarily encountered by families.

For severely disabled children, reality stress occurs over the lifetime of a disabled child. Parents experience stigmatized social interactions (Voysey, 1972), a prolonged burden of care, lack of information, and periodic grieving (Birenbaum, 1970; Voysey, 1975; Wikler, 1980). These stresses originate from the non-normal nature of the child as well as from the unusual experience of parenting a disabled child. Even close friendships may suffer in the confines of such an event, given public fears and misunderstandings about disabled people. For LD children, who are without physical stigma, but who may not meet age-appropriate norms for behaviors, social interactions, and school performance, there may be even greater public intolerance.

Parents of nondisabled children can rely on a variety of sources to give them information about raising a child. Personal developmental experiences, observations of siblings, conversations with grandparents, neighbors, friends, and pediatricians are generally sufficient and supportive enough to provide a feeling of competence and well being. For many parents of LD children, there is the opportunity to participate in parent support groups, which offer the opportunity for shared experience and understanding. However, many professionals may have mislabeled early signs of learning disability. Adding to the difficulty for the parent of a learning-disabled child is establishing mutuality in parenting. Mutuality in parenting is affected by opportunities and resources. All other things being equal, it is assumed that the mother-child relationship will provide reciprocal satisfactions (Bentovim, 1972; Strickler, 1969). In fact, this very intimate relationship has been named: *symbiosis*. It is both necessary and normal for the successful development of mother and child. Learning-disabled children may not have the resources to participate successfully in symbiotic relationships. Their own particular make-up may cause them to be irritable and difficult to nurture.

The transition away from the normal parenting role to one in which professionals play a critical role in decision making forces parents into prolonged, often difficult, encounters with the service delivery system. Obtaining adequate services is difficult enough without the reminder, at each step, that had this child been "normal" this process would not have been necessary. Given the service options available in the marketplace, parents may have few, if any choices.

Although LD children typically move into full independence with adulthood, their impact on family life prior to that point may be similar to that faced by families of more severely disabled children. Farber (1960) postulated an arrest in the family life cycle as the process by which severely retarded children affect their families. Individual family members move through a series of roles that are subjectively experienced as a process of self-identification, and that Farber referred to broadly as domestic careers. The mentally retarded child does not move through the anticipated career progression, thereby causing parents in particular to experience frustration as their own life cycle progression is halted. Essentially, these parents are unable to give up their parenting roles. Farber looked at family integration as a measure of domestic values and a lack of tension in roles in interpersonal family and community relationships.

This perspective on family serves to highlight the disruption of the normal flow of events that can occur within a family caring for a developmentally disabled child. Generally, children "force" changes in their parents as they develop. They become more independent and move toward increasing physical, emotional, and social maturity. Their parents constantly revise their expectations and views of their child's capabilities. Parents' views of themselves, their roles, and obligations adjust to the changing roles of the child. With respect to a severely disabled child, the parental role is fairly constant. Regardless of birth order in the family, the severely disabled child eventually becomes the youngest child socially. In the progressive move to the youngest-child role, the severely disabled child first slows down movement in the family life-cycle, then ultimately prevents the development of later stages. For the parents of the LD child, this perspective offers insight into the impact on family life of their protracted advocacy role in behalf of their child. This is particularly critical throughout the child's educational career. Parents may need to act as a protective buffer for the LD child against repeated school failure and may be involved in repeated negotiations with teachers and others. This pattern, once started, may make it difficult for parents to let go of the protective role and allow the LD child timely independence.

The family's perception of its situation as a crisis was seen by Farber (1960) as common to families having a disabled child. He distinguished two types of crisis. The first is precipitated by the initial diagnosis and is referred to as a *tragic crisis* (similar to Wolfensberger's novelty shock). The second is caused by a family's inability to cope with the disabled child over a long period of time and is called a *role reorganization crisis*. Farber suggested that families attempt to deal with these crises through a series of minimal adaptations. In this process, the family is viewed as a system attempting to cope with an offensive situation while maintaining its integrity. Events affecting the family life cycle are interpreted according to their impact on family values and roles. What is perceived as critical at one life stage may not be critical at another, and what worked to maintain equilibrium at one life stage may not work at another.

Opportunities and resources differ for individuals and families at specific life stages. These events generally impact particular family members to a greater or lesser extent. As the roles of individual family members are affected by the increased care needed by the disabled child, role tension is experienced and renegotiation is necessary to return to a state of family integrity (Farber, 1979). The ability of parents to role bargain with each other, and with their children, is important to their sense of competence as parents. Parents' perceptions of themselves as powerless greatly influence their ability to continue to carry out culturally prescribed parenting roles (Boggs, 1979).

The nature and severity of a child's disability are, of course, crucial in this framework. The crisis is perceived to the extent that the disability is expected to alter the normal progression of the family's life cycle.

INDIVIDUAL AND FAMILY LIFE CYCLES

Proponents of the life cycle approach to understanding individual dynamics suggest that intersections of biological and psychological development mark important life milestones. Erikson (1963) suggested that the tasks and needs facing individuals at a particular time can be understood in terms of an interactive process through which individuals seek to balance their own intrinsic drive toward self-actualization with societal expectations. Similarly, within a family, there are average expectable milestones characterized by phase-specific tasks and needs (Rhodes, 1977). Tasks of a given life stage are accomplished through utilizing opportunities and available resources. When there is a deficit in opportunities and/or resources, tasks cannot be accomplished. A family life cycle plan integrates the developmental needs of parents and children in a way that allows professionals to look at the family's expectable needs and behavior at a given time. This model promotes a perspective that permits diagnosis of a problem distinguishing normal family tension from that originating from, or exacerbated by, a disabling condition.

These individual and family life cycle frameworks have been combined in Appendix A (see page 231) to show, for each stage, the individual and family psychosocial tasks required for continued family functioning, stability, and growth. When there is a deficit in opportunities and/or resources, the tasks of a given stage are not likely to be accomplished. This leads to problem levels that Appendix A subdivides into those that reflect inadequate life stage resolution and those that reflect extra needs resulting from a disability. Use of Appendix A involves comparing simultaneous developmental tasks for individuals, as well as for the family as an entity, to see how individuals impact each other and family stability at any given time. Appendix A has been designed to help professionals anticipate needs and services that should be considered when working with developmentally disabled people and their families (O'Hara, Chaiklin, & Mosher, 1980). This proactive approach to service delivery can be critical. It provides a normalizing frame of reference for many of the critical transitions encountered by families. Also, it permits design of a service array that anticipates and plans for changing needs (Litman, 1974).

SOURCES OF STRESS

What sets learning disability apart from other developmental disabilities is the relatively nonvisible nature of this handicap. There are no obvious physical differences and the degree of disability may only become manifest when a child enters school. However, prior to that time, parent-child interaction may well have encountered significant problems because somehow this infant or young child is "different" to the parents, although the difference is not easily recognized or described. The mutuality expected by most parents is not easily established by parents of LD children. In infancy, these children may have seemed irritable or unresponsive. As toddlers and young children, they may have been slower to achieve gross-and fine-motor milestones such as walking and self-feeding. There may have been a general sense of clumsiness in many of the children's activities.

If children are language delayed, they may be unresponsive to their parents' verbal attempts to engage them. If they are hypersensitive to touch, they may shrink from the parents' attempts to cuddle them. Parents may interpret these behaviors narcissistically and perceive that the child is rejecting them (Wetter, 1972).

A mother may sense that something is abnormal about her child and ask her pediatrician for an opinion, only to be reassured that nothing is wrong. Facile reassurances that a child is developing normally to a mother experiencing difficulty only serve to foster resentment and anger. The anger may be directed at the physician, a spouse, or the child.

Willner and Crane (1979) noted that parental difficulties derive largely from the prevailing ignorance and confusion about the disabling condition, which in turn is derived mainly from the amorphous nature of the disability itself. For the most part, LD children look normal. In addition, there is a long delay before the diagnosis and ambivalence about it once it is made. Parents receive conflicting opinions from professionals. They frequently go to more than one for an opinion. This "shopping" behavior is generally viewed negatively by professionals as an attempt to deny the reality of the disability. In fact, it may merely be an effort to obtain a majority opinion and some clarity about the diagnosis. For most parents who have suspected that something is wrong, the confirmation of a recognized diagnosis is a relief. It is also, in some cases, a catalyst for the expression of the anger and resentment parents have been storing when their fears have been discounted in the past.

Mourning the loss of the fantasized child is difficult, given contrasting information and uncertainty. Since there is no clear message, parents continue to hope that perhaps the diagnosis is wrong and denial of the problem prevails. Willner and Crane (1979) believed that parents of LD children experience chronic disappointment rather than chronic sorrow. In response to ambivalent information about learning disability, parents are inconsistent in their parenting, ranging from overprotective to rejecting (Kaslow, 1979). Effective management of the child requires a heavy investment of time and energy from parents, frequently leading to major modifications of a family's patterns of interactions and lifestyle (Balkwell & Halverson, 1980; Silver, 1974).

Perhaps more than children with other developmental disabilities, LD children suffer secondary emotional problems. Because the first symptoms of learning disability are frequently defined behaviorally by both parents and professionals, parents may have reacted negatively to the child prior to full diagnosis (Faerstein, 1981). These parents then have the additional burden of having to cope with the possibility that they contributed to these secondary emotional problems. In various ways, most parents probably put the differences down to just the normal variability of children. However, over time, the pattern of compensation for the child's differences becomes accepted. It is only when the child's behavior becomes extreme or entry into school highlights the differences that the presence of the learning disability begins to be acknowledged. Sometimes, the long delay before diagnosis strengthens the denial of reality. Parents may have adjusted to their child's deficits in ways that make them unrecognizable and a normal part of the child's make-up. Language delays may be compensated for by using simple language and frequent gesturing. Parents may instinctively ask children to do only what they are capable of and therefore are not in a position to notice failures at expectable tasks. Parents may be unaware that they are making these adjustments.

The lack of early visibility of a learning disability creates its own sources of stress. In a study of children with various physical illnesses, Stein and Jessop (1982) found that the social and psychological consequences of the illness were more negative when there was poor functioning but the condition was not visible. Stein (1984) offered the concept of uncertainty as an explanation for the finding that marginal illness can have a much greater impact on psychosocial adjustment than those illnesses that are clearly debilitating:

> Lack of visible difference between a chronically impaired child and well peers may make it more difficult to recognize that a child has a chronic condition. If the physical difference is not obvious to the outside world, a child may need to be "sicker" before the condition can be fully acknowledged. This may produce an uncertainty that is psychologically unsettling and associated (a) with more negative psychological consequences for the mother and (b) with greater perceived impact on the family. (p. 5b)

LIFE CYCLE ISSUES FOR THE LEARNING-DISABLED CHILD

A life cycle perspective offers insight into critical developmental issues facing LD children and their families. The general tasks for normal families and the needs and problems facing families of developmentally disabled children can be modified to capture the distinguishing characteristics of learning disability (Adamson, 1979; Erikson, 1963).

Infancy: Trust versus Mistrust

Subtle but disruptive differences in the behavior of LD infants may occur. Such infants may be more irritable, restless, and active and may need less sleep. Parental expectations for increasing maturation in gross and fine motor skills may not be met. The child's high activity level and general clumsiness are seen as the child's failure, but with some unspoken parental guilt present in parent-child interaction. Even when parents attribute this behavior to the normal variability of children, they may still see management problems as a shared failure of themselves and the child. As a consequence, the necessary mutuality and reciprocity in parent-child interaction does not occur and the child fails to resolve this first psychosocial crisis of trust versus mistrust. This lack of parent-child reciprocity lays the early roots of poor self-concept and low self-esteem in the child. Thus far, the parents faith in having given birth to the ideal child is not seriously challenged, although they may have increasing doubts.

Preschool and School Age: Autonomy versus Shame and Doubt, Initiative versus Guilt

During this period, poor motor coordination and general clumsiness become noticeable in comparison with age peers and normal siblings. Also, exposure to formal testing reveals significant performance and behavioral differences. Shame and doubt are experienced as the child fails to reach expected standards. Any unspoken parental guilt will tend to be subconsciously absorbed by the child and lead to paralysis in the movement toward independence and initiative. For parents, their expectations are now seriously challenged, but competing professional diagnoses create uncertainty and insecurity. Parents begin to make the rounds of diagnosticians, seeking a consensus diagnosis. The long delay before a definitive diagnosis is made allows parents to acclimatize themselves to the deviant behavior as normal. Therefore, they may need a good deal of education before congruence can be achieved between themselves and professionals (Willner & Crane, 1979).

Teenage Years and Early Adulthood: Identity versus Role Diffusion, Intimacy versus Isolation

The invisibility of their disability continues to be a source of difficulty and misunderstanding for LD teenagers in establishing peer relationships. As difficult as it is for adults to understand the diagnosis of learning disability, it is that much more difficult for peers. Aspirations toward professional careers may be frustrated by the as yet undeveloped educational strategies that can compensate for the learning disability. Also, the severity of the disability itself may preclude certain career goals. Unless the teenagers' families help plan realistically within their competencies, teenagers may pursue career options aimlessly, in a no-win situation, unable to satisfy either themselves or their families. For some young adults raised within a particular class and social group with its own values, the choice of a potential marriage partner with similar background and aspirations may prove difficult. By now, continued failure and frustration have produced a chronic loss of self-esteem and poor self-image.

SIBLING ADJUSTMENT

There are several reasons for concern about the adjustments of non-disabled siblings. First, because they present a key focus for preventive intervention. If emotional neglect of siblings by parents can be avoided, then the presence of a disabled child need not lead to the whole family being disabled. Healthy siblings help neutralize any family disappointment centered on the disabled child (Grossman, 1972). Siblings can often be extremely helpful in furthering the social and emotional development of the disabled child. Finally, despite their high vulnerability, siblings have a good potential for normal adjustment (Adams, 1960; Kew, 1975; Trevino, 1979).

Although they may not experience grief in the same way as their parents, the chronic sorrow described by Olshansky (1962) is a pervasive backdrop to the lives of nondisabled siblings. Pressures placed on nondisabled siblings occur in various ways. There may be some degree of neglect of nondisabled siblings by parents because of the disproportionate amount of attention given to the disabled child. Siblings may encounter pressure to succeed, in part to compensate for the defects of the disabled sibling. Some may experience a sense of personal guilt at being normal in comparison with the disabled child. There may be some degree of distortion of the normal sibling role in order to help with care of the disabled child. Often, social life for the whole family is restricted because of the family's obligation to meet the unusual demands of the disability (Adams, 1960; Farber, 1960).

Of particular concern is the stress specific to the younger sibling, who ultimately surpasses the mentally and/or physically disabled brother or sister. Age grading within a culture is determined primarily by psychological and social capabilities. The severely retarded child ultimately becomes the "youngest" child in the family. Role expectations and responsibilities for the nondisabled sibling are both heavier and experienced earlier than one would predict given chronological age. As siblings reach a level of intellectual, social, or emotional maturity greater than that of the disabled child, they may have already had to deal with differing expectations of themselves versus the expectations held for the disabled brother or sister (Farber, 1960; Gath, 1972).

Within the life cycle perspective, the potential problems faced by siblings of the LD child are a consideration of anxiety reactions to parental concerns and role distortions occurring as a result of the increased attention given to the LD child.

During the preschool period (up to 5 years of age), parental neglect of the nondisabled sibling may lead to the child's withdrawal, a negative protest behavior. Deliberate irritation of parents by the child may be an attempt to stimulate increased parental attention and affection. These are normal reactions to the stress of a difficult situation and often can be dealt with easily (Adams, 1960).

In the early school period (5 to 8 years of age), a disability takes on many social implications. Younger siblings not only have to contend with separation from home, but they may enter a school in which the older LD child is already labeled and stigmatized. Thus, school adjustment and exposure to the larger world of teachers and peers may be made more dif-

ficult by the associational stigma (Grossman, 1972). The usual sibling ri-
valry sometimes leads to guilt feelings if the nondisabled child sees himself
as somehow the cause of the disability (Trevino, 1979).

By the mid-school period (8 to 12 years of age), older siblings in particular may begin to take some responsibility for the care of the LD child
(Gath, 1973). They must explain to friends about the LD sibling's behavior
and special treatment. Sometimes, the nondisabled sibling feels a need to
make it up to the parents for the LD child and so may become an over-
achiever in school. Others may feel guilty about being normal and become
reluctant to show their ability.

In adolescence, siblings often become concerned about the possibility
of an inherited defect affecting their marital prospects (Farber & Jenne,
1963). They may experience some ostracism by peers because of the disabled brother or sister, and they may begin to see themselves as disabled
by association. Siblings formerly described by their parents as relating very
positively to the disabled child may begin to reject any responsibility for
their sibling and avoid contact with him or her (Graliker, Fishler, & Koch,
1962). These issues can become problems of self-acceptance and compli-
cate the process of identity formation.

INTERVENTION

The issue for professional intervention with families of LD children is
that of preventing the disability from becoming a total family handicap
(Tew, Payne, & Lawrence, 1974). Thus far, we have presented the factors impinging on a family's ability to cope with disability, specifically a learning
disability. Problems presented by the child and the family are due to brain
dysfunction and a combination of intrapsychic and intrafamilial dynamic
factors (Abrams & Kaslow, 1976). In addition to the obvious need to remediate the learning disability, the LD child may need direct treatment to resolve secondary emotional problems, and the parents may need counseling
to help them understand and cope with their own emotions. This chapter
has emphasized a normal developmental framework for understanding
families faced with the crisis of having a learning disabled child. This suggests that it is reasonable for a family to need help with this problem periodically throughout the life of the child and, in fact, that some of those periods
are predictable. Often, the person making the initial suggestion to the family
that they seek counseling for themselves is in a unique and crucial position
to influence the attitude of the family toward obtaining help (Briard, 1976).
This may be the person who is first involved in making the diagnosis of
learning disability, but not necessarily. It is crucial to be able to reassure
both the child and parents that they are not deficient in their abilities to

care for themselves, but rather they are dealing with a very difficult situation without a great deal of support. The goal of counseling is to shore up their familial strengths so that they are able to cope with the pressures placed on them by the child's disability. With this perspective, the referring person can go a long way toward enlisting family members as allies in the treatment plan.

It is of major importance to understand how the parents of a disabled child define their situation. How do they perceive and understand what is happening to them? It is a critical first step in planning intervention to know the degree of congruence between parents on the meaning of this child for them, and the extent of the parents' uncertainty about the child's problems. The following questions can serve as a guide to understanding how parents define their situation.

- How do parents describe their child? Do they use primarily positive or negative terms?
- What is their statement of the problem?
- What do parents expect from professionals? Remediation or cure?
- What do parents understand about the etiology of the problem? Is it their fault that the child is learning disabled? Is it the fault of one parent? Is it genetically linked? Are parents blaming each other? Are they blaming professionals?
- What do parents understand about the child's ability to influence the problem?
- What diagnostic information have they heard previously?
- What is their understanding of the above information?
- What is their perception of their own relationship to the ongoing nature of the problem? To what extent do they feel they they can influence the course of the disability? What have they tried in the past to influence the situation?
- What has their experience been with other persons presenting problems similar to those of their child.
- What is the parents' assessment of how this problem affects their lives?
- How do they regard previous experiences associated with this problem? What was it like for them to take this child for diagnostic testing? Was their pediatrician supportive? What was diagnostic counseling like for them? How was the information presented? Were both parents present for the informing session? Were they able to support one another? What have their experiences been like with the school system thus far?
- What are their expectations for their own performance as it relates to the problem?
- How do the parents feel about this situation? Are they angry or sad? Are they able to express any feelings at all?

Many of these same questions can be applied to the children themselves to ascertain how they perceive the situation in which they find themselves. It is important to remember that a family's definition of their situation is likely to change over time.

Families referred for treatment are typically experiencing feelings of self-denial, anger, anxiety, and perhaps disappointment, all of which can cause dysfunctional interaction patterns between parents and children (Amerikaner & Omizio, 1984). Initially, the therapist needs to assess four areas of family functioning:

1. Does the family accept differences among family members and promote the growth of individuals as well as the family as a whole?
2. Is the family able to perform roles efficiently while still supporting each other emotionally?
3. Is the family able to establish effective patterns of leadership, or are there problems of control?
4. What is the family's effectiveness in developing the ways and means for clear commuincation? (Abrams & Kaslow, 1977, Margalit, 1982).

Given the cultural attitudes toward difference in the United States, one might predict that it is the exemplary, and probably rare, family that finds it easy to accept and promote a difference in one of its members. A parent experiences a narcissistic blow to the ego on learning the diagnosis of a learning disability in his or her child (Kornblum, 1982). It is hard to imagine that a parent can efficiently perform culturally expected roles and still have enough energy left over to provide the emotional support needed by other family members. As noted previously, parents of disabled children are faced with such uncertainty about the diagnosis, appropriate interventions, and guidelines for the future, that their parenting is frequently inconsistent and control is difficult to maintain. Guilt over etiology, as well as the parents' knowledge that they have felt rejection toward the child, causes parents to switch between extreme overprotection and rejection, from free rein to excessive control. Without insight into the dynamics of their behavior, it is difficult for them to set appropriate limits or to communicate effectively. Parents need to recognize their denial of the situation and understand its roots. It is important that they are able to ventilate their anger as well as their sad feelings, and that they are encouraged to mourn the loss of their ideal child. The guilt they experience over having rejected or felt negatively toward the child should be explored, not discounted. The underlying issues should be aired. The therapist must help a parent address the underlying issues and the difficulty in setting limits (Adamson, 1972; Barsch, 1961; Ohrenstein, 1979). Another major treatment issue is the anxiety felt by most parents about their child's future.

Parents are often able to help each other in this process. Frequently, however, each parent is at a different point in his or her adaptation to the diagnosis and, therefore, it is hard for one parent to summon the energy to help the other or even to be aware of the other's discomfort. Parents' groups may help provide mutual support and information. Sharing information can give parents perspective on their own experiences.

The disabled child is likely to suffer a poor self-image and low self-esteem. Children with chronic conditions exhibit twice the rates of mental disturbance as healthy children. An important variable in children's adjustment is their subjective definition of the severity of their condition as well as their perception of their parents' estimation of the severity of their condition (Stein, 1984). The children's perception that they are supported by their families is very important to functional adaptation. A family that can integrate a child's differences with dignity goes a long way toward forming a positive self-image.

Although some families enter family treatment to help them cope with raising an LD child, many more do not. It is necessary for professionals involved with LD children and their families to have guidelines at hand to help them interact positively and supportively. Every contact between family, child, and professional has its effect and adds to the child and family experience (Cornfort, 1985).

It is worth reiterating that disability is a family affair. If parents are not in agreement with or invested in a particular treatment plan, children will know it either directly or indirectly. It is a no-win situation for children to feel caught in the middle of a conflict between their parents and professionals. Besides feeling torn by loyalties, if the adults in their lives cannot agree on what to do about their problems, it must be a very bad problem indeed. Children are left feeling even more uncertain and anxious (Kozloff, 1979).

Good communication between professionals and parents, as well as among professionals on the treatment team, is essential for good management of a disability. Conflict between parents and professionals is frequently the result of differing perceptions of the situation. Without good, straightforward communication, conflicts are not articulated or resolved (Dembinski, 1977).

Most parents want to do what is best for their children. However, several factors interfere with parents' good intentions: parents have little time to devote to individual children; they feel estranged from the school and its personnel; parents would like to help their children but they don't know how; and it is very hard to "work" with your own children (Gollub, 1977).

These findings have implications for our expectations of families. Family time is precious and extra time is rare, particularly today when over half of the nation's children live in homes where both parents are employed. If, in fact, families do feel estranged from community resources, then we must provide them with consistent support and encourage them to be members of their child's treatment team. Parents generally know their children well. When conflicts arise between parents and professionals, the aim must be resolution rather than efforts to convince parents that the professional knows best (Wolfensberger, 1967). The fact that parents of disabled children may suffer from low self-esteem with regard to their parenting has been discussed previously. Professionals can help by teaching parents independent problem-solving techniques (Ferholt & Solnit, 1978). Parents need acceptance of their efforts and recognition of the fact that not only is their job more difficult and stressful than that of most parents, but more is expected of them. Parental identification with their children is too great to allow for the objectivity necessary to make teaching easy or conflict-free (Levy & Strobino, in press).

Educating parents to the nondisabled siblings' predicament and involving siblings in any therapeutic program are the responsibilities of the professional who wants to encourage positive family adaptation to the disabled child. Parents and professionals can present information about the etiology of the disability (to the extent known) and reassurance about the normalcy of the siblings' feelings and thoughts. Additionally, it is important to explain why the LD child needs a different educational approach. Ensuring that the nondisabled siblings each have some individual quality time alone with one or both parents also can be a very successful coping strategy. Siblings groups, individual counseling sessions, and continued discussion of the LD child's disability and its treatment are all strategies to assist in the adjustment of the nondisabled sibling.

SUMMARY

Families of children with learning disabilities experience similar stresses to those faced by families of other developmentally disabled children. On the other hand, there are substantial differences. Identification of the learning disability usually occurs much later, when patterns of family adaptation to early behavioral differences have become established. Added to the difficulty and ongoing uncertainty parents may experience in achieving a definitive diagnosis, the child has often begun to exhibit secondary emotional problems for which parents feel guilty.

Siblings may have been neglected by parents and yet have been expected to take on a substitute parenting role. The whole life cycle of the family has shifted perspective. Most families learn to make necessary adjustments and balance the demands and needs of children as well as of parents. Often family members can find positives as well as negatives in the uncertainty they face.

We would all like to have a crystal ball to predict the future, but no one does. Thus, we have to learn to live with a degree of uncertainty about almost everything. The parents of LD children must live with much more. The advantage is that uncertainty leaves room for hope. Many parents find this easier than predictions of well-defined limits to potential.

APPENDIX A

Life Stages of the Learning Disabled and Their Families

Life Stage A

	Establishing Family	**Parents**
Tasks and needs	Establish concensus of values & role organization Plan pregnancy & prenatal care	Intimacy versus isolation * Separation from family of origin Incorporating spousal role into identity
Problems and crises	High-risk pregnancy Poor prenatal care Adolescent parent	

Life Stage B

	LD Infant	**Family**	**Parents**
Tasks and needs	Basic trust versus mistrust * Effective parenting Early diagnosis and treatment	Maintain consensus on values & role organization	Generativity versus stagnation * Establishing identity as parent
Problems and crises	Temperamental and behavioral problems Irregular feeding & sleeping patterns	Adjustment of roles and responsibilities	Assessment of emotional ability to parent a "difficult" child

(continued)

* Adapted from Erikson (1963).
** Adapted from Rhodes (1977).

Life Stage B *(continued)*

	LD Infant	Family	Parents
		Failure to establish mutuality in parent/child interaction	Development of ability to provide adequate care Possible self-doubt in parenting role Decisions about more children

Life Stage C

	LD Toddler (18 months to 3 years)	Family	Parents
Tasks and needs	Autonomy versus shame and doubt * Effective parenting Early socialization and play Early identification as an "at risk" child	Replenishment versus turning inward ** Maintain consensus on values & role organization	Generativity versus stagnation * Support development in spouse & self & maintain community ties Recognition of individual needs of siblings
Problems and crises	Inability to master task of autonomy given developmental failures Beginning of self-doubt	Possible disproportionate use of family emotional resources for "difficult" child Ongoing shift in focus of family life Possible increasing frustration with child's inability to attain normal milestones	Ability to meet needs of spouse and/or siblings Coping with sense of inadequacy

* Adapted from Erikson (1963).
** Adapted from Rhodes (1977).

Life Stage D

	LD Child (3-13 years)	**Family**	**Parents**
Tasks and needs	Initiative versus guilt * Industry versus inferiority * Management of differentness Diagnosis & treatment of learning disability Appropriate educational planning	Replenishment versus turning inward ** Necessary adaptations in values & role organization Incorporate "difference" into family value system	Generativity versus stagnation * Achieve and maintain marital stability Maintain career opportunity
Problems and crises	Social inclusion Inadequate learning resources	"Arrested family" Acceptance of child & family limitations Inadequate financial resources Family breakdown Lack of parental & family support services	Loss of career & developmental opportunities Dealing with ongoing isolation Protection of siblings & maintenance of normal expectations for them

Life Stage E

	LD Adolescent (13-18 years)	**Family**	**Parents**
Tasks and needs	Group identity versus alienation * Individual identity versus role diffusion * Achieve healthy sexual identity	Individuation of family members versus pseudomutual organization **	Generativity versus stagnation * Preparation for eventual separation from children

(continued)

* Adapted from Erikson (1963).
** Adapted from Rhodes (1977).

Life Stage E *(continued)*

	LD Adolescent (13–18 years)	Family	Parents
	Acquire skills for maximum independence Appropriate educational placement Vocational assessment & counseling		
Problems and crises	School & vocational failure	Continued overprotection of LD child	Allowing independence

Life Stage F

	LD Young Adult (18–21 years)	Family	Parents
Tasks and needs	Intimacy versus isolation * Preparation for independence Recognition of exploitation versus ability for self-protection	Regrouping versus binding or expulsion **	Companionship versus isolation ** Renewing marital relationship
Problems and crises	Lack of vocational and/or employment opportunity Lack of transition resources	Family inability to follow full independence	Decision for separation versus continued protection

* Adapted from Erikson (1963).
** Adapted from Rhodes (1977).

Life Stage G

	LD Adult (21–65 years)	**Family**	**Parents**
Tasks and needs	Intimacy versus isolation * Generativity versus stagnation * Appropriate community supports for independence Expanding opportunities for self-development in life roles	Regrouping versus binding or expulsion **	Rediscovery versus despair ** Planning for & meeting death
Problems and crises	Preparation for parents' death	Transition from familial support system to community/friend support network Need for family to provide extended financial & emotional support	

* Adapted from Erikson (1963).
** Adapted from Rhodes (1977).

References

Aaron, P. G., Baker, C., & Hickox, G. L. (1982). In search of the third dyslexia. *Neuropsychologia, 20,* 203–208.

Abbott, R. C., & Frank, B. E. (1975). A follow-up of LD children in a private special school. *Academic Therapy, 10,* 291–298.

Abrams, J. C., & Kaslow, F. W. (1976). Learning disability and family dynamics: A mutual interaction. *Journal of Clinical Child Psychology, 5,* 35–40.

Abrams, J. C., & Kaslow, F. W. (1977). Family systems and the learning-disabled child: Intervention and treatment. *Journal of Learning Disabilities, 10,* 86–90.

Ackerman, P. T., & Dykman, R. A. (1982). Automatic and effortful information-processing deficits in children with learning and attention disorders. *Topics in Learning and Learning Disabilities, 2,* 12–22.

Ackerman, P. T., Dykman, R. A., & Peters, J. E. (1977). Learning-disabled boys as adolescents: Cognitive factors and achievement. *Journal of the American Academy of Child Psychiatry, 16,* 296–313.

Ackerman, P. T., Elardo, P. T., & Dykman, R. A. (1979). A psychosocial study of hyperactive and learning disabled boys. *Journal of Abnormal Child Psychology, 7,* 91–99.

Adams, M. (1960). *The mentally subnormal.* London: Heineman.

Adamson, W. C. (1972). Helping parents of children with learning disabilities. *Journal of Learning Disabilities, 5,* 327–330.

Adamson, W. C. (1979). Individual psychotherapy: An illustrative case study. In W. C. Adamson & K. K. Adamson (Eds.), *A handbook for specific learning disabilities* (pp. 193–236). New York: Gardner Press.

Adelman, H. S., & Taylor, L. (1982). Enhancing the motivation and skills needed to overcome interpersonal problems. *Learning Disability Quarterly, 5,* 438–446.

Adelman, H. S. & Taylor, L. (1985). The future of the LD field. *Journal of Learning Disabilities, 18,* 422–427.

Alberman, E. (1973). The early prediction of learning disorders. *Developmental Medicine and Child Neurology, 15,* 202–204.

Algozzine, B., & Korinek, J. (1985). Where is special education for students with high prevalence handicaps going? *Exceptional Children, 51,* 388–394.

Algozzine, B., & Ysseldyke, J. (1981). Special education for normal children: Better safe than sorry? *Exceptional Children, 48,* 238–243.

Allen, R. V., & Allen, P. (1970). *Language experience in reading.* Chicago: Encyclopaedia Brittanica.

Alley, G., & Deshler, D. (1979). *Teaching the learning-disabled adolescent: Strategies and methods.* Denver: Love

Alley, G., Deshler, D., Clark, F., Schumaker, J., & Warner, M. (1983). Learning disabilities in adolescent and adult populations: Part II: Research Implications. *Focus on Exceptional Children, 15*(9), 1–14.

Allington, R. L., & Flemming, J. T. (1978). The misreading of high-frequency words. *Journal of Special Education, 12,* 417–421.

Altwerger, B., & Bird, L. (1982). The learner or the curriculum? *Topics in Learning and Learning Disabilities, 1,* 69–78.

Aman, M. G. (1978). Drugs, learning, and the psychotherapies. In J. S. Werry (Ed.), *Pediatric psychopharmacology: The use of behavior modifying drugs in children* (pp. 79–108). New York: Brunner/Mazel.

Aman, M. G. (1980). Psychotropic drugs and learning problems — A selective review. *Journal of Learning Disabilities, 13,* 87–97.

Aman, M. G. (1982). Psychotropic drugs in the treatment of reading disorders. In R. N. Malatesha & P. G. Aaron (Eds.), *Reading disorders: Varieties and treatments.* New York: Academic Press.

Aman, M. G., & Werry, J. S. (1982). Methylphenidate and diazepam in severe reading retardation. *Journal of the American Academy of Child Psychiatry, 1,* 31–37.

Ambrose, A. (1974). Personality. In R. Sears & S. Feldman (Eds.), *The seven ages of man* (pp. 10–14). Los Altos, CA: Kaufmann.

Americaner, M. H., & Omizo, M. M. (1984). Family interaction and learning disability. *Journal of Learning Disabilities, 17*(9), 540–543.

Anderson, C. A., & Jennings, D. L. (1980). When experiences of failure promote expectations of success. The impact of attributing failure to ineffective strategies. *Journal of Personality, 48,* 393–407.

Anderson, D. (1976). Pruning the fuzziness and flab from learning disabilities research. *Journal of Special Education, 10,* 157–161.

Anderson, J. R. (1975). *Cognitive psychology and its implications.* San Francisco: Freeman.

Anderson, R. C. (1977). The notion of schemata and the educational enterprise. In R. Anderson, R. Spiro, & W. Montague (Eds.), *Schooling and the acquisition of knowledge* (pp. 415–531). Hillsdale, NJ: Lawrence Erlbaum.

Anderson, T. H. (1980). Study strategies and adjunct aids. In R. J. Spiro, B. B. Bruce, & W. F. Brewer (Eds.), *Theoretical issues in reading comprehension* (pp. 484–502). Hillsdale, NJ: Lawrence Erlbaum.

André, M. E. D. A., & Anderson, T. H. (1978-1979). The development and evaluation of a self-questioning study technique. *Reading Research Quarterly, 14,* 605–623.

Andrews, N., & Shaw, J. E. (1986). *Child Care, Health and Development, 12*(1), 53–62.

Applebee, A. N. (1971). Research in reading retardation: Two critical problems. *Journal of Child Psychology and Psychiatry, 12,* 91–113.

Application for admission Ben D. Caudle Special Learning Center. (Undated). Clarksville, AR: The College of the Ozarks.

Arkowitz, H. (1981). Assessment of social skills. In M. Hersen & A. S. Bellack (Eds.), *Behavioral assessment* (pp. 296–327). New York: Pergamon Press.

Armstrong, J. (1973). A generalized model for the evaluation of instructional materials and media. In J. Armstrong (Ed.), *A sourcebook for the evaluation of instructional materials and media.* Madison: University of Wisconsin, Special Education Instructional Materials Center.

Arter, J. A., & Jenkins, J. R. (1977). Examining the benefits and prevalence of modality considerations in special education. *Journal of Special Education, 11,* 281–298.

Arter, J. A., & Jenkins, J. R. (1979). Differential diagnosis — prescriptiive teaching: A critical appraisal. *Review of Educational Research, 49,* 517–555.

Asher, S., & Hymel, S. (1981). Children's social competence in peer relations: Sociometric and behavioral assessment. In J. D. Wine & M. D. Syme (Eds.), *Social competence.* New York: Guilford Press.

Ashlock, R. B. (1976). *Error patterns in computation: A semi-programmed approach.* Columbus, OH: Merrill.

Ashlock, R. B. (1986). *Error patterns in computation: A semi-programmed approach* (4th ed.). Columbus, OH: Merrill.

Ashlock, R. B., & Washbon, C. A. (1978). Games: Practice activities for the basic facts. In M. N. Suydam & R. E. Reys (Eds.), *Developing computational skills: 1978 yearbook* (pp. 39–50). Reston, VA: National Council of Teachers of Mathematics.

Averch, H. A., Carroll, S. J., Donaldson, T. S., Kiesling, H. J., & Pincus, J. (1984). *How effective is schooling? A critical review and synthesis of the research.* Englewood Cliffs, NJ: Educational Technology Publications.

Axelrod, L. (1982). Social perception in learning disabled adolescents. *Journal of Learning Disabilities, 15,* 610–613.

Ayllon, T., Layman, D., & Kandel, H. J. (1975). A behavioral-educational alternative to drug control of hyperactive children. *Journal of Applied Behavior Analysis, 8,* 137–146.

Ayllon, T., & Roberts, M. D. (1974). Eliminating discipline problems by strengthening academic performance. *Journal of Applied Behavior Analysis, 7,* 71–76.

Ayres, L. P. (1917). *Ayres scales for measuring handwriting.* Princeton, NJ: Educational Testing Service.

Bachara, G. (1976). Empathy in learning disabled children. *Perceptual and Motor Skills, 43,* 541–542.

Badian, N. A. (1983). Dyscalculia and nonverbal disorders of learning. In H. R. Myklebust (Ed.), *Progress in learning disabilities* (Vol. V, pp. 235–264). New York: Grune & Stratton.

Bailey, J., & Bostow, D. (1979). *Research methods in applied behavioral analysis.* Tallahassee: Behavior Management Consultants.

Bain, A. M. (1980). *Handwriting survey.* Unpublished paper, Loyola College, Baltimore.

Baker, H. J., & Leland, B. (1967). *Detroit Tests of Learning Aptitude* (rev. ed.). Indianapolis: Bobbs-Merrill.

Baker, L. (1979, July). *Do I understand or do I not understand: That is the question.* (Reading Education Report No. 10). Urbana: University of Illinois, Center for the Study of Reading.

Baker, L., & Brown, A. (1984a). Metacognitive skills and reading. In P. D. Pearson (Ed.), *Handbook of reading research* (pp. 353–394). New York: Longman.

Baker, L., & Brown, A. L. (1984b). Cognitive monitoring in reading. In J. Flood (Ed.). *Understanding reading comprehension* (pp. 21–44). Newark, DE: International Reading Association.

Balkwell, C., & Halverson, C. F., Jr. (1980). The hyperactive child as a source of stress in the family: Consequences and suggestions for intervention. *Family Relations, 29,* 550–557.

Balow, B. (1965). The long-term effects of remedial reading. *The Reading Teacher, 18,* 581–586.

Banikowski, A. L. (1981). *The verbal cognitive-socialization and strategies used by learning disabled and non-learning disabled junior high school adolescents in a peer-to-peer interaction activity.* Unpublished doctoral dissertation, University of Kansas, Lawrence.

Bannatyne, A. (1974). Diagnosis: A note on recategorization of the WISC scaled scores. *Journal of Learning Disabilities, 7,* 272–273.

Barat College Learning Opportunities Program case history. (1982, April). Lake Forest, IL: Barat College.

Barbaro, F. (1982). The learning disabled college student: Some considerations in setting objectives. *Journal of Learning Disabilities, 15,* 559–603.

Barkley, R. A. (1981a). *Hyperactive children: A handbook for diagnosis and treatment.* New York: Guilford Press.

Barkley, R. A. (1981b). Learning disabilities. In E. J. Mash & L. G. Terdal (Eds.), *Behavioral assessment of childhood disorders.* New York: Guilford Press.

Barkley, R. A., & Cunningham, C. E. (1978). Do stimulant drugs improve the academic performance of hyperkinetic children? *Clinical Pediatrics, 17,* 85–92.

Barkley, R. A., Cunningham, C. E., & Karlsson, J. (1983). The speech of hyperactive children and their mothers: Comparison with normal children and stimulant drug effects. *Journal of Learning Disabilities, 16,* 105–110.

Barsch, R. W. (1961). Counseling the parent of the brain-injured child. *Journal of Rehabilitation, 37,* 26–27, 40–42.

Barsch, R. (1967). *Achieving perceptual-motor efficiency.* Seattle: Special Child Publication.

Bateman, B. (1964). Learning disabilities — Yesterday, today, and tomorrow. *Exceptional Children, 31,* 167–177.

Bateman, R. J. (1966). Learning disorders. *Review of Educational Research, 36,* 93–119.

Battle, J. (1979). Self-esteem of students in regular and special classes. *Psychological Reports, 44,* 212–214.

Beattie, I. D., & Scheer, J. K. (1982). *Using the diagnostic stamp kit.* Port Roberts, WA: Janian Educational Materials.

Beck, R. J. (1977). *Remediation of learning deficits through precision teaching: A follow-up study.* Unpublished doctoral dissertation, University of Montana.

Becker, H. (1983). How schools use microcomputers. *Computer Room Learning,* 41–144.

Becker, W. C. (1977). Teaching reading and language to the disadvantaged — what we have learned from field research. *Harvard Educational Review, 47,* 518–543.

Becker, W. C., & Carnine, D. W. (1981). Direct instruction: A behavior theory model for comprehensive educational intervention with the disadvantaged. In S. W. Bijou & R. Ruis (Eds.), *Behavior modification: Contributions to education.* Hillsdale, NJ: Lawrence Erlbaum.

Becker, W. C., & Engleman, S. (1977). *The Oregon Direct Instruction Model: Comparative results in project Follow Through, a summary of nine years work.* Eugene: University of Oregon.

Beers, C. S. (1980). The relationship of cognitive development to spelling and reading abilities. In E. H. Henderson & J. W. Beers (Eds.), *Developmental and cognitive aspects of learning to spell.* Newark, DE: International Reading Associates.

Beers, J. W. (1980). Developmental strategies of spelling competence in primary school children. In E. H. Henderson & J. W. Beers (Eds.), *Developmental and cognitive aspects of learning to spell.* Newark, DE: International Reading Associates.

Beery, K. E., & Buktenica, N. A. (1967). *Developmental Test of Visual Motor Integration.* Chicago: Follett.

Begle, S. G. (1979). *Critical variables in mathematics education.* Washington, DC: Mathematics Association of America and the National Council of Teachers of Mathematics.

Beland, R. (1980). *An analysis of role perception and needs assessment of selected special edu-*

cators toward leisure education for the handicapped. Unpublished doctoral dissertation, University of Maryland.

Ben D. *Caudle Special Learning Center student handbook.* (1981, September) Clarkesville, AR: The College of the Ozarks.

Bennett, A. B. (1982). *Decimal squares: Step by step teacher's guide to readiness to advanced levels in decimals.* Fort Collins, CO: Scott Resources.

Bennett, K. (1981). The effects of syntax and verbal mediation on learning disabled students' verbal mathematical problem solving. *Dissertation Abstracts International, 42,* 1093. (University Microfilms No. 04-19, 4209)

Benton, A. L. (1974). *The revised visual retention test.* New York: Psychological Corporation.

Benton, A. L. (1978). Some conclusions about dyslexia. In A. L. Benton & D. Pearl (Eds.), *Dyslexia: An appraisal of current knowledge* (pp. 451–476). New York: Oxford University Press.

Bentovin, A. (1972). Emotional disturbance of handicapped pre-school children and their families: Attitudes to the child. *British Medical Journal, 3,* 579–581.

Berkell, D. E. (1984). Choosing the right software. *Journal of Learning Disabilities, 19*(4), 431–439.

Berler, E. S., Gross, A. M., & Drabman, R. S. (1982). Social skills training with children: Proceed with caution. *Journal of Applied Behavior Analysis, 15,* 41–53.

Bersoff, D. N., Kabler, M., Fiscus, E., & Ankney, R. (1972). Effectiveness of special class placement for children labeled neurologically handicapped. *Journal of School Psychology, 10,* 157–163.

Bickel, W. E., & Bickel, D. D. (1986). Effective schools, classrooms, and instruction: Implications for special education. *Exceptional Children, 52*(6), 489–500.

Bijou, D. W., Birnbrauer, J. S., Kidder, J. D., & Tague, C. (1966). Programmed instruction as an approach to teaching of reading, writing, and arithmetic to retarded children. *Psychological Record, 16,* 505–522.

Bingham, A. (1981). Exploratory process in career development: Implications for learning disabled students. *Career Development for Exceptional Individuals, 4*(2), 77–80.

Bingham, G. (1978). Career attitudes among boys with and without specific learning disabilities. *Exceptional Children, 44,* 341–342.

Bireley, M., & Manley, E. (1980). The learning disabled student in a college environment: A report of Wright State University's program. *Journal of Learning Disabilities, 13,* 12–15.

Birenbaum, A. (1970). On managing courtesy stigma. *Journal of Health and Social Behavior, 11,* 196–206.

Blackwell, P. M., Engen, E., Fischgrund, J. E., & Zarcadoolas, C. (1978). *Sentences and other systems: A language and learning curriculum for hearing impaired children.* Washington, DC: The Alexander Graham Bell Association for the Deaf.

Blair, J. R. (1972). The effects of differential reinforcement on the discrimination learning of normal and low-achieving middle class boys. *Child Development, 43,* 251–255.

Blalock, J. (1982a). Residual learning disabilities in young adults: Implications for rehabilitation. *Journal of Applied Rehabilitation Counseling, 13*(2), 9–13.

Blalock, J. (1982b). Persistent auditory language deficits in adults with learning disabilities. *Journal of Learning Disabilities, 15,* 604–609.

Blankenship, C., & Lilly, M. S. (1981). *Mainstreaming students with learning and behavioral problems: Techniques for the classroom teacher.* New York: Holt, Rinehart & Winston.

Blankenship, C. S. (1985). Linking assessment to curriculum assessment. In J. F. Cawley (Ed.), *Mathematics appraisal of the learning disabled.* Rockville, MD: Aspen Publications.

Blatt, B. (1958). The physical, personality, and academic status of children who are mentally retarded attending special classes as compared with children who are mentally retarded attending regular classes. *American Journal of Mental Deficiency, 62,* 810–818.

Blatt, B. (1980). Why educational research fails. *Journal of Learning Disabilities, 13,* 3–4.

Blau, H., & Loveless, E. (1982). Specific hemispheric routing — TAK/V to teach spelling to dyslexics: VAK and VAKT challenged. *Journal of Learning Disabilities, 15,* 461–466.

Bley, N. S., & Thornton, C. A. (1981). *Teaching mathematics to the learning disabled.* Rockville, MD: Aspen Publications.

Bloom, B. (1976). *Human characteristics and school learning.* New York: McGraw-Hill.

Bloomer, C. H. (1978). *A six year follow-up study on learning disabled children in a resource room program.* Unpublished doctoral dissertation, Columbia University, New York.

Blouin, A., Bornstein, R., & Trites, R. (1978). Teenage alcohol use among hyperactive children: A 5-year follow-up study. *Journal of Pediatric Psychology, 3,* 188–194.

Boder, E. (1971). Developmental dyslexia: A diagnostic screening procedure based on three characteristic patterns of reading and spelling. In B. Bateman (Ed.), *Learning disorders* (Vol. 4). Seattle: Special Child Publications.

Boersma, F. J., & Chapman, J. W. (1981). Academic self-concept, achievement expectations, and locus of control in elementary learning-disabled children. *Canadian Journal of Behavioural Science, 13,* 349–358.

Boggs, E. (1979). Economic factors in family care. In R.H. Bruininks & G. C. Krantz (Eds.), *Family care of developmentally disabled members: Conference proceedings.* Minneapolis: University of Minnesota.

Bognar, C., & Martin, W. R. W. (1982). A sociological perspective on diagnosing learning difficulties. *Journal of Learning Disabilities, 15,* 347–351.

Bork, A., & Franklin, S. (1979). Personal computers in learning. *Educational Technology, 19,* 7–12.

Borkowski, J. G., & Cavanaugh, J. C. (1979). Maintenance and generalization of skills and strategies by the retarded. In N. R. Ellis (Ed.), *Handbook of mental deficiency: Psychological theory and research* (2nd ed., pp. 569–618). Hillsdale, NJ: Lawrence Erlbaum.

Borkowski, J. G., Johnston, M. B., & Reid, M. K. (in press). Metacognition, motivation, and the transfer of control processes. In S. J. Ceci (Ed.), *Handbook of cognition, social and neuropsychological aspects of learning disabilities.* Hillsdale, NJ: Lawrence Erlbaum.

Borkowski, J. G., & Konarski, E. A. (1981). Educational implications of efforts to train intelligence. *Journal of Special Education, 15*(2), 289–305.

Borland, B. L., & Heckman, H. K. (1976). Hyperactive boys and their brothers: A 25-year follow-up study. *Archives of General Psychiatry, 33,* 669–675.

Bose, A. (1970). *Information system design methodology based on PERT/CPN networking.* (ERIC Document Reproduction Service No. AR 711 670).

Bracht, G. H. (1970). Experimental factors related to aptitude-treatment interactions. *Review of Educational Research, 40,* 627–645.

Bradley, C. (1937). The behavior of children receiving benzedrine. *American Journal of Psychiatry, 94,* 577–585.

Bradley, C. (1957). Characteristics and management of children with behavior problems associated with organic brain damage. *Pediatric Clinics of North America, 4,* 1049–1060.

Bradley, C., & Bowen, M. (1940). School performance of children receiving amphetamine (Benzedrine) sulfate. *American Journal of Orthopsychiatry, 10,* 782–788.

Brannan, R., & Schaaf, O. (1983). An instructional approach to problem solving. In G. Schfelt (Ed.), *The agenda in action.* Reston, VA: National Council of Teachers of Mathematics.

Brannan, S. A. (1977). A special education viewpoint: Consultation in the public schools. In J. Goldstein (Ed.), *Consultation: Enhancing leisure service delivery to handicapped children and youth* (pp. 51–79). Arlington, VA: National Recreation and Park Association.

Brannan, S., Chinn, K., & Verhoven, P. (1981). *What is leisure education?... A primer for persons working with handicapped children and youth.* Washington, DC: Hawkins and Associates.

Braun, C. (1976). Teacher expectations: Socio-psychological dynamics. *Review of Educational Research, 46,* 185–213.

Brewer, G., & Kakalik, J. (1979). *Handicapped children: Strategies for improving services.* New York: McGraw-Hill.

Briard, F. K. (1976). Counseling parents of children with learning disabilities. *Social Casework, 57,* 581–585.

Brightbill, C. (1961). *Man and leisure: A philosophy of recreation.* Englewood Cliffs, NJ: Prentice-Hall.

Broden, M., Hall, R. V., Dunlap, A., & Clark, R. (1970). Effects of teacher attention and a token reinforcement system in a junior high school special education class. *Exceptional Children, 36,* 341–349.

Broden, M., Hall, R. V., & Mitts, B. (1971). The effect of self-recording on the classroom behavior of two eighth-grade students. *Journal of Applied Behavioral Analysis, 4,* 191–199.

Brolin, D. E. (Ed.). (1978, 1983). *Life-centered career education: A competency based approach.* Reston, VA: Council for Exceptional Children.

Brolin, D. E. (1982). Life-centered career education for exceptional children. *Focus on Exceptional Children, 14*(7), 1–15.

Brolin, D. E. (1983). Career education: Where do we go from here? *Career Development for Exceptional Individuals, 6*(1), 3–14.

Brolin, D. E. (1985). Preparing handicapped students to be productive adults. [Special issue: Transition from school to the world of work]. *Technique, 1*(6), 447–454.

Brolin, D. E., & Carver, J. T. (1982). Lifelong career development for adults with handicaps: A new model. *Journal of Career Education, 8*(4), 280–282.

Brolin, D. E., & Kokaska, C. (1979). *Career education for handicapped children and youth.* Columbus, OH: Merrill.

Brolin, D. E., McKay, D., & West, L. (1978). *Trainer's guide for life-centered career education.* Reston, VA: Council for Exceptional Children.

Broughton, S. F., & Lahey, B. B. (1978). Direct and collateral effects of positive reinforcement, response cost, and mixed contingencies for academic performance. *Journal of School Psychology, 16,* 126–136.

Brown, A. L. (1978). Knowing when, where, and how to remember. A problem of metacognition. In R. Glaser (Ed.), *Advances in instructional psychology.* Hillsdale, NJ: Lawrence Erlbaum.

Brown, A. L. (1980). Metacognitive development and reading. In R. J. Spiro, B. B. Bruce, & W. F. Brewer (Eds.), *Theoretical issues in reading comprehension* (pp. 453–481). Hillsdale, NJ: Lawrence Erlbaum.

Brown, A. L., Campione, J. C., & Barclay, C. R. (1979). Training self-checking routines for estimating test readiness: Generalization from list learning to prose recall. *Child Development, 50,* 501–512.

Brown, D. (1982). *Counseling and accommodating the student with learning disabilities.* Washington, DC: President's Committee on Employment of the Handicapped. (ERIC Document Reproduction Service No. ED 214 338).

Brown, J. S., & Burton, R. R. (1978). Diagnostic models for procedural bugs in basic mathematical skills. *Cognitive Science, 2,* 155–192.

Brown, L. & Perlmutter, L. (1971). Teaching functional reading to trainable level retarded students. *Education and Training of the Mentally Retarded, 6,* 74–84.

Bruck, M., & Hebert, M. (1982). Correlates of learning disabled students' peer-interaction patterns. *Learning Disability Quarterly, 5,* 353–362.

Bruininks, V. L. (1978a). Actual and perceived peer status of learning disabled students in mainstream programs. *Journal of Special Education, 12,* 51–58.

Bruininks, V. L. (1978b). Peer status and personality characteristics of learning disabled and non-disabled students. *Journal of Learning Disabilities, 11,* 29–34.

Bruno, R. M. (1981). Interpretation of pictorially presented social situations by learning disabled and normal children. *Journal of Learning Disabilities, 14,* 350–352.

Bryan, J. H., & Perlmutter, B. (1979). Immediate impressions of LD children by female adults. *Learning Disability Quarterly, 2*(1), 80–88.

Bryan, J. H., & Sherman, R. (1981). Immediate impressions of nonverbal ingratiation attempts by learning disabled boys. *Learning Disability Quarterly, 3*(2), 19–28.

Bryan, J. H., Sherman, R., & Fisher, A. (1980). Learning disabled boys' nonverbal behaviors within a dyadic interview. *Learning Disability Quarterly, 3*(1), 65–72.

Bryan, J. H., & Sonnefeld, J. J. (1981). Children's social desirability ratings of ingratiation tactics. *Learning Disability Quarterly, 4,* 287–293.

Bryan, J. H., Sonnefeld, L. J., & Greenberg, F. Z. (1981). Children's and parents' views on ingratiation tactics. *Learning Disability Quarterly, 4,* 170–179.

Bryan, T. (1982). Social skills of learning disabled children and youth: An overview. *Learning Disability Quarterly, 5,* 332–333.

Bryan, T., Pearl, R., Donahue, M., Bryan, J., & Pflaum, S. (1983). The Chicago Institute for the study of learning disabilities. *Exceptional Education Quarterly, 4*(1), 1–22.

Bryan, T. H. (1974a). An observational study of classroom behaviors of children with learning disabilities. *Journal of Learning Disabilities, 7,* 26–34.

Bryan, T. H. (1974b). Peer popularity of learning disabled children. *Journal of Learning Disabilities, 7,* 621–625.

Bryan, T. H. (1976). Peer popularity of learning disabled children: A replication. *Journal of Learning Disabilities, 9,* 307–311.

Bryan, T. H. (1977). Learning disabled children's comprehension of nonverbal communication. *Journal of Learning Disabilities, 10,* 501–506.

Bryan, T. H., & Bryan, J. H. (1977). Research: The perpetual revolution. In R. D. Kneedler & S. G. Tarver (Eds.), *Changing perspectives in special education* (pp. 273–294). Columbus, OH: Merrill.

Bryan, T. H., & Bryan, J. H. (1978). Social interactions of learning disabled children. *Learning Disability Quarterly, 1*(1), 33–38.

Bryan, T. H., Cosden, M., & Pearl, R. (1982). The effects of cooperative models on LD and NLD students. *Learning Disability Quarterly, 5,* 415–421.

Bryan, T. H., Donahue, M., & Pearl, R. (1981). Learning disabled children's peer interactions during a small-group problem solving task. *Learning Disability Quarterly, 4,* 13–22.

Bryan, T. H., Donahue, M., Pearl, R., & Sturm, C. (1981). Learning disabled children's conversational skills — the "T.V. talk show." *Learning Disability Quarterly, 4,* 250–259.

Bryan, T. H., & Pflaum, S. (1978). Social interactions of learning disabled children: A linguistic, social, and cognitive analysis. *Learning Disability Quarterly, 1*(3), 70–79.

Bryan, T. H., Werner, M., & Pearl, R. (1982). Learning disabled students' conformity responses to prosocial and antisocial situations. *Learning Disability Quarterly, 5,* 344–352.

Bryan, T. H., & Wheeler, R. (1972). Perception of children with learning disabilities: The eye of the observer. *Journal of Learning Disabilities, 5,* 484–488.

Bryan, T. H., Wheeler, R., Felcan, J., & Henek, T. (1976). "Come on Dummy" An observational study of children's communications. *Journal of Learning Disabilities, 9,* 661–669.

Budoff, M., & Gottlieb, J. (1976). Special-class EMR children mainstreamed: A study of an aptitude (learning potential) x treatment interaction. *American Journal of Mental Deficiency, 81,* 1–11.

Burstein, L., & Guiton, G. W. (1984). Methodological perspectives on documenting program impact. In B. K. Keogh (Ed.), *Advances in Special Education* (Vol. 4, pp. 21–42). Greenwich, CT: JAI Press.

Burton, L., & Bero, F. (1984). Is career education really being taught? *Academic Therapy, 19*(4), 389–395.

Bush, W. J., & Giles, M. T. (1969). *Aids to psycholinguistic teaching.* Columbus, OH: Merrill.

Butkowsky, I. S., & Willows, D. M. (1980). Cognitive-motivational characteristics of children varying in reading ability: Evidence for learned helplessness in poor readers. *Journal of Educational Psychology, 72,* 408–422.

Calfee, R., & Drum, P. (1978). Learning to read: Theory, research and practice. *Curriculum Inquiry, 8,* 183–249.

Calfee, R., Venezky, R., & Chapman, R. (1969). *Pronunciation of synthetic words with predictable and unpredictable letter-sound correspondences* (Tech. Rep. 71). Madison: Wisconsin Research and Development Center for Cognitive Learning.

Campbell, D. T. (1969). Reforms as experiments. *American Psychologist, 24,* 409–429.

Campbell, D. T., & Stanley, J. C. (1969). *Experimental and quasi-experimental designs for research.* Chicago: Rand McNally.

Campbell, L. (1968). *Study of curriculum planning.* Sacramento: California Department of Education.

Canney, G., & Winograd, P. (1979). *Schemata for reading and reading comprehension performance* (Tech. Rep. No. 120). Urbana: University of Illinois, Center for the Study of Reading.

Cantwell, D. P., & Carlson, G. R. (1978). Stimulants. In J. S. Werry (Ed.), *Pediatric psychopharmacology: The use of behavior modifying drugs in children* (pp. 171–207). New York: Brunner/Mazel.

Cantwell, D. P., & Satterfield, J. H. (1978). The prevalence of academic underachievement in hyperactive children. *Journal of Pediatric Psychology, 3,* 161–168.

Carlberg, C., & Kavale, K. (1980). The efficacy of special versus regular class placement for exceptional children: A meta-analysis. *Journal of Special Education, 14,* 295–309.

Carnine, D. (1983). Direct instruction: In search of instructional solutions for educational problems. In *Interdisciplinary voices in learning disabilities and remedial education* (pp. 1–66). Austin, TX: Pro-Ed.

Carnine, D. A. (1987). A response to "False standards, a distorting and disintegrating effect on education, turning away from useful purposes, being inevitably unfulfilled, and remaining unrealistic and irrelevant." *Remedial and Special Education, 8*(1), 42–43.

Caroll, A. W. (1967). The effects of segregated and partially integrated school programs on self-concept and academic achievement of educable mentally retarded. *Exceptional Children, 34,* 93–99.

Carpenter, T. P., Corbitt, M. K., Keprer, H. S., Lindquist, M. M., & Reys, R. E. (1981). Decimals: Results and implications from national assessment. *Arithmetic Teacher, 28,* 34–37.

Carpenter, T. P., Hiebert, J., & Moser, J. (1981). The effect of problem structure on first grader's initial solution procedures for simple addition and subtraction problems. *Journal for Research in Mathematics Education, 12,* 27–39.

Carr, T. H. (1982). What's in a model: Reading theory and reading instruction. In M. Singer (Ed.), *Competent reader, disabled reader: Research and application* (pp. 119–140). Hillsdale, NJ: Lawrence Erlbaum.

Carroll, J. A. (1984). Process into product: Teacher awareness of the writing process affects students' written products. In R. Beach & L. S. Bridwell (Eds.), *New directions in composition research.* New York: Guilford Press.

Carver, R. P. (1978). The case against statistical significance testing. *Harvard Educational Review, 48,* 378–399.

Case, R. (1982). General developmental influences on the acquisition of elementary concepts and algorithms in arithmetic. In T. P. Carpenter, J. M. Moser, & T. A. Romberg (Eds.), *Addition and subtraction: A cognitive perspective.* Hillsdale, NJ: Lawrence Erlbaum.

Cawley, J. F. (1981). Commentary. *Topics in Learning and Learning Disabilities, 1,* 3.

Cawley, J. R. (1984). *Developmental teaching of mathematics for the learning disabled.* Rockville, MD: Aspen Publications.

Cegelka, W. J. (1978). Educational materials: Curriculum guides for the mentally retarded: An analysis and recommendations. *Education and Training of the Mentally Retarded, 13,* 187–188.

Cegelka, W. J., & Tyler, J. L. (1970). The efficacy of special class placement for the mentally retarded in proper perspective. *Training School Bulletin, 67,* 33–68.

Chadwick, B. A., & Day, R. C. (1971). Systematic reinforcement: Academic performance of underachieving students. *Journal of Applied Behavior Analysis, 4,* 311–319.

Chalfant, J., & Scheffelin, M. (1969). *Central processing dysfunctions in children* (NINDS Monograph No. 9). Washington, DC: U.S. Government Printing Office.

Chall, J. S. (1979). The great debate: Ten years later with a modest proposal for reading stage. In L. Resnick & P. Weaver (Eds.), *Theory and practice of early reading* (Vol. 1, pp. 29–55). Hillsdale, NJ: Lawrence Erlbaum.

Charles, L., & Schain, R. (1981). A four-year follow-up study of the effects of methylphenidate on the behavior and academic achievement of hyperactive children. *Child Psychology, 9,* 495–505.

Chassan, J. B. (1979). *Research design in clinical psychology and psychiatry* (2nd ed.). New York: Irvington.

Chesler, B. M. (1980). *A talking mouth speaks about learning disabled college students.* Sacramento: Author.

Chi, M. T. H. (1985). Interactive roles of knowledge and strategies in development. In S. Chipman, J. Segal, & R. Glaser (Eds.), *Thinking and learning skills: Current research and open questions* (Vol. 2, pp. 457–483). Hillsdale, NJ: Lawrence Erlbaum.

Childs, R. E. (1979). A drastic change in curriculum for the educable mentally retarded child. *Mental Retardation, 17,* 299–301.

Chomsky, C. (1970). Reading, writing, and phonology. *Harvard Educational Review, 40*(2), 287–309.

Chomsky, N. (1965). *Aspects of the theory of syntax.* Cambridge, MA: MIT Press.

Christopolos, F., & Renz, P. (1969). A critical examination of special education programs. *Journal of Special Education, 3,* 371–379.

Church, G., & Bender, M. (1984). A pilot survey on computer awareness. Unpublished manuscript, Johns Hopkins University, Baltimore.

Clark, C. A., & Walberg, H. J. (1979). The use of secondary reinforcement in teaching inner-city school children. *Journal of Special Education, 3,* 177–185.

Clark, G. M. (1979). *Career education for the handicapped child in the elementary classroom.* Denver: Love Publishing.

Clark, L. (1980). *Instructions for implementing and maintaining the exceptional education management and information system (EEMIS).* Jacksonville, FL: Duval County Schools.

Clift, J., Edwards, M., Reese, S., & Vincent, R. (1977). Therapeutic recreation with hyperactive children. *Therapeutic Recreation Journal, 11,* 165–171.

Cobb, R. M., & Crump, W. D. (1984). *Post-school status of young adults identified as learning disabled while enrolled in public schools: A comparison of those enrolled and not enrolled in learning disabilities programs.* Washington, DC: U.S. Department of Education, Research Projects Section.

Cohen, A. (1969). Studies in visual perception and reading in disadvantaged children. *Journal of Learning Disabilities, 2,* 298–303.

Cohen, S. (1976). The last word. *Journal of Special Education, 10,* 167–170.

Cohen, S. A. (1976). The fuzziness and the flab: Some solutions to research problems in learning disabilities. *Journal of Special Education, 10,* 129–139.

Cohn, R. (1971). Arithmetic and learning disabilities. In H. R. Myklebust (Ed.), *Progress in learning disabilities* (Vol. 2, pp. 322–389). New York: Grune & Stratton.

Colarusso, R., & Hammill, D. (1972). *Motor-Free Visual Perception Test.* San Rafael, CA: Academic Therapy.

Coleman, N., & Harmer, W. (1982). A comparison of standardized reading tests and informal placement procedures. *Journal of Learning Disabilities, 19,* 396–398.

Coles, G. S. (1978). The learning-disabilities test battery: Empirical and social issues. *Harvard Educational Review, 48,* 313–340.

Coles, R. E., & Goodman, Y. (1980). Do we really need those oversized pencils to write with? *Theory into Practice, 19*(3), 194–196.

Collard, K. (1981). Leisure education in the schools: Why, who, and the need for advocacy. *Therapeutic Recreation Journal, 15,* 8–16.

Collins, A., & Smith, E. E. (1980, Sept.) *Teaching the process of reading comprehension* (Tech. Rep. No. 182). Urbana: University of Illinois, Center for the Study of Reading.

Conners, C. K. (1970). Symptom patterns in hyperkinetic, neurotic, and normal children. *Child Development, 41,* 667–682.

Cooke, T. P., & Apolloni, L. (1976). Developing positive social emotional behaviors: A study of training and generalization effects. *Journal of Applied Behavior Analysis, 9,* 65–78.

Cooper, C. R. (1977). Holistic evaluation of writing. In C. R. Cooper & L. Odell (Eds.), *Evaluating writing* (pp. 3–31). Urbana, IL: NCTE.

Cordoni, B. K. (1979). Assisting dyslexic college students: An experimental program design at a university. *Bulletin of the Orton Society, 29,* 261–268.

Cordoni, B. K. (1980). College options for the learning disabled. *Learning Disabilities, 4*(11).

Cordoni, B. K. (1982a). Services for college dyslexics. In R. M. Malatesha & P. G. Aaron (Eds.), *Neuropsychology of developmental dyslexia and acquired alexia and treatment. Perspectives in neurolinguistics* (Vol. 21). New York: Academic Press.

Cordoni, B. K. (1982b). Personal adjustment: The psycho-social aspects of learning disabilities. In M. R. Schmidt & H. Z. Sprandel (Eds.), *New directions for student services: Helping the learning disabled student* (No. 18). San Francisco: Jossey-Bass.

Cordoni, B. K., O'Donnell, J. P., Ramaniah, N. V., Kurtz, J., & Rosenshein, K. (1981). Wechsler Adult Intelligence score patterns for learning disabled young adults. *Journal of Learning Disabilities, 14,* 404–407.

Cornfort, R. L. (1985). Social work with unconventional children and their families. *Social Work, 30*(4), 367–368, 384.

Corno, L., & Mandinach, E. B. (1983). The role of cognition engagement in classroom learning and motivation. *Educational Psychologist, 18*(2), 88–108.

Council for Exceptional Children Ad Hoc Committee. (1984). Reply to "A Nation at Risk." *Exceptional Children, 50,* 484–494.

Coval, T., Gilhool, T., & Laski, F. (1977). Rules and tactics in institutionalization proceedings for mentally retarded persons: The role of the courts in assuring access to services in the community. *Education and Training of the Mentally Retarded, 12,* 177–185.

Cowen, E. L., Pederson, A., Babigian, H., Izzo, L. D., & Trost, M. A. (1973). Long-term follow-up of early detected vulnerable children. *Journal of Consulting and Clinical Psychology, 41,* 438–446.

Coyne, P. (1981). The status of recreation as a related service in P.L. 94-142. *Therapeutic Recreation Journal, 14,* 4–15.

Cratty, B. (1969). *Perceptual motor behavior and educational process.* Springfield, IL: Thomas.

Cratty, B. (1970). *Motor activities, motor ability, and the education of children.* Springfield, IL: Thomas.

Creager, R., & Van Riper, C. (1967). The effect of methylphenidate on the verbal productivity of children with cerebral dysfunction. *Journal of Speech and Hearing Research, 10,* 623–628.

Crimando, W., & Nichols, B. (1982). A model for vocational explanation and selective placement of the learning disabled. *Vocational Evaluation and Work Adjustment Bulletin, 15*(3), 98–102.

Crnic, K. A., Friedrich, W. N., & Greenberg, M. T. (1983). Adaptation of families with mentally retarded children: A model of stress, coping and family ecology. *American Journal of Mental Deficiency, 88,* 125–138.

Cromer, R. F. (1980). Spontaneous spelling of language-disordered children. In Ute Frith (Ed.), *Cognitive processes in spelling.* London: Academic Press.

Cronin, M. E., & Gerber, P. J. (1982). Preparing the learning disabled adolescent for adulthood. *Topics in Learning and Learning Disabilities, 2,* 55–68.

Cruickshank, W. (1967). *The brain-injured child in the home, school, and community.* Syracuse, NY: Syracuse University Press.

Cruickshank, W., Morse, W., & Johns, J. (1980). *Learning disabilities: The struggle from adolescence toward adulthood.* Syracuse, NY: Syracuse University Press.

Cullinan, D., Gadow, K. D., & Epstein, M. H. (in press). Psychotropic drug treatment among learning disabled, educable mentally retarded, and seriously emotionally disturbed students. *Journal of Abnormal Child Psychology.*

Cullinan, D., Lloyd, J, & Epstein, M. H. (1981). Strategy training: A structured approach to arithmetic instruction. *Exceptional Education Quarterly, 2,* 41–49.

Cunningham, C., & Barkley, R. (1979). The interactions of normal and hyperactive children with their mothers in free play and structured tasks. *Child Development, 50,* 217–224.

Daiute, C. (1985). *Writing and computers.* Reading, MA: Addison-Wesley.

Delacatto, C. (1959). *Treatment and prevention of reading problems.* Springfield, IL: Thomas.

Dembinski, R. J. (1977). What parents of the learning disabled really want from professionals. *Journal of Learning Disabilities, 10,* 578.

Denckla, M. B. (1977). Minimal brain dysfunction and dyslexia: Beyond diagnosis and exclusion. In M. E. Blaw, I. Rapin, & M. Kinsbourne (Eds.), *Topics in child neurology.* New York: Spectrum Publications.

Denckla, M. B., & Rudel, R. C. (1976). Rapid "automized" naming (R.A.N.): Dyslexia differentiated from other learning disabilities. *Neuropsychologia, 14,* 471–479.

Denham, C., & Lieberman, A. (1980). *Time to learn.* Washington, DC: National Institute of Education.

Deno, E. (1970). Special education as developmental capital. *Exceptional Children, 37,* 229–237.

Deno, S., Mirkin, P., & Chiang, B. (1982). Identifying valid measures of reading. *Exceptional Children, 49,* 36–45.

Department of Education. (1982). Independent study sheds light on employment statistics. *Programs for the Handicapped, July/August*(4), 13(b).

Deshler, D. D. (1978). Issues related to the education of learning disabled adolescents. *Learning Disability Quarterly, 1,* 2–10.

Deshler, D. D., Alley, G. R., Warner, M. M., & Schumaker, J. B. (1981). Instructional practices for promoting skill acquisition and generalization in severely learning disabled adolescents. *Learning Disability Quarterly, 4,* 415–421.

Deshler, D. D., & Schumaker, J. B. (1983). Social skills of learning disabled adolescents: Characteristics and intervention. *Topics in Learning and Learning Disabilities, 3*(2), 15–23.

Deshler, D., Schumaker, J., Alley, G., Warner, M., & Clark, F. (1982). Learning disabilities in adolescent and young adult populations: Research implications. *Focus on Exceptional Children, 15*(1), 1–12.

Deschler, D. D., Schumaker, J. B., & Lenz, B. K. (1984). Academic and cognitive interventions for LD adolescents: Part I. *Journal of Learning Disabilities, 17,* 108–117.

Dickstein, E. B., & Warren, D. R. (1980). Role-taking deficits in learning disabled children. *Journal of Learning Disabilities, 13,* 378–382.

Dil, N. (1983). Affective curricula: Theory, models and implementation. *Topics in Early Childhood Special Education, 2,* 25–33.

Dinsmore, J. A., & Isacson, D. K. (1986). Tactics for teaching dyslexic students. *Academic Therapy, 21*(3), 293–300.

Disimoni, F. (1978). *The Token Test for Children.* New York: Teaching Resources.

Dobbert, D. (1973). Procedures for the selection of instructional material at various stages of the evaluative process. In J. Armstrong (Ed.), *A sourcebook for the evaluation of instructional materials and media* (pp. 453–462). Madison: University of Wisconsin, Special Education Instructional Materials Center.

Dobbins, D. A. (1985). A classification of poor readers. *Early Child Development and Care, 19*(3), 183–198.

Doehring, D. G., & Hoshko, I. M. (1977). Classification of reading problems by the Q-technique of factor analysis. *Cortex, 13,* 281–292, 284.

Doehring, D. G., Hoshko, I. M., & Bryans. (1979). Statistical classification of children with reading problems. *Journal of Clinical Neuropsychology, 1,* 5–16.

Doehring, D. G., Trites, R. L., Patel, P. G., & Fiedorowicz, C. A. M. (1981). *Reading disabilities: The interaction of reading, language, and neuropsychological deficits.* New York: Academic Press.

Donahue, M., & Bryan, T. (1983). Conversational skills and modeling in learning disabled boys. *Applied Psycholinguistics, 4,* 251–278.

Donahue, M., Pearl, R., & Bryan, T. (1980). Learning disabled children's conversational competence: Responses to inadequate messages. *Applied Psycholinguistics, 1,* 387–403.

Donahue, M., Pearl, R., & Bryan, T. (1982). Learning disabled children's syntactic proficiency during a communicative task. *Journal of Speech and Hearing Disorders, 47,* 397–403.

Donahue, M. L. (1981). Requesting strategies of learning disabled children. *Applied Psycholinguistics, 2,* 213–234.

Donmoyer, R. (1985). The rescue from relativism: Two failed attempts and an alternative strategy. *Educational Researcher, 14,* 13–20.

Douglas, V. I. (1972). Stop, look, and listen: The problem of sustained attention and impulse control in hyperactive and normal children. *Canadian Journal of Behavioural Science, 4,* 259–282.

Downing, J. (1970). Children's concepts of language in learning to read. *Educational Research, 12,* 106–112.

Downing, J. (1972). Children's developing concepts of spoken and written language.

Journal of Reading Behavior, 4, 1–19.

Downing, J. (1978). Linguistic awareness. English orthography and reading instruction. *Journal of Reading Behavior, 10,* 103–114.

Downing, J. (1979). *Reading and reasoning.* New York: Springer-Verlag.

Downing, J., & Oliver, P. (1974). The child's concept of 'a word.' *Reading Research Quarterly, 9,* 568–582.

Drabman, R. S., Spitalnik, R., & O'Leary, K. D. (1973). Teaching self-control to disruptive children. *Journal of Abnormal Psychology, 82,* 10–16.

Duffy, F. H., Denckla, M. B., Bartels, P. H., & Sandini, G. (1980). Dyslexia: Automated diagnosis by computerized classification of brain electrical activity. *Annals of Neurology,* 421–428.

Duffy, J. (1974). *Type it.* Cambridge, MA: Educators Publishing Service.

Dunkin, M. J., & Biddle, B. J. (1974). *The study of teaching.* New York: Holt, Rinehart & Winston.

Dunn, L. M. (1968). Special education for the mildly retarded — is much of it justifiable? *Exceptional Children, 35,* 5–22.

Dunn, L. M., & Markwardt, F. C. (1970). *Peabody Individual Achievement Test.* Circle Pines, NM: American Guidance Service.

Dweck, C. S. (1975). Achievement. In M. E. Lamb (Ed.), *Social and personality development* (pp. 114–130). New York: Holt, Rinehart & Winston.

Dykman, R. A., Ackerman, P. T., & McCray, D. S. (1980). Effects of methylphenidate on selective and sustained attention in hyperactive, reading-disabled and presumably attention-disordered boys. *Journal of Nervous and Mental Diseases, 168,* 745–752.

Edgington, R. E. (1975). SLD children: A ten-year follow-up. *Academic Therapy, 11,* 53–64.

Egelman, C. D. (1981). Career workshops for the disabled. *Journal of College Student Personnel, 22*(6), 567–568.

Ehri, L. C. (1979). Linguistic insight: Threshold of reading acquisition. In T. G. Waller & G. E. MacKinnon (Eds.), *Reading research: Advances in theory and practice* (Vol. 1). New York: Academic Press.

Elenbogen, M. L. (1957). A comparative study of some aspects of academic and social adjustment of two groups of mentally retarded children in special classes and in regular classes (Doctoral dissertation, Northwestern University, 1957). *Dissertation Abstracts, 17,* 2496.

Elkind, D. (1983). Viewpoint: The curriculum disabled child. *Topics in Learning and Learning Disabilities, 3,* 71–78.

Ellington, C., & Winskoff, L. (1982). Low cost implementation of a career education program for elementary school children with handicaps. *Journal of Career Education, 8,* 246–255.

Engelmann, S. (1969). *Preventing failure in the primary grades.* Chicago: SRA.

Englert, C. S. (1983). Measuring special education teacher effectiveness. *Exceptional Children, 50*(3), 247–254.

Entwisle, D. R. (1976). Young children's expectations for reading. In J. Guthrie (Ed.), *Aspects of reading acquisition* (pp. 37–38). Baltimore: Johns Hopkins University Press.

Epps, S., Ysseldyke, J. E., & Algozzine, B. (1983). Impact of different definitions of learning disabilities on the number of students identified. *Journal of Psychoeducational Assessment, 1,* 341–352.

Epps, S., Ysseldyke, J. E., & Algozzine, B. (1985). An analysis of the conceptual framework underlying definitions of learning disabilities. *Journal of School Psychology, 23,* 133–144.

Erikson, E. H. (1963). *Child and society* (2nd ed.). New York: Norton.

Evans, G. W., & Oswalt, G. L. (1968). Acceleration of academic progress through the manipulation of peer influence. *Behavior Research and Therapy, 6,* 189–195.

Evenson, T. L., & Evenson, M. L. (1983). An innovative approach to career development of disabled college students. *Journal of Rehabilitation, 49*(2), 64–67.

Faerstein, L. M. (1981). Stress and coping in families of learning disabled children: A literature review. *Journal of Learning Disabilities, 14,* 420–423.

Fafard, M. B., & Haubrich, P. A. (1981). Vocational and social adjustment of learning disabled young adults: A follow-up study. *Learning Disability Quarterly, 4,* 122–130.

Farber, B. (1960). Family organization and crisis: Maintenance of integration in families with a severely retarded child. *Monographs of the Society for Research in Child Development, 25,* 1–25.

Farber, B. (1979). Sociological ambivalence and family care. In R. H. Bruininks & G. C. Krantz (Eds.), *Family care of developmentally disabled members: Conference proceedings.* Minneapolis: University of Minnesota.

Farber, B., & Jenne, W. (1963). Interaction with retarded siblings and life goals of children. *Marriage and Family Living, 25,* 96–98.

Farber, B., & Jenne, W. (1979). Sociological ambivalence and family care. In R. H. Bruininks & G. C. Krantz (Eds.), *Family care of developmentally disabled members: Conference proceedings.* Minneapolis: University of Minnesota.

Farnham–Diggory, S. (1972). The development of an equivalence system. In S. Farnham–Diggory (Ed.), *Information processing in children.* New York: Academic Press.

Farnham–Diggory, S., & Nelson, B. (1984). Cognitive analyses of basic school tests. *Applied Developmental Psychology, 1,* 21–74.

Favell, J. (1973). Reduction of stereotypes by reinforcement of toy play. *Mental Retardation, 11,* 21–23.

Fayne, H., & Bryant, N. D. (1981). Relative effects of various word synthesis strategies on phonics achievement of the learning disabled. *Journal of Educational Psychology, 73,* 616–623.

Feagans, L. (1983). Discourse processes in learning disabled children. In J. D. McKinney & L. Feagans (Eds.), *Current topics in learning disabilities* (Vol. 1, pp. 87–115). Norwood, NJ: Ablex.

Feagans, L., & Applebaum, M. I. (1986). Language subtypes and their validation in learning disabled children. *Journal of Educational Psychology, 78*(5), 358–364.

Feagans, L., & McKinney, J. D. (1981). The pattern of exceptionality across domains in learning disabled children. *Journal of Applied Developmental Psychology, 1,* 313–328.

Federal Register. (1977, Wednesday, May 4). Nondiscrimination on basis of handicap. Washington, DC, pp. 22676–22702.

Federal Register. (1977, December 29). Washington, DC, pp. 65082–65085.

Feingold, B. F. (1976). Hyperkinesis and learning disabilities linked to the ingestion of artificial food colors and flavors. *Journal of Learning Disabilities, 9,* 551–559.

Feldman, K. A. (1971). Using the work of others: Some observations of reviewing and integrating. *Sociology of Education, 44,* 86–102.

Ferhold, J. B., & Solnit, A. J. (1978). Counseling parents of mentally retarded and learning disabled children. In L. E. Arnold (Ed.), *Helping parents help their children.* New York: Brunner/Mazel.

Fernald, G. (1943). Remedial techniques in basic school subjects. New York: McGraw-Hill.

Ferritor, D. E., Buckholdt, D., Hamblin, R. L., & Smith, L. (1972). The non-effects of contingent reinforcement for attending behavior on work accomplished. *Journal of Applied Behavior Analysis, 5,* 7–17.

Fincham, F. (1977). A comparison of moral judgment in learning disabled and normal-achieving boys. *Journal of Psychology, 96,* 153–160.

Fisher, C. W., & Berliner, D. C. (1985). *Perspectives on instructional time.* White Plaines, NY: Longman.

Fisk, J., & Rourke, B. (1979). Identification of subtypes of learning disabled children at three age levels: A multivariate approach. *Journal of Clinical Neuropsychology, 1,* 289–310.

Fitzgerald, E. (1966). *Straight language for the deaf.* Washington, DC: Volta Bureau.

Fitzmaurice–Hayes, A. M. (1984). Curriculum and instructional activities grade 2 through grade 4. In J. F. Cawley (Ed.), *Developmental teaching of mathematics for the learning disabled.* Rockville, MD: Aspen Publications.

Fitzmaurice–Hayes, A. M. (1985). Whole numbers: Concepts and skills. In J. F. Cawley (Ed.), *Secondary school mathematics for the learning disabled.* Rockville, MD: Aspen Publications.

Flack, V. (1973). Application of management principles to instructional methods. *Exceptional Children, 39*(5), 401–407.

Flavell, J. H. (1976). Metacognitive aspects of problem solving. In L. B. Resnick (Ed.), *The nature of intelligence* (pp. 231–235). Hillsdale, NJ: Lawrence Erlbaum.

Fleischner, J. E. (1983). *Arithmetic Task Force progress report.* Unpublished manuscript, Columbia University, Teacher's College, Institute for the Study of Learning Disabilities, New York.

Fleischner, J. E. (1985). Arithmetic instruction for handicapped children in elementary grades. *Focus on Learning Problems in Mathematics, 7,* 23–24.

Fleischner, J. E., & Garnett, K. (1983). Arithmetic difficulties among learning-disabled children: Background and current directions. *Learning Disabilities, 2,* 111–124.

Fleischner, J. E., Garnett, K., & Preddy, D. (1982). *Mastery of basic number facts by learning disabled students: An intervention study* (Tech. Rep. No. 17). New York: Columbia University, Teachers College.

Fleischner, J. E., Garnett, K., & Shepherd, M. J. (1982). Proficiency in arithmetic basic fact computation of learning disabled and nondisabled children. *Focus on Learning problems in Mathematics, 4,* 47–55.

Fleischner, J. E., Nuzum, M. B., & Marzola, E. S. (1987). Devising an instructional program to teach arithmetic problem solving skills to students with learning disabilities. *Journal of Learning Disabilities, 20,* 214–217.

Fleischner, J. E., & Shepherd, M. J. (1980). *Improving the performance of children with learning disabilities: Instruction matters* (Tech. Rep. No. 27). New York: Columbia University, Teachers College, The Research Institute for the Study of Learning Disabilities.

Fleisher, L. A., & Jenkins, J. R. (1983). The effect of word- and comprehension-emphasis instruction on reading performance. *Learning Disability Quarterly, 6*(2), 146–154.

Fleisher, L. S., Jenkins, J. R., & Pany, D. (1979). Effects on poor readers' comprehension of training in rapid decoding. *Reading Research Quarterly, 15,* 30–48.

Flower, L. (1985). *Problem-solving strategies for writing* (2nd ed.). San Diego: Harcourt Brace Jovanovich.

Flynn, P. A. (1985). Adapting computer software to accommodate the learning disabled student. *Journal of Reading, Writing, and Learning Disabilities International, 1*(4), 93–97.

Fokes, J. (1976). *Fokes sentence builder.* New York: Teacher Resources.

Ford, A., Brown, L., Pumpian, I., Baumgart, D., Nisbet, J., Schroeder, J., & Loomis, R. (1980). *Strategies for developing individualized recreation/leisure plans for adolescent and young adult severely handicapped students.* Madison: University of Wisconsin.

Forness, S. (1981). Concepts of school learning and behavior disorders: Implications for research and practice. *Exceptional Children, 48,* 56–64.

Forness, S. R. (1982). Diagnosing dyslexia: A note on the need for ecologic assessment. *American Journal of Diseases of Children, 134,* 237-242.

Forness, S. R. (1983). Diagnostic schooling for children or adolescents with behavior disorders. *Behavior Disorders, 8,* 176-190.

Forness, S. R., & Esveldt, K. C. (1975). Prediction of high-risk kindergarten children through observation. *Journal of Special Education, 9,* 375-388.

Forness, S. R., Guthrie, D., & Hall, R. J. (1976). Follow-up of high-risk children identified in kindergarten through direct classroom observation. *Psychology in the Schools, 13,* 45-49.

Forness, S. R., Hall, R. J., & Guthrie, D. (1977). Eventual school placement of kindergartners observed as high risk in the classroom. *Psychology in the Schools, 14,* 315-317.

Forness, S. R., & Kavale, K. A. (1984). Education of the mentally retarded: A note on policy. *Education and Training of the Mentally Retarded, 19,* 239-245.

Forness, S. R., & Kavale, K. A. (1987). Holistic inquiry and the scientific challenge in special education: A reply to Iano. *Remedial and Special Education, 8*(1), 47-51.

Forrest, D. L., & Waleer, T. G. (1980). *What do children know about their reading and study skills?* Paper presented at the annual meeting of the American Educational Resource Association, Boston.

Foster, G. E. (1972). *A short-term follow-up study of the academic, social, and vocational adjustment and achievement of children five to ten years following placement in a perceptual development program.* Unpublished doctoral dissertation, Wayne State University, Detroit.

Fox, B., & Routh, D. K. (1975). Analyzing spoken language into words, syllables and phonemes: A developmental study. *Journal of Psycholinguistic Research, 4,* 331-342.

Francis-Williams, J. (1976). Early identification of children likely to have specific learning difficulties. Report of a follow-up. *Developmental Medicine and Child Neurology, 18,* 71-77.

Franklin, G. S., & Sparkman, W. E. (1978). The cost effectiveness of two program delivery systems for exceptional children. *Journal of Educational Finance, 3,* 305-314.

Frauenheim, J. G. (1978). Academic achievement characteristics of adult males who were diagnosed as dyslexic in childhood. *Journal of Learning Disabilities, 11,* 476-483.

Frederickson, C. H. (1979). Discourse comprehension and early reading. In L. Resnick & P. Weaver (Eds.), *Theory and practice of early reading* (Vol. 1). Hillsdale, NJ: Lawrence Erlbaum.

Freeman, D. J., Kuhs, T. M., Knappen, L. B., & Porter, A. C. (1982). A closer look at standardized tests. *The Arithmetic Teacher, 29,* 50-54.

Friars, E., & Gelmann, N. (1981). *Special education management by information: A design handbook.* Washington, DC: National Association of State Directors of Special Education.

Frostig, M., & Horn, D. (1964). *The Frostig program for the development of visual perception.* Chicago: Follett Education Corporation.

Fuchs, L. S., & Fuchs, D. (1986). Effects of systematic formative evaluation: A meta-analysis. *Exceptional Children, 53*(3), 199-208.

Gable, R., Hendrickson, J., Young, C., Shores, R., & Stowitschek, J. (1983). A comparison of teacher approved statements across categories of exceptionality. *Journal of Special Education Technology, 6,* 15-22.

Gadow, K. D. (1981). Prevalence of drug treatment for hyperactivity and other childhood behavior disorders. In K. D. Gadow & J. Loney (Eds.), *Psychosocial aspects of drug treatment for hyperactivity.* Boulder, CO: Westview Press.

Gadow, K. D. (1983). Effects of stimulant drugs on academic performance in hyperactive and learning disabled children. *Journal of Learning Disabilities, 16,* 290–299.

Gadow, K. D. (1985). Relative efficacy of pharmacological, behavioral, and combination treatments for enhancing academic performance. *Clinical Psychology Review, 5,* 513–533.

Gadow, K. D. (1986). *Children on medication: I. Hyperactivity, learning disabilities, and mental retardation.* San Diego: College-Hill Press.

Gadow, K. D., & Sprague, R. L. (1980, September). *An anterospective followup of hyperactive children into adolescence: Licit and illicit drug use.* Paper presented at the meeting of the American Psychological Association, Montreal.

Gadow, K. D., & Swanson, H. L. (1985). Assessing drug effects on academic performance. *Psychopharmacology Bulletin, 21,* 877–886.

Gadow, K. D., Torgeson, J., Greenstein, J., & Schell, R. (1985). Learning disabilities. In M. Hersen (Ed.), *Pharmacological and behavioral treatment: An integrated approach.* New York: Wiley & Sons.

Gage, N. L. (Ed.). (1976). *The psychology of teaching methods: The 75th yearbook of the National Society for the Study of Education, Part I.* Chicago: University of Chicago Press.

Gagne, R. (1965). *The conditions of learning.* New York: Holt, Rinehart & Winston.

Gagne, R. (1968). Instructional variables and learning outcomes. CSE Report No. 16.

Garmezy, N. (1974). Children at risk — the search for antecedents of schizophrenia: I. Conceptual models and research methods. *Schizophrenia Bulletin, 1,* 14–90.

Garner, R. (1980). Monitoring of understanding: An investigation of good and poor readers' awareness of induced miscomprehension of text. *Journal of Reading Behavior, 12,* 55–63.

Garner, R. (1981). Monitoring of passage inconsistency among poor comprehenders: A preliminary text of the "Piecemeal Processing" explanation. *Journal of Educational Research, 74,* 159–162.

Garner, R., & Kraus, C. (1982). Good and poor comprehender differences in knowing and regulating reading behaviors. *Educational Research Quarterly, 6,* 5–12.

Garner, R., & Reis, R. (1981). Monitoring and resolving comprehension obstacles: An investigation of spontaneous text lookbacks among upper-grade good and poor comprehenders. *Reading Research Quarterly, 14,* 569–582.

Garner, R., & Taylor, N. (1982). Monitoring of understanding: An investigation of attentional assistance needs at different grade and reading proficiency levels. *Reading Psychology, 3,* 1–6.

Garnett, K., & Fleischner, J. E. (1987). Mathematical disabilities. *Pediatric Annals, 16,* 159–176.

Garnett, K., Frank, B., & Fleischner, J. A. (1983a). *A strategies generalization approach to basic fact learning (Addition and subtraction lessons)* (Manual No. 3). New York: Columbia University, Teachers College, Research Institute for the Study of Learning Disabilities.

Garnett, K., Frank, B., & Fleischner, J. (1983b). *A mastery/motivation approach to basic fact learning (Addition and subtraction lessons)* (Manual No. 4). New York: Columbia University, Teachers College, Research Institute for the Study of Learning Disabilities.

Garnett, K., Frank, B., & Fleischner, J. (1983c). *A strategies generalization approach to basic fact learning (Multiplication lessons).* New York: Columbia University, Teachers College, Research Institute for the Study of Learning Disabilities.

Garnett, K., Frank, B., & Fleischner, J. (1983d). *A mastery/motivation approach to basic fact learning* (Multiplication lessons). New York: Columbia University, Teachers College, Research Institute for the Study of Learning Disabilities.

Garrett, M. K., & Crump, W. D. (1980). Peer acceptance, teacher preferences, and self-appraisal of social status among learning disabled students. *Learning Disability Quarterly, 3,* 42–48.

Gath, A. (1973). The school age siblings of Mongol children. *British Journal of Psychiatry, 123,* 161–167.

Geiger, W. L., Brownsmith, K., & Forgonne, C. (1978). Differential importance of skills for TMR students as perceived by teachers. *Education and Training of the Mentally Retarded, 13,* 259–264.

Geist, C. S., & McGrath, C. (1983). Psychosocial aspects of the adult learning disabled person in the world of work: A vocational rehabilitation perspective. *Rehabilitation Literature, 44*(7–8), 210–213.

Gelman, R., & Gallistel, C. R. (1978). *The child's understanding of numbers.* Cambridge, MA: Harvard University Press.

Gerber, M. M. (1984). The Department of Education's Sixth Annual Report to Congress on PL 94-142: Is Congress getting the full story? *Exceptional Children, 51,* 209–224.

Gerber, M. M. (1983). Learning disabilities and cognitive strategies: A case for training or constraining problem solving? *Journal of Learning Disabilities 16*(5), 255–260.

Gerber, M. M., & Semmel, M. I. (1984). Teacher as imperfect test: Reconceptualizing the referral process. *Educational Psychologist, 19,* 137–148.

Gerber, P. J., & Zinkgraf, S. A. (1982). A comparative study of social-perceptual ability in learning disabled and non-handicapped students. *Learning Disability Quarterly, 5,* 374–378.

Gershman, J. (1976). *A follow-up study of graduates of the perceptual and behavioral special classes* (Research Report No. 143). Toronto, Canada: Board of Education. (ERIC Document Reproduction Service No. ED 135 169)

Gibson, E. (1972). Reading for some purpose. In J. Kavanaugh & I. Mattingly (Eds.), *Language by ear and by eye: The relationship between speech and reading* (pp. 3–19). Cambridge, MA: MIT Press.

Gibson, E. J., & Levin, H. (1975). *The psychology of reading.* Cambridge, MA: MIT Press.

Gilhool, T. (1976). Changing public policies in the individualization of instruction: Roots and force. *Education and Training of the Mentally Retarded, 11,* 180–188.

Gillet, P. (1978). *Career education for children with learning disabilities.* San Rafael, CA: Academic Therapy Publications.

Gillet, P. (1980). Career education and the learning disabled student. *Career Development for Exceptional Individuals, 3,*(2) 67–73.

Gillet, P. (1981). *Of work and worth: Career education for the handicapped.* Salt Lake City: Olympus Publishing.

Gillingham, A., & Stillman, B. W. (1960). *Remedial training for children with specific disability in reading, spelling, and penmanship.* Cambridge, MA: Educators Publishing Service.

Ginsburg, H. P. (Ed.). (1983). *The development of mathematical thinking.* New York: Academic Press.

Giordano, G. (1978). Convergent research on language and teaching reading. *Exceptional Children, 44,* 604–611.

Gittelman, R. (1985). Controlled trials of remedial approaches to reading disability. *Journal of Child Psychology and Psychiatry and Applied Disciplines, 26*(6), 843–846.

Gittelman, R., Klein, D. F., & Feingold, I. (1983). Children with reading disorders — II. Effects of methylphenidate in combination with reading remediation. *Journal of Child Psychology and Psychiatry, 24,* 193–212.

Gittelman–Klein, R., & Klein, D. F. (1976). Methylphenidate effects in learning disabilities. *Archives of General Psychiatry, 33,* 655–664.

Glaser, R. (1972). Individuals and learning: The new aptitudes. *Educational Researcher, 6,* 5–13.

Glass, G. (1973). *Teaching decoding as separate from reading.* Garden City, NY: Adelphi

University Press.

Glass, G. V. (1979). Policy for the unpredictable (uncertainty research and policy). *Educational Researcher, 8,* 12-14.

Glass, G. V., McGaw, B., & Smith, M. L. (1981). *Meta-analysis in social research.* Beverly Hills, CA: Sage.

Glass, G. V., & Robbins, M. P. (1967). A critique of experiments of the role of neurological organization in reading performance. *Reading Research Quarterly, 3,* 5-52.

Glavin, J. P. (1974). Behaviorally oriented resource rooms: A follow-up. *The Journal of Special Education, 8,* 337-347.

Glavin, J. P., Quay, H. C., Annesley, R. F., & Werry, J. S. (1971). An experimental resource room for behavior problem children. *Exceptional Children, 38,* 131-137.

Glazzard, P. (1982). Long-range kindergarten prediction of reading achievement in first through sixth grades. *Learning Disability Quarterly, 5,* 85-88.

Gleason, G. (1981). Microcomputers in education: The state of the art. *Educational Technology, 2*(1), 7-18.

Gleitman, L., & Rozin, P. (1977). The structure and acquisition of reading. I: Relations between orthographics and the structure of reading. In A. Reber & D. Scarborough (Eds.), *Toward a psychology of reading* (pp. 1-54). Hillsdale, NJ: Lawrence Erlbaum.

Glenwick, D. S., & Barocas, R. (1979). Training impulsive children in verbal self-control by the use of natural change agents. *Journal of Special Education, 13,* 387-398.

Glusker, P. (1968). An integrational approach to spelling. In J. Arens (Ed.), *Building spelling skills in dyslexic children.* San Rafael, CA: Academic Therapy Press.

Goldman, R., & Hardin, V. (1982). The social perception of learning disabled and non-learning disabled children. *The Exceptional Child, 29*(1), 57-63.

Goldstein, H. (1975). *The social learning curriculum.* Columbus, OH: Merrill.

Goldstein, H., Moss, J. W., & Jordan, L. J. (1965). *The efficacy of special class training on the development of mentally retarded children* (Cooperative Research Progress Report No. 619). Urbana: University of Illinois, Institute for Research on Exceptional Children. (ERIC Document Reproduction Service No. ED 002 907)

Goldstein, H., & Siegle, D. (1958). *A curriculum guide for teachers of the educable mentally handicapped.* Springfield, IL: Department of Public Instruction.

Golick, M. (1973). *Deal me in! The use of playing cards in teaching learning.* New York: Jeffrey Norton.

Gollub, W. L. (1977). Family communication rituals to aid children's learning. *Langauge Arts, 54,* 655-660.

Good, T. L. (1983). Classroom research: A decade of progress. *Educational Psychologist, 18,* 127-144.

Goodlad, J. I., & Klein, M. F. (1970). *Behind the classroom door.* Worthington, OH: Jones.

Goodman, K., & Goodman, Y. (1979). Learning to read is natural. In L. Resnick & P. Weaver (Eds.), *Theory and practice in early reading* (Vol. 1). Hillsdale, NJ: Lawrence Erlbaum.

Goodman, K. S. (1967). Reading: A psycholinguistic guessing game. *Journal of the Reading Specialist, 6,* 126-133.

Goodman, L., & Hammill, D. (1973). The effectiveness of Kephart-Getman activities in developing perceptual-motor and cognitive skills. *Focus on Exceptional Children, 4,* 1-9.

Goodstein, H. A. (1984). Measurement and assessment group and individual techniques. In J. F. Cawley (Ed.), *Secondary school mathematics for the learning disabled.* Rockville, MD: Aspen Publications.

Goodstein, H. A., & Kahn, H. (1974). Pattern of achievement among children with learning difficulties. *Exceptional Children, 5,* 47-49.

Gorman, R. (1974). *The psychology of classroom learning: An inductive approach.* Columbus, OH: Merrill.

Gorney–Krupsaw, B., Atwater, J., Powell, L., & Morris, E. K. (1981). *Improving social interactions between learning disabled adolescents and teachers: A child effects approach* (Research Report No. 45). Lawrence: University of Kansas, Institute for Research in Learning Disabilities.

Gottesman, R. L. (1978). *Follow-up study of reading achievement in learning disabled children* (Final Report). Washington, DC: Department of Health, Education, and Welfare. (ERIC Document Reproduction Service No. ED 155 833)

Gottesman, R. L. (1979). Follow-up of learning disabled children. *Learning Disability Quarterly, 2,* 60–69.

Gough, P. (1972). One second of reading. In J. Kavanaugh & I. Mattingly (Eds.), *Language by ear and by eye: The relationship between speech and reading.* Cambridge, MA: MIT Press.

Gough, P., & Hillinger, M. (1980). Learning to read: An unnatural act. *Bulletin of the Orton Society, 30,* 179–196.

Gough, P. B., & Turner, W. E. (1986). Decoding, reading, and reading disability. *Remedial and Special Education, 7*(1).

Graham, F. K., & Kendall, B. S. (1960). Memory-For-Designs Test: Revised General Manual. *Perceptual and Motor Skills Monograph* (Suppl. 2), 6, 147–188.

Gralicker, B., Fishler, K., & Koch, R. (1962). Teenage reaction to a mentally retarded sibling. *American Journal of Mental Deficiency, 66,* 838–843.

Graves, D. H. (1985). All children can write. *Learning Disabilities Focus, 1*(1), 36–43.

Gray, W. S. (1952). *The twenty-fourth yearbook of the National Society for the Study of Education: Part I.* Bloomington, IL: Public School Publishing.

Green, T. (1968). *Work, leisure, and the American Schools.* New York: Random House.

Greenan, J. R. (1982). Problems and issues in delivering vocational education instruction and support services to students with learning disabilities. *Journal of Learning Disabilities, 15,* 231–235.

Greene, V. E., & Enfield, M. (1979). *Framing your thoughts.* Bloomington, MN: Winston Press.

Gregg, L. W., & Farnham–Diggory, S. (1979). How to study reading: An information processing analysis. In L. Resnick & P. Weaver (Eds.), *Theory and practice of early reading* (Vol. 3, pp. 53–70). Hillsdale, NJ: Lawrence Erlbaum.

Gresham, F. M. (1981). Social skills training with handicapped children: A review. *Review of Educational Research, 51,* 139–176.

Groen, G., & Parkman, L. A. (1972). Chronometric analysis of simple addition. *Psychological Review, 79,* 329–343.

Grossman, F. (1972). *Brothers and sisters of retarded children: An exploratory study.* Syracuse, NY: Syracuse University Press.

Gunn, S., & Peterson, C. (1978). *Therapeutic recreation program design: Principles and practices.* Englewood Cliffs, NJ: Prentice-Hall.

Guskin, S., & Spicker, H. (1968). Educational research in mental retardation. In N. O. Ellis (Ed.), *International review of mental retardation* (Vol. 3, pp. 217–278). New York: Academic Press.

Guthrie, J. T. (1973). Models of reading and reading disability. *Journal of Educational Psychology, 65,* 9–18.

Guthrie, J. T. (1978). Principles of instruction: A critique of Johnson's "Remedial Approaches to Dyslexia." In A. L. Benton & D. Pearl (Eds.), *An appraisal of current knowledge* (pp. 423–433). New York: Oxford University Press.

Guthrie, J. T., Martuza, V., & Seifert, M. (1979). Impacts of instructional time in reading. In L. Resnick & P. Weaver (Eds.), *Theory and practice of early reading* (Vol. 3, pp. 153–

178). Hillsdale, NJ: Lawrence Erlbaum.

Guthrie, J. T., & Seifert, M. (1978). Education for children with reading disabilities. In H. Myklebust (Ed.), *Progress in learning disabilities* (Vol. 4, pp. 223–225). New York: Grune & Stratton.

Hakes, D., Evans, J., & Tunmer, W. (1980). *The development of metalinguistic abilities in children.* New York: Springer-Verlag.

Hall, R. J. (1980). An information processing approach to the study of exceptional children. In B. Keogh (Ed.), *Advances in special education* (Vol. 2, pp. 79–110). Greenwich, CT: JAI.

Hall, R. J., & Humphreys, M. (1982). Research on specific learning disabilities: Deficits and remediation. *Topics in Learning and Learning Disabilities, 2,* 68–78.

Hallahan, D. P. (Ed.). (1980). Teaching exceptional children to use cognitive strategies. *Exceptional Education Quarterly, 1.*

Hallahan, D. P., & Cruickshank, W. M. (1973). *Psychoeducational foundations of learning disabilities.* Englewood Cliffs, NJ: Prentice-Hall.

Hallahan, D. P., Hall, R. J., Ianna, S. O., Kneedler, R. D., Lloyd, J. W., Loper, A. B., & Reeve, R. E. (1983). Summary of the research findings at the University of Virginia Learning Disabilities Research Institute. *Exceptional Education Quarterly, 4*(1), 95–114.

Hallahan, D. P., & Kauffman, J. (1976). *Introduction to learning disabilities: A psychobehavioral approach.* Englewood Cliffs, NJ: Prentice-Hall.

Hallahan, D. P., Lloyd, J. W., Kauffman, J. M., & Loper, A. B. (1983). Academic problems. In R. J. Morris & T. R. Kratochiwill (Eds.), *The practice of child therapy.* New York: Pergamon.

Hallahan, D. P., Lloyd, J., Kosiewicz, M. M., Kauffman, J. M., & Graves, A. W. (1979). Self-monitoring of attention as a treatment for a learning-disabled boy's off-task behavior. *Learning Disability Quarterly, 2,* 24–34.

Hallahan, D. P., & Reeve, R. C. (1980). Selective attention and distractability. In B. K. Keogh (Ed.), *Advances in special education* (Vol. 1, pp. 141–181). Greenwich, CT: JAI Press.

Halpern, N. (1984). Artificial intelligence and the education of the learning disabled. *Journal of Learning Disabilities, 17*(2), 118–120.

Hambleton, R. A. (1973). A review of testing and decision-making procedures for selected instructional programs. *ACT Technical Bulletin,* No. 15.

Hammil, D., & Bartel, N. R. (1975). *Teaching students with learning and behavioral problems.* Boston: Allyn and Bacon.

Hammill, D. D., Brown, V. I., Larsen, S. C., & Wiederholt, J. L. (1980). *Test of adolescent language.* Austin, TX: Pro-Ed.

Hammill, D. D., & Larsen, S. (1974). The effectiveness of psycholinguistic training. *Exceptional Children, 41,* 5–15.

Hammill, D. D., & Larsen, S. C. (1978). The effectiveness of psycholinguistic training: A reaffirmation of position. *Exceptional Children, 44,* 402–414.

Hammill, D. D., & Larsen, S. C. (1983). *Test of written language.* Austin, TX: Pro-Ed.

Hanna, P. R., Hodges, R. F., & Hanna, J. S. (1971). *Spelling: Structures and strategies.* Boston: Houghton Mifflin.

Hannaford, A., & Sloane, E. (1981). Microcomputers: Powerful learning tool with proper programming. *Teaching Exceptional Children, 14*(2), 54–56.

Hardin, V. (1978). Ecological assessment and interaction for learning disabled students. *Learning Disability Quarterly, 1,* 15–20.

Hargis, C. H. (1982). Word recognition development. *Focus on Exceptional Children, 14*(9), 1–8.

Haring, N. G., & Hauck, M. A. (1969). Improved learning conditions in the establishment of reading skills with disabled readers. *Exceptional Children, 35,* 34–352.

Harris, A., & Sarver, B. (1966). The CRAFT project: Instructional time in reading research. *Reading Research Quarterly, 2,* 27–57.

Harris, A. J. (1982). How many kinds of reading disability are there? *Journal of Learning Disabilities, 19,* 456–460.

Harris, F. C., & Lahey, B. B. (1978). A method for combining occurrence and nonoccurrence interobserver agreement scores. *Journal of Behavior Analysis, 11,* 523–527.

Harris, K. R. (1985). Conceptual, methodological, and clinical issues in cognitive-behavioral assessment. *Journal of Abnormal Child Psychology, 13,* 373–390.

Harris, L. A., & Sherman, J. A. (1972). Effects of homework assignments and consequences on performance in social studies and mathematics. *Journal of Applied Behavior Analysis, 7,* 505–519.

Harris, L. A., Sherman, J. A., Henderson, D. G., & Harris, M. S. (1973). *Effects of peer tutoring on the spelling performance of elementary classroom students. A new direction for education: Behavior analysis.* Lawrence: University of Kansas, Support and Development Center for Follow Through.

Hart, B. M., & Risley, T. R. (1968). Establishing use of descriptive adjectives in the spontaneous speech of disadvantaged preschool children. *Journal of Applied Behavior Analysis, 1,* 109–120.

Hartman, D. P. (1977). Considerations in the choice of interobserver reliability estimates. *Journal of Applied Behavioral Analysis, 10,* 103–116.

Harvey, B. (1983). Stop saying "computer literacy." One man's controversial opinion. *Classroom Computer News, 3*(6), 56–57.

Haworth, M. (1971). The effects of rhythmic-motor training and gross-motor training on the reading and writing abilities of educable mentally retarded children. *Dissertation Abstracts International, 31,* 3391-A.

Hayden, D. A., Vance, H. B., & Irwin, J. J. (1982). A special education management system. *Journal of Learning Disabilities, 15*(7), 428–429.

Hayden, D. L. (1972). *NRRC/P Diagnostic prescriptive instructional data bank for teachers of handicapped children.* Harrisburg, PA: The National Regional Resource Center of Pennsylvania.

Hazel, J. S., Schumaker, J. B., & Sheldon, J. (1984). *Evaluation of a training program for court service officers for the treatment of learning disabled and other social skill deficient adolescents* (Research Report #62). Lawrence: The University of Kansas, Research Institute for Research in Learning Disabilities.

Hazel, J. S., Schumaker, J. B., Sherman, J. A., & Sheldon, J. (1982). Application of a group training program in social skills and problem solving skills to learning disabled and non-learning disabled youth. *Learning Disability Quarterly, 5,* 398–408.

Hazel, J. S., Schumaker, J. B., Sherman, J. A., & Sheldon-Wildgen, J. (1981). The development and evaluation of a group training program for teaching social and problem solving skills to court-adjudicated youth. In D. Upper & S. M. Ross (Eds.), *Behavioral group therapy.* Champaign, IL: Research Press.

Hazel, J. S., Smalter, M. C., & Schumaker, J. B. (1983, October). *A learner-managed social skills curriculum for mildly handicapped young adults.* Presentation at the International Conference on Learning Disabilities, San Francisco.

Hechtman, L., Weiss, G., & Perlman, T. (1984). Young adult outcome of hyperactive children who received long-term stimulant treatment. *Journal of the American Academy of Child Psychiatry, 23,* 261–269.

Hechtman, L., Weiss, G., Perlman, T., Hopkins, J., & Wener, A. (1979). Hyperactive children in young adulthood: A controlled prospective ten-year follow-up. *International Journal of Mental Health, 8,* 52–66.

Hedges, L. V., & Olkin, I. (1980). Vote-counting methods in research synthesis. *Psy-*

chological Bulletin, 88, 359–369.

Hegge, T. G., Kirk, S., & Kirk, W. (1936). *Remedial reading drills.* Ann Arbor, MI: Wahr.

Heller, K. A., Holtzman, W. H., & Messick, S. (1982). *Placing children in special education: A strategy for equity.* Washington, DC: National Academy Press.

Helms, H. B. (1970). Big chalkboard for big movement. In J. Arena (Ed.), *Building handwriting skills in dyslexic children.* San Rafael, CA: Academic Therapy.

Helwig, J. (1976). Measurement of visual-verbal feedback on changes in manuscript letter formation. *Dissertation Abstracts International, 36,* 5196-A.

Hemry, F. P. (1973). Effect of reinforcement conditions on a discrimination learning task for impulsive versus reflective children. *Child Development, 44,* 657–660.

Henderson, E. H. (1980). Word knowledge and reading disability. In E. J. Henderson & J. W. Beers (Eds.), *Developmental aspects of learning to spell.* Newark, DE: International Reading Associates.

Heron, T. E., & Heward, N. (1982). Ecologic assessment: Implications for teachers of learning disabled students. *Learning Disability Quarterly, 5,* 117–125.

Herr, C. M. (1976). Mainstreaming — Is it effective: A follow-up study of learning disabled children. *Division for Children with Learning Disabilities Newsletter, 2,* 22–29.

Hersen, M., & Barlow, D. (1976). *Strategies for studying behavioral change.* New York: Pergamon Press.

Heshusius, L. (1982). At the heart of the advocacy dilemma: A mechanistic word view. *Exceptional Children, 49,* 6–13.

Heshusius, L. (1986). Paradigm shifts and special education: A response to Ulman and Rosenberg. *Exceptional Children, 52,* 461–465.

Hewett, F. M., Taylor, F., & Artuso, A. (1968). The Madison plan really swings. *Today's Education, 59,* 15–17.

Hiebert, B., Wong, B. Y. L., & Hunter, M. (1982). Affective influences on learning-disabled adolescents. *Learning Disability Quarterly, 5*(4), 334–343.

Hillman, H. H., & Snowdon, R. L. (1960). Part-time classes for young backward readers. *British Journal of Educational Psychology, 30,* 168–172.

Hines, C. W., & Bruno, G. (1985). LD career success after high school. *Academic Therapy, 21*(2), 171–176.

Hines, C. W., & Hohenshil, T. A. (1985). Career development and career education for handicapped students: A reexamination. *Vocational Guidance Quarterly, 34*(1), 31–40.

Hinton, G. G., & Knights, R. M. (1971). Children with learning problems: Academic prediction and adjustment three years after assessment. *Exceptional Children, 37,* 513–519.

Hodges, R. E. (1977). *Learning to spell — Theory and research into practice.* Urbana, IL: NCTE.

Hofmeister, A., & Thorkildsen, R. (1981). Videodisc technology and the preparation of special education teachers. *Teacher Education and Special Education, 4*(3), 34–39.

Holt, M., Kocsis, J., & Reisman, K. (1980). *Special education data base information retrieval system.* Dallas, TX: Central Dallas Independent School District, Research and Evaluation Department.

Holyoak, K. J., & Gordon, P. C. (1984). Information processing and social cognition. In R. S. Wyer, Jr., & T. K. Srull (Eds.), *Handbook of social cognition* (pp. 39–70). Hillsdale, NJ: Lawrence Erlbaum.

Holznagel, D. (1981). Which courseware is right for you? *Microcomputing, 5*(10), 38–40.

Hopps, H. (1981). Behavioral assessment of exceptional children's development. *Exceptional Education Quarterly, 4,* 31–43.

Horn, W. F., O'Donnell, J. P., & Vitulano, L. A. (1983). Long-term follow-up studies of learning disabled persons. *Journal of Learning Disabilities, 16,* 542–555.

Horowitz, E. C. (1981). Popularity, decentering ability and role-taking skills in learning disabled and normal children. *Learning Disability Quarterly, 4,* 23–30.

Howe, C. (1981). From leisure ethic to reindustrialization. *Leisure Today, 12,* 23–39.

Hoyt, K. B. (1980, June 24). *Career education for persons with visual handicaps.* Paper presented at the Helen Keller Centennial Conference, Boston.

Huessy, H. R., Metoyer, M., & Townsend, M. (1974). 8-10 year follow-up of 84 children treated for behavioral disorder in rural Vermont. *Acta Paedopsychiatrica, 40,* 230–235.

Huey, E. B. (1968). *The psychology and pedagogy of reading.* Cambridge, MA: MIT Press.

Humes, C. W., & Bronner, G. (1985). LD career success after high school. *Academic Therapy, 21*(2), 171–176.

Hummel, J. W., & Balcom, F. W. (1984). Microcomputers: Not just a place for a practice. *Journal of Learning Disabilities, 17*(7), 432–434.

Hummel, J. W., & Farr, S. D. (1985). Options for creating and modifying CAI software for the handicapped. *Journal of Learning Disabilities, 18*(3), 166–168.

Hunt, K. W. (1977). Early blooming and late blooming syntactic structures. In C. R. Cooper & L. Odell (Eds.), *Evaluating writing.* Urbana, IL: NCTE.

Iano, R. P. (1986). The study of development of teaching: With implications for the advancement of special education. *Remedial and Special Education, 7*(5), 50–61.

Ingram, C. P. (1935). *Education of the slow-learning child.* Yonkers: World Book Co.

Ingram, T. T. S. (1969). Developmental disorders of speech. In P. Vinken & G. Bruyn (Eds.), *Handbook of clinical neurology* (Vol. 4). Amsterdam: North Holland.

Institute for Career and Leisure Development. (1979). *Special education for leisure fulfillment — A facilitator's instructional guide.* Washington, DC.

Ito, H. R. (1980). Long-term effects of resource room programs on learning disabled children's reading. *Journal of Learning Disabilities, 13,* 322–326.

Ito, H. R. (1981). After the resource room — then what? *Academic Therapy, 16,* 283–287.

Iwata, B. A., & Bailey, J. S. (1974). Reward versus cost token systems: An analysis of the effects on students and teacher. *Journal of Applied Behavior Analysis, 7,* 564–576.

Jackson, G. B. (1980). Methods for integrative reviews. *Review of Educational Research, 50,* 438–460.

Jastak, J. F., & Jastak, S. R. (1978). *The Wide Range Achievement Test* (Rev. Ed.). Wilmington, DE: Guidance Associates.

Jastak, S., & Wilkinson, G. (1984). *The Wide Range Achievement Test—Revised: Administration manual.* Wilmington, DE: Jastak Associates.

Jenkins, J. R., & Pany, D. (1978). Standardized achievement tests: How useful for special education? *Exceptional Children, 44,* 448–453.

Jennings, D. L. (1981). *The effects of attributions in social settings: Changes in strategy use, expectations, and performance quality following failure.* Unpublished manuscript.

Johnson, D. J. (1978). Remedial approaches to dyslexia. In A. L. Benton & D. Pearl (Eds.), *Dyslexia: An appraisal of current knowledge* (pp. 397–421). New York: Oxford University Press.

Johnson, D. J., & Myklebust, H. (1967). *Learning disabilities: Educational principles and practices.* New York: Grune & Stratton.

Johnson, G. O. (1962). Special education for the mentally handicapped — A paradox. *Exceptional Children, 29,* 62–69.

Johnson, W. T. (1977). *The Johnson handwriting program.* Cambridge, MA: Educators Publishing Service.

Jones, J. C., Trap, J., & Cooper, J. (1977). Technical report: Students self-recording of manuscript letter strokes. *Journal of Applied Behavior Analysis, 10,* 509–514.

Jones, R. L. (1974). Student views of special placement and their own special classes: A clarification. *Exceptional Children, 41,* 22–29.

Jongsma, E. (1971). *The cloze procedure as a teaching technique.* Newark, DE: International Reading Association.

Joyce, B., & Weil, M. (1972). *Models of teaching.* Englewood Cliffs, NJ: Prentice–Hall.

Kagan, J. (1966). Reflection-impulsivity: The generality and dynamics of conceptual tempo. *Journal of Abnormal Psychology, 71,* 17–24.

Kaliski, L., & Iohga, R. (1970). A musical approach to handwriting. In J. Arena (Ed.), *Building handwriting skills in dyslexic children.* San Rafael, CA: Academic Therapy.

Kaplan, __. (1964). *The conduct of inquiry.* San Francisco: Chandler.

Kaslow, F. W. (1979). Therapy within the family constellation. In W. Adamson & K. K. Adamson (Eds.), *A handbook for specific learning disabilities* (pp. 313–332). New York: Gardner Press.

Katz, J. (1986). *Arithmetic problem solving strategies of kindergarten children.* Unpublished doctoral dissertation, Teachers College, Columbia University, New York.

Kaufman, K. F., & O'Leary, K. D. (1972). Reward, cost, and self-evaluation procedures for disruptive adolescents in a psychiatric hospital school. *Journal of Applied Behavior Analysis, 5,* 293–309.

Kaufman, M. E., & Alberto, P. A. (1976). Research on efficacy of special education for the mentally retarded. In N. R. Ellis (Ed.), *International review of research in mental retardation* (Vol. 8, pp. 225–255). New York: Academic Press.

Kaufman, M. J., Gottlieb, J., Agard, J. A., & Kukic, M. B. (1975). Mainstreaming: Toward an explication of the construct. In E. Meyen, G. Vergason, & R. Whelan (Eds.), *Alternatives for teaching exceptional children* (pp. 35–54). Denver: Love.

Kavale, K., & Schreiner, R. (1978). Psycholinguistic implications for beginning reading instruction. *Language Arts, 55,* 34–40.

Kavale, K. A. (1981a). Functions of the Illinois Test of Psycholinguistic Abilities (ITPA): Are they trainable? *Exceptional Children, 47,* 496–510.

Kavale, K. A. (1981b). The relationship between auditory perceptual skills and reading ability: A meta-analysis. *Journal of Learning Disabilities, 14,* 539–546.

Kavale, K. A. (1982a). The efficacy of stimulant drug treatment for hyperactivity: A meta-analysis. *Journal of Learning Disabilities, 15,* 280–289.

Kavale, K. A. (1982b). Meta-analysis of the relationship between visual perceptual skills and reading achievement. *Journal of Learning Disablities, 15,* 42–51.

Kavale, K. A. (1982c). Psycholinguistic training programs: Are there differential treatment effects? *The Exceptional Child, 29,* 21–30.

Kavale, K. A., & Andreassen, E. (1984). Factors in diagnosing the learning disabled: Analysis of judgmental policies. *Journal of Learning Disabilities, 17,* 273–278.

Kavale, K. A., & Forness, S. R. (1983). Hyperactivity and diet treatment: A meta-analysis of the Feingold hypothesis. *Journal of Learning Disabilities, 16,* 324–330.

Kavale, K. A., & Forness, S. R. (1984). A meta-analysis assessing the validity of Wechsler scale profiles and recategorizations: Patterns or parodies? *Learning Disability Quarterly, 7,* 136–156.

Kavale, K. A., & Forness, S. R. (1985). *The science of learning disabilities.* San Diego: College-Hill Press.

Kavale, K. A., & Forness, S. R. (1987). The far side of heterogeneity: A critical analysis of empirical subtyping research in learning disabilities. *Journal of Learning Disabilities, 20,* 274–382.

Kavale, K. A., & Forness, S. R. (1987). Substance over style: A quantitative synthesis assessing the efficacy of modality testing and teaching. *Exceptional Children, 54,* 228–234.

Kavale, K. A., & Glass, G. V. (1981). Meta-analysis and the integration of research in special education. *Journal of Learning Disabilities, 14,* 531–538.

Kavale, K. A., & Matson, P. D. (1983). One jumped off the balance beam: Meta-analysis of perceptual–motor training. *Journal of Learning Disabilities, 16,* 165–173.

Kazdin, A., & Erickson, B. (1975). Developing responsiveness to instructions in severely and profoundly retarded residents. *Journal of Behavior Therapy and Experimental Psychiatry, 6,* 17–21.

Keeney, A. H., & Keeney, M. T. (1968). *Dyslexia: Diagnosis and treatment of reading disorders.* St. Louis: Mosby.

Kendall, C. R., Borkowski, J. G., & Cavanaugh, J. C. (1980). Maintenance and generalization of an interrogative strategy by EMR children. *Intelligence, 4,* 270.

Kendall, J. R., & Mason, J. M. (1982). Metacognition from the historical context of teaching reading. *Topics in Learning and Learning Disabilities, 2,* 82–89.

Kent, R. M., & O'Leary, K. D. (1976). A controlled evaluation of behavior modification with conduct problem children. *Journal of Consulting and Clinical Psychology, 44,* 586–596.

Keogh, B. K., Major-Kingsley, S., Omori-Gordon, H., & Reid, H. (1982). *A system of marker variables for the field of learning disabilities.* Syracuse, NY: Syracuse University Press.

Kephart, N. C. (1971). *The slow learner in the classroom.* Columbus, OH: Merrill.

Kerns, K., & Decker, S. (1985). Multifactorial assessment of reading disability: Identifying the best predictors. *Perceptual and Motor Skills 60*(3), 747–753.

Kew, S. (1975). *Handicap and family crisis: A study of siblings of handicapped children.* London: Longman.

Kimmel, G. M. (1968). Teaching spelling in a splash of color. In J. Arena (Ed.), *Building spelling skills in dyslexic children.* San Rafael, CA: Academic Therapy.

Kimmel, G. M. (1970). Handwriting readiness: Motor-coordinative practices. In J. Arena (Ed.), *Building handwriting skills in dyslexic children.* San Rafael, CA: Academic Therapy.

King, D. (1985). *Writing skills for the adolescent.* Cambridge, MA: Educators Publishing Service.

Kirby, F. D., & Shields, F. (1972). Modification of arithmetic response rate and attending behavior in a seventh grade student. *Journal of Applied Behavior Analysis, 5,* 78–84.

Kirk, S. A. (1964). Research in education. In H. A. Stevens & R. Heber (Eds.), *Mental retardation: A review of research* (pp. 57–99). Chicago: University of Chicago Press.

Kirk, S. A., & Elkins, J. (1975). Characteristics of children enrolled in child service demonstration centers. *Journal of Learning Disabilities, 8,* 630–637.

Kirk, S. A., & Kirk, W. D. (1971). *Psycholinguistic learning disabilities: Diagnosis and remediation.* Urbana: University of Illinois Press.

Kirk, S. A., McCarthy, J. J., & Kirk, W. D. (1968). *Illinois Test of Psycholinguistic Abilities.*(Rev. ed.). Urbana: University of Illinois Press.

Kirk, U. (1978). Rule-based instruction: A cognitive approach to beginning handwriting instruction. *Dissertation Abstracts International, 39,* 113-A.

Klein, N. K., Pasch, M., & Frew, T. W. (1979). *Curriculum analysis and design for retarded learners.* Columbus, OH: Merrill.

Knapczyk, D., & Yoppi, J. (1975). Development of cooperative and competitive play responses in developmentally disabled children. *American Journal on Mental Deficiency, 80,* 245–255.

Knight, E. (1975). *KISP: Knight Individualized Spelling Program.* Cambridge, MA: Educators Publishing Service.

Kohn, M. (1977). *Social competence, symptoms and underachievement in childhood: A longitudinal perspective.* Washington, DC: Winston.

Kohn, M., & Rosman, B. L. (1972). Relationship of preschool social–emotional functioning to later intellectual development. *Developmental Psychology, 6,* 445–452.

Kolich, E. (1985). Microcomputer technology with the learning disabled: A review of the literature. *Journal of Learning Disability, 18*(7), 428–431.

Koppell, S. (1979). Testing the attentional deficit notion. *Journal of Learning Disablities, 12,* 43–48.

Koppitz, E. M. (1971). *Children with learning disabilities: A five year follow-up study.* New York: Grune & Stratton.

Kornblum, H. (1982). A social worker's role with mothers of language disordered preschool children. *Journal of Learning Disabilities, 15,* 406–408.

Kornetsky, C. (1975). Minimal brain dysfunction and drugs. In W. Cruickshank & D. Hallahan (Eds.), *Perceptual learning disabilities in children: Research and theory* (Vol. 2, pp. 447–481). Syracuse, NY: Syracuse University Press.

Kosc, L. (1974). Developmental dyscalculia. *Journal of Learning Disabilities, 7,* 164–177.

Kottmeyer, W. (1959). *Teacher's guide for remedial reading.* St. Louis: Webster Publishing.

Kozloff, M. A. (1979). *A program for families of children with learning and behavioral problems.* New York: Wiley.

Kraus, R. (1978). *Recreation and leisure in a modern society.* Santa Monica, CA: Goodyear Publishing.

Kubie, L. S. (1964). Research on protecting preconscious functions in education. In A. H. Passow (Ed.), *Nurturing individual potential.* Washington, DC: Association for Supervision and Curriculum Development.

Kubler–Ross, E. (1969). *On death and dying.* New York: Macmillan.

LaBerge, D., & Samuels, S. J. (1974). Toward a theory of automatic information processing in reading. *Cognitive Psychology, 6,* 293–323.

Labouvie, E. W. (1975). The dialectical nature of measurement activities in the behavioral sciences. *Human Development, 18,* 205–222.

LaGreca, A. M., & Mesibov, G. B. (1981). Facilitating interpersonal functioning with peers in learning disabled children. *Journal of Learning Disabilities, 14,* 197–199, 238.

Lahey, B. B. (1976). Behavior modification with learning disabilities and related problems. In M. Hersen, R. Eisler, & P. Miller (Eds.), *Progress in behavior modification* (Vol. 3, pp. 173–206). New York: Academic Press.

Lahey, B. B. (1977). Research on the role of reinforcement in reading instruction: Some measurement and methodological difficulties. *Corrective and Social Psychiatry, 23,* 27–32.

Lahey, B. B. (1979). *Behavior therapy with hyperactive and learning disabled children.* New York: Oxford University Press.

Lahey, B. B., Busemeyer, M., O'Hara, C., & Beggs, V. E. (1977). Treatment of severe perceptual-motor disorders in children diagnosed as learning disabled. *Behavior Modification, 1,* 123–140.

Lahey, B. B., Delameter, A., Kupfer, D. L., & Hobbs, S. A. (1978). Behavioral aspects of learning disabilities and hyperactivity. *Education and Urban Society, 10,* 447–499.

Lahey, B. B., & Drabman, R. S. (1974). Facilitation of the acquisition and retention of sight-word vocabulary through token reinforcement. *Journal of Applied Behavior Analysis, 7,* 307–312.

Lahey, B. B., Kupfer, D. L., Beggs, V. E., & Landon, D. (1982). Do learning-disabled children exhibit peripheral deficits in selective attention?: Analysis of eye movements during reading. *Journal of Abnormal Child Psychology, 10,* 1–10.

Lahey, B. B., McNees, M. P., & Brown, S. C. (1973). Modification of deficits in reading for comprehension. *Journal of Applied Behavior Analysis, 6,* 475–480.

Lahey, B. B., McNees, M. P., & Schnelle, J. F. (1977). The functional independence of three reading behaviors: A behavior systems analysis. *Corrective and Social Psychiatry, 23,* 44–47.

Lahey, B. B., Vosk, B. N., & Habif, V. L. (1981). Behavioral assessment of learning disabled children: A rationale and strategy. *Behavioral Assessment, 3,* 3–14.

Lahey, B. B., Weller, D. R., & Brown, W. R. (1973). The behavior analysis approach to reading: Phonics discriminations. *Journal of Reading Behavior, 5,* 200–206.

Lambert, N., & Sandoval, J. (1980). The prevalence of learning disabilities in a sample of children considered hyperactive. *Journal of Abnormal Child Psychology, 8,* 33–50.

Lamkin, J. S. (1980). *Getting started: Career education activities for exceptional students (K–9).* Reston, VA: The Council for Exceptional Children.

Landers, S. (1987). Researchers struggling to understand learning disabilities. *APA Monitor, 18*(3), 28–29.

Larsen, S. C., & Hammill, D. D. (1976). *Test of written spelling.* Austin, TX: Pro-Ed.

Larson, C. H. (1981, January). *EBCE State of Iowa dissemination model for MD and LD students.* Ft. Dodge: Iowa Central Community College.

Larson, S. C. (1976). The learning disabilities specialist: Roles and responsibilities. *Journal of Learning Disabilities, 9,* 37–47.

Lasagna, L. (1974). A plea for the "naturalistic" study of medicine (Editorial). *European Journal of Clinical Pharmacology, 7,* 153.

Lee, L. (1974). *Developmental sentence analysis.* Evanston, IL: Northwestern University Press.

Lee, L. (1975). *Interactive language developmental teaching.* Evanston, IL: Northwestern University Press.

Lefton, L. A., Nagle, R. J., Johnson, G., & Fisher, D. G. (1979). Eye movement dynamics of good and poor readers: Then and now. *Journal of Reading Behavior, 11,* 319–328.

Leggett, C. L. (1978). Special education and career education: A call for a new partnership. *Education and Training of the Mentally Retarded, 13,* 430–431.

Lehtinen–Rogan, L., & Hartman, L. D. (1976). *A follow-up study of learning disabled children as adolescents* (Final Report). Washington, DC: Department of Health, Education, and Welfare, Bureau of Education of the Handicapped. (ERIC Document Reproduction Service No. ED 163 728)

Leinhardt, G., & Pallay, A. (1982). Restrictive educational settings. *Review of Educational Research, 52,* 557–578.

Leinhardt, G., Zigmond, N., & Cooley, W. (1981). Reading instruction and its effects. *American Educational Research Journal, 18,* 343–361.

Leisure Information Service (1976). *A systems model for developing a leisure education program for handicapped children and youth (K–12).* Washington, DC: Hawkins and Associates.

Leone, P., Lovitt, T., & Hansen, C. (1981). A descriptive followup study of learning disabled boys. *Learning Disability Quarterly, 4,* 152–162.

Lerer, R. M., Lerer, M. P., & Artner, J. (1977). The effects of methylphenidate on the handwriting of children with minimal brain dysfunction. *Journal of Pediatrics, 91,* 127–132.

Lesgold, A. M., & Perfetti, C. A. (1981). *Interactive processes in reading.* Hillsdale, NJ: Lawrence Erlbaum.

Levin, E. K., Zigmond, N., & Birch, J. W. (1985). A follow-up study of 52 learning disabled adolescents. *Journal of Learning Disabilities, 18,* 2–7.

Levin, J. R. (1973). Inducing comprehension in poor readers: A test of a recent model. *Journal of Educational Psychology, 65,* 19–24.

Levy, B. A. (1978). Speech processing during reading. In A. Lesgold, J. Pellegrino, S. Fokkema, & R. Glaser (Eds.), *Cognitive psychology and instruction.* New York: Plenum.

Levy, B. A. (1980). Interactive processes during reading. In A. Lesgold & C. Perfetti (Eds.), *Interactive processes in reading* (pp. 1–35). Hillsdale, NJ: Lawrence Erlbaum.

Levy, H. B. (1973). *Square pegs, round holes: The learning-disabled child in the classroom and the home.* Boston: Little, Brown.

Levy, J. (1982). Behavioral observation techniques in assessing change in therapeutic recreation/play settings. *Therapeutic Recreation Journal, 5,* 170-173.

Lew, F. (1977). The Feingold diet, experienced [letter]. *Medical Journal of Australia, 1,* 190.

Liberman, I., & Shankweiler, D. (1979). Speech, the alphabet, and teaching to read. In L. Resnick & P. Weaver (Eds.), *Theory and practice of early reading* (Vol. 2, pp. 109-132). Hillsdale, NJ: Lawrence Erlbaum.

Liberman, I., Shankweiler, D., Liberman, A., Fowler, C., & Fischer, F. (1977). Phonetic segmentation and recording in the beginning reader. In A. Reber & D. Scarborough (Eds.), *Toward a psychology of reading* (pp. 207-225). Hillsdale, NJ: Lawrence Erlbaum.

Liberman, I. Y. (1973). Segmentation of the spoken word and reading acquisition. *Bulletin of the Orton Society, 23,* 65-77.

Liberman, I. Y. (1982). A language-oriented view of reading and its disabilities. In H. Myklebust (Ed.), *Progress in learning disabilities* (Vol. 5, pp. 81-101). New York: Grune & Stratton.

Libet, J. M., & Lewinsohn, P. M. (1973). Concept of social skills with special reference to the behavior of depressed persons. *Journal of Consulting and Clinical Psychology, 40,* 304-312.

Licht, B. G. (1983). Cognitive-motivational factors that contribute to the achievement of learning-disabled children. *Journal of Learning Disabilities, 16,* 483-490.

Lieber, J., & Semmel, M. (1985). Effectiveness of computer application to instruction with mildly handicapped learners: A review. *Remedial and Special Education, 6*(5), 5-12.

Lieby, J. (1981). *Automatization, cognitive style, and the selection of an instructional method for teaching basic facts to learning disabled and compensatory education students.* Unpublished doctoral dissertation, Teachers College, Columbia University, New York.

Light, R. J., & Smith, P. V. (1971). Accumulating evidence: procedures for resolving contradictions among different research studies. *Harvard Educational Review, 41,* 429-471.

Lincoln, A. L. (1949). *Diagnostic Spelling Test, Form 3.* New York: Educational Records Bureau.

Lincoln, A. L. (1959). *Lincoln Intermediate Spelling Test, Form A for grades 4-8.* New York: Educational Records Bureau.

Lindquist, M. M., Carpenter, T. P., Silver, E. A., & Matthews, W. (1983). The third national mathematics assessment: Results and implications for elementary and middle schools. *Arithmetic Teacher, 31,* 14-19.

Lindsey, J. D., & Kerlin, M. A. (1979). Learning disabilities and reading disorders: A brief review of the secondary level literature. *Journal of Learning Disabilities, 12,* 408-415.

Lindvall, C., & Cox, R. (1970). The IPI evaluation program. AERA monograph series on *Curriculum Evaluation.* Chicago: Rand McNally.

Litman, T. (1974). The family as a basic unit in health and medical care: A social-behavioral overview. *Social Science and Medicine, 8,* 495-519.

Lloyd, J. (1975). The pedagogical orientation: An argument for improving instruction. *Journal of Learning Disabilities, 8*(2), 74-78.

Lloyd, J. (1980). Academic instruction and cognitive behavior modification: The need for attack strategy training. *Exceptional Education Quarterly, 1*(1), 53-63.

Lloyd, J., Cullinan, D., Heins, E. D., & Epstein, M. H. (1980). Direct instruction: Effects on oral and written language comprehension. *Learning Disability Quarterly, 3*(4), 70-76.

Lloyd, J., Saltzman, N. J., & Kauffman, J. M. (1981). Predictable generalization in academic learning as a result of preskills and strategy training. *Learning Disablity Quarterly, 4,* 203–216.

Lloyd, J. W. (1984). How shall we individualize instruction — Or should we? *Remedial and Special Education, 5*(1), 7–15.

Lloyd, J. W. (1987). The art and science of research on teaching. *Remedial and Special Education, 8*(1), 44–46.

Lloyd–Jones, R. (1977). Primary trait scoring. In C. R. Cooper & L. Odell (Eds.), *Evaluation writing.* Urbana, IL: NCTE.

Loney, J., Kramer, J., & Kosier, T. (1981, August). *Medicated vs. unmedicated hyperactive adolescents: Academic, delinquent and symptomatological outcome.* Paper presented at the meeting of the American Psychological Association, Los Angeles.

Loney, J., Kramer, J., & Milich, R. (1981). The hyperactive child grows up: Predictors of symptoms, delinquency, and achievement at followup. In K. D. Gadow & J. Loney (Eds.), *Psychosocial aspects of drug treatment for hyperactivity.* Boulder, CO: Westview Press.

Lopez, M., & Clyde-Snyder, M. (1983). Higher education for learning disabled students. *NASPA Journal, 20*(4), 34–39.

Lovitt, T. C., & Smith, D. D. (1974). Using withdrawal of positive reinforcement to alter subtraction performance. *Exceptional Children, 40,* 357–358.

Ludlow, C., Rapoport, J., Bessich, S., & Mikkelsen, E. (1980). The differential effects dextroamphetamine on the language and performance in hyperactive and normal children. In R. Knights & D. Bakker (Eds.), *Treatment of hyperactive and learning disordered children: Current research* (pp. 185–206). Baltimore: University Park Press.

Lund, K. A., Foster, G. E., & McCall-Perez, F. C. (1978). The effectiveness of psycholinguistic training: A reevaluation. *Exceptional Children, 44,* 310–319.

Lyon, G. R., (1983). Learning disabled readers: Identification of subgroups. In H. Myklebust (Ed.), *Progress in learning disabilities* (Vol. 5, pp. 103–134). New York: Grune & Stratton.

Lyon, G. R. (1985a). Educational validation of learning disability subtypes. In B. Rourke (Ed.), *The neuropsychology of learning disabilities: Essentials of subtype analysis* (pp. 228–253). New York: Guilford Press.

Lyon, G. R. (1985b). Neuropsychology and learning disabilities. *Neurology and Neurosurgery Update, 5,* 2–8.

Lyon, G. R., & Risucci, D. (in press). Classification issues in learning disabilities. In K. Kavale (Ed.), *Learning disabilities: State of the art and practice.* San Diego: College-Hill Press.

Lyon, G. R., Rietta, S., Watson, B., Porch, B., & Rhodes, J. (1981). Selected linguistic and perceptual abilities of empirically derived subgroups of learning disabled readers. *Journal of School Psychology, 19,* 152–166.

Lyon, G. R., Stewart, N., & Freedman, D. (1982) Neuropsychological characteristics of empirically derived subgroups of learning disabled readers. *Journal of Clinical Neuropsychology, 4,* 343–365.

Lyon, R., & Watson, B. (1981). Empirically derived subgroups of learning-disabled readers: Diagnostic characteristics. *Journal of Learning Disabilities, 14,* 256–261.

Mackenzie, D. E. (1983). Research for school improvement: An appraisal of some recent trends. *Educational Researcher, 12*(4), 5–17.

Mackworth, J., & Mackworth, N. (1974). How children read: Matching by sight and sound. *Journal of Reading Behavior, 6,* 295–305.

MacMillan, D. L. (1971). Special education for the mildly retarded: Servant or savant? *Focus on Exceptional Children, 2,* 1–11.

MacMillan, D. L., & Semmel, M. I. (1977). Evaluation of mainstreaming programs. *Focus on Exceptional Children, 9,* 1-14.

Madden, N. A., & Slavin, R. E. (1983). Mainstreaming students with mild handicaps: Academic and social outcomes. *Review of Educational Research, 53*(4), 519-569.

Madison, B. D. (1970). A kinesthetic technique for handwriting development. In J. Arena (Ed.), *Building handwriting skills in dyslexic children.* San Rafael, CA: Academic Therapy.

Madsen, C. H., Becker, W. C., & Thomas, D. R. (1968). Rules, praise, and ignoring: Elements of elementary classroom control. *Journal of Applied Behavior Analysis, 1,* 139-150.

Mager, R. (1962). *Preparing instructional objectives.* San Francisco: Fearon.

Maheady, L., & Maitland, G. E. (1982). Assessing social perception abilities in learning disabled students. *Learning Disability Quarterly, 5,* 363-370.

Major-Kinglsey, S. (1982). *Learning disabled boys as young adults: Achievement, adjustment, and aspirations.* Unpublished doctoral dissertation, University of California, Los Angeles.

Mandler, G. (1981, August). *What's cognitive psychology? What isn't?* Invitational address, Division of Philosophical Psychology, American Psychological Association convention, Los Angeles.

Mangrum, C. T., & Strichart, S. S. (1984). *College and the learning disabled student.* Orlando, FL: Grune & Stratton

Mangrum, C. T., & Strichart, S. S. (1985). *Peterson's guide to colleges with programs for learning-disabled students.* Princeton, NJ: Peterson's Guides.

Margalit, M. (1982). Learning disabled children and their families: Strategies of extension and adaptation of family therapy. *Journal of Learning Disabilities, 15,* 594-595.

Marholin, D., & Steinman, W. M. (1977). Stimulus control in the classroom as a function of the behavior reinforced. *Journal of Applied Behavior Analysis, 10,* 465-478.

Markman, E. M. (1977). Realizing that you don't understand: A preliminary investigation. *Child Development, 43,* 986-992.

Markman, E. M. (1979). Realizing that you don't understand: Elementary school children's awareness of inconsistencies. *Child Development, 50,* 643-655.

Marland, S. P., Jr. (1971). Career education now. Speech presented before the annual convention of the National Association of Secondary School Principals, Houston.

Martin, F. (1971). TRIC — A computer-based information storage and retrieval for the field of therapeutic recreation service. *Therapeutic Recreation Journal, 5,* 170-173.

Martin, F. (1977). Therapeutic recreation research: An analysis of research content area, methodology and setting. In G. Fain & G. Hitzhusen (Eds.), *Therapeutic recreation: State of the art* (pp. 83-91). Arlington, VA: National Recreation and Park Association.

Martino, L., & Johnson, D. W. (1979). Cooperative and individualistic experiences among disabled and normal children. *Journal of Social Psychology, 107,* 177-183.

Marzola, E. S. (1985). *An arithmetic problem solving model based on a plan for steps to solution, mastery learning, and calculator use in a resource room for learning disabled students.* Unpublished doctoral dissertation, Teachers College, Columbia University, New York

Massari, D. J., & Schack, M. L. (1972). Discrimination learning by reflective and impulsive children as a funciton of reinforcement schedule. *Developmental Psychology, 6,* 183.

Massaro, D. W. (Ed.). (1975). *An information-processing analysis of speech perception, reading, and psycholinguistics.* New York: Academic Press.

Masson, M. A. (1982). A framework of cognitive and metacognitive determinants of reading skill. *Topics in Learning and Learning Disabilities, 2,* 37–43.

Mathews, R., Whang, P., & Fawcett, S. B. (1982). Behavioral assessment of occupational skills of learning disabled adolescents. *Journal of Learning Disabilities, 15,* 41–83.

Mathews, R. M., Whang, P., & Fawcett, S. B. (1980). *Behavioral assessment of job-related skills: Implications for learning disabled young adults* (Research Report No. 6). Lawrence: The University of Kansas, Institute for Research in Learning Disabilities.

Mattingly, I. G. (1972). Reading, the linguistic process, and linguistic awareness. In J. Kavanaugh & I. Mattingly (Eds.), *Language by ear and by eye: The relationship between speech and reading* (pp. 133–148). Cambridge, MA: MIT Press.

Mattis, S. (1978). Dyslexia syndromes: A working hypothesis that works. In A. L. Benton & D. Pearl (Eds.), *Dyslexia: An appraisal of current knowledge* (pp. 43–58). New York: Oxford University Press.

Mattis, S. (1981). Dyslexia syndromes in children: Toward the development of syndrome-specific treatment patterns. In F. J. Pirozzolo & M. C. Wittrock (Eds.), *Neuropsychological and cognitive processes in reading* (pp. 93–107). New York: Academic Press.

Mattis, S., French, J. H., & Rapin, I. (1975). Dyslexia in children and adults: Three independent neuropsychological syndromes. *Developmental Medicine and Child Neurology, 17,* 150–163.

Mayer, W. V. (1982). Curriculum development: A process and a legacy. *Focus on Exceptional Children, 14,* 1–12.

McCormick, S., & Moe, A. J. (1982). The language of instructional materials: A source of reading problems. *Exceptional Children, 49,* 48–53.

McDowell, R. L., & Brown, G. B. (1978). The emotionally disturbed adolescent: Development of program alternatives in secondary education. *Focus on Exceptional Children, 10,* 1–16.

McIntyre, R. B., & Nelson, C. C. (1969). Empirical evaluation of instructional materials. *Educational Technology, 9*(2), 24–27.

McKinney, J. D., & Feagans, L. (1980). *Learning disabilities in the classroom* (Final Project Report). Chapel Hill: University of North Carolina, Frank Porter Graham Child Development Center.

McKinney, J. D., & Feagans, L. (1984). Academic and behavioral characteristics of learning disabled children and average achievers: Longitudinal studies. *Learning Disability Quarterly, 7,* 251–265.

McKinney, J. D., & Kreuger, M. (1974). *Models for educating the learning disabled (MELD): Project period 1971–1974: Final evaluation report.* Washington, DC: Bureau of Elementary and Secondary Education (DHEW/OE). (ERIC Document Reproduction Service No. ED 108 402)

McKinney, J. D., Mason, J., Perkerson, K., & Clifford, M. (1975). Relationship between classroom behavior and academic achievement. *Journal of Educational Psychology, 67,* 198–203.

McKinney, J. D., McClure, S., & Feagans, L. (1982). Classroom behavior of learning disabled children. *Learning Disability Quarterly, 5,* 45–52.

McKinney, J. D., Short, E. J., & Feagans, L. (1985). Academic consequences of perceptual-linguistic subtypes of learning disabled children. *Learning Disability Quarterly, 1*(1), 6–17.

McKinney, J. D., & Speece, D. L. (1983). Classroom behavior and the academic progress of learning disabled students. *Journal of Applied Developmental Psychology, 4,* 149–161.

McLeod, T. M., & Armstrong, S. W. (1982). Learning disabilities in mathematics skill deficits and remedial approaches at the intermediate and secondary level. *Learning*

Disability Quarterly, 5, 303–311.

McNeil, J. D. (1976). *Designing curriculum of self-instructional modules.* Boston: Little, Brown.

Meichenbaum, D. (1977). *Cognitive-behavior modification: An integrative approach.* New York: Plenum.

Meichenbaum, D., & Asarnow, J. (1978). Cognitive-behavioral modification and meta-cognitive development: Implications for the classroom. In P. Kendall & S. Hollon (Eds.), *Cognitive-behavioral interventions: Theory, research and procedure.* New York: Academic Press.

Meichenbaum, D., & Goodman, J. (1971). Training impulsive children to talk to themselves: A means of developing self-control. *Journal of Abnormal Psychology, 77,* 115–126.

Mendelson, W. B., Johnson, N. E., & Stewart, M. A. (1971). Hyperactive children as teenagers: A follow-up study. *Journal of Nervous and Mental Disease, 153,* 273–279.

Mercer, C. D., & Mercer, A. R. (1981). *Teaching students with learning problems.* Columbus, OH: Merrill.

Meyen, E. L. (1972). *Developing units of instruction: For the mentally retarded and other children with learning problems.* Dubuque, IA: Brown.

Meyen, E. L., & Horner, R. D. (1976). Curriculum development. In J. Wortis (Ed.), *Mental retardation and developmental disabilities.* New York: Grune & Stratton.

Meyen, E. L., & Schumaker, J. B. (1981). *A learner-managed social skills curriculum development project.* Washington, DC: U.S. Office of Education (Contract No. 300-81-0349).

Meyen, E. L., & White, W. J. (1980). Career education and PL 94-142: Some views. In G. M. Clark & W. J. White (Eds.), *Career education for the handicapped: Current perspectives for teachers.* Boothwyn, PA: Educational Resources Center.

Meyers, C. E., MacMillan, D. L., & Yoshida, R. K. (1980). Regular class education of EMR students, from efficacy to mainstreaming: A review of issues and research. In J. Gottlieb (Ed.), *Educating mentally retarded persons in the mainstream* (pp. 176–206). Baltimore: University Park Press.

Miccinati, J. (1979). The Fernald technique: Modifications increase the probability of success. *Journal of Learning Disabilities, 12,* 139–142.

Michelson, L., Foster, S., & Ritchey, W. (1981). Behavioral assessment of children's social skills. In B. B. Lahey & A. E. Kazdin (Eds.), *Advances in clinical child psychology* (Vol. 3). New York: Plenum.

Milazzo, T. C. (1970). *Special class placement or how to destroy in the name of help.* Paper presented at the 49th annual international convention of the Council for Exceptional Children, Chicago. (ERIC Document Reproduction Service No. ED 039 383)

Miller, C. D., McKinley, D. L., & Ryan, M. (1979). College students: Learning disabilities and services. *The Personnel and Guidance Journal, 58,* 154–158.

Miller, G. A., Galanter, E., & Pribram, K. H. (1960). *Plans and the structure of behavior.* New York: Holt, Rinehart & Winston.

Miller, L. G. (1968). Toward a greater understanding of the parents of the mentally retarded child. *Pediatrics, 73,* 699–705.

Miller, L. K., & Schneider, R. (1970). The use of a token system in project Head Start. *Journal of Applied Behavior Analysis, 3,* 213–220.

Millman, J. (1973). Passing scores and test lengths for domain-referenced measures. *Review of Educational Research, 43*(2), 205–215.

Minde, K., Lewin, D., Weiss, G., Lavigueur, H., Douglas, V., & Sykes, E. (1971). The hyperactive child in elementary school: A 5 year, controlled followup. *Exceptional Children, 38,* 215–221.

Minde, K. K., Weiss, G., & Mendelson, N. A. (1972). A 5-year follow-up study of 91 hyperactive school children. *Journal of the American Academy of Child Psychiatry, 11,* 595–610.

Mineo, B., & Cavalier, A. R. (1985). From idea to implementation: Cognitive software for students with learning disabilities. *Journal of Learning Disabilities, 18*(10), 613–618.

Minskoff, E. (1975). Research on psycholinguistic training: Critique and guidelines. *Exceptional Children, 42,* 136–144.

Mitchell, G. D. (1981). *School related achievement of high risk learning disabled students: A follow-up study.* Unpublished doctoral dissertation, Duke University, Durham, NC.

Miyake, N., & Norman, D. A. (1979). To ask a question, one must know enough to know what is not known. *Journal of Verbal Learning and Verbal Behavior, 18,* 357–364.

Molitch, M., & Sullivan, J. P. (1937). Effect of benzedrine sulfate on children taking New Stanford Achievement Test. *American Journal of Orthopsychiatry, 7,* 519–522.

Moore, S. R., & Simpson, R. L. (1984). Reciprocity in the teacher–pupil and peer verbal interactions of learning disabled, behavior-disordered and regular education students. *Learning Disability Quarterly, 7,* 30–38.

Mori, A. A. (1980). Career education for the learning disabled — where are we now? *Learning Disability Quarterly, 1*(3), 91–101.

Mori, A. A. (1982a). Career attitudes and job knowledge among junior high school regular, special, and academically talented students. *Career Development for Exceptional Individuals, 5*(1), 62–69.

Mori, A. A. (1982b). School-based career assessment programs: Where are we now and where are we going? *Exceptional Education Quarterly, 3,* 41–48.

Mori, A. A., & Neisworth, J. T. (1983). Curricula in early childhood education: Some generic and special condsiderations. *Topics in Early Childhood Special Education, 2,* 1–8.

Morrison, G. M., Lieber, J., & Morrison, R. L. (in press). A multi-dimensional view of teacher perceptions of special education episodes. *Remedial and Special Education.*

Morrison, G. M., & MacMillan, D. L. (1983). Defining, describing, and explaining the social status of mildly handicapped children: A discussion of methodological problems. In J. M Berg (Ed.), *Prospectives and progress in mental retardation: I. Social, psychological, and educational aspects* (pp. 43–52). Baltimore: University Park Press.

Morrison, G. M., MacMillan, D. L., & Kavale, K. (1985). System identification of learning disabled children: Implications for research sampling. *Learning Disability Quarterly, 8,* 1–10.

Morsink, C. V., Soar, R. S., Soar, R. M., & Thomas, R. (1986). Research on teaching: Opening the door to special education classrooms. *Exceptional Children, 53*(1), 32–40.

Moulton, J. R., & Bader, M. S. (1985). The writing process: A powerful approach for the language-disabled student. *Annals of Dyslexia, 35,* 161–173.

Muenster, G. E. (1982). The career development process at the elementary level. *Journal of Career Development, 8,* 238–245.

Mullen, F., & Itkin, W. (1961). The value of special classes for the mentally handicapped. *Chicago Schools Journal, 42,* 353–363.

Mullins, J., Joseph, F., Turner, C., Zawadyski, R., & Saltzman, L. (1972). A handwriting model for children with learning disabilities. *Journal of Learning Disabilities, 5,* 306–311.

Mullis, I. (1980). *The primary trait system for scoring writing tasks* (NAEP Report No. 05-W-50). Denver, CO: Education Commission of the United States.

Mundy, J. (1975). *Systems approach to leisure education.* Tallahassee: Florida State University.

Munester, G. E. (1982). The career development process at the elementary level. *Journal of Career Development, 8,* 238–245.

Muraski, J. A. (1982). Designing career education programs that work. *Academic Therapy, 18,* 65–71.

Myers, A. C., & Thornton, C. A. (1977). The learning disabled child: Learning the basic facts. *Arithmetic Teacher, 24,* 46–50.

Myers, J. K. (1976). The efficacy of the special day school for EMR pupils. *Mental Retardation, 14,* 3–11.

Myers, P. I., & Hammill, D. (1982). *Learning disabilities: Basic concepts, assessment practices, and instructional strategies.* Austin, TX: Pro-Ed.

Myklebust, H. (1965). *Development and disorders of written language: Picture story language test* (Vol. 1). New York: Grune & Stratton.

Myklebust, H. R., & Johnson, D. J. (1962). Dyslexia in children. *Exceptional Children, 29,* 14–25.

Nagle, R. J., & Thwaite, B. C. (1979). Modeling effects of impulsivity with learning disabled children. *Journal of Learning Disabilities, 12,* 331–336.

Nash, K., & Geyer, C. (1983). *Touch to type.* North Billerica, ME: Curriculum Associates.

National Assessment of Educational Progress. (1977). *Write/rewrite: An assessment of revision skills* (Writing Report No. 05-W-04). Washington, DC: U. S. Government Printing Office.

National Council of Teachers of Mathematics. (1980). *An agenda for action: Recommendations for school mathematics of the 1980's.* Reston, VA: Author.

National Joint Committee for Learning Disabilities. (1981). *Learning disabilities: Issues on definition.* Unpublished position paper. (Available from NJCLD Committee Chairperson, c/o Orton Society, 8419 Bellona Lange, Touson, MD 21204).

Neal, L. (1970). *Recreation's role in the rehabilitation of the mentally retarded.* Eugene: University of Oregon Rehabilitation and Training Center in Mental Retardation.

Neeley, M. D., & Lindsley, O. R. (1978). Phonetic, linguistic, and sight readers produce similar learning with exceptional children. *Journal of Special Education, 12,* 423–441.

Nelson, H. E. (1980). Analysis of spelling errors in normal dyslexic children. In U. Frith (Ed.), *Cognitive processes in spelling.* London: Academic Press.

Newcombe, F., & Marshall, J. (1981). On psycholinguistic classification of the acquired dyslexias. *Bulletin of the Orton Society, 31,* 29–46.

Newcomer, P., Larsen, S., & Hammill, D. (1975). A response. *Exceptional Children, 42,* 144–148.

Nichols, P. L., & Chen, T. C. (1981). *Minimal brain dysfunction: A prospective study.* Hillsdale, NJ: Lawrence Erlbaum.

Noel, M. M. (1980). Referential communication abilities of learning disabled children. *Learning Disability Quarterly, 3,* 70–75.

Novak, A., & Heal, L. (Eds.). (1980). *Integration of developmentally disabled individuals into the community.* Baltimore: Paul H. Brookes.

Novy, P., Burnett, J., Powers, M., & Sulzer–Azaroff, B. (1973). Modifying attending-to-work behavior of a learning disabled child. *Journal of Learning Disabilities, 6,* 217, 221.

Nuzum, M. (1982). *The effects of a curriculum based on the information processing paradigm on the arithmetic problem solving performance of four learning disabled students.* Unpublished doctoral dissertation, Teachers College, Columbia University, New York.

Oakland, T. (Ed.). (1981). *Psychological assessment of minority children.* New York: Bruner/Mazel.

Oden, S., & Asher, S. R. (1977). Coaching children in social skills for friendship making. *Child Development, 48,* 459–506.

O'Hara, D. M., Chaiklin, H., & Mosher, B. M. (1980). A family life cycle plan for delivery services for the developmentally disabled. *Child Welfare, 59,* 80–90.

Ohrenstein, D. F. (1979). Parent counseling. In W. C. Adamson (Ed.), *A handbook for specific learning disabilities.* New York: Gardner Press.

Oldesen, C. F. (1974). Instructional materials. In *Thesaurus for special education* (2nd ed.). Education IMC/RMC Network. (ERIC Reproduction Document Service No. EC 070 639.

O'Leary, K. D. (1980). Pills or skills for hyperactive children. *Journal of Applied Behavior Analysis, 13,* 191–204.

O'Leary, K. D., & Becker, W. C. (1967). Behavior modification of an adjustment class: A token reinforcement program. *Exceptional Children, 9,* 637–642.

Olsen, J., & Midgett, J. (1984). Alternative placements: Does a difference exist in the LD population? *Journal of Learning Disabilities, 17*(2), 101–103.

Olsen, K. (1973). *SER-LARS-I. Users manual.* Harrisburg, PA: National Regional Resource Center of Pennsylvania.

Olshansky, S. (1962). Chronic sorrow: A response to having a mentally defective child. *Social Casework, 43,* 190–193.

O'Morrow, G. (1976). *Therapeutic recreation: A helping profession.* Reston, VA: Reston Publishing.

O'Neill, D. R., & Jensen, R. S. (1981). Some aids for teaching place value. *Arithmetic Teacher, 28,* 6–9.

Orton, S. (1937). *Reading, writing, and speech problems in children.* New York: Norton.

Osburn, W. (1953). Handwriting. In O. Buros (Ed.), *Fourth mental measurement yearbook.* Highland Park, NJ: The Gryphon Press.

Osman, B. (1982). *No one to play with: The social side of learning disabilities.* New York: Random House.

Otto, W., McMenemy, R. A., & Smith, P. J. (1973). *Corrective and remedial teaching* (2nd ed.). Boston: Houghton Mifflin.

Otto, W., & Smith, R. J. (1983). Skill-centered and meaning-centered conceptions of remedial instruction: Striking a balance. *Topics in Learning and Learning Disabilities, 2,* 20–26.

Palincsar, A. S. (1982). Improving the reading comprehension of junior high students through reciprocal teaching of comprehension-monitoring strategies. Unpublished doctoral dissertation, University of Illinois, Urbana.

Palmer, D. J. (1980). Factors to consider in placing handicapped children in regular education classes. *Journal of School Psychology, 18,* 163–171.

Palmer, D. J. (1985). The microcomputer and the learning disabled: A useful tool. *Journal of Reading, Writing, and Learning Disabilities International, 1*(1), 24–40.

Palmer, D. J., Drummond, F., Tollison, P., & Zinkgraff, S. (1982). An attributional investigation of performance outcomes for learning disabled and normal-achieving pupils. *Journal of Special Education, 16,* 207–216.

Palmer, D. J., & Goetz, E. T. (1985). Selection and the use of study strategies: The role of the studier's beliefs about self and strategies. Unpublished manuscript, Texas A & M University, College Station.

Palmer, J. T. (1985). The microcomputer and the learning disabled: A useful tool. *Journal of Reading, Writing, and Learning Disabilities, 1*(1), 24–40.

Paloutzian, R., Hasazi, J., Streitel, R., & Edgar, C. (1971). Promotion of positive social interaction in severely retarded young children. *American Journal on Mental Defi-*

ciency, 75, 519–524.

Pany, D., Jenkins, J., & Schreck, J. (1982). Vocabulary instruction: Effects of word knowledge and reading comprehension. *Learning Disability Quarterly, 5,* 203–215.

Parker, J. (1975). A photo-electric pen for producing action feedback to aid development in handicapped children of fine visual-motor skills: Tracing and writing. *Slow Learning Child, 22,* 13–22.

Parker, S., Friars, E., Gelman, N., & Kowacki, W. (1980). *Special education: Management information.* Washington, DC: National Association of State Directors of Special Education.

Parten, M. (1932). Social play among school children. *Journal of Abnormal Psychology, 28,* 136–147.

Parten, M., & Newhall, S. (1943). Social behavior of preschool children. In R. Barker, J. Kounin, & H. Wright (Eds.), *Child behavior and development.* New York: McGraw-Hill.

Pearl, R. (1982). Learning-disabled children's attributions for success and failure: A replication with a labeled learning-disabled sample. *Learning Disability Quarterly, 5,* 173–176.

Pearl, R. (1985). Cognitive behavioral interventions for increasing motivation. *Journal of Abnormal Child Psychology, 13,* 443–454.

Pearl, R., Bryan, T., & Donahue, M. (1980). Learning-disabled children's attributions for success and failure. *Learning Disability Quarterly, 3,* 3–9.

Pearl, R., Bryan, T., & Donahue, M. (1983). Social behaviors of learning disabled children: A review. *Topics in Learning and Learning Disabilities, 3*(2), 1–14.

Pearl, R., Bryan, T., & Herzog, A. (1983). Learning-disabled and nondisabled children's strategy analyses under high and low success conditions. *Learning Disability Quarterly, 6,* 67–74.

Pearl, R., & Cosden, M. (1982). Sizing up a situation: LD children's understanding of social interactions. *Learning Disability Quarterly, 5,* 371–373.

Pearl, R., Donahue, M., & Bryan, T. (1983). The development of tact: Children's strategies for delivering bad news. Unpublished manuscript. University of Illinois at Chicago.

Pearson, P. D. (1978). Some practical applications of psycholinguistic models of reading. In S. J. Samuels (Ed.), *What research has to say about reading instruction* (pp. 84–95). Newark, DL: International Reading Association.

Peck, D. M., & Jencks, S. M. (1981). Conceptual issues in the teaching and learning of fractions. *Journal of Research in Mathematics Education, 12,* 339–348.

Peck, M., & Fairchild, S. H. (1980). Another decade of research in handwriting: Progress and prospect in the 1970s. *Journal of Educational Research, 73*(5), 283–298.

Pelham, W. E. (1983). The effects of psychostimulants on academic achievement in hyperactive and learning-disabled children. *Thalamus, 3,* 1–49.

Pelham, W. E. (1985). The effects of psychostimulant drugs on learning and academic achievement in children with attention deficit disorders and learning disabilities. In J. K. Torgeson & B. Wong (Eds.), *Psychological and educational perspectives on learning disabilities* (pp. 259–295). Orlando, FL: Academic Press.

Pelham, W. E., Bender, M. E., Caddell, J., Booth, S., & Moorer, S. H. (1985). Methylphenidate and children with attention deficit disorder: Dose effects on classroom academic and social behavior. *Archives of General Psychiatry, 42,* 948–952.

Pelham, W. E., Milich, R., & Walker, J. L. (1986). The effects of continuous and partial reinforcement and methylphenidate on learning in children with attention deficit disorder. *Journal of Abnormal Psychology, 95,* 319–325.

Pelham, W. E., & Murphy, H. A. (1985). Behavioral and pharmacological treatment of attention deficit and conduct disorders. In M. Hersen (Ed.), *Pharmacological and behavioral treatment: An integrative approach.* New York: Wiley.

Pelham, W. E., Swanson, J., Bender, M., & Wilson, J. (1980, September). *Effects of pemoline on hyperactivity: Laboratory and classroom measures.* Paper presented at the annual meeting of the American Psychological Association, Montreal.

Pennhurst State School and Hospital v. Halderman. (1981). 451 US 1.

Pepe, H. J. (1974). A comparison of the effectiveness of itinerant and resource room model programs designed to serve children with learning disabilities. Doctoral dissertation, University of Kansas. *Dissertation Abstracts International, 1,* 75–92.

Perfetti, C. A., & Lesgold, A. M. (1977). *Coding and comprehension in skilled reading and implications for reading instruction.* Pittsburgh, PA: University of Pittsburgh, Learning Research and Development Center.

Perfetti, C. A., & Lesgold, A. M. (1979). Coding and comprehension in skilled reading and implications for reading instruction. In L. Resnick & P. Weaver (Eds.), *Theory and practice of early reading* (Vol. 1, pp. 57–84). Hillsdale, NJ: Lawrence Erlbaum.

Perlmutter, B. F., Crocker, J., Cordray, D., & Garstecki, D. (1983). Sociometric status and related personality characteristics of mainstreamed learning disabled adolescents. *Learning Disability Quarterly, 6,* 20–30.

Perry, D. C. (1981). The disabled student and college counseling centers. *Journal of College Student Personnel, 22*(6), 533–538.

Peterson, P. L., & Walberg, H. J. (Eds.). *Research on teaching: Concepts, findings, and implications.* Berkeley, CA: McCutchan.

Petrauskas, R., & Rourke, B. (1979). Identification of subgroups of retarded readers: A neuropsychological multivariate approach. *Journal of Clinical Neuropsychology, 1,* 17–37.

Pflaum, S. W., & Pascarella, E. T. (1980). Interactive effects of prior reading achievement and training in context on the reading of learning disabled children. *Reading Research Quarterly, 16,* 138–158.

Phelps, J., Stempel, L., & Speck, G. (1982). *Children's handwriting evaluation scale: A new diagnostic tool.* Unpublished manuscript.

Phelps–Gunn, T., & Phelps–Terasaki, D. (1982). *Written language instruction.* Rockville, MD: Aspen Publications.

Phelps–Terasaki, D., & Phelps, T. (1980). *Teaching written expression: The Phelps sentence guide program.* Novato, CA: Academic Therapy.

Phillips, D. (1983). After the wake: Post positivistic educational thought. *Educational Researcher, 12,* 4–12.

Phillips, D. C. (1980). What do the researcher and the practitioner have to offer each other? *Educational Researcher, 9,* 17–20, 24.

Piaget, J. (1951). *Dreams and imitation in childhood.* New York: Norton.

Piers, M. (1972). *Play and development.* New York: Norton.

Pirozzolo, F. (1979). *The neuropsychology of developmental reading disorders.* New York: Praeger.

Polloway, E. A. (1984). The integration of mildly retarded students in the schools: A historical review. *Remedial and Special Education, 5*(4), 18–19.

Polloway, E. A., Payne, J. S., Patton, J. R., & Payne, R. A. (1985). *Strategies for teaching retarded and special needs learners* (3rd ed.). Columbus, OH: Merrill.

Polsgrove, L. (1979). Self-control: Methods for child training. *Behavioral Disorders, 4,* 116–130.

Popham, W., Eisner, E., Sullivan, H., & Tyler, L. (1969). Instructional objectives. *AERA Monograph Series of Curriculum Evaluation.* Chicago: Rand McNally.

Poplin, M. (1979). The science of curriculum development applied to special education and the IEP. *Focus on Exceptional Children, 12,* 1–16.

Poplin, M., & Gray, R. (1980). A conceptual framework for assessment of curriculum and student progress. *Exceptional Education Quarterly, 1,* 75–86.

Posner, M. I. (1979). Applying theories and theorizing about applications. In L. Resnick & P. Weaver (Eds.), *Theory and practice of early reading* (Vol. 1, pp. 331–342)). Hillsdale, NJ: Lawrence Erlbaum.

Poteet, J. A. (1980). Informal assessment of written expression. *Learning Disability Quarterly, 3,* 88–98.

President's Committee on Mental Retardation. (1974). *America's needs in habilitation and employment of the mentally retarded.* Washington, DC: U.S. Government Printing Office.

Pratt, D. (1980). *Curriculum design and development.* New York: Harcourt Brace Jovanovich.

Prillaman, D. (1981). Acceptance of learning disabled students in the mainstream environment: A failure to replicate. *Journal of Learning Disabilities, 14,* 344–346.

Project Achieve case information. (Undated). Carbondale: Southern Illinois University.

Public Law 94-142. (1977, August 23). Education for All Handicapped Children Act. *Federal Register, 42.*

Purkey, S. C., & Smith, M. S. (1983). Effective schools: A review. *Elementary School Journal, 83,* 427–452.

Quandt, D. F. (1985). *Mathematical problem solving performance of learning disabled, low achieving, and average achieving children.* Unpublished doctoral dissertation, Teachers College, Columbia University, New York.

Quay, H. C., Glavin, J. R., Annesley, F. R., & Werry, J. S. (1972). The modification of problem behavior and academic achievement in a resource room. *Journal of School Psychology, 10,* 187–198.

Quinn, P., & Rapoport, J. (1975). One-year follow-up of hyperactive boys treated with imipramine and methylphenidate. *American Journal of Psychiatry, 132,* 241–245.

Rabinovitch, R. D. (1962). Dyslexia: Psychiatric considerations. In J. Money (Ed.), *Reading disability: Progress and research needs in dyslexia.* Baltimore: Johns Hopkins Press.

Ramming, J. (1970). Using the chalkboard to overcome handwriting difficulties. In J. Arena (Ed.), *Building handwriting skills in dyslexic children.* San Rafael, CA: Academic Therapy Publications.

Rapoport, J. L. (1980). The "real" and "ideal" management of stimulant drug treatment for hyperactive children: Recent findings and a report from clinical practice. In C. K. Whalen & B. Henker (Eds.), *Hyperactive children: The social ecology of identification and treatment.* New York: Academic Press.

Rapoport, J. L., Quinn, P. O., Bradbard, G., Riddle, K. D., & Brooks, E. (1974). Imipramine and methylphenidate treatments of hyperactive boys. *Archives of General Psychiatry, 30,* 789–793.

Rapport, M. .D., Murphy, A., & Bailey, J. S. (1980). The effects of a response cost treatment tactic on hyperactive children. *Journal of School Psychology, 18,* 98–111.

Rapport, M. D., Murphy, H. A., & Bailey, J. S. (1982). Ritalin vs. response cost in the control of hyperactive children.: A within-subject comparison. *Journal of Applied Behavior Analysis, 15,* 205–216.

Rapport, M. D., Stoner, G., DuPaul, G. J., Birmingham, B. K., & Tucker, S. (1985). Methylphenidate in hyperactive children: Differential effects of dose on academic learning and social behavior. *Journal of Abnormal Child Psychology, 13,* 227–244.

Raskind, M. H., Drew, D. E., & Regan, J. O. (1983). Nonverbal communication signals in behavior-disordered and non-disordered LD boys and NLD boys. *Learning Disability Quarterly, 6,* 12–19.

Rasmussen, S. (1980). *Key to fractions.* Berkeley, CA: Key Curriculum Project.

Raven, J. C. (1956). *Standard progresive matrices.* London: H. K. Lewis.

Read, C. (1980). Pre-school children's knowledge of English phonology. In M. Wolf, M.

McQuillan, & E. Radwin (Eds.), Thought & language/language and reading. *Har vard Educational Review* (Reprint Series No. 14, pp. 150–179).

Redden, M. R., Levering, C., & DiQuinzio, D. (1978). *Recruitment, admissions and handicapped students.* Washington, DC: The American Association of College Registrars and Admissions Officers and the American Council on Education.

Reed, J. C. (1968). The ability deficits of good and poor readers. *Journal of Learning Disabilities, 1,* 134–139.

Reeves, R. A., & Brown, A. L. (1985). Metacognition reconsidered: Implications for intervention research. *Journal of Abnormal Child Psychology, 13,* 343–356.

Reid, D. K., & Hresko, W. P. (1981a). *A cognitive approach to learning disabilities.* New York: McGraw-Hill.

Reid, D. K., & Hresko, W. P. (1981b). From the editors. *Topics in Learning and Learning Disabilities, 1,* viii–ix.

Reisman, F. K., & Kauffman, S. H. (1980). *Teaching mathematics to children with special needs.* Columbus, OH: Merrill.

Resnick, L., & Beck, I. (1976). Designing instruction in reading: Interaction of theory and practice. In J. Guthrie (Ed.), *Aspects of reading acquisition* (pp. 180–204). Baltimore: Johns Hopkins University Press.

Resnick, L. B. (1981). Instructional psychology. In M. R. Rosenzweig & L. W. Porter (Eds.), *Annual review of psychology* (Vol. 32, pp. 741–704) Palo Alto, CA: Annual Review.

Reynolds, M. C., & Birch, J. W. (1982). *Teaching exceptional children in all America's schools* (rev. ed.). Reston, VA: The Council for Exceptional Children.

Rhodes, L. K., & Shannon, J. L. (1982). Psycholinguistic principles in operation in a primary learning disabilities classroom. *Topics in Learning and Learning Disabilities, 1,* 1–10.

Rhodes, S. L. (1977). A developmental approach to the life cycle of the family. *Social Casework, 58,* 301–304.

Rhodes, S. S. (1985). Mini-assessment: A practical approach to classroom identification of learning disabled readers. *Reading Horizons, 25*(3), 186–193.

Riddle, D., & Rapoport, J. (1976). A 2-year follow-up of 72 hyperactive boys. *Journal of Nervous and Mental Disease, 162,* 126–134.

Rie, H. E., Rie, E. D., Stewart, S., & Ambuel, J. P. (1976). Effects of methylphenidate on underachieving children. *Journal of Consulting and Clinical Psychology, 44,* 250–260.

Risner, M. T. (1979). *NICSEM special education thesaurus.* Los Angeles: The National Information Center for Special Education Media.

Ritter, D. R. (1978). Surviving in the regular classroom: A follow-up of mainstreamed children with learning disabilities. *Journal of School Psychology, 16,* 253–256.

Roberts, G. H. (1968). The failure strategies of third grade arithmetic pupils. *The Arithmetic Teacher, 15,* 442–446.

Robins, L. N. (1977). Problems in follow-up studies. *American Journal of Psychiatry, 134,* 904–907.

Robins, L. N. (1979). Follow-up studies of behavior disorders in children. In H. C. Quay & J. S. Werry (Eds.), *Psychopathological disorders of childhood* (pp. 483–513). New York: Wiley.

Robinson, S. P. (1974). *Study skills for superior students in secondary schools* (2nd ed.). New York: Macmillan.

Roddy, E. A. (1984). When are resource rooms going to share in the declining enrollment trend? Another look at mainstreaming. *Journal of Learning Disabilities, 17*(5), 279–281.

Roff, M., Sells, S. B., & Golden, M. M. (1972). *Social adjustment and personality develop-*

ment in children. Minneapolis: University of Minnesota Press.

Rose, T., Lessen, E., & Gottlieb, J. (1982). A discussion of transfer of training in mainstreaming progress. *Journal of Learning Disabilities, 15*(3), 162–165.

Rosegrant, T. (1985). Using the microcomputer as a tool for learning to read and write. *Journal of Learning Disabilities, 18*(2), 113–115.

Rosen, L. A., O'Leary, S. G., & Conway, G. (1983). *The withdrawal of stimulant medication for hyperactivity: A case study.* Unpublished manuscript, SUNY, Department of Psychology, Stony Brook, NY.

Rosenshine, B. V., & Berliner, D. C. (1978). Academic engaged time. *British Journal of Teacher Education, 4,* 3–16.

Rosenthal, R., & Jacobson, L. (1968). *Pygmalion in the classroom.* New York: Holt, Rinehart & Winston.

Rosenthal, R., & Rubin, D. B. (1978). Interpersonal expectancy effects: The first 345 studies. *The Behavioral and Brain Sciences, 3,* 377–415.

Rosenthal, R., & Rubin, D. R. (1982). A simple, general purpose display of the magnitude of experimental effect. *Journal of Educational Psychology, 74,* 166–169.

Ross, A. O. (1976). *Psychological aspects of learning disabilities and reading disorders.* New York: McGraw-Hill.

Ross, A. O. (1981). *Child behavior therapy.* New York: Wiley.

Ross, S. K., & O'Brien, M. B. (1981). *504 and admissions: Making the law work for the applicant and the college.* Minneapolis, MN: St Mary's College. (ERIC Document Reproduction Service No. ED 206 335)

Rourke, B. P. (1978). Reading, spelling, arithmetic disabilities: A neuropsychological perspective. In H. R. Myklebust (Ed.), *Progress in learning disabilities* (Vol. 4, pp. 97–120). New York: Grune & Stratton.

Rourke, B. P. (Ed.). (1985). *Neuropsychology of learning disabilities: Advances in subtype analysis.* New York: Guilford Press.

Rourke, B. P., & Finlayson, M. A. (1978). Neuropsychological significance of variations patterns of academic performance: Verbal and visual spatial abilities. *Journal of Abnormal Child Psychology, 6,* 121–133.

Rourke, B. P., & Orr, R. R. (1977). Prediction of the reading and spelling performances of normal and retarded readers: A four-year follow-up. *Journal of Abnormal Child Psychology, 5,* 9–20.

Rubin, L. J. (Ed.). (1977). *Curriculum handbook.* Boston: Allyn and Bacon.

Rumelhart, D. E. (1977). Toward an interactive model of reading. In S. Dornic (Ed.), *Attention and performance* (Vol. 6). New York: Wiley.

Russell, R. L., & Ginsburg, H. P. (1981). *Cognitive analysis of children's mathematics difficulties.* Rochester, NY: University of Rochester.

Rutter, M. (1978). Prevalence and types of dyslexia. In A. L. Benton & D. Pearl (Eds.), *Dyslexia: An appraisal of current knowledge* (pp. 3–28). New York: Oxford University Press.

Rutter, M., & Yule, W. (1975). The concept of specific reading retardation. *Journal of Child Psychology and Psychiatry, 16,* 181–197.

Ryback, D., & Staats, A. W. (1970). Parents as behavior-therapy technicians in treating reading deficits (dyslexia). *Journal of Behavior Therapy and Experimental Psychiatry, 1,* 109–119.

Sabatino, D. A. (1971). An evaluation of resource rooms for children with learning disabilities. *Journal of Learning Disabilities, 4,* 27–35.

Sabatino, D. (1976). *Learning disabilities handbook: A technical guide to program development.* Dekalb: Northern Illinois University.

Safer, D., & Allen, R. (1976). *Hyperactive children: Diagnosis and management.* Baltimore:

University Park Press.

Safer, D. J., & Krager, J. M. (1984). Trends in medication treatment of hyperactive school children. In K. D. Gadow (Ed.), *Advances in learning and behavioral disabilites* (Vol. 3, pp. 125–149). Greenwich, CT: JAI Press.

Salend, S. J. (1984). Factors contributing to the development of successful mainstreaming programs. *Exceptional Children, 50,* 409–416.

Salend, S. J., & Lutz, J. G. (1984). Mainstreaming or maintaining: A competency based approach to mainstreaming. *Journal of Learning Disabilities, 17,* 27–29.

Salend, S. J., & Salend, S. M. (1985). The implications of using microcomputers in classroom testing. *Journal of Learning Disabilities, 18*(1), 51–53.

Salomon, G. (1972). Heuristic models for the generation of aptitude-treatment interaction hypotheses. *Review of Educational Research, 42,* 327–343.

Salvia, J., & Ysseldyke, J. E. (1985). *Assessment in special and remedial education* (3rd ed.). Boston: Houghton Mifflin.

Samaras, M., & Ball, T. (1975). Reinforcement of cooperation between profoundly retarded adults. *American Journal on Mental Deficiency, 80,* 63–71.

Samuels, S. J. (1986). Why children fail to learn and what to do about it. *Exceptional Children, 53*(1), 7–16.

Satterfield, J. H., Cantwell, D. P., & Satterfield, B. T. (1979). Multimodality treatment: A one-year follow-up of 84 hyperactive boys. *Archives of General Psychiatry, 35,* 965–974.

Satterfield, J. H., Satterfield, B. T., & Cantwell, D. P. (1980). Multimodality treatment: A two year evaluation of 61 hyperactive boys. *Archives of General Psychiatry, 37,* 915–918.

Satterfield, J. H., Satterfield, B. T., & Cantwell, D. P. (1981). Three-year multimodality treatment study of 100 hyperactive boys. *Journal of Pediatrics, 98,* 650–655.

Satz, P., & Morris, R. (1981). Learning disability subtypes: A review. In F. J. Pirozzolo & M. C. Wittrock (Eds.), *Neuropsychological and cognitive processes in reading* (pp. 109–141). New York: Academic Press.

Satz, P., Taylor, H. G., Friel, J., & Fletcher, J. (1978). Some developmental and predictive precursors of reading disabilities: A six-year follow-up. In A. L. Benton & D. Pearl (Eds.), *Dyslexia: An appraisal of current knowledge* (pp. 313–348). New York: Oxford University Press.

Savage, J. F., & Mooney, J. F. (1979). *Teaching reading to children with special needs.* Boston: Allyn and Bacon.

Schacht, E. J. (1967). A study of the mathematical errors of low achievers in elementary school mathematics. *Dissertation Abstracts International, 29A,* 920–921.

Schaefer, E. S. (1981). Development of adaptive behavior: Conceptual models and family correlates. In M. Begab, H. Garber, & H. C. Haywood (Eds.), *Prevention of retarded development in psychosocially disadvantaged children.* Baltimore: University Park Press.

Schain, R. J., & Reynard, C. L. (1975). Observations on the effects of central stimulant drug (methylphenidate) in children with hyperactive behavior. *Pediatrics, 55,* 709–716.

Schenck, S. J. (1980). The diagnostic-instructional link in individualized education programs. *Journal of Special Education, 14,* 337–345.

Schleien, S. (1982). *Effects of an individualized leisure education instructional program of cooperative leisure skill activities on severely learning disabled children.* Unpublished doctoral dissertation, University of Maryland.

Schleien, S., Porter, R., & Wehman, P. (1979). An assessment of the leisure skill needs of developmentally disabled individuals. *Therapeutic Recreation Journal, 13,* 16–21.

Schumaker, J., Hovell, M., & Sherman, J. (1977a). An analysis of daily report cards and

parent managed privileges in the improvement of adolescents' classroom performance. *Journal of Applied Behavior Analysis, 10,* 449–464.

Schumaker, J., Hovell, M., & Sherman, J. (1977b). *A home-based achievement system.* Lawrence, KS: Excel Enterprises.

Schumaker, J. B., Deshler, D. D., Alley, G. R., & Warner, M. M. (1983). Toward the
development of an intervention model for learning disabled adolescents: The University of Kansas Institute. *Exceptional Education Quarterly, 4*(1), 45–74.

Schumaker, J. B., & Ellis, E. (1982). Social skills training of LD adolescents: A generalization study. *Learning Disability Quarterly, 5,* 409–414.

Schumaker, J. B., Hazel, J. S., & Pederson, C. (1988). *Social skills for daily living.* Circle
Pines, MN: American Guidance Service.

Schumaker, J. B., Hazel, J. S., Pederson, C. S., & Nolan, S. (in preparation). *Evaluation of a
method for promoting generalization of newly learned social skills* (Research Report). Lawrence: The University of Kansas Institute for Research in Learning Disabilities.

Schumaker, J. B., Hazel, J. S., Sherman, J. A., & Sheldon, J. (1982). Social skill performances of learning disabled and non-learning disabled, and delinquent adolescents.
Learning Disability Quarterly, 5, 409–414.

Schumaker, J. B., Pederson, C. S., Hazel, J. S., & Meyen, E. L. (1983). Social skills
curricula for mildly handicapped adolescents: A review. *Focus on Exceptional
Children, 16*(4), 1–16.

Schumaker, J. B., Sheldon-Wildgen, J., & Sherman, J. A. (1980). *An observational study of
the academic and social behaviors of learning disabled adolscents in the regular classroom*
(Research Report No. 22). Lawrence: The University of Kansas Institute for
Research in Learning Disabilities.

Schwartz, J. S. (1977). *A longitudinal study to determine the effectiveness of a special program
for the learning disabled child.* Unpublished doctoral dissertation, Fordham University, Bronx, NY.

Schworm, R. W. (1979). The effects of selective attention on the decoding skills of
children with learning disabilities. *Journal of Learning Disabilities, 12,* 639–644.

Scranton, T., & Ryckman, D. (1979). Sociometric status of learning disabled children in
an interactive program. *Journal of Learning Disabilities, 12,* 402–407.

Scribner, W. (1953). Evaluation of the Lincoln diagnostic spelling tests. In O. Buros
(Ed.), *The fourth annual mental measurements yearbook.* Highland Park, NJ: Gryphon
Press.

Seabaugh, G. O., & Schumaker, J. B. (1981). *The effects of self-regulation training on the
academic productivity training of LD and NLD adolescents* (Research Report No. 37).
Lawrence: University of Kansas Institute for Research in Learning Disabilities.

Semmel, M. I., Gottlieb, J., & Robinson, N. M. (1979). Mainstreaming: Perspectives on
educating handicapped children in the public school. In D. C. Berliner (Ed.),
Review of research in education (pp. 223–279). Washington, DC: American Educational Research Association.

Senf, G. M. (1972). An information-integration theory and its application to normal
reading acquisition and reading disability. In N. D. Bryant & C. E. Kass (Eds.),
Leadership training institute in learning disabilities (Vol. 2, pp. 305–391, Final Report).
Tucson, AZ: University of Arizona.

Senf, G. M. (1978). Implications of the final procedures for evaluating specific learning
disabilities. *Journal of Learning Disabilities, 11,* 124–126.

Serna, L., Hazel, S., Schumaker, J. B., & Sheldon, J. (1984, May). Training reciprocal
skills to parents of problem adolescents. In L. Serna (Chair), *Parent-adolescent communication programs and family data analysis.* Symposium conducted at the Tenth
Annual Convention of the Association for Behavioral Analysis, Nashville, TN.

Serna, L. A., Schumaker, J. B., Hazel, J. S., & Sheldon, J. B. (1986). Teaching reciprocal social skills to parents and their delinquent adolescents. *Journal of Clinical Psychology, 15,* 64–77.

Seymour, D. (1970). What do you mean "auditory perception"? *Elementary School Journal, 70,* 175–179.

Seymour, P. H., & Porpodas, C. D. (1980). Lexical and non-lexical processing in dyslexia. In U. Frith (Ed.), *Cognitive processes in spelling.* London: Academic Press.

Sharma, M. (1979). Children at risk for disabilities in mathematics. *Focus on Learning Problems, 1,* 63–94.

Shattuck, M. (1946). Segregation versus non-segregation of exceptional children. *Journal of Exceptional Children, 12,* 235–240.

Sheehan, R., & Keogh, B. K. (1984). Approaches to evaluation in special education. In B. K. Keogh (Ed.), *Advances in special education* (Vol. 4, pp. 1–20). Greenwich, CT: JAI Press.

Sheridan, J. J., & Meister, K. A. (1982). *Food additives and hyperactivity.* New York: American Council on Science and Health.

Shulman, R. (1976). Recreation programming for children with specific learning disabilities. *Leisurability, 3,* 13.

Siefferman, L. D. (1983). Vocational education — the post-secondary connection for learning disabled students. *The Journal for Vocational Special Needs Education, 5*(2), 28–29.

Siegel, S. (1956). *Nonparametric statistics for the behavioral sciences.* New York: McGraw-Hill.

Silberberg, N. E., Iverson, I. A., & Goins, J. T. (1973). Which remedial method works best? *Journal of Learning Disabilities, 6,* 547–555.

Silberberg, N. E., & Silberberg, M. C. (1969). Myths in remedial education. *Journal of Learning Disabilities, 2,* 209–217.

Silbert, J., Carnine, D., & Stein, M. (1981). *Direct instruction mathematics.* Columbus, OH: Merrill.

Silver, A. A., & Hagin, R. A. (1976). *SEARCH.* New York: Walker Educational Book Corp.

Silver, A. A., Hagin, R. A., & Beecher, R. (1978). Scanning, diagnosis, and intervention in the prevention of reading disabilities: I. SEARCH: The scanning measure; II. TEACH: Learning tasks for the prevention of learning disabilities. *Journal of Learning Disabilities, 11,* 439–449.

Silver, A. A., Hagin, R. A., & Beecher, R. (1981). A program for secondary prevention of learning disabilities: Results in academic achievement and in emotional adjustment. *Journal of Preventive Psychiatry, 1,* 77–87.

Silver, L. B. (1974). Emotional and social problems of the family with a child who has developmental disabilities. In R. W. Weber (Ed.), *Handbook on learning disabilities: A prognosis for the child, the adolescent, the adult.* Englewood Cliffs, NJ: Prentice-Hall.

Simches, G., & Bohn, R. (1963). Issues in curriculum: Research and responsibility. *Mental Retardation, 1,* 84–87.

Sinclair, A., Jarvella, R., & Levelt, W. (1978). *The child's conception of language.* New York: Springer-Verlag.

Sindelar, P. T., & Deno, S. L. (1978). The effectiveness of resource programming. *The Journal of Special Education, 12,* 17–28.

Singer, M. H. (1982). Reading disability research: A misguided search for difference. In M. Singer (Ed.), *Competent reader, disabled reader: Research and application* (pp. 39–54). Hillsdale, NJ: Lawrence Erlbaum.

Siperstein, G. N., Bopp, M. J., & Bak, J. J. (1978). Social status of learning disabled children. *Journal of Learning Disabilities, 11,* 98–102.

Sleator, E. K. (1985). Measurement of compliance. *Psychopharmacology Bulletin, 21,*

1089–1093.

Sleator, E. K., Ullman, R. K., & von Neumann, A. (1982). How do hyperactive children feel about taking stimulants and will they tell the doctor? *Clinical Pediatrics, 21*, 474–479.

Sleator, E. K., von Neumann, A. W., & Sprague, R. L. (1974). Hyperactive children: A continuous long-term placebo controlled follow-up. *Journal of the American Medical Association, 229*, 316–317.

Slingerland, B. (1970). *Slingerland screening tests for identifying children with specific language disability.* Cambridge, MA: Educators Publishing Service.

Slingerland, B. (1981). *A multi-sensory approach to language arts for specific language disability children.* Cambridge, MA: Educators Publishing Service.

Smiley, A., & Bryan, T. (1983a). *Learning disabled boys' problem solving and visual interactions during raft building.* Chicago: Chicago Institute for the Study of Learning Disabilities.

Smiley, A., & Bryan, T. (1983b). *Learning disabled junior high boys' motor performance and trust during obstacle course activities.* Unpublished manuscript, University of Illinois at Chicago.

Smith, C. R. (1983). *Learning disabilities: The interaction of learner, task, and setting.* Boston: Little, Brown.

Smith, D. D., Lovitt, T. C., & Kidder, J.S. (1972). Using reinforcement contingencies and teaching aids to alter the subtraction performance of children with learning disabilities. In G. Semb (Ed.), *Behavior analysis and education.* Lawrence: University of Kansas Department of Human Development.

Smith, F. (1971). *Understanding reading: A psycholinguistic analysis of reading and learning to read.* New York: Holt, Rinehart & Winston.

Smith, F. (1977). Making sense of reading — And of reading instruction. *Harvard Educational Review, 47*, 386–395.

Smith, F., & Goodman, K. S. (1971). On the psycholinguistic method of teaching reading. *Elementary School Journal, 71*, 177–181.

Smith, G., & Smith, D. (1985). A mainstreaming program that really works. *Journal of Learning Disabilities, 18*, 369–372.

Smith, H. W., & Kennedy, W. A. (1967). Effects of three educational programs on mentally retarded children. *Perceptual and Motor Skills, 24*, 174.

Smith, J. D., & Dexter, B. L. (1980). The basics movement: What does it mean for the education of the mentally retarded students? *Education and Training of the Mentally Retarded, 15*, 72–74.

Smith, M. D., Coleman, J. M., Dokecki, P. R., & Davis, E. E. (1977). Intellectual characteristics of school labeled learning disabled children. *Exceptional Children, 43*, 352–357.

Smith, P. L., & Tomkins, G. E. (1984). Selecting software for your LD students. *Academic Therapy, 20*(2), 221–224.

Smith, T. E. C., Flexter, R. W., & Sigelman, C. K. (1980). Attitudes of secondary principals toward the learning disabled, mentally retarded and workstudy program. *Journal of Learning Disabilities, 13*, 62–64.

Snodgrass, G. (1980). *Computerized IEP and management information system.* Washington, DC: National Association of State Directors of Special Education.

Snowling, M. J. (1980). The development of grapheme-phoneme correspondence in normal and dyslexic readers. *Journal of Experimental Child Psychology, 29*, 294–305.

Soltis, J. (1984). On the nature of educational research. *Educational Researcher, 13*, 5–10.

Søvik, N. (1976). The effects of different principles of instruction in children's copying performance. *Journal of Experimental Education, 45*, 38–45.

Spache, G. D. (1963). *Toward better reading.* Champaign, IL: Garrard.

Spache, G. D. (1976). *Investigating the issue of reading disabilities.* Boston: Allyn and Bacon.

Speece, D. L. (1985). *Information processing and reading in subtypes of learning disabled children.* Unpublished manuscript, University of Maryland, Department of Special Education.

Speece, D. L., McKinney, J. D., & Applebaum, M. I. (1984). Classification and validation of behavior subtypes of learning disabled children. *Journal of Educational Psychology, 77,* 67–77.

Spekman, N. J. (1981). Dyadic verbal communication abilities of learning disabled and normally achieving fourth- and fifth-grade boys. *Learning Disability Quarterly, 4,* 139–151.

Spollen, J. C., & Ballif, B. F. (1971). Effectiveness of individualized instruction for kindergarten children with a developmental lag. *Exceptional Children, 38,* 205–209.

Sprague, R. L., & Berger, B. D. (1980). Drug effects on learning performance: Relevance of animal research to pediatric psychopharmacology. In R. M. Knights & B. J. Bakker (Eds.), *Treatment of hyperactive and learning disordered children: Current research* (pp. 167–184). Baltimore: University Park Press.

Sprague, R. L., & Sleator, E. K. (1973). Effects of psychopharmacologic agents on learning disorders. *Pediatric Clinics of North America, 20,* 719–735.

Sprague, R. L., & Sleator, E. K. (1975). What is the proper dose of stimulant drugs in children? *International Journal of Mental Health, 4,* 75–104.

Sprague, R. L., & Sleator, E. K. (1977). Methylphenidate in hyperactive children: Differences in dose effects on learning and social behavior. *Science, 198,* 1274–1276.

Spuck, D., Junter, S. N., Owen, S. P., & Belt, S. L. (1975). *Computer management of individualized instruction* (Tech. Report 55). Madison: University of Wisconsin, Wisconsin Research and Development Center for Cognitive Learning.

Squires, D. (1983). *Effective schools and classrooms: A research-based perspective.* Alexandria, VA: Association for Supervision and Curriculum Development.

Staats, A. W., & Butterfield, W. H. (1965). Treatment of nonreading in a culturally deprived juvenile delinquent: An application of reinforcement principles. *Child Development, 36,* 925–942.

Stainback, W., Stainback, S., Courtnage, L., & Jaben, T. (1985). Facilitating mainstreaming by modifying the mainstream. *Exceptional Children, 52,* 144–152.

Stanovich, K. E. (1982a). Individual differences in the cognitive processes of reading: I. Word decoding. *Journal of Learning Disabilities, 15,* 485–493.

Stanovich, K. E. (1982b). Individual differences in the cognitive process of reading: II. Text level processes. *Journal of Learning Disabilities, 15,* 549–554.

Stanovich, K. E. (1980). Toward an interactive compensatory model of individual differences in the development of reading fluency. *Reading Research Quarterly, 16,* 32–71.

Stanovich, K. E. (1981). Relationships between word decoding speed, general name-retrieval ability and reading progress in first-grade children. *Journal of Educational Psychology, 73,* 809–815.

Stanovich, K. E. (1985). Explaining variance in reading ability in terms of psychological processes: What have we learned? *Annals of Dyslexia, 35,* 67–69.

Stanton, J. E., & Cassidy, V. M. (1964). Effectiveness of special classes for the educable mentally retarded. *Mental Retardation, 2*(1), 8–13.

Stauffer, R. G. (1975). *Directing the reading-thinking process.* New York: Harper & Row.

Stearns, P. H. (1986). Problem solving and the learning disabled: Looking for answers. *Journal of Learning Disabilities, 19*(2), 116–120.

Stein, R. (1984). Growing up with a physical difference. *Journal of the Association for the Care of Children's Health, 12,* 53-61.

Stein, R. E. K., & Jessup, D. J. (1982). A non-categorical approach to chronic childhood illness. *Public Health Report, 97,* 354-362.

Stephens, R. S., Pelham, W. E., & Skinner, R. (1984). The state-dependent and main effects of methylphenidate and pemoline on paired-associates learning and spelling in hyperactive children. *Journal of Consulting and Clinical Psychology, 523,* 104-113.

Stern, C., & Stern, M. B. (1971). *Children discover arithmetic.* New York: Harper & Row.

Stevens, R., & Rosenshine, B. (1981). Advances in research on teaching. *Exceptional Education Quarterly, 2,* 1-9.

Sticht, T. C. (1979). Applications of the audread model to reading evaluation and instruction. In L. Resnick & P. Weaver (Eds.), *Theory and practice of early reading* (Vol. 1, pp. 209-226). Hillsdale, NJ: Lawrence, Erlbaum.

Stokes, T. F., & Baer, D. M. (1977). An implicit technology of generalization. *Journal of Applied Behavior Analysis, 10,* 349-367.

Stone, M. (1972). Problems with research designs in studies of sensory-response patterns in remedial reading. *Journal of the Association for the Study of Perception, 8,* 8-15.

Strain, P. (1975). Increasing social play of severely retarded preschoolers through socio-dramatic activities. *Mental Retardation, 13,* 7-9.

Strain, P. S. (1977). An experimental analysis of peer social initiations on the behavior of withdrawn preschool children: Some training and generalization effects. *Journal of Abnormal Child Psychology, 5,* 445-455.

Strain, P. S., Cooke, T. P., & Apolloni, T. (1976). *Teaching exceptional children: Assessing and modifying social behavior.* New York: Academic Press.

Strain, P. S., Shores, R. E., & Timm, M. A. (1977). Effects of peer social initiations on the behavior of withdrawn preschool children. *Journal of Applied Behavior Analysis, 10,* 289-298.

Strauss, A., & Lehtinen, L. (1947). *Psychopathology and education of the brain-injured child.* New York: Grune & Stratton.

Strickler, E. (1969). Family interaction factors in psychogenic learning disturbance. *Journal of Learning Disabilities, 2,* 31-38.

Stromer, R. (1975). Modifying letter and number reversals in elementary school children. *Journal of Applied Behavior Analysis, 8,* 211.

Stromer, R. (1977). Remediating academic deficiencies in learning disabled children. *Exceptional Children, 43,* 432-440.

Sulzbacher, S. I. (1972). Behavior analysis of drug effects in the classroom. In G. Semb (Ed.). *Behavior analysis and education.* Lawrence, KS: University of Kansas.

Swanson, H. L. (1984a). Semantic and visual memory codes in learning disabled readers. *Journal of Experimental Child Psychology, 37,* 124-140.

Swanson, H. L. (1984b). Does theory guide practice? *Remedial and Special Education, 5(5),* 7-16.

Swanson, J. M., & Kinsbourne, M. (1978). Should you use stimulants to treat the hyperactive child? *Modern Medicine, 46,* 71-80.

Swanson, J. M., & Kinsbourne, M. (1979). The cognitive effects of stimulant drugs on hyperactive children. In G. A. Hale & M. Lewis (Eds.), *Attention and cognitive development.* New York: Plenum Press.

Swanson, J. M., Kinsbourne, M., Roberts, W., & Zucker, K. (1978). Time-response analysis of the effect of stimulant medication on the learning ability of children referred for hyperactivity. *Pediatrics, 61,* 21-29.

Swanson, L. (1982). A multidirectional model for assessing learning disabled students' intelligence: An information processing framework. *Learning Disability Quarterly, 6,* 313-326.

Swift, C., & Lewis, R. (1985). Leisure preferences of elementary aged learning disabled boys. *Remedial and Special Education, 6*(1), 37–42.

Taber, F. (1983). *Microcomputers in special education: Selection and decision making process.* Reston, VA: The Council for Exceptional Children.

Tannenbaum, A. (1970). *The taxonomic instruction process.* New York: Columbia University.

Tarver, S., & Hallahan, D. (1976). Children with learning disabilities: An overview. In J. Kauffman & D. Hallahan (Eds.), *Teaching children with learning disabilities: Personal perspectives* (pp. 2–57). Columbus, OH: Merrill.

Taylor, B. M. (1982). Text structure and children's comprehension and memory for expository material. *Journal of Educational Psychology, 74,* 323–340.

Taylor, B. M., & Beach, R. W. (1984). The effects of text structure on middle-grade students' comprehension and production of expository text. *Reading Research Quarterly, 19,* 134–146.

Taylor, E. (1979). The use of drugs in hyperkinetic states: Clinical issues. *Neuropharmacology, 18,* 951–958.

Tew, B. J., Payne, H., & Lawrence, J. M. (1974). Must a family with a handicapped child be a handicapped family. *Developmental Medicine and Child Neurology, 16,* 95–98.

Texas Department of Mental Health and Mental Retardation. (1976). *Behavioral characteristics progression (BCP).* Fort Worth: Education Service Center, Region XI.

Thomas, S. (1981). Impact of the 1981 rehabilitation regulations on vocatonal evaluation of learning disabled. *Vocational Evaluation and Workshop Bulletin, 14*(1), 28–31.

Thompson, B. J. (1980). Computers in reading. A review of applications and implications. *Educational Technology, 20,* 20–28.

Thorndike, E. L. (1917). Reading as reasoning: A study of mistakes in paragraph reading. *Journal of Educational Psychology, 8,* 323–332.

Thorsell, M. (1961). Organizing experience units for the educable mentally retarded. *Exceptional Children, 27,* 177–185.

Thurlow, M. L., Graden, J., Greener, J. W., & Ysseldyke, J. E. (1982). *Academic responding for learning disabled and non-learning disabled students* (Research Report No. 72). Minneapolis: University of Minnesota, Institute for Research on Learning Disabilities.

Tindal, G. (1985). Investigating the effectiveness of special education: An analysis of methodology. *Journal of Learning Disabilities, 18,* 101–112.

Torgesen, J. K. (1977). The role of nonspecific factors in the task performance of learning-disabled children: A theoretical assessment. *Journal of Learning Disabilities, 10,* 27–34.

Torgesen, J. K. (1979). Factors related to poor performance on memory tasks in reading disabled children. *Learning Disability Quarterly, 2,* 17–23.

Torgesen, J. K. (1980). Implications of the LD child's use of efficient task strategies. *Journal of Learning Disabilities, 13,* 364–371.

Torgesen, J. K. (1981). The study of short-term memory in learning disabled children: Goals, methods, and conclusions. In K. D. Gadow & I. Bialer (Eds.), *Advances in learning and behavior disabilities* (pp. 117–149). Greenwich, CT: JAI Press.

Torgesen J. K. (1982). The learning-disabled child as an inactive learner: educational implications. In B. Y. L. Wong (Ed.), Metacognition and learning disabilities, *Topics in Learning and Learning Disabilities, 2,* 45–52.

Torgesen, J. K., & Licht, B. C. (1983). The learning disabled child as an inactive learner: Retrospect and prospects. In J. D. McKinney, & L. Feagans (Eds.), *Topics in learning disabilities* (pp. 3–31). Norwood, NJ: Ablex.

Torgesen, J. K., Murphy, L. A., & Ivey, C. I. (1979). The influence of an orienting task on the memory performance of children with reading problems. *Journal of Learning Disabilities, 12,* 396–401.

Torgesen, J. K., & Young, K. A. (1983). Priorities for the use of microcomputers with learning disabled children. *Journal of Learning Disabilities, 16*(4), 234–237.

Trammel, C. A. (1974). *A comparison of expressed play interests of children with language and/or learning disabilities and normal children.* Unpublished master's study, Texas Woman's University, Denton.

Traub, N. (1985). *Recipe for math.* North Bergen, NJ: Book Lab.

Traub, M., & Bloom, F. (1975). *Recipe for reading.* Cambridge, MA: Educators Publishing Service.

Treiber, F. A., & Lahey, B. B. (1983). Toward a behavioral model of academic remediation with learning disabled children. *Journal of Learning Disabilities, 16,* 73–136.

Trevino, F. (1979). Siblings of handicapped children: Identifying those at risk. *Social Casework, 60,* 488–492.

Trieber, F., & Lahey, B. (1982). Toward a model of academic remediation with learning disabled children. *Journal of Learning Disabilities, 16,* 111–116.

Trifiletti, J., Frith, G., & Armstrong, S. (1984). Microcomputers versus resource rooms for LD students: A preliminary investigation of the effects on math. *Learning Disability Quarterly, 7,* 69–76.

Trower, P., Bryant, B., & Argyle, M. (1978). *Social skills and mental health.* Pittsburgh: University of Pittsburgh Press.

Tucker, J., Stevens, L., & Ysseldyke, J. (1983). Learning disabilities: The experts speak out. *Journal of Learning Disabilities, 16,* 6–14.

Tucker, J. A. (1980). Ethnic proportions in classes for the learning disabled: Issues in nonbiased assessment. *The Journal of Special Education, 14,* 93–105.

U.S. Department of Education. (1980). *Second annual report to Congress on implementation of the Education of the Handicapped Act.* Washington, DC: U.S. Government Printing Office.

U.S. Department of Health and Human Services. (1979). *Plain talk about children with learning disabilities.* Rockville, MD: Alcohol, Drug Abuse, and Mental Health Administration.

U.S. News & World Report. (1981, August 10). Happiness. *U.S. News & World Report, 58.*

Ulman, J. D., & Rosenberg, M. S. (1986). Science and superstition in special education. *Exceptional Children, 52,* 459–460.

Ullman, C. A. (1957). Teachers, peers, and tests as predictors of adjustment. *Journal of Educational Psychology, 48,* 257–267.

Vacc, N. A. (1968). A study of emotionally disturbed children in regular and special education classes. *Exceptional Children, 35,* 197–204.

Valtin, R. (1974). German studies of dyslexia: Implications for education. *Journal of Research in Reading, 7*(2), 79–109.

Valtin, R. (1978–1979). Dyslexia: Deficit in reading or deficit in research? *Reading Research Quarterly, 14,* 201–221.

Van Hassalt, V. B., Hersen, M., & Bellack, A. S. (1981). The validity of role play tests for assessing social skills in children. *Behavior Therapy, 12,* 202–216.

Van Reusen, A. (1984). *A study of the effects of training learning disabled adolescents in self-advocacy procedures for use in the IEP conference.* Unpublished doctoral dissertation, University of Kansas, Lawrence.

Van Reusen, A., Bos, C., Schumaker, J. B., Deshler, D. D. (1987). *The education planning strategy.* Lawrence, KS: EXCELLENTERPRISES.

Varnen, J. (1983, March). The schoolhouse apple. *Softalk, 4,* 135–136.

Varnen, J. (1983, April). When Rich Hofmann's apple talks, children listen. *Softalk, 3,* 194–199.

Vaughn, S., & Bos, C. S. (1987). Basic knowledge and perception of the resource room: The student's perspective. *Journal of Learning Disabilities, 20*(4), 218–223.

Vellutino, F. R. (1979). *Dyslexia: Theory and research.* Cambridge, MA: MIT Press.

Vellutino, F. R., Steger, B. M., Moyer, G. C., Harding, C. J., & Niles, J. A. (1977). Has the perceptual deficit hypothesis led us astray? *Journal of Learning Disabilities, 10,* 54–64.

Venezky, R. (1970). *The structure of English orthography.* The Hague: Mouton.

Venezky, R., & Massaro, D. (1979). The role of orthographic regularity in word recognition. In L. Resnick & P. Weaver (Eds.), *Theory and practice of early reading* (Vol. 1, pp. 85–108). Hillsdale, NJ: Lawrence Erlbaum.

Verhoven, P., & Goldstein, J. (1976). *Leisure activity participation and handicapped populations.* Arlington, VA: National Recreation and Park Association.

Vetter, A. (1983). *A comparison of the characteristics of learning disabled and non-learning disabled young adults.* Unpublished doctoral dissertation, University of Kansas, Lawrence.

Visonhaler, J., Weinshank, A., Wagner, C., & Polin, R. (1982). Diagnosing children with educational problems: Characteristics of reading and learning disabilities specialists and classroom teachers. *Reading Research Quarterly, 18,* 134–164.

Voeltz, L. M., Evans, I. M., Freedland, K., & Donellon, S. (1982). Teacher decision making in the selection of educational programming priorities for severely handicapped children. *Journal of Special Education, 16,* 179–198.

Vogel, S. A. (1982). On developing LD college programs. *Journal of Learning Disabilities, 15,* 518–528.

Vogel, S. A., & Adelman, P. (1981). Personal development: College and university programs designed for learning disabled adults. *ICEC Quarterly, 1,* 12–18.

Vogel, S. A., & Moran, M. R. (1982). Written language disorders in learning disabled students: A preliminary report. In W. M. Cruickshank & J. W. Lerner (Eds.), *Coming of age: The best of ACLD* (Vol. 3). Syracuse, NY: Syracuse University Press.

Vogel, S. A., & Sattler, J. L. (1981). *The college student with a learning disability: A handbook for college and university admissions officers, faculty, and administration.* Springfield: Illinois Council for Developmental Disabilities.

Voss, J. F. (1982, March). Knowledge and social science problem solving. Paper presented at the AERA meeting, New York.

Voysey, M. (1972). Impression management by parents with disabled children. *Journal of Health and Social Behavior, 13,* 80–89.

Voysey, M. (1975). *A constant burden: The reconstitution of family life.* London: Rutledge and Kegan Paul.

Wadsworth, H. G. (1971). A motivational approach toward the remediation of learning disabled boys. *Exceptional Children, 37,* 33–42.

Walker, V. S. (1974). The efficacy of the resource room for educating retarded children. *Exceptional Children, 40,* 288–289.

Wallace, G., & Larsen, S. C. (1978). *Educational assessment of learning problems: Testing for teaching.* Boston: Allyn and Bacon.

Wallace, G., & McLoughlin, J. A. (1979). *Learning disabilities: Concepts and characteristics.* Columbus, OH: Merrill.

Wallach, M., & Wallach, L. (1976). *Teaching all children to read.* Chicago: University of Chicago Press.

Wallbrown, F. H., Wherry, R. J., Blaha, J., & Counts, D. H. (1974). An empirical test of Myklebust's cognitive structure hypothesis for 70 reading-disabled children. *Journal of Consulting and Clinical Psychology, 42,* 211–218.

Wang, M. C., & Baker, E. T. (1985–1986). Mainstreaming programs design features and effect. *Journal of Special Education, 19,* 503–521.

Wang, M. C., & Birch, J. W. (1984). Comparison of a full-time mainstreaming program and a resource room approach. *Exceptional Children, 51,* 33–40.

Warner, F., Thrapp, R., & Walsh, S. (1973). Attitudes of children toward their special class placement. *Exceptional Children, 40,* 37-38.

Warwick, N. (1968). Notes on spelling tests. In J. Arena (Ed.), *Building spelling skills in dyslexic children.* San Rafael, CA: Academic Therapy Publications.

Webb, G. M. (1974). The neurologically impaired youth goes to college. In R. E. Weber (Ed.), *Handbook on learning disabilities.* Englewood Cliffs, NJ: Prentice-Hall.

Wehman, P. (1977). *Helping the mentally retarded acquire play skills.* Springfield, IL: Thomas.

Wehman, P. (1979). *Recreation programming for developmentally disabled persons.* Baltimore: University Park Press.

Wehman, P., & Schleien, S. (1980). Assessment and selection of leisure skills for severely handicapped individuals. *Education and Training of the Mentally Retarded, 15,* 50-57.

Wehman, P., & Schleien, S. (1981). *Leisure programs for handicapped persons: Adaptations, techniques, and curriculum.* Baltimore: University Park Press.

Weiner, L. H. (1969). An investigation of the effectiveness of resource rooms for children with specific learning disabilities. *Journal of Learning Disabilities, 2,* 223-229.

Weir, S., & Watt, D. (1981). Logo: A computer environment for learning-disabled students. *The Computer Teacher, 8*(5), 11-17.

Weisberg, K. (1984). How consistent is the clinical diagnosis of reading specialists. *Reading Teacher, 38*(2), 205-212.

Weisgerber, R. A., & Rubin, D. P. (1985). Designing and using software for the learning disabled. *Journal of Reading, Writing, and Learning Disabilities International, 1*(2), 133-138.

Weiss, C. (1976). Learning and planning for retirement. *Leisure Today,* 27-28.

Weiss, G. (1979). Controlled studies of efficacy of long-term treatment with stimulants of hyperactive children. In E. Denhoff & L. Stern (Eds.), *Minimal brain dysfunction: A developmental approach.* New York: Masson.

Weiss, G. (1981). Controverial issues of the pharmacotherapy of the hyperactive child. *Canadian Journal of Psychiatry, 26,* 385-392.

Weiss, G., Hechtman, L., Perlman, T., Hopkins, J., & Wener, A. (1979). Hyperactive children as young adults: A controlled prospective 10 year follow-up of the psychiatric status of 75 hyperactive children. *Archives of General Psychiatry, 36,* 675-681.

Weiss, G., Kruger, E., Danielson, U., & Elman, M. (1975). Effects of long-term treatment of hyperactive children with methylphenidate. *Canadian Medical Association Journal, 112,* 159-165.

Wender, E. H. (1977). Food additives and hyperkinesis. *American Journal of Diseases of Children, 131,* 1204-1206.

Wepman, J. M. (1975). *Auditory discrimination test* (rev. 1973). Palm Springs, CA: Research Associates.

Werner, E. E., Blerman, J. M., & French, F. E. (1971). *The children of Kauai: A longitudinal study from the prenatal period to age ten.* Honolulu: University of Hawaii Press.

Werner, E. E., Simonian, K., & Smith, R. S. (1967). Reading achievement, language functioning, and perceptual-motor development of 10 and 11 year olds. *Perceptual and Motor Skills, 25,* 409-420.

Werner, E. E., & Smith, R. S. (1977). *Kauai's children come of age.* Honolulu: University of Hawaii Press.

Werner, E. E., & Smith, R. S. (1979). An epidemiologic perspective on some antecedents and consequences of childhood mental health problems and learning disabilities: A report from the Kauai longitudinal study. *Journal of the American Academy of Child Psychiatry, 18,* 292-306.

Werner, E. E., & Smith, R. S. (1982). *Vulnerable but invincible: A longitudinal study of resilient children and youth.* New York: McGraw-Hill.

Wetter, J. (1972). Parent attitudes toward learning disability. *Exceptional Children, 38,* 490–491.

Whalen, C., Collins, B., Henker, B., Alkus, S., Adams, D., & Stapp, J. (1978). Behavior observations of hyperactive children and methylphenidate effects in systematically structured classroom environments: Now you see them, now you don't. *Journal of Pediatric Psychology, 3,* 177–187.

Whalen, C. K., & Henker, B. (1976). Psychostimulants and children: A review and analysis. *Psychological Bulletin, 83,* 1113–1130.

Whalen, C. K., Henker, B., Collins, B. E., Finck, D., & Dotemoto, S. (1979). A social ecology of hyperactive boys: Medication effects in structured classroom environments. *Journal of Applied Behavior Analysis, 12,* 65–81.

Whalen, C. K., Henker, B., & Finck, D. (1981). Medication effects in the classroom: Three naturalistic indicators. *Canadian Journal of Psychiatry, 26,* 385–392.

Whang, P. L., Fawcett, S. B., & Mathews, R. M. (1981). Teaching job-related social skills to learning disabled adolescents. *Analysis and Intervention in Developmental Disabilities, 4,* 29–38.

White, O. (1971). *A glossary of behavioral terminology.* Champaign, IL: Research Press.

White, O. (1972). *A manual for the calculation and use of the median slope — A technique of progress estimation and prediction in the single case.* Eugene: University of Oregon, Regional Resource Center for Handicapped Children.

White, O. (1974). *The "split middle" — A "quickie" method of trend estimation.* Seattle: University of Washington, Child Development and Mental Retardation Center, Experimental Education Unit.

White, W. J., Alley, G. R., Deshler, D. D., Schumaker, J. B., Warner, M. M., & Clark, F. (1982). Are there learning disabilities after high school? *Exceptional Children, 49,* 273–274.

White, W. J., Deshler, D., Schumaker, J., Warner, M., Alley, G., & Clark, F. (1983). The effects of learning disabilities on postschool adjustment. *Journal of Rehabilitation, 49*(1), 46–50.

White, W. J., Schumaker, J. B., Warner, M. M., Alley, G. R., & Deshler, D. D. (1980). *The current status of young adults identified as learning disabled during their school career* (Research Report No. 21). Lawrence: University of Kansas Institute for Research in Learning Disabilities.

Whitman, T., Mercurio, J., & Caponigri, V. (1970). Development of social responses in two severely retarded children. *Journal of Applied Behavior Analysis, 3,* 133–138.

Wiederholt, J. (1976). Learning disability research in special education. *Journal of Special Education, 10,* 127–128.

Wiener, M., & Cromer, W. (1967). Reading and reading difficulty: A conceptual analysis. *Harvard Educational Review, 37,* 620–643.

Wiig, E. H., & Harris, S. P. (1974). Perception and interpretation of nonverbally expressed emotions by adolescents with learning disabilities. *Perceptual Motor Skills, 38,* 239–245.

Wikler, L. (1980). Chronic stresses of families of mentally retarded children. *Family Relations, 30,* 281–288.

Wikler, L., Wasow, M., & Hatfield, E. (1981). Chronic sorrow revisited: Parent vs. professional depiction of the adjustment of parents of mentally retarded children. *Americal Journal of Orthopsychiatry, 51,* 63–70.

Will, M. C. (1984). Let us pause and reflect — but not too long. *Exceptional Children, 51,* 11–16.

Williams, J. (1979). The ABDs of reading: A program for the learning disabled. In L. Resnick & P. Weaver (Eds.), *Theory and practice of early reading* (Vol. 3, pp. 399–416).

Hillsdale, NJ: Lawrence Erlbaum.

Williams, J. P. (1986). The role of phonemic analysis in reading. In J. K. Torgeson & B. Y. L. Wong (Eds.), *Psychological and educational perspectives in learning diabilities* (pp. 399–416)., New York: Academic Press.

Williams, M., & Lahey, B. B. (1977). The functional independence of response latency and accuracy: Implications for the concept of conceptual tempo. *Journal of Abnormal Child Psychology, 5,* 371–378.

Willner, S. K., & Crane, R. (1979). A parental dilemma: The child with a marginal handicap. *Social Casework, 60,* 30–35.

Willoughby–Herb, S. J. (1983). Selecting relevant curricular objectives. *Topics in Early Childhood Special Education, 2,* 9–14.

Wilson, G. (1969). Status of recreation for the handicapped school centered. *Therapeutic Recreation Journal, 3,* 10–12.

Wilson, K. (1981). Managing the administrative morals of special needs. *Classroom Computer News, 1*(4), 8–9.

Winograd, P. (1984). Strategic difficulties in summarizing texts. *Reading Research Quarterly, 19*(4), 404–425.

Winter, A., & Wright, E. N. (1983). *A follow-up of pupils who entered learning disabilities self-contained classes in 1981–1982* (Research Report No. 171). Toronto, Canada: Board of Education. (ERIC Document Reproduction Service No. ED 238 224)

Wittrock, M. C. (1978). The cognitive movement in instruction. *Educational Psychologist, 13,* 15–30.

Wolf, M. M., Giles, D. K., & Hall, R. V. (1968). Experiments with token reinforcement in a remedial classroom. *Behavior Research and Therapy, 6,* 51–64.

Wolfensberger. W. (1967). Counseling the parents of the retarded. In A. A. Baumeister (Ed.), *Mental retardation: Appraisal, education and rehabilitation* (pp. 329–400). Chicago: Aldine.

Wolraich, M., Drummond, T., Salomon, M. K., O'Brien, M., & Sivage, C. L. (1978). Effects of methylphenidate alone and in combination with behavior modification procedures on the behavior and academic performance of hyperactive children. *Journal of Abnormal Child Psychology, 6,* 149–161.

Wong, B. (1979). The role of theory in learning disabilities research. Part 1. An analysis of problems. *Journal of Learning Disabilities, 12,* 19–28.

Wong, B. (1980). Activating the inactive learner: Use of questions/prompts to enhance comprehension and retention of implied information in learning disabled children. *Learning Disability Quarterly, 3,* 29–37.

Wong, B. Y. (1985). Potential means of enhancing content skill acquisition in learning disabled adolescents. *Focus on Exceptional Children, 17*(5), 1–8.

Wong, B. Y. L. (1985a). Metacognition and learning disabilities. In T. G. Waller, D. Forrest–Pressley, & E. MacKinnon (Eds.), *Metacognition, cognition and human performance* (pp. 137–180). New York: Academic Press.

Wong, B. Y. L. (1985b). Potential means of enhancing content skills acquisition in learning-disabled adolescents. *Focus on Exceptional Children, 17,* 1–8.

Wong, B. Y. L. (1985c). Self-questioning instructional research. *Review of Educational Research, 55*(2), 227–268.

Wong, B. Y. L., & Jones, W. (1982). Increasing metacomprehension in learning-disabled and normally-achieving students through self-questioning training. *Learning Disability Quarterly, 5,* 228–240

Wong, B. Y. L., & Wong, R. (1980). Role-taking skills in normal achieving and learning disabled children. *Learning Disability Quarterly, 3*(2), 11–18.

Wood, M. M., & Hurley, O. L. (1977). Curriculum and instruction. In J. B. Jordan, A. H. Hayden, M. B. Karnes, & M. M. Wood (Eds.), *Early childhood education for excep-*

tional children: A handbook of ideas and exemplary practices. Reston, VA: Council for Exceptional Children.

Woodcock, R. (1973). *Woodcock reading mastery test.* Circle Pines, NM: American Guidance Service.

Woodcock, R., & Johnson, M. (1977). *Woodcock–Johnson psycho-educational battery.* Allen, TX: DLM Teaching Resources.

Worcester, L. H. (1981). *The Canadian Franco-American learning disabled college student at the University of Maine at Orono.* Orono: University of Maine. (ERIC Document Reproduction Service No. ED 204 881)

Wright, L. S., & Stimmel, T. (1984). Perceptions of parents and self among college students reporting learning disabilities. *Exceptional Child, 31*(3), 203–208.

Yates, J. M. (1983). *Research implications for writing in the content areas.* Washington, DC: National Education Association.

Yellin, A. M., Hopwood, J. H., & Greenberg, L. M. (1982). Adults and adolescents with attention deficit disorders: Clinical and behavioral response to psychostimulants. *Journal of Clinical Psychopharmacology, 2,* 133–136.

Yoshida, R. K., Fenton, K. S., Maxwell, J. P., & Kaufman, M. J. (1978). Group decision making in the planning team process: Myth or reality? *Journal of School Psychiatry, 16,* 237–244.

Youngberg v. Romeo. (1982). 102 S.Ct. 2452.

Ysseldyke, J. E. (1983). Current practices in making psychoeducational decisions about learning disabled students. *Journal of Learning Disabilities, 16,* 226–233.

Ysseldyke, J. E., & Algozzine, B. (1982). *Critical issues in special and remedial education.* Boston: Houghton Mifflin.

Ysseldyke, J. E., Algozzine, B., & Richey, L. (1982). Judgment under uncertainty: How many children are handicapped? *Exceptional Children, 48,* 531–534.

Ysseldyke, J. E., Algozzine, B., Richey, L., & Gardner, J. (1982). Declaring students eligible for learning disability services: Why bother with the data? *Learning Disability Quarterly, 5,* 37–44.

Ysseldyke, J. E., & Thurlow, M. L. (1983). *Identification/classifcation research: An integrative summary of findings* (Research Report No. 142). Minneapolis: University of Minnesota, Institute for Research on Learning Disabilities.

Zajonc, R. B. (1980). Feeling and thinking: Preferences need no inferences. *American Psychologist, 35,* 151–175.

Zigmond, N. (1978a). A prototype of comprehensive service for secondary students with learning disabilities: A preliminary report. *Learning Disability Quarterly, 1,* 39–49.

Zigmond, N. (1978b). Remediation of dyslexia: A discussion. In A. L. Benton & D. Pearl (Eds.), *Dyslexia: An appraisal of current knowledge* (pp. 425–448). New York: Oxford University Press.

Zutell, J. (1980). Children's spelling strategies and their cognitive development. In E. H. Henderson & J. W. Beers (Eds.), *Developmental and cognitive aspects of learning to spell.* Newark, DE: International Reading Association.

Zweng, M. J., Garaghty, J., & Turner, J. (1979). *Children's strategies of solving verbal problems* (Final Report). Washington, DC: National Institute of Education. (ERIC Document Reproduction Service No. ED 178 359)

Index

A

Academic behavior, deficient, behavioral approach to remediation of, 5
Academic behavior deficits, identification of functional units of, 11–15
  goal of, 11
  research on, 11–12
  treatment, 12
    molecular intervention, 13–14, 15–16
    stimulus-fading techniques, 15
    tutoring methods, 12, 13–14
Academic performance, as appropriate target for behavioral remediation, 8–9
Adolescent, LD, 224, 233–234(t)
Algorithms, difficulty of LD students applying, 102
Amphetamine sulfate (Benzedrine), 210
Arithmetic, behavioral intervention with, 9
Arithmetic deficits
  instruction principles
    assessment issues, 90–94
    conceptual base, establishing, 93–94
    directive instruction and mastery learning, 94–95
  instruction, topics of
    basic operations, 96–101

    part-whole representation, 103–105
    precomputational skills, 95–96
    problem solving, 105–106
    related topics, 106–107
    whole number computations, 101–103
  research on, 89–90
  summary of, 108
Arithmetic, use of stimulant drugs to enhance academic productivity of, 107
Assessment
  social skills, 134–135. *See also* Social skills deficit, remediation of
  sociometric, 138–139
Atomistic assessment of written language
  Picture Story Language Test, 83, 83–84
  TOAL, 83, 85
  TOWL, 83, 84, 85
  Woodcock-Johnson Psycho-Educational Battery, 83, 85
Attention deficit, as inappropriate target for behavioral remediation, 6–7
Attention deficit LD subtype, 38
Attention problems, techniques for, 68
Auditory discrimination deficit, 58
Auditory memory deficits, 43, 44(t), 46, 50, 52
Auditory and visual perceptual skills, assessment of, 180–185
Ayres Handwriting Scale, 75

Key: (t) indicates *table*.